Student Solutions Manual

NANCY J. GARDNER
California State University, Long Beach

INTRODUCTION TO

Chemical Principles

H. STEPHEN STOKER

PEARSON

Prentice
Hall

Upper Saddle River, NJ 07458

Project Manager: Kristen Kaiser
Editor-in-Chief, Science: John Challice
Vice President of Production & Manufacturing: David W. Riccardi
Executive Managing Editor: Kathleen Schiaparelli
Assistant Managing Editor: Becca Richter
Production Editor: Donna Crilly
Supplement Cover Manager: Paul Gourhan
Supplement Cover Designer: Joanne Alexandris
Manufacturing Buyer: Ilene Kahn
Cover Photograph: Warren Bolster/Stone/Getty Images, Inc.

© 2005 Pearson Education, Inc.
Pearson Prentice Hall
Pearson Education, Inc.
Upper Saddle River, NJ 07458

Printed in the United States of America

10 9 8 7 6 5 4 3 2 1

ISBN 0-13-144941-9

Pearson Education Ltd., *London*
Pearson Education Australia Pty. Ltd., *Sydney*
Pearson Education Singapore, Pte. Ltd.
Pearson Education North Asia Ltd., *Hong Kong*
Pearson Education Canada, Inc., *Toronto*
Pearson Educación de Mexico, S.A. de C.V.
Pearson Education—Japan, *Tokyo*
Pearson Education Malaysia, Pte. Ltd.

Table of Contents

CHAPTER ONE
The Science of Chemistry

PRACTICE PROBLEMS

Scientific Disciplines (Sec. 1.1)

1.1   a) true   b) false   c) false   d) true

The Scientific Method (Sec. 1.4)

1.3   c, b, e, a, and d

1.5   a) fact   b) hypothesis   c) fact   d) natural law

1.7   a) false   b) false   c) true   d) false

1.9   While a theory may not be an absolute answer, it is the best answer available. It may be supplanted only if repeated experimental evidence conclusively disproves it and a new theory is developed.

1.11   a) 4 is eliminated   b) 1 is eliminated
           c) 1 and 4 are eliminated   d) 1 and 2 are eliminated

1.12   a) 1 is eliminated   b) 1 and 3 are eliminated
           c) 1 and 4 are eliminated   d) 1, 3 and 4 are eliminated

1.13   a) qualitative   b) quantitative   c) quantitative   d) qualitative

1.15   The product of the pressure times the volume is a constant; or the pressure of the gas is inversely proportional to its volume; $P_1V_1 = P_2V_2$

1.17   Scientific or natural laws are discovered by research. Researchers have no control over what the laws turn out to be. Societal laws are arbitrary conventions that can be and are changed by the society when necessary.

1.19   Publishing scientific data provides access to that data enabling scientists to develop new theories based on a wider range of knowledge including all relevant data.

1.21   Conditions under which an experiment is conducted often affect the results of the experiment. If the conditions are uncontrolled the data resulting from that experiment is not validated.

1.23   A qualitative observation is a non-nummerical general observation about a system under study. A quantitative observation is a numerical observation about a system under study.

CHAPTER TWO
Numbers from Measurements

PRACTICE PROBLEMS

Exact and Inexact Numbers (Sec. 2.2)

2.1 a) exact (counting integer) b) exact (definition)
c) inexact (measurement) d) exact (counting integer)

2.3 a) exact (counting integer) b) inexact (measurement)
c) exact (counting integer) d) exact (coins are counted)

Accuracy and Precision (Sec. 2.3)

2.5 Student A: low precision, low accuracy
Student B: high precision, high accuracy
Student C: high precision, low accuracy

Uncertainty in Measurements (Sec. 2.4)

2.7 The reading should have one estimated digit beyond the markings on the measuring device.
a) 0.1 degree   b) 0.1 fluid ounce   c) 1 milliliter   d) 0.1 millimeter

2.9 The uncertainty in the first reading is ±0.1 second and the uncertainty in the second reading is ±0.01 second.

2.11 a) Thermometer A is marked with 1° markings, so readings should be recorded to tenths: 42.1° and 61.5°.
b) Thermometer B is marked with 0.1° markings, so readings should be recorded to hundredths: 35.03° and 47.98°.

Significant Figures (Sec. 2.5)

2.13 a) 2   b) 6   c) 8   d) 7

2.15 a) 2   b) 4   c) 5   d) 6

2.17 a) 6   b) 5   c) 6   d) 6

2.19 a) confined zeros = 2, leading zeros = 0, significant trailing zeros = 0, trailing zeros not significant = 0
b) confined zeros = 2, leading zeros = 0, significant trailing zeros = 1, trailing zeros not significant = 0
c) confined zeros = 2, leading zeros = 1, significant trailing zeros = 1, trailing zeros not significant = 0
d) confined zeros = 3, leading zeros = 0, significant trailing zeros = 0, trailing zeros not significant = 2

2.21   a) 3031.02, **2** is the estimated digit   b) 3.0030, **0** is the estimated digit
      c) 0.706050, **0** is the estimated digit   d) 46,000,**3**00, **3** is the estimated digit

2.23   a) ± 0.01   b) ± 0.0001   c) ± 0.000001   d) ± 100

2.25   a) same number of significant figures   b) different number of significant figures
      c) same number of significant figures   d) same number of significant figures

2.27   a) same uncertainty, ± 0.01   b) different uncertainties, ± 1, ± 10
      c) same uncertainty, ± 0.00001   d) different uncertainties, ± 0.000001, ± 10,000

2.29   a) 23,000   b) 23,$\overline{0}$ 00   c) 23,000.0   d) 23,000.000

2.31   a) 3   b) 4   c) 2   d) 5

Rounding Off (Sec. 2.6)

2.33   a) 0.351   b) 653.9   c) 22.556   d) 0.2777

2.35   a) 3.630502   b) 3.6305   c) 3.631   d) 3.63

2.37   a) 30,427.3   b) 30,427   c) 30,430   d) 3$\overline{0}$,000

2.39   a) 0.035   b) 2.50   c) 1,500,000   d) 1$\overline{0}$0

2.41   a) 0.12   b) 120,000   c) 12   d) 0.00012

Significant Figures in Multiplication and Division (Sec. 2.6)

2.43   a) 2   b) 1   c) 3   d) 3

2.45   a) 3   b) 2   c) 4 or more   d) 4 or more

2.47   a) 0.029889922 (calc), 0.0299 (corr)   b) 136,900 (calc), 140,000 (corr)
      c) 1277.2522 (calc), 1280 (corr)   d) 0.98816568 (calc), 0.988 (corr)

2.49   a) 3.9265927 (calc), 3.9 (corr)   b) 4.8410309 (calc), 4.84 (corr)
      c) 63.13492 (calc), 63 (corr)   d) 1.1851852 (calc), 1 (corr)

Significant Figures in Addition and Subtraction (Sec. 2.6)

2.51   a) tenths, ±0.1   b) tenths, ±0.1   c) units, ±1   d) hundreds, ±100

2.53   a) 162 (calc and corr)   b) 9.321 (calc), 9.3 (corr)
      c) 1260.72 (calc), 1261 (corr)   d) 19.95 (calc), 20.0 (corr)

2.55   a) 957 (calc), 957.0 (corr)   b) 342.63 (calc), 343 (corr)
       c) 1250 (calc), 1200 (corr)   d) 131.9927 (calc), 132 (corr)

Significant Figures and Exact Numbers (Sec. 2.6)

2.57   14.56 (calc), 14.6 centimeters (corr)

2.59   a) 267.3 (calc and corr)   b) 257,140 (calc); 260,000 (corr)
       c) 201.3 (calc and corr)   d) 3.8038461 (calc); 3.8 (corr)

Exponents and Orders of Magnitude (Sec. 2.7)

2.61   a) 5^3 b) 10^4 c) 3^{-4} d) 10^{-3}

2.63   a) 10^7 b) 10^{-1} c) 10^{-3} d) 10^{-7}

Scientific Notation (Sec. 2.7)

2.65   a) negative   b) positive   c) zero   d) positive

2.67   a) four   b) one   c) five   d) two

2.69   a) four   b) five   c) four   d) five

2.71   a) 4   b) 2   c) 4   d) 5

2.73   a) 4.732×10^2 b) 1.234×10^{-3} c) 2.3100×10^2 d) 2.31×10^8

2.75   a) 7×10^4 b) 6.70×10^4 c) 6.7000×10^4 d) 6.700000×10^4

2.77   a) 0.000170   b) 573   c) 0.5550   d) 11,1$\overline{0}$0,000,000

2.79   a) 3.42×10^6 b) 2.36×10^{-3} c) 3.2×10^2 d) 1.2×10^{-4}

Multiplication and Division in Scientific Notation (Sec. 2.8)

2.81   a) 10^8 b) 10^{-8} c) 10^2 d) 10^{-2}

2.83   a) 2.991905×10^8 (calc), 2.992×10^8 (corr)   b) 9.1290×10^2 (calc), 9.1×10^2 (corr)
       c) 2.7×10^{-9} (calc and corr)   d) 2.7×10^{11} (calc and corr)

2.85   a) 10^2 b) 10^8 c) 10^{-8} d) 10^{-2}

2.87   a) 2.8649608×10^1 (calc), 2.86×10^1 (corr)   b) 8.9991001×10^{17} (calc), 8.999×10^{17} (corr)
       c) 3.4904491×10^{-2} (calc), 3.49×10^{-2} (corr)   d) $1.1112222 \times 10^{-18}$ (calc), 1.111×10^{-18} (corr)

2.89 a) 10^1 b) 10^{-1} c) 10^{20} d) 10^2

2.91 a) 1.5×10^0 (calc and corr)   b) 6.6666666×10^{-1} (calc), 6.7×10^{-1} (corr)
c) $8.5073917 \times 10^{-19}$ (calc), 8.51×10^{-19} (corr)   d) 7.7775×10^{15} (calc), 8×10^{15} (corr)

Addition and Subtraction in Scientific Notation (Sec 2.8)

2.93 a) 4.415×10^3 (calc), 4.42×10^3 (corr)   b) 9.3×10^{-2} (calc), 9.30×10^{-2} (corr)
c) 9.683×10^5 (calc and corr)   d) 1.9189×10^4 (calc), 1.919×10^4 (corr)

2.95 a) 7.713×10^7 (calc and corr)   b) 8.253×10^7 (calc and corr)
c) 8.307×10^7 (calc and corr)   d) 8.31294×10^7 (calc), 8.313×10^7 (corr)

ADDITIONAL PROBLEMS

2.97 12 pizzas is an exact number, 12 inch rope is a measured number.

2.99 a) 3   b) 4   c) 4   d) 4

2.101 a) no   b) yes   c) yes   d) yes

2.103 a) $6\overline{0}\,\overline{0}$ pounds   b) 600.0 pounds   c) $6\overline{0}\,\overline{0}$ pounds   d) 600.000 pounds

2.105 a) yes   b) no   c) no   d) yes

2.107 a) 6.326×10^5 b) 3.13×10^{-1} c) 6.300×10^7 d) 5.000×10^{-1}

2.109 a) 2   b) 4 or more   c) 3   d) 3

2.111 a) $2.3 + 4.5 = 6.8$ (calc and corr)   b) $3.7 - 3.4 - 0.3$ (calc and corr)
   $4.0 \times 6.8 = 27.2$ (calc), $= 27$ (corr) $3.0 \times 0.3 = 0.9$ (calc and corr)

   c) $34 - 4.23 = 29.77$ (calc) $= 3\overline{0}$ (corr)   d) $0.0001 + 0.01 = 0.0101$ (calc) $= 0.01$ (corr)
   $6.0 \times 3\overline{0} = 180$ (calc) $= 1.8 \times 10^2$ (corr) $7.02 \times 0.01 = 0.0702$ (calc) $= 0.07$ (corr)

2.113 An exact number is a whole number; it cannot possess decimal digits.

2.115 a) $4.2 + 5.30 = 9.52$ (calc) $= 9.5$ (corr)
   $28 + 11 = 39$ (exact)
   $39 \times 9.5 = 370.5$ (calc) $= 3.7 \times 10^2$ (corr)
   b) $28 - 11 = 17$ (exact)
   $4.2 \times 5.30 \times 17 = 378.42$ (calc) $= 3.8 \times 10^2$ (corr)
   c) 28. (exact) $- 4.2 - 23.8$ (calc and corr)
   5.30×11 (exact) $= 58.30$ (calc) $= 58.3$ (corr)

   $$\frac{23.8}{58.3} = 0.40823328 \text{ (calc)} = 0.408 \text{ (corr)}$$

   d) 28. (exact) $- 4.2 = 23.8$ (calc and corr)
   11 (exact) $- 5.30 = 5.70$ (calc and corr)

$$\frac{23.8}{5.70} = 4.1754386 \text{ (calc)} = 4.18 \text{ (corr)}$$

2.117   a) 2.07×10^2, 243, 1.03×10^3 b) 2.11×10^{-3}, 0.0023, 3.04×10^{-2}
         c) 23,000, 9.67×10^4, 2.30×10^5 d)   0.000014, 0.00013, 1.5×10^{-4}

CHAPTER THREE
Unit Systems and Dimensional Analysis

PRACTICE PROBLEMS

Metric System Units (Sec. 3.1 through 3.4)

3.1   a) no   b) yes   c) no   d) yes

3.3   a) kilo   b) centi   c) micro   d) 10^{-9} e) 10^6 f) 10^{-3}

3.5   a) μg   b) km   c) cL   d) decimeter   e) milliliter   f) picogram

3.7   a) n (nano)   b) μ (micro)   c) k (kilo)   d) G (giga)

3.9   a) smaller by 100 (10^2) times   b) smaller by 1000 (10^3) times
         c) larger by 10,000 (10^4) times   d) smaller by 1,000,000,000 (10^9) times

3.11   a) volume   b) length   c) volume   d) area

3.13   a) 1 inch   b) 1 meter   c) 1 pound   d) 1 gallon

Units and Mathematical Operations (Sec. 3.4 and 3.5)

3.15   a) mm^3 b) nm^2 c) km   d) cm

3.17   a) A = $(4.52 \text{ cm})^2$ = 20.4304 (calc) = 20.4 cm^2 (corr)
         b) A = (3.5 m) x (9.2 m) = 32.2 (calc) = 32 m^2 (corr)
         c) A = 3.142 x $(4.579 \text{ mm})^2$ = 65.879071 (calc) = 65.88 mm^2 (corr)
         d) A = ½ x (5.5 mm) x (3.0 mm) = 8.25 (calc) = 8.2 mm^2 (corr)

3.19   a) V = (5.4 cm) x (0.52 cm) x (3.4 cm) = 9.5472 (calc) = 9.5 cm^3 (corr)
         b) V = 3.142 x $(2.4 \text{ cm})^2$ x (7.5 cm) = 135.7344 (calc) = 1.4×10^2 cm (corr)
         c) V = 4/3 x 3.142 x $(87 \text{ mm})^3$ = 2.7586886×10^6 (calc) = 2.8×10^6 mm^3 (corr)
         d) V = $(7.2 \text{ cm})^3$ = 373.248 (calc) = 3.7×10^2 cm^3

Conversion Factors (Sec. 3.6)

3.21   a) 24 hr = 1 day $\dfrac{1 \text{ day}}{24 \text{ hr}}$ $\dfrac{24 \text{ hr}}{1 \text{ day}}$

         b) 60 sec = 1 min $\dfrac{1 \text{ min}}{60 \text{ sec}}$ $\dfrac{60 \text{ sec}}{1 \text{ min}}$

         c) 10 decades = 1 century $\dfrac{1 \text{ century}}{10 \text{ decades}}$ $\dfrac{10 \text{ decades}}{1 \text{ century}}$

         d) 365.25 days = 1 yr $\dfrac{1 \text{ yr}}{365.25 \text{ day}}$ $\dfrac{365.25 \text{ day}}{1 \text{ yr}}$

3.23 a) $\dfrac{1 \text{ kL}}{10^3 \text{ L}}$ b) $\dfrac{10^3 \text{ L}}{1 \text{ kL}}$ $\dfrac{1 \text{ mg}}{10^{-3} \text{ g}}$ $\dfrac{10^{-3} \text{ g}}{1 \text{ mg}}$ c) $\dfrac{1 \text{ cm}}{10^{-2} \text{ m}}$ $\dfrac{10^{-2} \text{ m}}{1 \text{ cm}}$ d) $\dfrac{1 \text{ μsec}}{10^{-6} \text{ sec}}$ $\dfrac{10^{-6} \text{ sec}}{1 \text{ μsec}}$

3.25 a) 4 significant figures   b) exact   c) 4 significant figures   d) exact

3.27 a) exact   b) inexact   c) exact   d) exact

Dimensional Analysis: Metric-Metric Unit Conversion (Sec. 3.7)

3.29

a) $25 \text{ mg} \times \dfrac{10^{-3} \text{ g}}{1 \text{ mg}} = 0.025 \text{ g}$

b) $323 \text{ km} \times \dfrac{10^3 \text{ m}}{1 \text{ km}} = 3.23 \times 10^5 \text{ m}$

c) $25.0 \text{ L} \times \dfrac{1 \text{ dL}}{10^{-1} \text{ L}} = 2.50 \times 10^2 \text{ dL}$

d) $0.010 \text{ g} \times \dfrac{1 \text{ pg}}{10^{-12} \cdot \text{g}} = 1.0 \times 10^{10} \text{ pg}$

3.31

a) $23 \text{ dL} \times \dfrac{10^{-1} \text{ L}}{1 \text{ dL}} \times \dfrac{1 \text{ cL}}{10^{-2} \text{ L}} = 2.3 \times 10^2 \text{ cL}$

b) $6.00 \text{ kg} \times \dfrac{10^3 \text{ g}}{1 \text{ kg}} \times \dfrac{1 \text{ mg}}{10^{-3} \text{ g}} = 6.00 \times 10^6 \text{ mg}$

c) $6 \times 10^{-3} \text{ μL} \times \dfrac{10^{-6} \text{ L}}{1 \text{ μL}} \times \dfrac{1 \text{ nL}}{10^{-9} \text{ L}} = 6 \text{ nL}$

d) $25 \text{ Mm} \times \dfrac{10^6 \text{ m}}{1 \text{ Mm}} \times \dfrac{1 \text{ nm}}{10^{-9} \text{ m}} = 2.5 \times 10^{16} \text{ nm}$

3.33

a) $\dfrac{55 \text{ L}}{1 \text{ sec}} \times \dfrac{60 \text{ sec}}{1 \text{ min}} \times \dfrac{60 \text{ min}}{1 \text{ hr}} = 198{,}000 \text{ (calc)} = 2.0 \times 10^5 \text{ L/hr (corr)}$

b) $\dfrac{55 \text{ L}}{1 \text{ sec}} \times \dfrac{1 \text{ kL}}{10^3 \text{ L}} = 5.5 \times 10^{-2} \dfrac{\text{kL}}{\text{sec}}$

c) $\dfrac{55 \text{ L}}{1 \text{ sec}} \times \dfrac{1 \text{ dL}}{10^{-1} \text{ L}} \times \dfrac{60 \text{ sec}}{\text{min}} = 33{,}000 \text{ (calc)} = 3.3 \times 10^4 \text{ dL/min (corr)}$

d) $\dfrac{55 \text{ L}}{1 \text{ sec}} \times \dfrac{1 \text{ mL}}{10^{-3} \text{ L}} \times \dfrac{60 \text{ sec}}{1 \text{ min}} \times \dfrac{60 \text{ min}}{1 \text{ hr}} \times \dfrac{24 \text{ hr}}{1 \text{ day}}$
$= 4.752 \times 10^9 \text{ (calc)} = 4.8 \times 10^9 \dfrac{\text{mL}}{\text{day}} \text{ (corr)}$

3.35

a) $365 \text{ m}^2 \times \left(\dfrac{1 \text{ km}}{10^3 \text{ m}} \right)^2 = 3.65 \times 10^{-4} \text{ km}^2$

b) $365 \text{ m}^2 \times \left(\dfrac{1 \text{ cm}}{10^{-2} \text{ m}} \right)^2 = 3.65 \times 10^6 \text{ cm}^2$

c) $365 \text{ m}^2 \times \left(\dfrac{1 \text{ dm}}{10^{-1} \text{ m}} \right)^2 = 3.65 \times 10^4 \text{ dm}^2$

d) $365 \text{ m}^2 \times \left(\dfrac{1 \text{ Mm}}{10^6 \text{ m}} \right)^2 = 3.65 \times 10^{-10} \text{ Mm}^2$

3.37 a) $6.0 \text{ cm}^2 \times \left(\dfrac{10^{-2} \text{ m}}{1 \text{ cm}} \right)^2 = 6.0 \times 10^{-4} \text{ m}^2$

b) $7.2 \text{ mm}^3 \times \left(\dfrac{10^{-3} \text{ m}}{1 \text{ mm}} \right)^3 = 7.2 \times 10^{-9} \text{ m}^3$

c) $25 \text{ } \mu\text{m}^2 \times \left(\dfrac{10^{-6} \text{ m}}{1 \text{ } \mu\text{m}} \right)^2 \times \left(\dfrac{1 \text{ dm}}{10^{-1} \text{ m}} \right)^2 = 2.5 \times 10^{-9} \text{ dm}^2$

d) $0.023 \text{ km}^3 \times \left(\dfrac{10^3 \text{ m}}{1 \text{ km}} \right)^3 \times \left(\dfrac{1 \text{ nm}}{10^{-9} \text{ m}} \right)^3 = 2.3 \times 10^{34} \text{ nm}^3$

Dimensional Analysis: Metric-English Unit Conversions (Sec. 3.7)

3.39 a) $100.0 \text{ yd} \times \dfrac{3 \text{ ft}}{1 \text{ yd}} \times \dfrac{12 \text{ in.}}{1 \text{ ft}} \times \dfrac{2.540 \text{ cm}}{1 \text{ in.}} \times \dfrac{10^{-2} \text{ m}}{1 \text{ cm}} = 91.44 \text{ m}$ (calc and corr)

b) $100.0 \text{ yd} \times \dfrac{3 \text{ ft}}{1 \text{ yd}} \times \dfrac{12 \text{ in.}}{1 \text{ ft}} \times \dfrac{2.540 \text{ cm}}{1 \text{ in.}} = 9144 \text{ cm}$ (calc and corr)

c) $100.0 \text{ yd} \times \dfrac{3 \text{ ft}}{1 \text{ yd}} \times \dfrac{12 \text{ in.}}{1 \text{ ft}} \times \dfrac{2.540 \text{ cm}}{1 \text{ in.}} \times \dfrac{10^{-2} \text{ m}}{1 \text{ cm}} \times \dfrac{1 \text{ km}}{10^3 \text{ m}} = 0.09144 \text{ km}$ (calc and corr)

d) $100.0 \text{ yd} \times \dfrac{3 \text{ ft}}{1 \text{ yd}} \times \dfrac{12 \text{ in.}}{1 \text{ ft}} = 3600 \text{ (calc)} = 3.600 \times 10^3 \text{ in.}$ (corr)

3.41 a) $75 \text{ mL} \times \dfrac{10^{-3} \text{ L}}{1 \text{ mL}} \times \dfrac{1 \text{ qt}}{0.9463 \text{ L}} = 0.079256 \text{ (calc)} = 0.079 \text{ qt}$ (corr)

b) $75 \text{ mL} \times \dfrac{10^{-3} \text{ L}}{1 \text{ mL}} \times \dfrac{1 \text{ qt}}{0.9463 \text{ L}} \times \dfrac{1 \text{ gal}}{4 \text{ qt}} = 0.019814 \text{ (calc)} = 0.020 \text{ gal}$ (corr)

c) $75 \text{ mL} \times \dfrac{10^{-3} \text{ L}}{1 \text{ mL}} \times \dfrac{1 \text{ qt}}{0.9463 \text{ L}} \times \dfrac{32 \text{ fl oz}}{1 \text{ qt}} = 2.5361936 \text{ (calc)} = 2.5 \text{ fl oz}$ (corr)

d) $75 \text{ mL} \times \dfrac{1 \text{ cm}^3}{1 \text{ mL}} = 75 \text{ cm}^3$

3.43 a) $6.6 \times 10^{21} \text{ tons} \times \dfrac{2000 \text{ lb}}{1 \text{ ton}} \times \dfrac{453.6 \text{ g}}{1 \text{ lb}} = 5.98752 \times 10^{27} \text{ (calc)} = 6.0 \times 10^{27} \text{ g}$ (corr)

b) $6.6 \times 10^{21} \text{ tons} \times \dfrac{2000 \text{ lb}}{1 \text{ ton}} \times \dfrac{453.6 \text{ g}}{1 \text{ lb}} \times \dfrac{1 \text{ kg}}{10^3 \text{ g}} = 5.98752 \times 10^{24} \text{ (calc)} = 6.0 \times 10^{24} \text{ kg}$ (corr)

c) $6.6 \times 10^{21} \text{ tons} \times \dfrac{2000 \text{ lb}}{1 \text{ ton}} \times \dfrac{453.6 \text{ g}}{1 \text{ lb}} \times \dfrac{1 \text{ ng}}{10^{-9} \text{ g}} = 5.98752 \times 10^{36} \text{ (calc)}$

$= 6.0 \times 10^{36} \text{ ng}$ (corr)

d) $6.6 \times 10^{21} \text{ tons} \times \dfrac{2000 \text{ lb}}{1 \text{ ton}} \times \dfrac{16 \text{ oz}}{1 \text{ lb}} = 2.112000 \times 10^{26} \text{ (calc)} = 2.1 \times 10^{26} \text{ oz}$ (corr)

3.45 a) $A = 2.1 \text{ cm} \times 2.5 \text{ cm} = 5.25 \text{ (calc)} = 5.2 \text{ cm}^2$ (corr)

b) $A = 5.2 \text{ cm}^2 \times \left(\dfrac{1 \text{ in.}}{2.540 \text{ cm}} \right)^2 = 0.80600161 \text{ (calc)} = 0.81 \text{ in.}^2$ (corr)

3.47 $V = (95 \times 105 \times 145) \text{ cm}^3 \times \left(\dfrac{1 \text{ in.}}{2.540 \text{ cm}} \right)^3 \times \left(\dfrac{1 \text{ ft}}{12 \text{ in.}} \right)^3 = 51.078251 \text{ (calc)} = 51 \text{ ft}^3 \text{ (corr)}$

Density (Sec. 3.8)

3.49   density = mass (grams) divided by volume (mL)

a) $\dfrac{25.0 \text{ g}}{31.7 \text{ mL}} = 0.78864353 \text{ (calc)} = 0.789 \dfrac{\text{g}}{\text{mL}} \text{ (corr)}$

b) $\dfrac{25.0 \text{ g}}{3.48 \text{ cm}^3 \times \dfrac{1 \text{ mL}}{1 \text{ cm}^3}} = 7.1839080 \text{ (calc)} = 7.18 \dfrac{\text{g}}{\text{mL}} \text{ (corr)}$

c) $\dfrac{22.9 \text{ g}}{25.0 \text{ mL}} = 0.916 \dfrac{\text{g}}{\text{mL}} \text{ (calc and corr)}$

d) $\dfrac{37,200 \text{ g}}{25.0 \text{ L} \times \dfrac{1 \text{ mL}}{10^{-3} \text{ L}}} = 1.488 \times 10^6 \text{ (calc)} = 1.49 \times 10^6 \dfrac{\text{g}}{\text{mL}} \text{ (corr)}$

3.51   Use density as a conversion factor

a) $22.2 \text{ mL} \times \dfrac{1.027 \text{ g}}{1 \text{ mL}} = 22.7994 \text{ (calc)} = 22.8 \text{ g (corr)}$

b) $22.2 \text{ cm}^3 \times \dfrac{19.3 \text{ g}}{1 \text{ cm}^3} = 428.46 \text{ (calc)} = 428 \text{ g (corr)}$

c) $22.2 \text{ L} \times \dfrac{1.29 \text{ g}}{1 \text{ L}} = 28.638 \text{ (calc)} = 28.6 \text{ g (corr)}$

d) $22.2 \text{ L} \times \dfrac{1 \text{ mL}}{10^{-3} \text{ L}} \times \dfrac{1.027 \text{ g}}{1 \text{ mL}} = 22,799.4 \text{ (calc)} = 22,800 \text{ g (corr)}$

3.53   Use density as a conversion factor

a) $50.0 \text{ g} \times \dfrac{1 \text{ mL}}{0.791 \text{ g}} = 63.211125 \text{ (calc)} = 63.2 \text{ mL (corr)}$

b) $50.0 \text{ g} \times \dfrac{1 \text{ cm}^3}{10.40 \text{ g}} \times \dfrac{1 \text{ mL}}{1 \text{ cm}^3} = 4.8076923 \text{ (calc)} = 4.81 \text{ mL (corr)}$

c) $50.0 \text{ g} \times \dfrac{1 \text{ L}}{1.25 \text{ g}} \times \dfrac{1 \text{ mL}}{10^{-3} \text{ L}} = 40,000 \text{ (calc)} = 4.00 \times 10^4 \text{ mL (corr)}$

d) $50.0 \text{ g} \times \dfrac{1 \text{ cm}^3}{2.18 \text{ g}} \times \dfrac{1 \text{ mL}}{1 \text{ cm}^3} = 22.935780 \text{ (calc)} = 22.9 \text{ mL (corr)}$

3.55 $(5.261 - 3.006) \text{ g} = 2.255 \text{ g red liquid (calc and corr)}$

$d = \dfrac{2.255 \text{ g}}{2.171 \text{ mL}} = 1.0386918 \text{ (calc)} = 1.039 \dfrac{\text{g}}{\text{mL}} \text{ (corr)}$

3.57 pathway: gal → qt → L → mL → g → lb

$$13.0 \text{ gal} \times \frac{4 \text{ qt}}{1 \text{ gal}} \times \frac{0.9463 \text{ L}}{1 \text{ qt}} \times \frac{1 \text{ mL}}{10^{-3} \text{ L}} \times \frac{0.56 \text{ g}}{1 \text{ mL}} \times \frac{1 \text{ lb}}{453.6 \text{ g}} = \begin{array}{l} 60.750123 \text{ (calc)} \\ = 61 \text{ lb (corr)} \end{array}$$

3.59 Al = aluminum, Cr = chromium

$$100.0 \text{ g Al} \times \frac{1 \text{ cm}^3 \text{ Al}}{2.70 \text{ g Al}} \times \frac{1 \text{ cm}^3 \text{ Cr}}{1 \text{ cm}^3 \text{ Al}} \times \frac{7.18 \text{ g Cr}}{1 \text{ cm}^3 \text{ Cr}} = 265.92593 \text{ (calc)} = 266 \text{ g (corr)}$$

3.61 a) float   b) sink

Equivalence Conversion Factors (Sec. 3.9)

3.63 a) equivalence   b) equality   c) equality   d) equivalence

3.65 $225 \text{ kroner} \times \frac{1 \text{ dollar}}{7.65 \text{ kroner}} = 29.41176471 \text{ (calc)} = 29.4 \text{ dollar (corr)}$

3.67 $15.9 \text{ kg} \times \frac{32 \text{ mg antibiotic}}{1 \text{ kg}} = 508.8 \text{ (calc)} = 5.1 \times 10^2 \text{ mg antibiotic(corr)}$

3.69 $375 \text{ mg} \times \frac{1 \text{ kg}}{6.00 \text{ mg}} \times \frac{10^3 \text{ g}}{1 \text{ kg}} \times \frac{1 \text{ lb}}{453.6 \text{ g}} = 137.7866 \text{ (calc)} = 138 \text{ lb (corr)}$

3.71
a) $\frac{2.30 \text{ μg}}{1 \text{ L}} \times \frac{10^{-6} \text{ g}}{1 \text{ μg}} \times \frac{1 \text{ mg}}{10^{-3} \text{ g}} = 2.30 \times 10^{-3} \frac{\text{mg}}{\text{L}}$

b) $\frac{2.30 \text{ μg}}{1 \text{ L}} \times \frac{10^{-3} \text{ L}}{1 \text{ mL}} = 2.30 \times 10^{-3} \text{ μg/mL}$

c) $\frac{2.30 \text{ μg}}{1 \text{ L}} \times \frac{10^{-6} \text{ g}}{1 \text{ μg}} \times \frac{1 \text{ cg}}{10^{-2} \text{ g}} \times \frac{10^{-2} \text{ L}}{1 \text{ cL}} = 2.30 \times 10^{-6} \text{ cg/cL}$

d) $\frac{2.30 \text{ μg}}{1 \text{ L}} \times \frac{10^{-6} \text{ g}}{1 \text{ μg}} \times \frac{1 \text{ kg}}{10^3 \text{ g}} \times \frac{10^{-3} \text{ L}}{1 \text{ mL}} \times \frac{1 \text{ mL}}{1 \text{ cm}^3} \times \left(\frac{1 \text{ cm}}{10^{-2} \text{ m}}\right)^3 = 2.30 \times 10^{-6} \text{ kg/m}^3$

Percentage (Sec. 3.10)

3.73
a) % nickels = $\frac{5 \text{ nickels}}{40 \text{ coins (total)}} \times 100 = 12.5\%$ (calc and corr)

b) % quarters = $\frac{15 \text{ quarters}}{40 \text{ coins (total)}} \times 100 = 37.5\%$ (calc and corr)

c) % 10¢ or less = $\frac{17 \text{ pennies} + 5 \text{ nickels} + 2 \text{ dimes}}{40 \text{ coins total}} \times 100 = \frac{24}{40} \times 100 = 60.0 \%$ *(calc and corr)*

d) % smaller than nickel = $\frac{17 \text{ pennies} + 2 \text{ dimes}}{40 \text{ coins (total)}} \times 100 = \frac{19}{40} \times 100 = 47.5\%$ (calc and corr)

3.75 a) % copper = $\frac{2.902 \text{ g copper}}{3.053 \text{ g penny}} \times 100 = 95.054045 \text{ (calc)} = 95.05\%$ copper(corr)

b) mass zinc = 3.053 g penny − 2.902 g copper = 0.151 g zinc

$$\% \text{ zinc} = \frac{0.151 \text{ g zinc}}{3.053 \text{ g penny}} \times 100 \quad = 4.945948 \text{ (calc)} = 4.95\% \text{ zinc (corr)}$$

Alternate method:

% zinc = 100 − % copper = 100 − 95.05 = 4.95% zinc (calc and corr)

3.77 $65.3 \text{ g mixture} \times \dfrac{34.2 \text{ g water}}{100 \text{ g mixture}} = 22.3326 \text{ (calc)} = 22.3 \text{ g water (corr)}$

3.79 $437 \text{ g solution} \times \dfrac{15.3 \text{ g salt}}{100 \text{ g solution}} = 66.861 \text{ (calc)} = 66.9 \text{ g salt (corr)}$

3.81 $661 \text{ Gummi} \times \dfrac{30.9 \text{ bears}}{100 \text{ Gummi}} \times \dfrac{23.0 \text{ orange}}{100 \text{ bears}} \times \dfrac{6.4 \text{ one-ear}}{100 \text{ orange}} \quad = 3.0065453 \text{ (calc)}$
$= 3 \text{ one-ear (corr)}$

3.83   student 1: $\dfrac{(78.0\text{-}78.5)^\circ\text{C}}{78.5\,^\circ\text{C}} \times 100 = -0.63694267 \% \text{ (calc)} = -0.6\% \text{ (corr)}$

student 2: $\dfrac{(77.9\text{-}78.5)^\circ\text{C}}{78.5\,^\circ\text{C}} \times 100 = -0.76433121 \% \text{ (calc)} = -0.8\% \text{ (corr)}$

student 3: $\dfrac{(79.7\text{-}78.5)^\circ\text{C}}{78.5\,^\circ\text{C}} \times 100 = 1.5286624 \% \text{ (calc)} = 1.5\% \text{ (corr)}$

3.85 $72.6 \text{ yrs} - 53.6 \text{ yrs} = \dfrac{19.0 \text{ yrs}}{53.6 \text{ yrs}} \times 100 = 35.4477611 \% \text{ (calc)} = 35.4 \% \text{ (corr)}$

Temperature Scales (Sec. 3.11)

3.87   a) 32°F   b) 0 °C   c) 273 K

3.89   a) $1251\,^\circ\text{C} = 1251\,^\circ\text{C above FP} \times \dfrac{9\,^\circ\text{F}}{5\,^\circ\text{C}} = 2251.8 \text{ (calc)} = 2252 \text{ (corr) }^\circ\text{F above FP (32 }^\circ\text{F)}$
$= 2252 + 32 = 2284\,^\circ\text{F}$

b) $23.2\,^\circ\text{C} = 23.2\,^\circ\text{C above FP} \times \dfrac{9\,^\circ\text{F}}{5\,^\circ\text{C}} = 41.76 \text{ (calc)} = 41.8 \text{ (corr) }^\circ\text{F above FP (32 }^\circ\text{F)}$
$= 41.8 + 32.0 = 73.8\,^\circ\text{F}$

c) $-2\,^\circ\text{C} = 2\,^\circ\text{C below FP} \times \dfrac{9\,^\circ\text{F}}{5\,^\circ\text{C}} = 3.6 \text{ (calc)} = 4 \text{ (corr) }^\circ\text{F below FP (32 }^\circ\text{F)} = 32 - 4 = 28\,^\circ\text{F}$

d) $-87\,^\circ\text{C} = 87\,^\circ\text{C below FP} \times \dfrac{9\,^\circ\text{F}}{5\,^\circ\text{C}} = 156.6 \text{ (calc)} = 157 \text{ (corr) }^\circ\text{F below FP (32 }^\circ\text{F)}$
$= 32 - 157 = -125\,^\circ\text{F}$

3.91   a) $2450\,^\circ\text{F} = 2450 - 32 = 2418\,^\circ\text{F above FP} \times \dfrac{5\,^\circ\text{C}}{9\,^\circ\text{F}} = 1343.3333 \text{ (calc)}$
$= 1343 \text{ (corr) }^\circ\text{C above FP (0 }^\circ\text{C)}$
$= 1343\,^\circ\text{C}$

b) $337\,^\circ\text{F} = 337 - 32 = 305\,^\circ\text{F above FP} \times \dfrac{5\,^\circ\text{C}}{9\,^\circ\text{F}} = 169.4444 \text{ (calc)}$
$= 169 \text{ (corr) }^\circ\text{C above FP (0 }^\circ\text{C)} = 169\,^\circ\text{C}$

c) $11\,^\circ\text{F} = 11 - 32 = 21\,^\circ\text{F below FP} \times \dfrac{5\,^\circ\text{C}}{9\,^\circ\text{F}} = 11.66667 \text{ (calc)}$
$= 12 \text{ (corr) }^\circ\text{C below FP (0 }^\circ\text{C)} = -12\,^\circ\text{C}$

d) $-37\,^\circ\text{F} = -37 - 32 = 69\,^\circ\text{F below FP} \times \dfrac{5\,^\circ\text{C}}{9\,^\circ\text{F}} = 38.33333 \text{ (calc)}$
$= 38 \text{ (corr) }^\circ\text{C below FP (0 }^\circ\text{C)} = -38\,^\circ\text{C}$

3.93   a) K = 231 °C + 273.2 = 504.2 (calc) = 504 K (corr)
        b) K = 231.7 °C + 273.2 = 504.9 K (calc and corr)
        c) K = 231.74 °C + 273.15 = 504.89 K (calc and corr)

        d) 37.3 °F = 37.3 − 32 = 5.3 °F above FP x $\dfrac{5 \text{ °C}}{9 \text{ °F}}$ = 2.944444 (calc)
$$= 2.9 \text{ °C (corr) above FP } (0 \text{ °C}) = 2.9 \text{ °C}$$
$$K = 2.9 \text{ °C} \times 273.2 = 276.1 \text{ K (calc and corr)}$$

3.95   a) 101 °F = 101 − 32 = 69 °F above FP x $\dfrac{5 \text{ °C}}{9 \text{ °F}}$ = 38.33333 (calc) = 38 (corr) °C above FP (0 °C)
$$= 38 \text{ °C}$$

        b) −218.4 °C = 218.4 °C below FP x $\dfrac{9 \text{ °F}}{5 \text{ °C}}$ = 393.12 (calc) = 393.1 (corr) °F below FP (32 °F)
$$= (32 − 393.1) = −361.1 \text{ °F}$$

        c) 804 °C + 273.2 = 1077 K
        d) 77 K − 273.2 = −195.8 (calc) = −196 °C (corr)

        −196 °C = 196 °C below FP x $\dfrac{9 \text{ °F}}{5 \text{ °C}}$ = 352.8 (calc) = 353 (corr) °F below FP (32 °F)
$$= (32 − 353) = −321 \text{ °F}$$

3.97   −10 °C = 10 °C below the ice point

        10 C ° x $\dfrac{9 \text{ °F}}{5 \text{ °C}}$ = 18 °F below the ice point (calc and corr) 32 °F − 18 F ° = 14 °F

        ∴ −10 °C is a higher temperature than 10 °F

3.99   223 K − 273.2 = −50.2 (calc) = −50 °C (corr)   −50 °C = 50 °C below the ice point

        50 C° x $\dfrac{9 \text{ °F}}{5 \text{ °C}}$ = 90 °F below the ice point (calc and corr)

        32 °F − 90 ° F = −58 °F
        ∴ −60 °F is a lower temperature than 223 K

ADDITIONAL PROBLEMS

3.101   a) 2   b) 3   c) 5   d) 4

3.103   a) 6.301 km   b) 1.442 sec   c) 1.327 mg   d) 2.1 cL

3.105   a) 10^3 m   b) 10^{-9} m   c) 10^{12} pm   d) 10^{-6} Mm

3.107   Before adding, all values must have the same units; convert them all to centimeters.

    (1) 20.9 dm x $\dfrac{10^{-1} \text{ m}}{1 \text{ dm}}$ x $\dfrac{1 \text{ cm}}{10^{-2} \text{ m}}$ = 209 cm(2) 2030 mm x $\dfrac{10^{-3} \text{ m}}{1 \text{ mm}}$ x $\dfrac{1 \text{ cm}}{10^{-2} \text{ m}}$ = 203 cm

(3) $1.90 \text{ m} \times \dfrac{1 \text{ cm}}{10^{-2} \text{ m}} = 190 \text{ cm}$ (4) $0.00183 \text{ km} \times \dfrac{10^3 \text{ m}}{1 \text{ km}} \times \dfrac{1 \text{ cm}}{10^{-2} \text{ m}} = 183 \text{ cm}$

(5) 203 cm = 203 cm

209 cm + 203 cm + 190 cm + 183 cm + 203 cm = 988 cm

Average = $\dfrac{988 \text{ cm}}{5}$ = 197.6 (calc) = 198 cm (corr)

3.109   a) $4.67 \text{ L} \times \dfrac{1 \text{ qt}}{0.9463 \text{ L}} \times \dfrac{1 \text{ gal}}{4 \text{ qt}} = 1.2337525$ (calc) = 1.23 gal (corr)

b) $4.670 \text{ L} \times \dfrac{1 \text{ qt}}{0.9463 \text{ L}} \times \dfrac{1 \text{ gal}}{4 \text{ qt}} = 1.2337525$ (calc) = 1.234 gal (corr)

c) $4.6700 \text{ L} \times \dfrac{1 \text{ qt}}{0.94633 \text{ L}} \times \dfrac{1 \text{ gal}}{4 \text{ qt}} = 1.2337133$ (calc) = 1.2337 gal (corr)

d) $4.67000 \text{ L} \times \dfrac{1 \text{ qt}}{0.946333 \text{ L}} \times \dfrac{1 \text{ gal}}{4 \text{ qt}} = 1.2337094$ (calc) = 1.23371 gal (corr)

3.111 $8 \text{ } yrs \times \dfrac{365 \text{ days}}{1 \text{ yr}} \times \dfrac{24 \text{ hrs}}{1 \text{ day}} \times \dfrac{60 \text{ min}}{1 \text{day}} \times \dfrac{69 \text{ beats}}{1 \text{ min}} = 2.90076000 \times 10^8$ beats (calc)

$= 2.9 \times 10^8$ beats (corr)

3.113   pathway: pt → qt → L → mL → g

$1.00 \text{ pt} \times \dfrac{1 \text{ qt}}{2 \text{ pt}} \times \dfrac{0.9463 \text{ L}}{1 \text{ qt}} \times \dfrac{1 \text{ mL}}{10^{-3} \text{ L}} \times \dfrac{1.05 \text{ g}}{1 \text{ mL}} = 496.8075$ (calc) = 497 g (corr)

3.115 $325 \text{ g acid} \times \dfrac{10\overline{0} \text{ g solution}}{38.1 \text{ g acid}} \times \dfrac{1 cm^3 \text{ solution}}{1.29 \text{ g solution}} \times \dfrac{1 \text{ mL solution}}{1 cm^3 \text{ solution}} = 661.25455$ (calc)

$= 661 \text{ mL}$ (corr)

3.117

$\qquad\qquad\qquad\qquad\qquad\qquad \mu g \to g \to mg$

a) pathway $\searrow \quad mL \to L \to dL$

$5000 \text{ } \dfrac{1 \text{ } \mu g}{1 \text{ mL}} \times \dfrac{10^{-6} \text{ g}}{1 \text{ } \mu g} \times \dfrac{1 \text{ mg}}{10^{-3} \text{ g}} \times \dfrac{1 \text{ mL}}{10^{-3} \text{ L}} \times \dfrac{10^{-1} \text{ L}}{1 \text{ dL}} = 500 \dfrac{mg}{dL}$ (calc and corr)

∴ Yes, a life-threatening situation

$\qquad\qquad\qquad\qquad g \to mg$

b) pathway $\nearrow$

$\qquad\qquad\qquad \searrow \quad L \to dL$

$0.5 \text{ } \dfrac{1 \text{ g}}{1 \text{ L}} \times \dfrac{1 \text{ mg}}{10^{-3} \text{ g}} \times \dfrac{10^{-1} \text{ L}}{1 \text{ dL}} = 50 \dfrac{mg}{dL}$ (calc and corr)

∴ No, not a life-threatening situation

3.119 pathway: dimensions → volume → mass
$3.5 \text{ m} \times 3.0 \text{ m} \times 3.2 \text{ m} = 33.6 \text{ (calc)} = 34 \text{ m}^3 \text{ (corr)}$

$$34 \text{ m}^3 \times \left(\frac{1 \text{ cm}}{10^{-2} \text{ m}} \right)^3 \times 5.7 \times 10^{-3} \frac{1 \text{ μg}}{1 \text{ cm}^3} \times \frac{10^{-6} \text{ g}}{1 \text{ μg}} = 0.1938 \text{ (calc)} = 0.19 \text{ g (corr)}$$

3.121 $\text{Area (cm}^2) = 4.0 \text{ in.} \times 4.0 \text{ in.} \times \left(\frac{2.540 \text{ cm}}{1 \text{ in.}} \right)^2 = 103.2256 \text{ (calc)} = 1\bar{0}0 \text{ cm}^2 \text{ (corr)}$

$\text{Volume (cm}^3) = 0.466 \text{ g} \times \left(\frac{1 \text{ cg}}{10^{-2} \text{ g}} \times \frac{1 \text{ cm}^3}{269 \text{ cg}} \right) = 0.1732342 \text{ (calc)} = 0.173 \text{ cm}^3 \text{ (corr)}$

$\text{Thickness} = \frac{0.173 \text{ cm}^3}{1\bar{0}0 \text{ cm}^2} = 0.00173 \text{ cm} = 0.0173 \text{ mm (calc)} = 1.7 \times 10^{-2} \text{ mm (corr)}$

3.123 Conversion factor: $(212 - 32) \,^\circ\text{F} = [200 - (-200)] \,^\circ\text{H}; \quad 180 \,^\circ\text{F} = 400 \,^\circ\text{H}$
$20 \,^\circ\text{H} = 9 \,^\circ\text{F}$

$50 \,^\circ\text{F} = 50 - 32 = 18 \,^\circ\text{F} \text{ above FP} \times \frac{20 \,^\circ\text{H}}{9 \,^\circ\text{F}} = 40 \,^\circ\text{H} \text{ above FP} \, (-200 \,^\circ\text{H}) = 40 + (-200)$
$= -160 \,^\circ\text{H}$

3.125 Conversion factors: (1) $\dfrac{30.3 \text{ orange}}{100 \text{ bears}}$ (2) $\dfrac{8.10 \text{ one-ear orange}}{100 \text{ orange}}$ (3) $\dfrac{3 \text{ one-ear orange}}{1 \text{ bag}}$

$\dfrac{3 \text{ one-ear orange}}{1 \text{ bag}} \times \dfrac{100 \text{ orange}}{8.10 \text{ one-ear orange}} \times \dfrac{100 \text{ bears}}{30.3 \text{ orange}} = 122.23445 \text{ (calc)}$

$= 122 \dfrac{\text{bears}}{\text{bag}} \text{ (corr)}$

CUMULATIVE PROBLEMS

3.127 a) $d = \dfrac{2.000 \text{ g}}{4.000 \text{ mL}} = 0.5 \text{ (calc)} = 5.000 \times 10^{-1} \dfrac{\text{g}}{\text{mL}} \text{ (corr)}$

b) $d = \dfrac{2.00 \text{ g}}{4.0 \text{ mL}} = 0.5 \text{ (calc)} = 5.0 \times 10^{-1} \dfrac{\text{g}}{\text{mL}} \text{ (corr)}$

c) $d = \dfrac{2.0000 \text{ g}}{4.0000 \text{ mL}} = 0.5 \text{ (calc)} = 5.0000 \times 10^{-1} \dfrac{\text{g}}{\text{mL}} \text{ (corr)}$

d) $d = \dfrac{2.000 \text{ g}}{4.0000 \text{ mL}} = 0.5 \text{ (calc)} = = 5.000 \times 10^{-1} \dfrac{\text{g}}{\text{mL}} \text{ (corr)}$

3.129 a) $V = 1\bar{0} \text{ cm} \times 2\bar{0}0 \text{ cm} \times 4 \text{ cm} = 8000 \text{ (calc)} = 8 \times 10^3 \text{ cm}^3 \text{ (corr)}$
b) $V = 10.0 \text{ cm} \times 200.0 \text{ cm} \times 4.0 \text{ cm} = 8000 \text{ (calc)} = 8.0 \times 10^3 \text{ cm}^3 \text{ (corr)}$
c) $V = 10.00 \text{ cm} \times 200.00 \text{ cm} \times 4.00 \text{ cm} = 8000 \text{ (calc)} = 8.00 \times 10^3 \text{ cm}^3 \text{ (corr)}$
d) $V = 1\bar{0} \text{ cm} \times 2\bar{0}0 \text{ cm} \times 4.0 \text{ cm} = 8000 \text{ (calc)} = 8.0 \times 10^3 \text{ cm}^3 \text{ (corr)}$

3.131 Express each measurement as a decimal number with ± uncertainty, using the same units for the set.

a) 3.256×10^3 g $= 3256 \pm 1$ g

3.256×10^4 g $= 32{,}560 \pm 10$ g

3.256×10^5 g $= 325{,}600 \pm 100$ g

$\therefore 3.256 \times 10^3$ g has the greatest precision (least uncertainty)

b) 3.34 g $= 3.34 \pm 0.01$ g 3.34 kg $\times \dfrac{10^3 \text{ g}}{1 \text{ kg}} = 3.34 \times 10^3$ g $= 3{,}340 \pm 10$g

3.34 mg $\times \dfrac{10^{-3} \text{ g}}{1 \text{ mg}} = 3.34 \times 10^{-3}$ g $= 0.00334 \pm 0.00001$ g

$\therefore 3.34$ mg has the greatest precision (least uncertainty)

c) 4.31 ± 0.01 g 4.31×10^{-3} kg $\times \dfrac{10^3 \text{ g}}{1 \text{ kg}} = 4.31 \pm 0.01$ g

4.31×10^3 mg $\times \dfrac{10^{-3} \text{ g}}{1 \text{ mg}} = 4.31 \pm 0.01$ g $\therefore$ Each has the same precision

d) 325.0 cg $\times \dfrac{10^{-2} \text{ g}}{1 \text{ cg}} = 3.250 \pm 0.001$ g

3.2500 g $= 3.2500 \pm 0.0001$ g

0.00325 kg $\times \dfrac{10^3 \text{ g}}{1 \text{ kg}} = 3.25$ g $= 3.25 \pm 0.01$ g

$\therefore 3.2500$ g has the greatest precision (least uncertainty)

3.133 1.2120 ± 0.0001 g

a) 0.00121 kg $\times \dfrac{10^3 \text{ g}}{1 \text{ kg}} = 1.21 \pm 0.01$ g $\therefore$ Therefore is not equivalent.

b) 121.20 cg $\times \dfrac{10^{-2} \text{ g}}{1 \text{ cg}} = 1.2120 \pm 0.0001$ g $\therefore$ Therefore is equivalent.

c) 12120 mg $\times \dfrac{10^{-3} \text{ g}}{1 \text{ mg}} = 12.120$ g ± 0.001 g $\therefore$ Therefore is not equivalent.

d) 1212.0 µg $\times \dfrac{10^{-6} \text{ g}}{1 \text{ µg}} = 0.0012120 \pm 0.0000001$ g $\therefore$ Therefore is not equivalent.

CHAPTER FOUR
Basic Concepts About Matter

PRACTICE PROBLEMS

Physical States of Matter (Sec. 4.2)

4.1   a) shape (indefinite vs. definite)   b) indefinite shape

4.3   a) Does not take shape of the container, definite volume.
b) Takes on shape of container, indefinite volume.
c) Does not take shape of the container, definite volume.
d) Takes on shape of container, definite volume.

4.5   a) solid   b) solid   c) liquid   d) gas

Properties of Matter (Sec. 4.3)

4.7   a) chemical   b) chemical   c) physical   d) physical

4.9   a) chemical   b) physical   c) physical   d) physical

4.11 a) extensive b) intensive   c) intensive d) intensive

4.13 a) differ in extensive properties (amount)
b) differ in intensive properties (substance)
c) differ in intensive properties (temperature)
d) differ in extensive (amount) and intensive properties (temperature)

Changes in Matter (Sec. 4.4)

4.15 a) physical   b) physical   c) chemical   d) physical

4.17 a) physical   b) physical   c) chemical   d) chemical

4.19 a) physical   b) physical   c) chemical   d) physical

4.21 a) freezing   b) condensation   c) sublimation   d) evaporation

Pure Substances and Mixtures (Secs. 4.5 and 4.6)

4.23 a) heterogeneous and homogeneous mixtures
b) pure substance, homogeneous mixture

4.25 a) false   b) true   c) false   d) true

4.27   a) heterogeneous mixture   b) homogeneous mixture
           c) homogeneous mixture   d) heterogeneous mixture

4.29   a) homogeneous mixture, 1 phase   b) homogeneous mixture, 1 phase
           c) heterogeneous mixture, 2 phases   d) heterogeneous mixture, 2 phases

4.31   a) chemically homogeneous, physically homogeneous
           b) chemically heterogeneous, physically homogeneous
           c) chemically heterogeneous, physically heterogeneous
           d) chemically heterogeneous, physically heterogeneous

Elements and Compounds (Sec. 4.7)

4.33   a) compound   b) compound   c) no classification possible   d) no classification possible

4.35   a) true   b) false   c) false   d) false

4.37   a) A (no classification possible), B (no classification possible), C (compound)
           b) D (compound), E (no classification possible), F (no classification possible), G (no classification
             possible)

4.39   First box, mixture; second box, compound

4.41   a) element and compound   b) element and compound
           c) two elements   d) pure substance

Discovery and Abundance of the Elements (Sec. 4.8)

4.43   a) false   b) true   c) false   d) true

4.45   a) yes, silicon is more abundant   b) no, hydrogen is more abundant
           c) no, oxygen is more abundant   d) yes, sodium is more abundant

Names and Symbols of the Elements (Sec. 4.9)

4.47   a) nitrogen   b) nickel   c) lead   d) tin
           e) Al   f) Ne   g) H   h) U

4.49   a) Na and S   b) Mg and Mn   c) Ca and Cd   d) As and Ar

4.51   a) boron   b) barium   c) beryllium   d) bismuth
           e) berkelium   f) bromine

4.53   a) fluorine   b) zinc   c) potassium   d) sulfur

4.55   a) iron, Fe   b) tin, Sn   c) sodium, Na   d) gold, Au

4.57   a) Re-Be-C-Ca   b) Ra-Y-Mo-Nd   c) Na-N-C-Y
           d) Br-U-Ce or B-Ru-Ce   e) S-H-Ar-O-N   f) Al-I-Ce

ADDITIONAL PROBLEMS

4.59 a) colorless gas, odorless gas, colorless liquid, boils at 43 °C
b) toxic to humans, Ni reacts with CO.

4.61 a) compound b) mixture c) compound d) mixture

4.63 a) homogeneous mixture b) element c) heterogeneous mixture   d) homogeneous mixture

4.65 a) heterogeneous mixture   b) heterogeneous mixture
c) homogeneous mixture   d) heterogeneous, but not a mixture

4.67 (b) and (c)

4.69 Alphabetized: Bh, Bi, Bk, Cf, Co, Cs, Cu, Hf, Ho, Hs, In, Nb, Ni, No, Np, Os, Pb, Po, Pu, Sb, Sc, Si, Sn, Yb

CUMULATIVE PROBLEMS

4.71 a) solid   b) state determination not possible (boiling point not known)
c) gas   d) state determination not possible (two states present)

4.73 a) $\% = \dfrac{88}{110 \text{ total}} \times 100 = 80 \text{ (calc)} = 80.0 \% \text{ (corr)}$

b) $\% = \dfrac{14}{110 \text{ total}} \times 100 = 12.7277272 \text{ (calc)} = 12.8 \% \text{ (corr)}$

c) $\% = \dfrac{28}{110 \text{ total}} \times 100 = 25.45454545 \text{ (calc)} = 25.5 \% \text{ (corr)}$

d) $\% = (20.1 + 2.4 + 2.2)\% = 24.7 \% \text{ (calc and corr)}$

4.75 a) $\text{density(I)} = \dfrac{4.32 \text{ g}}{3.78 \text{ mL}} = 1.1428571 \text{ (calc)} = 1.14 \text{ g/mL (corr)}$

$\text{density(II)} = \dfrac{5.73 \text{ g}}{5.02 \text{ mL}} = 1.1414342 \text{ (calc)} = 1.14 \text{ g/mL (corr)}$

$\text{density(III)} = \dfrac{1.52 \text{ g}}{1.33 \text{ mL}} = 1.1428571 \text{ (calc)} = 1.14 \text{ g/mL (corr)}$

It is likely the students were all working with the same substance.
b) No, density alone will not distinguish between elements and compounds.

4.77 The substance analyzed is likely a compound. The percent composition to three significant figures is the same in each case. The substance cannot be an element because two substances, Q and X, were produced in the analysis.

CHAPTER FIVE

Atoms, Molecules, Formulas and Subatomic Particles

PRACTICE PROBLEMS

Atoms and Molecules (Secs. 5.1 and 5.2)

5.1   a) consistent   b) consistent   c) not consistent   d) consistent

5.3   a) heteroatomic, diatomic, compound   b) heteroatomic, triatomic, compound
        c) homoatomic, diatomic, element   d) heteroatomic, triatomic, compound

5.5   a) false. Molecules must contain two or more atoms.
        b) true
        c) false. Some compounds have molecules as their basic structural unit and others have ions as their basic structural unit.
        d) false, The diameter is approximately 10^{-10} meters.

Chemical Formulas (Sec. 5.4)

5.7   a) X_2Q or QX_2 b) XQZ   c) Z_2Q or QZ_2 d) Z_2

5.9   a) compound   b) compound   c) element   d) element

5.11   a) C_2H_3 b) H_2SO_4 c) HCN   d) $KMnO_4$

5.13   a) same, both 3   b) same, both 5   c) fewer, 5 and 7   d) more, 17 and 13

5.15   a) NO = 1 atom nitrogen, 1 atom oxygen   b) Cs_2 = 2 atoms cesium
        No = 1 atom Nobelium CS_2 = 1 atom carbon, 2 atoms sulfur
        c) $CoBr_2$ = 1 atom cobalt, 2 atoms bromine   d) H = 1 atom hydrogen
        $COBr_2$ = 1 atom carbon, 1 atom oxygen, H_2 = 2 atoms hydrogen
              2 atoms bromine

5.17   a) H_3PO_4 b) $SiCl_4$ c) NO_2 d) H_2O_2

Subatomic Particles (Sec. 5.5)

5.19   a) electron   b) proton   c) proton, neutron   d) neutron

5.21   a) false   b) false   c) false   d) true

Atomic Number and Mass Number (Sec. 5.6)

5.23   a) 50   b) 47   c) nickel   d) iodine

5.25   a) 24, 53   b) 44, 103   c) 101, 256   d) 16, 34

5.27   a) (1)   b) (3)   c) (2)   d) (3)

5.29   a) $^{11}_{5}B$ b) $^{16}_{8}O$ c) $^{27}_{13}Al$ d) $^{40}_{18}Ar$

5.31   a) 16 protons, 16 electrons, 16 neutrons   b) 29 protons, 29 electrons, 34 neutrons
        c) 22 protons, 22 electrons, 28 neutrons   d) 92 protons, 92 electrons, 146 neutrons

5.33   a) 27 protons, 27 electrons, 32 neutrons   b) 45 protons, 45 electrons, 58 neutrons
        c) 69 protons, 69 electrons, 100 neutrons   d) 9 protons, 9 electrons, 10 neutrons

5.35   a) 27   b) 45   c) 69   d) 9

5.37   a) atom has 15 protons; mass number = 15 + 16; $^{31}_{15}P$
        b) oxygen has 8 protons; mass number is 8 + 10 = 18; $^{18}_{8}O$
        c) chromium has 24 protons; $^{54}_{24}Cr$
        d) a gold atom has 79 protons and 79 electrons. 276 subatomic particles – 79 protons – 79
          electrons = 118 neutrons. ∴ mass # = 79 + 118 = 197; $^{197}_{79}Au$

5.39   a) same total number of subatomic particles, 60
        b) same number of neutrons, 16
        c) same number of neutrons, 12
        d) same number of electrons, 3

5.41   a) scandium   b) chlorine   c) strontium   d) arsenic

5.43   a) no   b) yes   c) no   d) yes

Isotopes and Isobars (Sec. 5.7)

5.45 $^{54}_{26}Fe$ $^{56}_{26}Fe$ $^{57}_{26}Fe$ $^{58}_{26}Fe$

5.47 $^{96}_{40}Zr$ $^{94}_{40}Zr$ $^{92}_{40}Zr$ $^{91}_{40}Zr$ $^{90}_{40}Zr$

5.49   a) no   b) yes   c) no   d) yes

5.51   a) isotopes   b) isobars   c) neither   d) isotopes

5.53   a) isotopes   b) isobars   c) neither   d) isotopes

5.55 $^{40}_{18}Ar$ $^{40}_{19}K$ $^{40}_{20}Ca$

Atomic Masses (Sec. 5.8)

5.57   a) 55.84 amu   b) 14.01 amu   c) calcium   d) iodine

5.59   Values on this hypothetical relative mass scale are Q = 8.00 bebs, X = 4.00 bebs, and Z = 2.00 bebs.

5.61   a) Z = ¾(12.) = 9 amu;   X = 3Z = 27 amu;   Q = 9(12) = 108 amu
        b) Z is Be, X is Al, Q is Ag

5.63

$$
\begin{array}{llll}
0.220 \times 271 \text{ lb} & = 59.62 \text{ (calc)} & = & 59.6 \text{ lb (corr)} \\
0.190 \times 175 \text{ lb} & = 33.25 \text{ (calc)} & = & 33.2 \text{ lb (corr)} \\
0.260 \times 263 \text{ lb} & = 68.38 \text{ (calc)} & = & 68.4 \text{ lb (corr)} \\
0.150 \times 182 \text{ lb} & = 27.3 \text{ (calc)} & = & 27.3 \text{ lb (corr)} \\
0.190 \times 191 \text{ lb} & = 36.29 \text{ (calc)} & = & \underline{36.3 \text{ lb}} \text{ (corr)} \\
 & & = & 224.8 \text{ lb (calc and corr)}
\end{array}
$$

5.65 $\begin{array}{ll} 0.7553 \times 34.9689 \text{ amu} = 26.41201 \text{ (calc)} & = 26.41 \text{ amu (corr)} \\ 0.2447 \times 36.9659 \text{ amu} = 9.0455557 \text{ (calc)} & = \underline{9.046 \text{ amu}} \text{ (corr)} \\ & = 35.456 \text{ amu (calc)} \\ & = 35.46 \text{ amu (corr)} \end{array}$

5.67

$$
\begin{array}{lll}
0.0793 \times 45.95263 \text{ amu} & = 3.6440435 \text{ (calc)} & = 3.64 \text{ amu (corr)} \\
0.0728 \times 46.9518 \text{ amu} & = 3.418091 \text{ (calc)} & = 3.42 \text{ amu (corr)} \\
0.7394 \times 47.94795 \text{ amu} & = 35.452714 \text{ (calc)} & = 35.45 \text{ amu (corr)} \\
0.0551 \times 48.94787 \text{ amu} & = 2.6970276 \text{ (calc)} & = 2.70 \text{ amu (corr)} \\
0.0534 \times 49.9448 \text{ amu} & = 2.6670523 \text{ (calc)} & = \underline{2.67 \text{ amu}} \text{ (corr)} \\
 & & = 47.88 \text{ amu (calc and corr)}
\end{array}
$$

5.69   a) ^{14}N b) ^{51}V c) ^{121}Sb d) ^{193}Ir

5.71   a) $\underline{35.45 \text{ amu}} = 0.414765$ (calc) = 0.415 (corr)   b) $\underline{2(35.45 \text{amu})} = 0.414765$ (calc) = 0.415 (corr)
        85.47 amu   2(85.47 amu)
        c) $\underline{107.87 \text{ amu}} = 0.848702$ (calc) = 0.849 (corr)   d) $\underline{10(1.01 \text{ amu})} = 1.12097$ (calc) = 1.12 (corr)
        2(63.55amu)   9.01amu

5.73   a) iron (Fe)   b) strontium (Sr)   c) beryllium (Be)   d) helium (He)

5.75   The number 12.0000 amu applies only to the ^{12}C isotope. The number 12.01 amu applies to naturally occurring carbon, a mixture of ^{12}C, ^{13}C, and ^{14}C.

Evidence Supporting the Existence of Subatomic Particles (Sec. 5.9)

5.77   a) true   b) false   c) false   d) false

ADDITIONAL PROBLEMS

5.79   a) $2 + x + 3 = 7$; $x = 2$
b) $1 + 2(1 + x) = 9$; $3 + 2x = 9$; $2x = 6$; $x = 3$
c) $x + x + 10 = 16$; $2x = 6$; $x = 3$
d) $x + 2x + x = 24$; $4x = 24$; $x = 6$

5.81   7 molecules x $\dfrac{6 \text{ C atoms}}{1 \text{ molecule}}$ x $\dfrac{6 \text{ protons}}{1 \text{ C atom}}$ = 252 protons (calc and corr)

7 molecules x $\dfrac{12 \text{ H atoms}}{1 \text{ molecule}}$ x $\dfrac{1 \text{ proton}}{1 \text{ H atom}}$ = 84 protons (calc and corr)

7 molecules x $\dfrac{6 \text{ O atoms}}{1 \text{ molecule}}$ x $\dfrac{8 \text{ protons}}{1 \text{ O atom}}$ = 336 protons (calc and corr)

Total protons = 252 + 84 + 336 = 672 total protons (calc and corr)

5.83   a) 4 (N_2O, H_2O, CCl_4, CH_2Br_2)
b) 2 (CCl_4 and CH_2Br_2)
c) 4 (N_2O, H_2O, CCl_4, CH_2Br_2)
d) 6 (O, N, H, C, Cl, and Br)
e) $(3 \times 2) + (3 \times 3) + (3 \times 3) + (3 \times 5) + (3 \times 5) = 54$

5.85   a) false   b) false   c) true   d) true

5.87   a) $^{37}_{18}Ar$, $^{39}_{19}K$, $^{42}_{20}Ca$, $^{44}_{21}Sc$, $^{43}_{22}Ti$ b) $^{44}_{21}Sc$, $^{42}_{20}Ca$, $^{43}_{22}Ti$, $^{39}_{19}K$, $^{37}_{18}Ar$

c) $^{37}_{18}Ar$, $^{39}_{19}K$, $^{42}_{20}Ca$, $^{44}_{21}Sc$, $^{43}_{22}Ti$ d) $^{44}_{21}Sc$, $^{43}_{22}Ti$, $^{42}_{20}Ca$, $^{39}_{19}K$, $^{37}_{18}Ar$

5.89   a) $^{8}_{5}B$ b) $^{12}_{5}B$ c) $^{12}_{5}B$ d) $^{16}_{5}B$

5.91   a) 29 and 29   b) 29 and 29   c) 34 and 36

5.93   a) 13   b) 27   c) 14   d) 27.0 amu

5.95   a) $1.679 \times 30.97\,\text{amu} = 51.99863$ (calc) = 52.00 amu = Cr
b) 30e x 3 = 90e = Th
c) 4p + 20p = 24p = Cr
d) [20e + 20p = 40e&p] x 2 = 80e&p = 40p = Zr

5.97   Nickel weighs 20.000 amu on the "new scale" and 58.6934 amu on the old carbon-12 scale. Therefore, 20.000 "new" amu units is equal to 58.6934 "old" amu units.

a) 107.87 old amu x $\dfrac{20.000 \text{ new amu}}{58.6934 \text{ old amu}}$ = 36.7592 (calc) = 36.759 new amu (corr)

b) 196.97 old amu x $\dfrac{20.000 \text{ new amu}}{58.6934 \text{ old amu}}$ = 67.118279 (calc) = 67.118 new amu (corr)

5.99   Let the units of this new relative atomic weight scale be in "bobs." Conversion factors derived from the data:

(1) atomic mass of Z = $\dfrac{80.000 \text{ bobs Z}}{\text{atom Z}}$; the units for atomic mass of X will be $\dfrac{\text{bobs X}}{\text{atom X}}$

(2) if compound is 43.2% X, it will be 100 - 43.2, or 56.8% Z.

%X = $\dfrac{43.2 \text{ bobs X}}{100 \text{ bobs XZ}_2}$ and %Y = $\dfrac{56.8 \text{ bobs Z}}{100 \text{ bobs Z}}$

(3) from the formula XZ$_2$: $\dfrac{2 \text{ atoms Z}}{1 \text{ molecule XZ}_2}$; $\dfrac{1 \text{ atom X}}{1 \text{ molecule XZ}_2}$ or $\dfrac{2 \text{ atoms Z}}{1 \text{ atom X}}$

Applying dimensional analysis (inverting some factors as needed),

$\dfrac{80.000 \text{ bobs Z}}{\text{atom Z}}$ x $\dfrac{2 \text{ atoms Z}}{1 \text{ atom X}}$ x $\dfrac{100 \text{ bobs XZ}_2}{56.8 \text{ bobs Z}}$ x $\dfrac{43.2 \text{ bobs X}}{100 \text{ bobs XZ}_2}$

= 121.69014 (calc) = 122 (corr)

5.101   Multiplying these ratios as conversion factors (applying dimensional analysis) gives

$\dfrac{^{81}\text{Br}}{^{12}\text{C}} = \dfrac{^{19}_{9}\text{F}}{^{12}_{6}\text{C}}$ x $\dfrac{^{35}_{17}\text{Cl}}{^{19}_{9}\text{F}}$ x $\dfrac{^{81}_{35}\text{Br}}{^{35}_{17}\text{Cl}}$ = 1.5832 x 1.8406 x 2.3140 = 6.7430837 (calc) = 6.7431 (corr)

Multiplying by mass of ^{12}C: 12.0000 amu x 6.7431 = 80.9172 (calc) = 80.917 amu (corr)

5.103   The BrCl product with the smallest mass (about 114 amu) must have come from the smaller Cl isotope (^{35}Cl - about 35 amu) and the smallest Br isotope. The smallest Br isotope has a mass of about (114 amu - 35 amu) or 79 amu. Hence, ^{79}Br is the smallest Br isotope.

The BrCl product with the largest mass (about 118 amu) must have come from the larger Cl isotope (^{37}Cl - about 37 amu) and the largest Br isotope, whose mass is (118 amu - 37 amu) = 81 amu. Hence, ^{81}Br is the largest Br isotope.

The *only* other BrCl product (about 116 amu) could have come from either ^{35}Cl with ^{81}Br or ^{37}Cl with ^{79}Br. Hence, only the two isotopes, ^{79}Br and ^{81}Br, exist.

5.105   Since the atomic mass (weighted average) is close to the mass number of the lightest isotope, ^{39}K, that one must be the most abundant of the three isotopes.

CUMULATIVE PROBLEMS

5.107   a) compound   b) mixture   c) element   d) mixture

5.109   92

5.111   3.22 cm^3 x $\dfrac{19.3 \text{ g}}{1 \text{ cm}^3}$ x $\dfrac{1 \text{ Au atom}}{3.27 \times 10^{-22} \text{ g}}$ = 1.9004892 x 10^{23} (calc) = 1.90 x 10^{23} Au atoms (corr)

5.113   pathway: atoms → cm → in → ft → mi

$$3.17 \times 10^{22} \text{ atoms} \times \frac{1.44 \times 10^{-8} \text{ cm}}{1 \text{ atom}} \times \frac{1 \text{ in.}}{2.540 \text{ cm}} \times \frac{1 \text{ ft}}{12 \text{ in.}} \times \frac{1 \text{ mi}}{5280 \text{ ft}}$$

$$= 2.8364352 \times 10^9 \text{ (calc)} = 2.84 \times 10^9 \text{ miles (corr)}$$

5.115   A Pb atom has 82 electrons.

$$\frac{82 \times 5.5 \times 10^{-4} \text{ amu}}{207 \text{ amu}} \times 100 = 0.021787439 \text{ (calc)} = 0.022\% \text{ (corr)}$$

5.117   pathway: in. (nucleus) → in. (atom) → ft (atom) → mi (atom)

$$1.5 \text{ in. (nucleus)} \times \frac{10^5 \text{ in. (atom)}}{1 \text{ in. (nucleus)}} \times \frac{1 \text{ ft}}{12 \text{ in.}} \times \frac{1 \text{ mile}}{5280 \text{ ft}} = 2.3674242 \text{ (calc)} = 2.4 \text{ miles (corr)}$$

CHAPTER SIX
Electronic Structure and Chemical Periodicity

PRACTICE PROBLEMS

Periodic Law and Periodic Table (Sec. 6.1 and 6.2)

6.1   a) Ga   b) Zr   c) Li   d) Cl

6.3   a) same period
b) neither same group nor same period
c) same group
d) same period

6.5   a) $_{19}$K and $_{37}$Rb
b) $_{15}$P and $_{33}$As
c) $_9$F and $_{53}$I
d) $_{11}$Na and $_{55}$Cs

6.7   a) group   b) periodic law   c) periodic law   d) period

6.9   a) fluorine   b) sodium   c) krypton   d) strontium

6.11   a) 3   b) 4   c) 4   d) 4

Terminology Associated with Electron Arrangements (Secs. 6.3–6.6)

6.13   a) 2   b) 10   c) 6   d) 14

6.15   Any orbital has a maximum capacity of 2 electrons. a) 2   b) 2   c) 2   d) 2

6.17   a) 3d subshell can hold 10; second shell can hold 8; $\therefore$ 3d subshell can hold more.
b) n = 1 shell can hold 2; 2p subshell can hold 6; $\therefore$ 2p subshell can hold more.
c) 3p orbital can hold 2; 3p subshell can hold 6; $\therefore$ 3p subshell can hold more.
d) 4f subshell can hold 14; third shell can hold 18; $\therefore$ third shell can hold more.

6.19   a) true   b) false   c) true   d) true   e) false

6.21   a) spherical   b) dumbbell   c) cloverleaf   d) spherical

6.23   a) allowed
b) not allowed, 3d is lowest allowed
c) not allowed, 2p is lowest allowed
d) allowed

Writing Electron Configurations (Sec. 6.7)

6.25 a) $3s$ b) $3d$ c) $7s$ d) $4p$

6.27 a) $1s^2 2s^2 2p^6 3s^2 3p^1$ b) $1s^2 2s^2 2p^3$
c) $1s^2 2s^2 2p^6 3s^2 3p^6$ d) $1s^2 2s^2 2p^6 3s^2$

6.29 a) $1s^2 2s^2 2p^6 3s^2 3p^6 4s^2 3d^6$
b) $1s^2 2s^2 2p^6 3s^2 3p^6 4s^2 3d^{10} 4p^6 5s^1$
c) $1s^2 2s^2 2p^6 3s^2 3p^6 4s^2 3d^{10} 4p^6 5s^2 4d^{10} 5p^5$
d) $1s^2 2s^2 2p^6 3s^2 3p^6 4s^2 3d^{10} 4p^6 5s^2 4d^{10} 5p^6 6s^2 4f^{14} 5d^{10} 6p^6$

6.31 a) $_{10}$Ne b) $_{19}$K c) $_{22}$Ti d) $_{30}$Zn

Orbital Diagrams (Sec. 6.8)

6.33 a)

↑↓	↑
1s	2s

b)

↑↓	↑↓	↑↓ ↑↓ ↑
1s	2s	2p

c)

↑↓	↑↓	↑↓ ↑↓ ↑↓	↑↓	↑ ↑ ↑
1s	2s	2p	3s	3p

d)

↑↓	↑↓	↑↓ ↑↓ ↑↓	↑↓	↑↓ ↑↓ ↑↓	↑↓	↑↓ ↑↓ ↑↓ ↑ ↑
1s	2s	2p	3s	3p	4s	3d

6.35 a)

↑↓	↑↓	↑ ↑
1s	2s	2p

b)

↑↓	↑↓	↑↓ ↑↓ ↑↓
1s	2s	2p

c)

↑↓	↑↓	↑↓ ↑↓ ↑↓	↑
1s	2s	2p	3s

d)

↑↓	↑↓	↑↓ ↑↓ ↑↓	↑↓	↑ ↑ ↑
1s	2s	2p	3s	3p

6.37 a) one b) one c) one d) none

6.39   a) paramagnetic (unpaired)   b) paramagnetic (unpaired)
        c) paramagnetic (unpaired)   d) diamagnetic (paired)

Electron Configurations and the Periodic Law (Sec. 6.9)

6.41   a) no b) yes c) no d) yes

Electron Configurations and the Periodic Table (Sec. 6.10)

6.43   a) d b) p c) s d) f

6.45   a) $4s$ b) $4p$ c) $4d$ d) $5d$

6.47   a) $_{35}$Br   b) $_{87}$Fr   c) $_{40}$Zr   d) $_{23}$V

6.49   a) 2   b) 2   c) 3   d) 4

6.51   a) Al   b) Li   c) La   d) Sc

6.53   a) Kr   b) Li   c) K   d) Lu

6.55   a) $1s^2 2s^2 2p^6 3s^2 3p^6 4s^2 3d^{10} 4p^3$

        b) $1s^2 2s^2 2p^6 3s^2 3p^6 4s^2 3d^{10} 4p^6 5s^2 4d^{10} 5p^3$

        c) $1s^2 2s^2 2p^6 3s^2 3p^6 4s^2 3d^{10} 4p^6 5s^1$

        d) $1s^2 2s^2 2p^6 3s^2 3p^6 4s^2 3d^{10} 4p^6 5s^2 4d^{10}$

6.57   a) Ti, $1s^2 2s^2 2p^6 3s^2 3p^6 4s^2 3d^2$ $\therefore$ 2 electrons in 3d

        b) Ni, $1s^2 2s^2 2p^6 3s^2 3p^6 4s^2 3d^8$ $\therefore$ 8 electrons in 3d

        c) Se, $1s^2 2s^2 2p^6 3s^2 3p^6 4s^2 3d^{10} 4p^4$ $\therefore$ 10 electrons in 3d

        d) Pd, $1s^2 2s^2 2p^6 3s^2 3p^6 4s^2 3d^{10} 4p^6 5s^2 4d^8$ $\therefore$ 10 electrons in 3d

6.59   a) 4   b) 9   c) 2   d) 0

Classification Systems for the Elements (Sec. 6.11)

6.61   a) transition   b) representative   c) noble gas   d) inner transition

6.63   a) metallic   b) nonmetallic   c) metallic   d) nonmetallic

6.65   a) (1) contains more metals   b) (1) contains more metals
        c) (2) contains more nonmetals   d) (2) contains more nonmetals

6.67   a) S   b) P   c) I   d) Cl

6.69   a) Li   b) K   c) Fe   d) Hg

6.71   a) H   b) He   c) Li   d) Ce

Chemical Periodicity (Sec. 6.12)

6.73   a) false   b) true   c) false

6.75   a) Ge   b) B   c) Po   d) Te

6.77   a) Mg   b) Au   c) S   d) Rb

6.79   a) F   b) P   c) Zn   d) Cl

6.81   a) N   b) Ga   c) K   d) Rb

ADDITIONAL PROBLEMS

6.83   a) The $2s$ subshell is more than filled. It has a maximum occupancy of 2 electrons.
b) The $2p$ subshell must be filled before the $3s^2$. It can accommodate 6 electrons.
c) The $2p$ subshell, which fills after the $2s$, is omitted.
d) The $3p$ and $4s$ subshells fill after the $3s$ and before the $3d$ subshell.

6.85   a) period 3, group IA   b) period 3, group IIIA
c) period 4, group IIIB   d) period 4, group VIIA

6.87   a) x = 6, y = 2   b) x = 2, y = 1   c) x = 2, y = 10   d) x = 2, y = 6

6.89   a) $1s^2 2s^2 2p^6 3s^2 3p^2$ (Si)   b) $1s^2 2s^2 2p^2$ (C)
c) $1s^2 2s^2 2p^3$ (N)   d) $1s^2 2s^2 2p^3$ (N)

6.91   a) Be   b) Be   c) Ne   d) Ar

6.93   a) 2   b) 4   c) 1   d) 2

6.95   a) 7 (He + group IIA)   b) 2 (group VIA in periods 2 & 3)
c) 4 (group IIIB)   d) 3 (group VA in periods 4-6)

6.97   a) groups IVA and VIA
b) group VB and middle column of group VIIIB
c) group IVB and last column of group VIIIB
d) group IA

6.99   a) (2)   b) (3)   c) (3)   d) (1)

6.101   a) Po   b) Cr   c) elements 88-112   d) elements 12-18

6.103   a) F   b) Ag

6.105 a) $1s^3 2s^3 2p^7$ b) $1s^3 2s^3 2p^9 3s^3 3p^9 4s^3 3d^5$

c) $1s^3 2s^3 2p^9 3s^1$ d) $1s^3 2s^3 2p^9 3s^3 3p^8$

CUMULATIVE PROBLEMS

6.107 a) O, Li, He, B, K   b) O, He, B (the nonmetals)
c) O, Li, He, B, Sr, K (all of them)   d) K

6.109 the same

6.111 Since the isotopic mass is 36.96590 amu, the mass number is 37. Since 17 electrons are present the atomic number is 17.
protons = electrons = 17; neutrons = 37 − 17 = 20
17 + 17 + 20 = 54

6.113 +38 (Sr)

6.115 a) 22   b) 16/22 x 100 = 72.7%   c)12/22 x 100 = 54.5%   d) 50% (#e + #p)

6.117 P, S, Cl, Se, Br

CHAPTER SEVEN
Chemical Bonds

PRACTICE PROBLEMS

Valence Electrons (Sec. 7.2)

7.1 Valence electrons are all of the *s* and *p* electrons in the highest shell.
a) $2 + 1 = 3$ b) $2 + 5 = 7$ c) 1   d) $2 + 1 = 3$

7.3 a) (1)   b) (3)   c) (1)   d) (2)

7.5 a) group IA, 1 valence electron   b) group VIIIA, 8 valence electrons
c) group IIA, 2 valence electrons   d) group VIIA, 7 valence electrons

7.7 a) C b) F c) Mg d) P

Lewis Structures for Atoms (Sec. 7.2)

7.9 a) $\overset{\displaystyle ..}{Be}:$ b) $\cdot \overset{\displaystyle ..}{\underset{\displaystyle ..}{O}} \cdot$ c) $\cdot \overset{\displaystyle ..}{\underset{\displaystyle ..}{Cl}}:$ d) $\cdot \overset{\displaystyle ..}{\underset{\displaystyle \cdot}{Se}}:$

7.11 a) B b) C c) F d) Li

7.13 a) $Li \cdot, Be:, \therefore$ (2) Li has fewer dots   b) $Mg:, Ca:, \therefore$ (3) same number dots

c) $\cdot \overset{\displaystyle \cdot}{Al} \cdot, K \cdot, \therefore$ (1) Al has more dots   d) $: \overset{\displaystyle ..}{\underset{\displaystyle ..}{Ar}}:, : \overset{\displaystyle ..}{\underset{\displaystyle ..}{Ne}}:, \therefore$ (3) same number dots

Notation for Ions (Sec. 7.4)

7.15 a) Li^+ b) P^{3-} c) Br^- d) Ba^{2+}

7.17 a) 3 protons, 2 electrons   b) 7 protons, 10 electrons
c) 20 protons, 18 electrons   d) 17 protons, 18 electrons

7.19 a) Al^{3+} b) O^{2-} c) Mg^{2+} d) Be^{2+}

7.21 a) (2), anion   b) (1), cation   c) (3), not an ion   d) (2), anion

Ionic Charge Magnitude (Sec. 7.5)

7.23 a) cation   b) anion   c) cation   d) cation

7.25 a) 2 lost   b) 1 gained   c) 3 gained   d) 1 lost

7.27 a) loss   b) loss   c) loss   d) gain

7.29 a) $1s^2 2s^2 2p^6 3s^2 3p^6$ b) $1s^2$ c) $1s^2 2s^2 2p^6$ d) $1s^2 2s^2 2p^6$

7.31 a) group IA   b) group VIA   c) group VA   d) group IVA

7.33 a) $_2$He   b) $_{54}$Xe   c) $_{36}$Kr   d) $_{54}$Xe

7.35 Neon has 10 electrons.   a) Na^+ b) F^- c) O^{2-} d) Mg^{2+}

7.37 a) yes   b) no   c) yes   d) no

Lewis Structures for Ionic Compounds (Sec. 7.6)

7.39 a)
$$
\overset{\cdot\cdot}{\cdot Br :} \\
Ca \cdot \quad \rightarrow \quad Ca^{2+} \\
\overset{\cdot\cdot}{\cdot Br :}
\qquad
\begin{bmatrix} : Br : \end{bmatrix}^-
\begin{bmatrix} : Br : \end{bmatrix}^-
$$

b) $Mg \cdot\cdot S : \rightarrow Mg^{2+} \begin{bmatrix} : \overset{\cdot\cdot}{\underset{\cdot\cdot}{S}} : \end{bmatrix}^{2-}$

c)
$$
Be \cdot \\
\cdot N : \qquad Be^{2+} \\
Be \cdot \quad \rightarrow \quad Be^{2+} \\
\cdot N : \qquad Be^{2+} \\
Be \cdot
$$
$$
Be^{2+} \begin{bmatrix} : N : \end{bmatrix}^{3-} Be^{2+} \begin{bmatrix} : N : \end{bmatrix}^{3-} Be^{2+}
$$

d)
$$
Na \cdot \\
Na \cdot \cdot P : \rightarrow \\
Na \cdot
$$
$$
Na^+ \\
Na^+ \begin{bmatrix} : P : \end{bmatrix}^{3-} \\
Na^+
$$

7.41 a) Lithium has 1 valence electron, (lose 1); nitrogen has five valence electrons, (gain 3)

$$
Li \cdot \\
Li \cdot \cdot N : \rightarrow \\
Li \cdot
$$
$$
Li^+ \\
Li^+ \begin{bmatrix} : N : \end{bmatrix}^{3-} \\
Li^+
$$

b) Mg has 2 valence electrons (lose 2); O has 6 valence electrons (gain 2)

$$
Mg \cdot \cdot O : \rightarrow Mg^{2+} \begin{bmatrix} : \overset{\cdot\cdot}{\underset{\cdot\cdot}{O}} : \end{bmatrix}^{2-}
$$

c) Cl has 7 valence electrons (gain 1); barium has 2 valence electrons (lose 2). Write Ba first.

$$\cdot \ddot{\underset{\cdot\cdot}{Cl}} : \qquad\qquad : \ddot{\underset{\cdot\cdot}{Cl}} :$$

$$Ba \cdot \qquad\qquad \rightarrow \qquad Ba^{2+}$$

$$\cdot \ddot{\underset{\cdot\cdot}{Cl}} : \qquad\qquad : \ddot{\underset{\cdot\cdot}{Cl}} : \; ^-$$

d) F has 7 valence electrons (gain 1); K has 1 valence electron (lose 1). Write K first.

$$K \cdot \quad \cdot \ddot{\underset{\cdot\cdot}{F}} : \; \rightarrow \; K^+ \; : \ddot{\underset{\cdot\cdot}{F}} : \; ^-$$

Formulas for Ionic Compounds (Sec. 7.7)

7.43   a) $CaCl_2$ b) BeO   c) AlN   d) K_2S

7.45   a) Mg^{2+}, S^{2-} b) Al^{3+}, N^{3-} c) $2Na^+$, O^{2-} d) $3Ca^{2+}$, $2N^{3-}$

7.47   a) X_2Z b) XZ_3 c) X_3Z d) ZX_2

Polyatomic-ion-containing Ionic Compounds (Sec. 7.9)

7.49   a) $Mg(CN)_2$ b) $CaSO_4$ c) $Al(OH)_3$ d) NH_4NO_3

7.51   a) $AlPO_4$ b) $Al_2(CO_3)_3$ c) $Al(ClO_3)_3$ d) $Al(C_2H_3O_2)_3$

Electron-dot Structures for Covalent Compounds (Secs. 7.10–7.15)

7.53   a) $: \ddot{\underset{\cdot\cdot}{I}} : \ddot{\underset{\cdot\cdot}{I}} :$ b) $: \ddot{\underset{\cdot\cdot}{Cl}} : \ddot{\underset{\cdot\cdot}{F}} :$

c) $H : \ddot{\underset{\cdot\cdot}{S}} : H$ d) $: \ddot{\underset{\cdot\cdot}{F}} : \ddot{\underset{: F :}{P}} : \ddot{\underset{\cdot\cdot}{F}} :$

7.55

a) $H : \ddot{\underset{\cdot\cdot}{Br}} :$ b) $\ddot{\underset{\cdot\cdot}{F}} : \ddot{\underset{\cdot\cdot}{O}} : F$ c) $: \ddot{\underset{: \ddot{Cl} :}{\underset{\cdot\cdot}{Cl}}} : \ddot{N} : \ddot{\underset{\cdot\cdot}{Cl}} :$ d) $: \ddot{\underset{: \ddot{I} :}{\underset{\cdot\cdot}{I}}} : \ddot{Si} : \ddot{\underset{: \ddot{I} :}{\underset{\cdot\cdot}{I}}} :$

7.57 a) 3 bonding pairs, 2 nonbonding pairs   b) 6 bonding pairs, 0 nonbonding pairs
c) 4 bonding pairs, 4 nonbonding pairs   d) 7 bonding pairs, 2 nonbonding pairs

7.59 a) 1 triple bond   b) 4 single, 1 double   c) 2 double   d) 2 triple, 1 single

7.61 a) yes   b) yes   c) no, C has to form 4 bonds   d) yes

7.63 A bond in which both electrons of the shared pair come from one of the two atoms.

7.65 a) the N–O bond   b) none   c) the O–Cl bond   d) the two O–Br bonds

7.67 Resonance structures are two or more electron-dot structures for a molecule or ion that have the same arrangement of atoms, contain the same number of electrons, and differ only in the location of the electrons.

7.69

$$\left[\ddot{\underset{\ddot{}}{O}}=N-\ddot{\underset{\ddot{}}{O}}\ :\ \underset{\ :\ddot{O}:}{|}\right]^{-} \leftrightarrow \left[:\ddot{O}-N=\ddot{O}\ :\ \underset{:\ddot{O}:}{|}\right]^{-}$$

Systematic Procedures for Drawing Electron-dot Structures (Sec. 7.16)

7.71 a) $1 + 5 + (3 \times 6) = 24$ b) $5 + (3 \times 7) = 26$
c) $3 + (4 \times 7) - 1 = 30$ d) $5 + (4 \times 6) + 3 = 32$

7.73 a) 1 bonding pair, 3 nonbonding pairs   b) 3 bonding pairs, 2 nonbonding pairs
c) 1 bonding pair, 3 nonbonding pairs   d) 3 bonding pairs, 2 nonbonding pairs

7.75 a) 1. There are 14 valence electrons
$(6 \times 1) + (2 \times 4)$.
2. The two C atoms are central atoms.
3. Attach hydrogens (all 14 electrons used).

b) 1. There are 14 valence electrons
$(4 \times 1) + (2 \times 5)$.
2. The two N atoms are central.
3. Attach H atoms on N's (8 electrons used).
4. Complete octet on each N by putting a nonbonding pair on each N (all 14 electrons used).

c) 1. There are 20 electrons
        $(2 \times 7) + 4 + (2 \times 1)$.
    2. The C is central.
    3. Attach H and F atoms (8 electrons used).
    4. Complete octet on F (all 20 electrons used).

d) 1. There are 32 electrons
        $(3 \times 1) + (2 \times 4) + (3 \times 7)$.
    2. The C atoms are central.
    3. Attach H and Cl atoms (12 electrons used).
    4. Complete octet on Cl (all 32 electrons used).

7.77

a) 1. There are 32 electrons
        $[5 + (4 \times 7) - 1]$.
    2. The N atom is central.
    3. Attach F atoms (8 electrons used).
    4. Complete octet on F (all 32 electrons used).

b) 1. There are 8 electrons
        $[2 + (4 \times 1) + 2]$.
    2. The Be atom is central.
    3. Attach H atoms (all 8 electrons used).

c) 1. There are 26 electrons
        $[7 + (3 \times 6) + 1]$.
    2. The Cl atom is central.
    3. Attach O atoms (6 electrons used).
    4. Complete octet on O atoms
        (24 electrons used).
    5. Complete octet on Cl with a nonbonding pair
        (all 26 electrons used).

d) 1. There are 32 electrons
        [7 + (4 x 6) + 1].
    2. The I atom is central.
    3. Attach O atoms (8 electrons used).
    4. Complete octet on O atoms (all 32 electrons used).

$$\left[\begin{array}{c} \ddot{\underset{\cdot\cdot}{O}} \\ | \\ \ddot{\underset{\cdot\cdot}{:O}} - I - \ddot{\underset{\cdot\cdot}{O:}} \\ | \\ \ddot{\underset{\cdot\cdot}{O:}} \end{array}\right]^{-}$$

7.79   a) 1. There are 24 electrons
            [(2 x 4) + (2 x 1) + (2 x 7)].
        2. Join 2 C atoms (2 electrons used).
        3. Attach H and Cl atoms (8 electrons).
        4. Complete octet on Cl atoms (12 electrons used).
        5. Complete octet on C atoms by double bond (all 24 electrons used).

$$\ddot{\underset{\cdot\cdot}{:Cl}} - C = C - H$$
$$\qquad\quad | \qquad |$$
$$\qquad\; :\ddot{Cl}: \quad H$$

    b) 1. There are 16 electrons
            [(2 x 4) + (3 x 1) + 5].
        2. Join 2 C atoms (2 electrons used).
        3. Attach 3 H atoms to a C (6 electrons used).
        4. Attach the N atom to other C (2 more electrons used).
        5. Complete octet on other C atom by triple bond (4 electron used to make triple bond).
        6. Complete octet on N atom (16 electrons used).

$$\qquad\quad H$$
$$\qquad\quad |$$
$$H - C - C \equiv N :$$
$$\qquad\quad |$$
$$\qquad\quad H$$

    c) 1. There are 16 electrons
            [(3 x 4) + (4 x 1)].
        2. Join 3 C atoms (4 electrons used).
        3. Attach the 4 H atoms (8 electrons).
        4. Complete octet on C atoms by triple bond (all 16 electrons used).

$$\qquad\qquad\qquad H$$
$$\qquad\qquad\qquad |$$
$$H - C \equiv C - C - H$$
$$\qquad\qquad\qquad |$$
$$\qquad\qquad\qquad H$$

    d) 1. There are 24 electrons
            [(2 x 5) + (2 x 7)].
        2. Join 2 N atoms (2 electrons).
        3. Attach 2 F atoms (4 electrons).
        4. Complete octet on 2 F atoms (12 electrons).
        5. Complete octet on 2 N atoms by making a double bond (2 electrons) and 1 nonbonding pair on each (all 24 electrons used).

$$:\ddot{\underset{\cdot\cdot}{F}} - \ddot{N} = \ddot{N} - \ddot{\underset{\cdot\cdot}{F}}:$$

7.81 Follow steps used in Problems 7.75-7.80.

a)
$$
\begin{array}{c}
\text{H} \\
| \\
\text{H} - \text{C} - \text{N} = \text{O} \\
| \\
\text{H} \quad :\text{O}:
\end{array}
\leftrightarrow
\begin{array}{c}
\text{H} \\
| \\
\text{H} - \text{C} - \text{N} - \text{O}: \\
| \\
\text{H} \quad :\text{O}:
\end{array}
$$

b) $:N \equiv N - O: \leftrightarrow :N = N = O: \leftrightarrow :N - N \equiv O:$

c)
$$
\left[O = C - O: \atop :O: \right]^{2-}
\leftrightarrow
\left[:O - C - O: \atop :O: \right]^{2-}
\leftrightarrow
\left[:O - C = O \atop :O: \right]^{2-}
$$

d)
$$
\left[:S - C \equiv N: \right]^{-}
\leftrightarrow
\left[S = C = N \right]^{-}
\leftrightarrow
\left[:S \equiv C - N: \right]^{-}
$$

7.83 Total electrons in structure = 32; total valence electrons = 4(6) + 7 = 31; 31 - 32 = -1; ∴ n = 1.

Molecular Geometry (VSEPR Theory) (Sec. 7.17)

7.85 a) angular b) linear c) angular d) linear (diatomic molecule)

7.87 a) The electron arrangement about the central atom involves 2 bonding locations and 2 nonbonding locations. This arrangement produces an angular geometry.
b) The electron arrangement about the central atom involves 2 bonding locations and no nonbonding locations. This arrangement produces a linear geometry.
c) The electron arrangement about the central atom involves 2 bonding locations and no nonbonding locations. This arrangement produces a linear geometry.
d) The electron arrangement about the central atom involves 2 bonding locations and 1 nonbonding location. This arrangement produces an angular geometry.

7.89 a) The electron arrangement about the central atom involves 3 bonding locations and 1 nonbonding location. This arrangement produces a trigonal pyramidal geometry.
b) The electron arrangement about the central atom involves 2 bonding locations and no nonbonding locations. This arrangement produces a linear geometry.
c) The electron arrangement about the central atom involves 3 bonding locations and no nonbonding locations. This arrangement produces a trigonal planar geometry.
d) The electron arrangement about the central atom involves 4 bonding locations and no nonbonding locations. This arrangement produces a tetrahedral geometry.

7.91 a) The electron arrangement about the central atom involves 4 bonding locations and no nonbonding locations. This arrangement produces a tetrahedral geometry.

b) The electron arrangement about the central atom involves 2 bonding locations and no nonbonding locations. This arrangement produces a linear geometry.

c) The electron arrangement about the central atom involves 3 bonding locations and 1 nonbonding location. This arrangement produces a trigonal pyramidal geometry.

d) The electron arrangement about the central atom involves 3 bonding locations and 1 nonbonding location. This arrangement produces a trigonal pyramidal geometry.

7.93 a) Each central atom has 3 bonding locations and 1 nonbonding location, giving a trigonal pyramid for each center. The centers are joined by one axis of each trigonal pyramid.

b) The C has 4 bonding locations and no nonbonding locations; tetrahedral. The O has two bonding and 2 nonbonding; angular.

Electronegativity (Sec. 7.18)

7.95 increases across a period; decreases down a group

7.97 a) O   b) O   c) S   d) Mg

7.99 a) Na, Mg, Al, and P   b) I, Br, Cl, and F
c) As, P, S, and O   d) Ca, Ge, C, and O

7.101 a) C = 2.5, ∴ elements N (3.0), O (3.5), F(4.0), Cl (3.0) are more electronegative.

b) 1.0 ∴ elements that are less electronegative include Na (0.9), K (0.8), Rb (0.8), Cs (0.7), Ba (0.9), Fr (0.7) and Ra (0.9)

c) 4 most electronegative elements include F (4.0), O (3.5), N and Cl (3.0)

d) For period 2, elements increase from left-to-right by 0.5 in electronegative values.

Bond Polarity (Sec. 7.19)

7.103 a) S   b) Br   c) N   d) N

7.105 Response c) has the symbol backwards; the H is the + end.

7.107 Calculating the difference in electronegativity between the two atoms in each pair gives:
a) H–Cl = 0.9; H–O = 1.4; H–Br = 0.7   ∴ H–O has the greatest polarity
b) O–F = 0.5; O–P = 1.4; O–Al = 2.0   ∴ O–Al has the greatest polarity
c) H–Cl = 0.9; Br–Br = 0; B–N = 1.0   ∴ B–N has the greatest polarity
d) Al–Cl = 1.5; C–N = 0.5; Cl–F = 1.0   ∴ Al–Cl has the greatest polarity

7.109 a) nonpolar covalent   b) ionic   c) polar covalent   d) nonpolar covalent

7.111 a) more covalent character   b) more ionic character
c) more covalent character   d) more ionic character

Molecular Polarity (Sec. 7.20)

7.113   a) nonpolar   b) polar   c) polar   d) nonpolar

7.115   a) nonpolar   b) polar   c) polar   d) nonpolar

7.117   a) F_2 is nonpolar, BrF is polar   b) HOCl and HCN are both polar
c) CH_4 and CCl_4 are both nonpolar   d) SO_3 is nonpolar and NF_3 is polar

ADDITIONAL PROBLEMS

7.119   a) Mg: $1s^2 2s^2 2p^6 3s^2$ Mg^{2+}: $1s^2 2s^2 2p^6$
b) F: $1s^2 2s^2 2p^5$ F^-: $1s^2 2s^2 2p^6$
c) N: $1s^2 2s^2 2p^3$ N^{3-}: $1s^2 2s^2 2p^6$
d) Ca^{2+}: $1s^2 2s^2 2p^6 3s^2 3p^6$ S^{2-}: $1s^2 2s^2 2p^6 3s^2 3p^6$

7.121   a) nonisoelectronic cations   b) nonisoelectronic anions
c) isoelectronic cations   d) nonisoelectronic anions

7.123   a) ionic   b) molecular   c) ionic   d) molecular

7.125   a) and d) are molecules; b) and c) are ionic compounds for which the formula unit is the simplest ratio of ions.

7.127   a) (1), CaF_2 contains only monoatomic ions
b) (3), $NaNO_3$ contains monoatomic and polyatomic ions
c) (2) $(NH_4)_2 SO_4$ contains only polyatomic ions
d) (1) BaO contains only monoatomic ions

7.129   a) CaO, Ca has charge of +2   b) MgF_2, Mg has a charge of +2
c) $Na_2 S$, neither ion contains charge of +2   d) NO, neither ion contains charge of +2

7.131   a) O b) N c) O d) F

7.133   a, b and d are not correct.
a) should be $BeCl_2$ b) should be $CaCl_2$ c) correct   d) should be Li_2S

7.135   a) correct number of electron dots, but improperly placed
b) not enough electron dots
c) correct number of electron dots, but improperly placed
d) correct number of electron dots, but improperly placed

7.137   BA, CA, DB, and DA

7.139   a) same, both single   b) different, single and triple
c) different, triple and double   d) different, triple and double

7.141 a) There are 26 electrons shown. The 3 oxygen and 1 hydrogen provide 19, so X must provide 7: X = Cl
b) There are 20 electrons shown. The 2 oxygen provide 12, the ionic charge provides 1, so X must provide 7: X = Cl

7.143 a) Ca^{2+} [structure of SO_4^{2-}] b) [structure of NH_4^+] [structure of NO_3^-]

Note that other resonance structures are possible for the SO_4^{2-} and NO_3^- ions!

7.145 a) tetrahedral electron pair geometry; tetrahedral molecular geometry
b) tetrahedral electron pair geometry; trigonal pyramidal molecular geometry
c) linear electron pair geometry; linear molecular geometry
d) tetrahedral electron pair geometry; tetrahedral molecular geometry

7.147 a) 109 ° because the electron pair arrangement about the oxygen atom is tetrahedral
b) 120 ° because the electron pair arrangement about the carbon atom is trigonal planar

7.149 a) H–F bond is more polar than H–Cl, so HF molecule is more polar.
b) C–F bond is more polar than C–Cl, so H_3CF is the more polar molecule.
c) the symmetry of the linear CO_2 makes it nonpolar, so HCN molecule is more polar.
d) the symmetry of the trigonal planar SO_3 makes it nonpolar, so the angular SO_2 is more polar.

7.151 a) HI, HBr, HCl   b) NH_3, H_2O, HF
c) SCl_2. PCl_3, $SiCl_4$ d) CI_4, NI_3, HI

7.153 CO_3^{2-}, CO_2, CO

CUMULATIVE PROBLEMS

7.155 A = Al, D = N, formula = AlN

7.157 D = Ca, A = S, formula = CaS

7.159 A= 0 and D = F. The electron-dot structure of the compound is : F : O : F :

7.161 A = H and D = O. x is 2 and y is 1. The formula is H_2O.

7.163 A= Be and D = F. The electron-dot structure is [structure of BeF_4^{2-}]

CHAPTER EIGHT
Chemical Nomenclature

PRACTICE PROBLEMS

Nomenclature Classifications for Compounds (Sec. 8.1)

8.1 A binary compound contains two kinds of atoms: a) and d)

8.3 Ionic compounds contain a metal and one or more nonmetals: a) and d)

8.5 a) yes b) yes c) no, both molecular d) no, both ionic

Types of Binary Ionic Compounds (Sec. 8.2)

8.7 a) fixed charge b) variable charge c) fixed charge d) variable charge

8.9 (a) and (d)

8.11 a) variable charge b) variable charge c) fixed charge d) fixed charge

Nomenclature of Binary Ionic Compounds (Sec. 8.3)

8.13 a) potassium ion b) magnesium ion c) copper (I) ion d) lead (IV) ion

8.15 a) bromide ion b) nitride ion c) sulfide ion d) selenide ion

8.17 a) Zn^{2+} b) Pb^{2+} c) Ca^{2+} d) N^{3-}

8.19 a) magnesium oxide b) lithium sulfide c) silver chloride d) zinc bromide

8.21 a) no b) no c) yes d) yes

8.23 a) +2 b) +2 c) +3 d) +2

8.25 a) iron (II) bromide, iron (III) bromide b) copper (I) oxide, copper (II) oxide
c) tin (II) sulfide, tin (IV) sulfide d) nickel (II) oxide, nickel (III) oxide

8.27 a) aluminum chloride b) nickel (III) chloride c) zinc oxide d) cobalt (II) oxide

8.29 a) plumbic oxide b) auric chloride c) iron (III) iodide d) tin (II) bromide

8.31 a) FeS b) SnS_2 c) Li_2S d) ZnS

8.33 In b and c both names denote the same compound

8.35   a) $CaCl_2$ b) Na_2O c) $FeBr_3$ d) Cu_2S

Nomenclature for Ionic Compounds Containing Polyatomic Ions (Sec. 8.4)

8.37   a) PO_4^{3-} b) MnO_4^- c) NO_3^- d) CN^-

8.39   a) peroxide   b) thiosulfate   c) oxalate   d) chlorate

8.41   a) SO_4^{2-}, SO_3^{2-} b) PO_4^{3-}, HPO_4^{2-} c) OH^-, O_2^{2-} d) CrO_4^{2-}, $Cr_2O_7^{2-}$

8.43   In b and c both compounds contain polyatomic ions

8.45   a) fixed-charge   b) fixed-charge   c) variable-charge   d) variable-charge

8.47   a) +2   b) +4   c) +3   d) +1

8.49   a) zinc sulfate   b) barium hydroxide   c) iron (III) nitrate   d) copper (II) carbonate

8.51   a) iron (III) carbonate, iron (II) carbonate   b) gold (I) sulfate, gold (III) sulfate
       c) tin (II) hydroxide, tin (IV) hydroxide   d) chromium (III) acetate, chromium (II) acetate

8.53   a) ammonium nitrate   b) ammonium chloride
       c) sodium phosphate   d) copper (I) phosphate

8.55   a) Ag_2CO_3 b) $AuNO_3$ c) $Cr_2(SO_4)_3$ d) $NH_4C_2H_3O_2$

8.57   a) $Fe_2(SO_4)_3$ b) $CuCN$ c) $Sn(CO_3)_2$ d) $Pb(OH)_2$

Nomenclature for Binary Molecular Compounds (Sec. 8.5)

8.59   a) 7   b) 5   c) 3   d) 10

8.61   a) tetraphosphorus decoxide   b) sulfur tetrafluoride
       c) carbon tetrabromide   d) chlorine dioxide

8.63   a) ICl b) NCl_3 c) SF_6 d) OF_2

8.65   a) hydrogen sulfide   b) hydrogen fluoride   c) ammonia   d) methane

8.67   a) PH_3 b) HBr c) C_2H_6 d) H_2Te

8.69   Chemical formulas for molecular compounds are always written with the least electronegative atom first. O is more electronegative than N, therefore, N is written first.

8.71 $NaNO_3$ is an ionic compound and is therefore named as two ions, sodium nitrate.

Nomenclature for Acids (Sec. 8.6)

8.73   a) no   b) yes   c) yes   d) no

8.75   a) cyanide comes from hydrocyanic acid   b) sulfate comes from sulfuric acid
c) nitrite comes from nitrous acid   d) borate comes from boric acid

8.77   a) HCN   b) H_2SO_4 c) HNO_2 d) H_3BO_3

8.79   a) nitric acid   b) hydriodic acid   c) hypochlorous acid   d) acetic acid

8.81   a) Cl^-, chloride ion   b) ClO_2^- chlorite ion
c) ClO_4^- perchlorate ion   d) SO_4^{2-}, sulfate ion

8.83   a) arsenous acid   b) periodic acid   c) hypophosphorous acid   d) bromous acid

8.85   a) hydrogen bromide   b) hydrocyanic acid   c) hydrogen sulfide   d) hydroiodic acid

8.87   a) $HClO_3$ b) HNO_2 c) HF   d) $HC_2H_3O_2$

ADDITIONAL PROBLEMS

8.89   a) 2   b) 1   c) 2   d) 2

8.91   a) no, +2 and +1   b) both +3   c) both +2   d) no, +3 and +1

8.93   a) no   b) no   c) yes   d) no

8.95   a) yes   b) no   c) no   d) yes

8.97   a) 4, $3K^+$ and N^{3-} b) 2, K^+ and N^{3-} c) 3, $2Na^+$ and O^{2-} d) 3, $2Na^+$ and O_2^{2-}

8.99   a) sulfate   b) perchlorate   c) peroxide   d) dichromate

8.101   a) Ca_3N_2 b) $Ca(NO_3)_2$ c) $Ca(NO_2)_2$ d) $Ca(CN)_2$

8.103   a) K_3P b) K_3PO_4 c) K_2HPO_4 d) KH_2PO_4

8.105   a) N_2O, CO_2 b) NO_2, SO_2 c) SF_2, SCl_2 d) N_2O_3

8.107   a) $CaCO_3$, HNO_2 b) $NaClO_4$, $NaClO_3$ c) $HClO_2$, $HClO$ d) Li_2CO_3, Li_3PO_4

8.109   a) sodium nitrate
b) aluminum sulfide, magnesium nitride, beryllium phosphide
c) iron (III) oxide
d) gold (I) chlorate

8.111   a) $Ni_2(SO_4)_3$ b) Ni_2O_3 c) $Ni_2(C_2O_4)_3$ d) $Ni(NO_3)_3$

8.113   The superoxide ion is O_2^-. The nitronium ion is NO_2^+. The formula of nitronium superoxide is NO_2O_2.

8.115   a) beryllium oxide   b) magnesium chloride   c) sodium carbonate   d) ammonium sulfate

8.117   a) SO_3 reacts with H_2O to form H_2SO_4.
b) $HClO_4$ reacts with Cd to produce $Cd(ClO_4)_2$.
c) $ZnCO_3$ decomposes to form ZnO and CO_3.
d) Mg reacts with $FeCl_2$ to produce $MgCl_2$ and Fe.

8.119   a) HCN, (4) ternary molecular   b) HBr, (3) binary molecular
c) Na_2O_2,, (1) binary ionic   d) H_2O_2, (3) binary molecular

CUMULATIVE PROBLEMS

8.121   a) magnesium chloride, $MgCl_2$ b) oxygen difluoride, OF_2

8.123   a) x = 4; silicon tetrachloride   b) x = 2; magnesium chloride
c) x = 3; potassium nitride   d) x = 3; nitrogen trichloride

8.125   beryllium bromate

8.127   aluminum nitride

8.129   carbon dioxide

8.131   beryllium cyanide

CHAPTER NINE
Chemical Calculations:
The Mole Concept and
Chemical Formulas

PRACTICE PROBLEMS

Law of Definite Proportions (Sec. 9.1)

9.1 The same: 33.4% S and 66.6% O. Any size sample of SO_2 will have that composition

9.3 According to the law of definite proportions, the percentage A in each sample should be the same and the percentage D should also be the same.

Sample I: $\%A = \dfrac{10.03 \text{ g}}{17.35 \text{ g}} \times 100 = 57.809798 \text{ (calc)} = 57.81\% \text{ (corr)}$

$\%D = \dfrac{7.32 \text{ g}}{17.35 \text{ g}} \times 100 = 42.190202 \text{ (calc)} = 42.2\% \text{ (corr)}$

Sample II: $\%A = \dfrac{13.17 \text{ g}}{22.78 \text{ g}} \times 100 = 57.813872 \text{ (calc)} = 57.81\% \text{ (corr)}$

$\%D = \dfrac{9.61 \text{ g}}{22.78 \text{ g}} \times 100 = 42.186128 \text{ (calc)} = 42.2\% \text{ (corr)}$

9.5 The mass ratio between X and Q present in the sample will be the same for samples of the same compound.

Experiment	Q/X mass ratio
1	$\dfrac{8.90 \text{ g}}{3.37 \text{ g}} = 2.6409496 \text{ (calc)} = 2.64 \text{ (corr)}$
2	$\dfrac{1.711 \text{ g}}{0.561 \text{ g}} = 3.0499109 \text{ (calc)} = 3.05 \text{ (corr)}$
3	$\dfrac{71.0 \text{ g}}{26.9 \text{ g}} = 2.6394052 \text{ (calc)} = 2.64 \text{ (corr)}$

∴Experiments 1 and 3 produced the same compound.

9.7 If all 42.9 g C is used, the mass of CO produced would be:

$42.9 \text{ g C} \times \dfrac{100. \text{ g CO}}{42.9 \text{ g C}} = 100. \text{ g CO}.$

If all 80.0 g O is used, the mass of CO produced would be:

$80.0 \text{ g O} \times \dfrac{100 \text{ g CO}}{57.1 \text{ g O}} = 140.10508 \text{ (calculator)} = 140. \text{ g CO}.$

But after making 100. g CO, all the C is used. ∴ The maximum possible is 100. g CO.

Formula Masses (Sec. 9.2)

9.9   a)

Na	4 x 22.99 amu =	91.96
Si	1 x 28.09 amu =	28.09
O	4 x 16.00 amu =	64.00
	Na_4SiO_4 =	184.05

  b)

H	3 x 1.01 amu =	3.03
B	1 x 10.81 amu =	10.81
O	3 x 16.00 amu =	48.00
	H_3BO_3 =	61.84

  c)

C	12 x 12.01 amu =	144.12
H	11 x 1.01 amu =	11.11
N	1 x 14.01 amu =	14.01
O	2 x 16.00 amu =	32.00
	$C_{12}H_{11}NO_2$ =	201.24

  d)

C	22 x 12.01 amu =	264.22
H	30 x 1.01 amu =	30.30
Cl	1 x 35.45 amu =	35.45
N	1 x 14.01 amu =	14.01
O	2 x 16.00 amu =	32.00
	$C_{22}H_{30}ClNO_2$ =	375.98

9.11   a)

C	2 x 12.01 amu =	24.02
H	6 x 1.01 amu =	6.06
O	2 x 16.00 amu =	32.00
	$C_2H_4(OH)_2$ =	62.08

  b)

H	4 x 1.01 amu =	4.04
N	2 x 14.01 amu =	28.02
C	1 x 12.01 amu =	12.01
O	1 x 16.00 amu =	16.00
	$(H_2N)_2CO$ =	60.07

  c)

Mg	3 x 24.30 amu =	72.90
Si	4 x 28.09 amu =	112.36
O	12 x 16.00 amu =	192.00
H	2 x 1.01 amu =	2.02
	$Mg_3(Si_2O_5)_2(OH)_2$	379.28

  d)

Al	2 x 26.98 amu =	53.96
Si	2 x 28.09 amu =	56.18
O	7 x 16.00 amu =	112.00
H	2 x 1.01 amu =	2.02
	$Al_2Si_2O_5(OH)_2$ =	224.16

9.13 y· (12.01 amu) + 8(1.01 amu) + 32.06 amu   =   88.19 amu

$\qquad$ (12.01)· y amu + 40.14 amu   =   88.19 amu

$\qquad$ (12.01)· y amu   =   48.05 amu

$\qquad$ y   =   4

9.15 $\dfrac{2 \text{ atoms O}}{1 \text{ molecule}}$ x $\dfrac{16 \text{ amu O}}{1 \text{ atom O}}$ x $\dfrac{100 \text{ amu molecule}}{51.5 \text{ amu O}}$ = 62.136922 (calc) = 62.1 amu (corr)

Percent Composition (Sec. 9.4)

9.17 a) 118.71 amu + 2(19.00) amu = 156.71 amu total

$\qquad$ %Sn = $\dfrac{118.71 \text{ amu Sn}}{156.71 \text{ amu total}}$ x 100 = 75.751388 (calc) = 75.751 % Sn (corr)

$\qquad$ %F = $\dfrac{2(19.00) \text{ amu F}}{156.71 \text{ amu total}}$ x 100 = 24.248612 (calc) = 24.25 % F (corr)

$\quad$ b) 55.84 amu + 32.06 amu + 4(16.00) amu = 151.90 total

$\qquad$ %F = $\dfrac{55.84 \text{ amu Fe}}{151.90 \text{ amu total}}$ x 100 = 36.761027 (calc) = 36.76 % Fe (corr)

$\qquad$ %S = $\dfrac{32.06 \text{ amu S}}{151.90 \text{ amu total}}$ x 100 = 21.105991 (calc) = 21.11 % S (corr)

$\qquad$ %O = $\dfrac{4(16.00) \text{ amu O}}{151.90 \text{ amu total}}$ x 100 = 42.132982 (calc) = 42.13 % O (corr)

$\quad$ c) 12(12.01) amu + 22(1.01) amu + 11(16.00) amu = 342.34 amu total

$\qquad$ %C = $\dfrac{12(12.01) \text{ amu C}}{342.34 \text{ amu total}}$ x 100 = 42.098499 (calc) = 42.10 % C (corr)

$\qquad$ %H = $\dfrac{22(1.01) \text{ amu H}}{342.34 \text{ amu total}}$ x 100 = 6.4906234 (calc) = 6.49% H (corr)

$\qquad$ %O = $\dfrac{11(16.00) \text{ amu O}}{342.34 \text{ amu total}}$ x 100 = 51.410878 (calc) = 51.41 % O (corr)

$\quad$ d) 14(12.01) amu + 9(1.01) amu + 5(35.45) amu = 354.48 amu total

$\qquad$ %C = $\dfrac{14(12.01) \text{ amu C}}{354.48 \text{ amu total}}$ x 100 = 47.432859 (calc) = 47.43 % C (corr)

$\qquad$ %H = $\dfrac{9(1.01) \text{ amu H}}{354.48 \text{ amu total}}$ x 100 = 2.564320 (calc) = 2.56 % H (corr)

$\qquad$ %Cl = $\dfrac{5(35.45) \text{ amu Cl}}{354.48 \text{ amu total}}$ x 100 = 50.002821 (calc) = 50.00 % Cl (corr)

9.19 a) 1.271 g Cu + 0.320 g O = 1.591 g compound

$\qquad$ %Cu = $\dfrac{1.271 \text{ g Cu}}{1.591 \text{ g compound}}$ x 100 = 79.886864 (calc) = 79.89 % Cu (corr)

$\qquad$ %O = $\dfrac{0.320 \text{ g O}}{1.591 \text{ g compound}}$ x 100 = 20.113136 (calc) = 20.1 % O (corr)

b) total = 49.31 g

$$\%Na = \frac{15.96 \text{ g Na}}{49.31 \text{ g total}} \times 100 = 32.366660 \text{ (calc)} = 32.37 \% \text{ Na (corr)}$$

$$\%S = \frac{11.13 \text{ g S}}{49.31 \text{ g total}} \times 100 = 22.571487 \text{ (calc)} = 22.57 \% \text{ S (corr)}$$

$$\%O = \frac{22.22 \text{ g O}}{49.31 \text{ g total}} \times 100 = 45.061854 \text{ (calc)} = 45.06\% \text{ O (corr)}$$

c) 25.00 g compound − 6.48 g N = 18.52 g O

$$\%N = \frac{6.48 \text{ g N}}{25.00 \text{ g total}} \times 100 = 25.92 \text{ (calc)} = 25.9 \% \text{ N (corr)}$$

$$\%O = \frac{18.52 \text{ g O}}{25.00 \text{ g total}} \times 100 = 74.08 \% \text{ O (calc and corr)}$$

d) mass compound = 10.00 g; mass O reacted = 10.00 g (initial) − 3.34 g (left over) = 6.66 g O

$$\%S = \frac{3.34 \text{ g S}}{10.00 \text{ g compound}} \times 100 = 33.4 \% \text{ S (calc and corr)}$$

$$\%O = \frac{6.66 \text{ g O}}{10.00 \text{ g compound}} \times 100 = 66.6 \% \text{ O (calc and corr)}$$

9.21   In order for the %O to be greater than 50%, the total mass of all O atoms must be greater than the total mass of the other atom(s) in the compound.
a) yes, 16 vs 12 and 32 vs 12
b) no, 16 vs 35 and 32 vs 35
c) no 3(16) vs (7 + 14) and 3(16) vs (85 + 14)
d) no, 4(16) vs [3(23) + 31] and 8(16) vs [3(9) + 2(31)]

9.23   for C_2H_2, $\%C = \dfrac{2(12.01) \text{ amu C}}{2(12.01) + 2(1.01) \text{ amu total}} \times 100 = 92.242704 \text{ (calc)} = 92.24\% \text{ C (corr)}$

$$\%H = \frac{2(1.01) \text{ amu H}}{2(12.01) + 2(1.01) \text{ amu total}} \times 100 = 7.757296 \text{ (calc)} = 7.76\% \text{ H (corr)}$$

for C_6H_6, $\%C = \dfrac{6(12.01) \text{ amu C}}{6(12.01) + 2(1.01) \text{ amu total}} \times 100 = 92.242704 \text{ (calc)} = 92.24\% \text{ C (corr)}$

$$\%H = \frac{6(1.01) \text{ amu H}}{6(12.01) + 2(1.01) \text{ amu total}} \times 100 = 7.757296 \text{ (calc)} = 7.76\% \text{ H (corr)}$$

Both compounds have the same ratio of carbon to hydrogen. Thus, the %C and %H will be the same in each.

9.25   2(14.01 amu) + 4(1.01 amu) = 32.06 amu (calc and corr)

$$\%H = \frac{4.04 \text{ amu H}}{32.06 \text{ amu total}} \times 100 = 12.601372 \text{ (calc)} = 12.6 \%H \text{ (corr)}$$

Using %H as a conversion factor,

$$52.34 \text{ g H} \times \frac{100 \text{ g compound}}{12.6 \text{ g H}} = 415.396825 \text{ (calc)} = 415 \text{ g compound (corr)}$$

mass N = total mass − mass H
= 415.4 g − 52.34 g = 363.06 (calc) = 363.1 g N (corr)

The Mole as a Counting Unit (Sec. 9.5)

9.27 a) 1.00 mole Ag x $\dfrac{6.022 \times 10^{23}\ \text{Ag atoms}}{1\ \text{mole Ag}}$ = 6.022 x 10²³ (calc) = 6.02 x 10²³ Ag atoms (corr)

b) 1.00 mole H₂O x $\dfrac{6.022 \times 10^{23}\ \text{H}_2\text{O molecules}}{1\ \text{mole H}_2\text{O}}$ = 6.022 x 10²³ (calc)

= 6.02 x 10²³ H₂O molecules (corr)

c) 1.00 mole NaNO₃ x $\dfrac{6.022 \times 10^{23}\ \text{NaNO}_3 \text{ formula units}}{1\ \text{mole NaNO}_3}$ = 6.022 x 10²³ (calc)

= 6.02 x 10²³ NaNO₃ formula units (corr)

d) 1.00 mole SO₄²⁻ ions x $\dfrac{6.022 \times 10^{23}\ \text{SO}_4^{2-} \text{ ions}}{1\ \text{mole SO}_4^{2-} \text{ ions}}$ = 6.022 x 10²³ (calc)

= 6.02 x 10²³ SO₄²⁻ ions (corr)

9.29 a) 2.50 moles C x $\dfrac{6.022 \times 10^{23}\ \text{C atoms}}{1\ \text{mole C}}$ = 1.5055 x 10²⁴ (calc) = 1.51 x 10²⁴ C atoms (corr)

b) 3.25 moles C x $\dfrac{6.022 \times 10^{23}\ \text{C atoms}}{1\ \text{mole C}}$ = 1.9572 x 10²⁴ (calc) = 1.96 x 10²⁴ C atoms (corr)

c) 0.23 mole C x $\dfrac{6.022 \times 10^{23}\ \text{C atoms}}{1\ \text{mole C}}$ = 1.3851 x 10²³ (calc) = 1.4 x 10²³ C atoms (corr)

d) 0.3114 mole C x $\dfrac{6.022 \times 10^{23}\ \text{C atoms}}{1\ \text{mole C}}$ = 1.8751 x 10²³ (calc) = 1.875 x 10²³ C atoms (corr)

9.31 a) 1.50 moles CO₂ x $\dfrac{6.022 \times 10^{23}\ \text{molecules CO}_2}{1\ \text{mole CO}_2}$ = 9.033 x 10²³ (calc)

= 9.03 x 10²³ molecules CO₂ (corr)

b) 0.500 mole NH₃ x $\dfrac{6.022 \times 10^{23}\ \text{molecules NH}_3}{1\ \text{mole NH}_3}$ = 3.011 x 10²³ (calc)

= 3.01 x 10²³ molecules NH₃ (corr)

c) 2.33 moles PF₃ x $\dfrac{6.022 \times 10^{23}\ \text{molecules PF}_3}{1\ \text{mole PF}_3}$ = 1.40313 x 10²⁴ (calc)

= 1.40 x 10²⁴ molecules PF₃ (corr)

d) 1.115 moles N₂H₄ x $\dfrac{6.022 \times 10^{23}\ \text{molecules N}_2\text{H}_4}{1\ \text{mole N}_2\text{H}_4}$ = 6.71453 x 10²³ (calc)

= 6.715 x 10²³ molecules N₂H₄ (corr)

Molar Mass (Sec. 9.6)

9.33 a) 1.00 mole Cu x $\dfrac{63.55\ \text{g Cu}}{1\ \text{mole Cu}}$ = 63.55 (calc)   b) 1.00 mole Ba x $\dfrac{137.33\ \text{g Ba}}{1\ \text{mole Ba}}$ = 137.33 (calc)

= 63.6 g Cu (corr)   = 137 g Ba (corr)

c) 1.00 mole Si x $\dfrac{28.09\ \text{g Si}}{1\ \text{mole Si}}$ = 28.09 (calc)   d) 1.00 mole U x $\dfrac{238.03\ \text{g U}}{1\ \text{mole U}}$ = 238.03 (calc)

= 28.1 g Si (corr)   = 238 g U (corr)

9.35   a) 26.98 amu + 3(16.00 amu) + 3(1.01 amu)   = 78.01 amu (calc and corr)

               mass of 1 $Al(OH)_3$ formula unit   = 78.01 amu

               molar mass of $Al(OH)_3$ formula units   = 78.01 g/mole

       b) 3(24.30 amu) + 2(14.01 amu)   = 100.92 amu (calc and corr)

               mass 1 Mg_3N_2 formula unit   = 100.92 amu

               molar mass of Mg_3N_2 formula units   = 100.92 g/mole

       c) 63.55 amu + 2(14.01 amu) + 6(16.00 amu)   = 187.57 amu (calc and corr)

               mass of 1 $Cu(NO_3)_2$ formula unit   = 187.57 amu

               molar mass of $Cu(NO_3)_2$ formula units   = 187.57 g/mole

       d) 2(138.91 amu) + 3(16.00 amu)   = 325.82 amu (calc and corr)

               mass of 1 La_2O_3 formula unit   = 325.82 amu

               molar mass of La_2O_3 formula units   = 325.82 g/mole

9.37   a) $1.357 \text{ moles NaCl} \times \dfrac{58.44 \text{ g NaCl}}{1 \text{ mole NaCl}} = 79.30308 \text{ (calc)} = 79.30 \text{ g NaCl (corr)}$

       b) $1.357 \text{ moles Na}_2\text{S} \times \dfrac{78.04 \text{ g Na}_2\text{S}}{1 \text{ mole Na}_2\text{S}} = 105.90028 \text{ (calc)} = 105.9 \text{ g Na}_2\text{S (corr)}$

       c) $1.357 \text{ moles NaNO}_3 \times \dfrac{85.00 \text{ g NaNO}_3}{1 \text{ mole NaNO}_3} = 115.345 \text{ (calc)} = 115.3 \text{ g NaNO}_3 \text{ (corr)}$

       d) $1.357 \text{ moles Na}_3\text{PO}_4 \times \dfrac{163.94 \text{ g Na}_3\text{PO}_4}{1 \text{ mole Na}_3\text{PO}_4} = 222.46658 \text{ (calc)} = 222.5 \text{ g Na}_3\text{PO}_4 \text{ (corr)}$

9.39   a) $2.00 \text{ moles Cu} \times \dfrac{63.55 \text{ g Cu}}{1 \text{ mole Cu}} = 127.1 \text{ (calc)} = 127 \text{ g Cu (corr)}$

          $2.00 \text{ moles O} \times \dfrac{16.00 \text{ g O}}{1 \text{ mole O}} = 32.00 \text{ (calc)} = 32.0 \text{ g O (corr)}$ ∴ 2.00 mole Cu greater

       b) $1.00 \text{ mole Br} \times \dfrac{79.90 \text{ g Br}}{1 \text{ mole Br}} = 79.90 \text{ (calc)} = 79.9 \text{ g Br (corr)}$

          $5.00 \text{ moles Be} \times \dfrac{9.01 \text{ g Be}}{1 \text{ mole Be}} = 45.05 \text{ (calc)} = 45.0 \text{ g Be}$ ∴ 1.00 mole Br greater

       c) $2.00 \text{ moles CO} \times \dfrac{28.01 \text{ g CO}}{1 \text{ mole CO}} = 56.02 \text{ (calc)} = 56.0 \text{ g CO (corr)}$

          $1.50 \text{ moles N}_2\text{O} \times \dfrac{44.02 \text{ g N}_2\text{O}}{1 \text{ mole N}_2\text{O}} = 66.03 \text{ (calc)} = 66.0 \text{ g N}_2\text{O (corr)}$

                                            ∴ 1.50 mole N_2O greater

       d) $4.87 \text{ moles B}_2\text{H}_6 \times \dfrac{27.68 \text{ g B}_2\text{H}_6}{1 \text{ mole B}_2\text{H}_6} = 134.802 \text{ (calc)} = 135 \text{ g B}_2\text{H}_6 \text{ (corr)}$

          $0.35 \text{ mole U} \times \dfrac{238.03 \text{ g U}}{1 \text{ mole U}} = 83.31 \text{ (calc)} = 83 \text{ g U (corr)}$ ∴ 4.87 moles B_2H_6 greater

Relationship Between Atomic Mass Units and Gram Units (Sec. 9.8)

9.41   Molar mass has units of $\dfrac{g}{mole}$, so take the number of grams and divide by the number of moles.

$$\dfrac{5.904 \text{ g}}{0.123 \text{ mole}} = 48 \text{ (calc)} = 48.0 \ \dfrac{g}{mole} \text{ (corr)}$$

9.43 $19.0 \text{ amu} \times \dfrac{1.00 \text{ g}}{6.022 \times 10^{23} \text{ amu}} = 3.155098 \times 10^{-23} \text{ (calc)} = 3.16 \times 10^{-23} \text{ g (corr)}$

9.45 $5.143 \times 10^{-23} \text{ g} \times \dfrac{6.022 \times 10^{23} \text{ amu}}{1.000 \text{ g}} = 30.971146 \text{ (calc)} = 30.97 \text{ amu (corr)}$

The element with an atomic mass of 30.97 amu is phosphorus.

9.47 $26.98 \text{ g Al} \times \dfrac{6.022 \times 10^{23} \text{ amu}}{1.00 \text{ g}} \times \dfrac{1 \text{ } atom \text{ } Al}{26.98 \text{ } amu} = 6.022 \times 10^{23} \text{ atoms Al (calc and corr)}$

Counting Particles by Weighing (Sec. 9.9)`--

9.49   The ratio of the atomic masses:

a) $\dfrac{107.87}{35.45} = 3.0428772 \text{(calc)} = 3.043:1 \text{ (corr)}$

b) $\dfrac{107.87}{1.01} = 106.80198 \text{ (calc)} = 106.8:1 \text{ (corr)}$

c) $\dfrac{107.87}{16.00} = 6.741875 \text{ (calc)} = 6.742:1 \text{ (corr)}$

d) $\dfrac{107.87}{30.97} = 3.4830481 \text{ (calc)} = 3.483:1 \text{(corr)}$

9.51   a)   the ratio of their atomic masses $= \dfrac{26.98}{9.01} = 2.994450 \text{ (calc)} = 2.99 \text{ (corr)}$

b)   twice as great as a) = 5.98

c)   half as much as a) = 1.50

d)   this is the same as having 4 times as many Al as Be atoms, so 4 times a) = 11.96

9.53   If the mass ratio between the two substances is the same as the ratio of formula masses for the substances, then an equal number of particles is present.

a) $\dfrac{\text{mass Si}}{\text{mass Cl}} = \dfrac{28.086 \text{ g}}{35.453 \text{ g}} = 0.79220376 \text{ (calc)} = 0.79220 \text{ (corr)}$

$\dfrac{\text{atomic mass Si}}{\text{atomic mass Cl}} = \dfrac{28.086 \text{ amu}}{35.453 \text{ amu}} = 0.79220376 \text{ (calc)} = 0.79220 \text{ (corr)}$

Since the two ratios are the same, the samples contain an equal number of atoms.

b) $\dfrac{\text{mass Ge}}{\text{mass Ga}} = \dfrac{72.59 \text{ g}}{74.72 \text{ g}} = 0.97149357 \text{ (calc)} = 0.9715 \text{ (corr)}$

$\dfrac{\text{atomic mass Ge}}{\text{atomic mass Ga}} = \dfrac{72.59 \text{ amu}}{69.72 \text{ amu}} = 1.0411646 \text{ (calc)} = 1.041 \text{ (corr)}$

Since the ratios differ, the samples do not contain an equal number of atoms.

c) $\dfrac{\text{mass } NH_3}{\text{mass } N_2H_4} = \dfrac{1.427 \text{ g}}{2.685 \text{ g}} = 0.53147113 \text{ (calc)} = 0.5315 \text{ (corr)}$

$\dfrac{\text{formula mass } NH_3}{\text{formula mass } N_2H_4} = \dfrac{17.04 \text{ amu}}{32.06 \text{ amu}} = 0.53150343 \text{ (calc)} = 0.5315 \text{ (corr)}$

Since the ratios are the same (to four significant figures), the samples contain an equal number of molecules (to four significant figures).

d) $\dfrac{\text{mass } S}{\text{mass } SO_2} = \dfrac{64.14 \text{ g}}{128.14 \text{ g}} = 0.50054627 \text{ (calc)} = 0.5005 \text{ (corr)}$

$\dfrac{\text{atomic mass } S}{\text{formula mass } SO_2} = \dfrac{32.06 \text{ amu}}{64.06 \text{ amu}} = 0.5004683 \text{ (calc)} = 0.5005 \text{ (corr)}$

Since the ratios are the same, the samples contain an equal number of particles (atoms for   S and molecules for SO_2).

9.55 a) $\dfrac{\text{atomic mass } Fe}{\text{atomic mass } Cu} = \dfrac{55.84 \text{ amu}}{63.55 \text{ amu}} = 0.8786782 \text{ (calc)} = 0.8787 \text{ (corr)}$

$\dfrac{\text{mass } Fe}{\text{mass } Cu} = \dfrac{24.3 \text{ g}}{23.6 \text{ g}} = 1.0296610 \text{ (calc)} = 1.03 \text{ (corr)}$

Since the mass ratio is greater than 0.879 (equal numbers of atoms) there are more Fe atoms than Cu atoms.

b) $\dfrac{\text{atomic mass } Ni}{\text{atomic mass } Cu} = \dfrac{58.69 \text{ amu}}{63.55 \text{ amu}} = 0.9235247 \text{ (calc)} = 0.9235 \text{ (corr)}$

$\dfrac{\text{mass } Ni}{\text{mass } Cu} = \dfrac{19.6 \text{ g}}{23.6 \text{ g}} = 0.83050848 \text{ (calc)} = 0.831 \text{ (corr)}$

Since the mass ratio is less than 0.924 (equal numbers of atoms) there are fewer Ni atoms than Cu atoms.

c) $\dfrac{\text{atomic mass } P}{\text{atomic mass } Cu} = \dfrac{30.97 \text{ amu}}{63.55 \text{ amu}} = 0.4873328 \text{ (calc)} = 0.4873 \text{ (corr)}$

$\dfrac{\text{mass } P}{\text{mass } Cu} = \dfrac{11.5 \text{ g}}{23.6 \text{ g}} = 0.48823559 \text{ (calc)} = 0.488 \text{ (corr)}$

Since the ratios are equal, the same number of atoms are present (to three significant figures).

d) $\dfrac{\text{atomic mass } Al}{\text{atomic mass } Cu} = \dfrac{26.98 \text{ amu}}{63.55 \text{ amu}} = 0.4245476 \text{ (calc)} = 0.4245 \text{ (corr)}$

$\dfrac{\text{mass } Al}{\text{mass } Cu} = \dfrac{11.2 \text{ g}}{23.6 \text{ g}} = 0.47457627 \text{ (calc)} = 0.475 \text{ (corr)}$

Since the mass ratio is greater than 0.425 (equal numbers of atoms) there are more Al atoms than Cu atoms.

9.57 a) $3 \times 10.00 \text{ g P} \times \dfrac{32.06 \text{ g S}}{30.97 \text{ g P}} = 31.055861 \text{ (calc)} = 31.06 \text{ g S (corr)}$

b) $3 \times 10.00 \text{ g P} \times \dfrac{9.012 \text{ g Be}}{30.97 \text{ g P}} = 8.7297384 \text{ (calc)} = 8.730 \text{ g Be (corr)}$

c) $3 \times 10.00 \text{ g P} \times \dfrac{238.03 \text{ g U}}{30.97 \text{ g P}} = 230.57474 \text{ (calc)} = 230.6 \text{ g U (corr)}$

d) $3 \times 10.00 \text{ g P} \times \dfrac{28.09 \text{ g Si}}{30.97 \text{ g P}} = 27.210203 \text{ (calc)} = 27.21 \text{ g Si (corr)}$

The Mole and Chemical Formulas (Sec. 9.10)

9.59 $\dfrac{3 \text{ moles Na}}{1 \text{ mole Na}_3\text{PO}_4}$ $\dfrac{1 \text{ mole P}}{1 \text{ mole Na}_3\text{PO}_4}$

$\dfrac{4 \text{ moles O}}{1 \text{ mole Na}_3\text{PO}_4}$ $\dfrac{3 \text{ moles Na}}{1 \text{ mole P}}$

$\dfrac{3 \text{ moles Na}}{4 \text{ moles O}}$ $\dfrac{1 \text{ mole P}}{4 \text{ moles O}}$

9.61   a) $1.0 \text{ mole Na}_2\text{SO}_4 \times \dfrac{1 \text{ mole S}}{1 \text{ mole Na}_2\text{SO}_4} = 1.0 \text{ mole S};$

$0.50 \text{ mole Na}_2\text{S}_2\text{O}_3 \times \dfrac{2 \text{ moles S}}{1 \text{ mole Na}_2\text{S}_2\text{O}_3} = 1.0 \text{ mole. Same moles of S}$

b) $2.00 \text{ moles S}_3\text{Cl}_2 \times \dfrac{3 \text{ moles S}}{1 \text{ mole S}_3\text{Cl}_2} = 6.00 \text{ moles S};$

$1.50 \text{ moles S}_2\text{O} \times \dfrac{2 \text{ moles S}}{1 \text{ mole S}_2\text{O}} = 3.00 \text{ moles. Not the same}$

c) $3.00 \text{ moles H}_2\text{S}_2\text{O}_5 \times \dfrac{2 \text{ moles S}}{1 \text{ mole H}_2\text{S}_2\text{O}_5} = 6.00 \text{ moles S};$

$6.00 \text{ moles H}_2\text{SO}_4 \times \dfrac{1 \text{ mole S}}{1 \text{ mole H}_2\text{SO}_4} = 6.00 \text{ moles S. Same moles of S}$

d) $1.00 \text{ mole Na}_3\text{Ag(S}_2\text{O}_3)_2 \times \dfrac{4 \text{ moles S}}{1 \text{ mole Na}_3\text{Ag(S}_2\text{O}_3)_2} = 4.00 \text{ moles S};$

$2.00 \text{ moles S}_2\text{F}_{10} \times \dfrac{2 \text{ moles S}}{1 \text{ mole S}_2\text{F}_{10}} = 4.00 \text{ moles S. Same moles of S}$

9.63   a) $2.00 \text{ moles NaAuBr}_4 \times \dfrac{6 \text{ moles total atoms}}{1 \text{ mole NaAuBr}_4} = 12.0 \text{ moles atoms}$

$2.00 \text{ moles Au}_2\text{Te}_3 \times \dfrac{5 \text{ moles total atoms}}{1 \text{ mole Au}_2\text{Te}_3} = 10.0 \text{ moles atoms} \therefore 2.00 \text{ moles NaAuBr}_4$

b) $1.00 \text{ mole C}_2\text{H}_2\text{Cl}_4 \times \dfrac{8 \text{ moles total atoms}}{1 \text{ mole C}_2\text{H}_2\text{Cl}_4} = 8.00 \text{ moles atoms}$

$1.00 \text{ mole CCl}_4 \times \dfrac{5 \text{ moles total atoms}}{1 \text{ mole CCl}_4} = 5.00 \text{ moles atoms} \therefore 1.00 \text{ mole C}_2\text{H}_2\text{Cl}_4$

c) $3.00 \text{ moles Ba(NO}_3)_2 \times \dfrac{9 \text{ moles total atoms}}{1 \text{ mole Ba(NO}_3)_2} = 27.0 \text{ moles atoms}$

$3.00 \text{ moles BaSO}_4 \times \dfrac{6 \text{ moles total atoms}}{1 \text{ mole BaSO}_4} = 18.0 \text{ moles atoms} \therefore 3.00 \text{ moles Ba(NO}_3)_2$

d) $1.20 \text{ moles NH}_4\text{CN} \times \dfrac{7 \text{ moles total atoms}}{1 \text{ mole NH}_4\text{CN}} = 8.40 \text{ moles atoms}$

$1.30 \text{ moles NH}_4\text{Cl} \times \dfrac{6 \text{ moles total atoms}}{1 \text{ mole NH}_4\text{Cl}} = 7.80 \text{ moles atoms} \therefore 1.20 \text{ moles NH}_4\text{CN}$

The Mole and Chemical Calculations (Sec. 9.11)

9.65   a) $7.500 \text{ g S} \times \dfrac{1 \text{ mole S}}{32.06 \text{ g S}} \times \dfrac{6.022 \times 10^{23} \text{ atoms S}}{1 \text{ mole S}}$

$$= 1.4087648 \times 10^{23} \text{ (calc)} = 1.408 \times 10^{23} \text{ atoms S (corr)}$$

     b) $7.500 \text{ g Be} \times \dfrac{1 \text{ mole Be}}{9.012 \text{ g Be}} \times \dfrac{6.022 \times 10^{23} \text{ atoms Be}}{1 \text{ mole Be}}$

$$= 5.0116511 \times 10^{23} \text{ (calc)} = 5.012 \times 10^{23} \text{ atoms Be (corr)}$$

     c) $7.500 \text{ g Ba} \times \dfrac{1 \text{ mole Ba}}{137.33 \text{ g Ba}} \times \dfrac{6.022 \times 10^{23} \text{ atoms Ba}}{1 \text{ mole Ba}}$

$$= 3.288788 \times 10^{22} \text{ (calc)} = 3.289 \times 10^{22} \text{ atoms Ba (corr)}$$

     d) $7.500 \text{ g Au} \times \dfrac{1 \text{ mole Au}}{196.97 \text{ g Au}} \times \dfrac{6.022 \times 10^{23} \text{ atoms Au}}{1 \text{ mole Au}}$

$$= 2.292984 \times 10^{22} \text{ (calc)} = 2.293 \times 10^{22} \text{ atoms Au (corr)}$$

9.67   a) $25.0 \text{ g HF} \times \dfrac{1 \text{ mole HF}}{20.01 \text{ g HF}} \times \dfrac{6.022 \times 10^{23} \text{ molecules HF}}{1 \text{ mole HF}}$

$$= 7.52374 \times 10^{22} \text{ (calc)} = 7.52 \times 10^{23} \text{ molecules HF (corr)}$$

     b) $25.0 \text{ g N}_2\text{H}_4 \times \dfrac{1 \text{ mole N}_2\text{H}_4}{32.06 \text{ g N}_2\text{H}_4} \times \dfrac{6.022 \times 10^{23} \text{ molecules N}_2\text{H}_4}{1 \text{ mole N}_2\text{H}_4}$

$$= 4.6958827 \times 10^{23} \text{ (calc)} = 4.70 \times 10^{23} \text{ molecules N}_2\text{H}_4 \text{ (corr)}$$

     c) $25.0 \text{ g SO}_2 \times \dfrac{1 \text{ mole SO}_2}{64.06 \text{ g SO}_2} \times \dfrac{6.022 \times 10^{23} \text{ molecules SO}_2}{1 \text{ mole SO}_2}$

$$= 2.3501405 \times 10^{23} \text{ (calc)} = 2.35 \times 10^{23} \text{ molecules SO}_2 \text{ (corr)}$$

     d) $25.0 \text{ g H}_2\text{SO}_4 \times \dfrac{1 \text{ mole H}_2\text{SO}_4}{98.08 \text{ g H}_2\text{SO}_4} \times \dfrac{6.022 \times 10^{23} \text{ molecules H}_2\text{SO}_4}{1 \text{ mole H}_2\text{SO}_4}$

$$= 1.5349715 \times 10^{23} \text{ (calc)} = 1.53 \times 10^{23} \text{ molecules H}_2\text{SO}_4 \text{ (corr)}$$

9.69   a) $6.022 \times 10^{23} \text{ atoms Ag} \times \dfrac{1 \text{ mole Ag}}{6.022 \times 10^{23} \text{ atoms Ag}} \times \dfrac{107.87 \text{ g Ag}}{1 \text{ mole Ag}} = 107.87 \text{ (calc)}$

$$= 107.9 \text{ g Ag (corr)}$$

     b) $1.750 \times 10^{23} \text{ atoms N} \times \dfrac{1 \text{ mole N}}{6.022 \times 10^{23} \text{ atoms N}} \times \dfrac{14.01 \text{ g N}}{1 \text{ mole N}}$

$$= 4.07132182 \text{ (calc)} = 4.071 \text{ g N (corr)}$$

     c) $6.5 \times 10^{30} \text{ molecules CO}_2 \times \dfrac{1 \text{ mole CO}_2}{6.022 \times 10^{23} \text{ molecules CO}_2} \times \dfrac{44.01 \text{ g CO}_2}{1 \text{ mole CO}_2}$

$$= 4.750332 \times 10^{8} \text{ (calc)} = 4.8 \times 10^{8} \text{ g CO}_2 \text{ (corr)}$$

     d) $2431 \text{ molecules CO} \times \dfrac{1 \text{ mole CO}}{6.022 \times 10^{23} \text{ molecules CO}} \times \dfrac{28.01 \text{ g CO}}{1 \text{ mole CO}}$

$$= 1.1307258 \times 10^{-19} \text{ (calc)} = 1.131 \times 10^{-19} \text{ g CO (corr)}$$

9.71   a) $1 \text{ atom Na} \times \dfrac{22.99 \text{ amu}}{1 \text{ atom Na}} \times \dfrac{1 \text{ g}}{6.022 \times 10^{23} \text{ amu}} = 3.8176685 \times 10^{-23} \text{ (calc)}$

$$= 3.818 \times 10^{-23} \text{ g Na (corr)}$$

b) $1 \text{ atom Mg} \times \dfrac{24.30 \text{ amu}}{1 \text{ atom Mg}} \times \dfrac{1 \text{ g}}{6.022 \times 10^{23} \text{ amu}} = 4.0352043 \times 10^{-23}$ (calc)

$= 4.035 \times 10^{-23} \text{ g Mg}$ (corr)

c) $1 \text{ molecule } C_4H_{10} \times \dfrac{[4(12.01) + 10(1.01)] \text{ amu}}{1 \text{ molecule } C_4H_{10}} \times \dfrac{1 \text{ g}}{6.022 \times 10^{23} \text{ amu}}$

$= 9.6545998 \times 10^{-23}$ (calc) $= 9.655 \times 10^{-23} \text{ g } C_4H_{10}$ (corr)

d) $1 \text{ molecule } C_6H_6 \times \dfrac{[6(12.01) + 6(1.01)] \text{ amu}}{1 \text{ molecule } C_6H_6} \times \dfrac{1 \text{ g}}{6.022 \times 10^{23} \text{ amu}}$

$= 1.2972434 \times 10^{-22}$ (calc) $= 1.297 \times 10^{-22} \text{ g } C_6H_6$ (corr)

9.73 a) $100.0 \text{ g NaCl} \times \dfrac{1 \text{ mole NaCl}}{58.44 \text{ g NaCl}} \times \dfrac{1 \text{ mole Cl}}{1 \text{ mole NaCl}} \times \dfrac{35.45 \text{ g Cl}}{1 \text{ mole Cl}} = 60.660506$ (calc)

$= 60.66 \text{ g Cl}$ (corr)

b) $980.0 \text{ g CCl}_4 \times \dfrac{1 \text{ mole CCl}_4}{153.81 \text{ g CCl}_4} \times \dfrac{4 \text{ moles Cl}}{1 \text{ mole CCl}_4} \times \dfrac{35.45 \text{ g Cl}}{1 \text{ mole Cl}} = 903.47832$ (calc)

$= 903.5 \text{ g Cl}$ (corr)

c) $10.0 \text{ g HCl} \times \dfrac{1 \text{ mole HCl}}{36.46 \text{ g HCl}} \times \dfrac{1 \text{ mole Cl}}{1 \text{ mole HCl}} \times \dfrac{35.45 \text{ g Cl}}{1 \text{ mole Cl}} = 9.7229841$ (calc)

$= 9.72 \text{ g Cl}$ (corr)

d) $50.0 \text{ g BaCl}_2 \times \dfrac{1 \text{ mole BaCl}_2}{208.23 \text{ g BaCl}_2} \times \dfrac{2 \text{ mole Cl}}{1 \text{ mole BaCl}_2} \times \dfrac{35.45 \text{ g Cl}}{1 \text{ mole Cl}} = 17.024444$ (calc)

$= 17.0 \text{ g Cl}$ (corr)

9.75 a) $25.0 \text{ g PF}_3 \times \dfrac{1 \text{ mole PF}_3}{87.97 \text{ g PF}_3} \times \dfrac{1 \text{ mole P}}{1 \text{ mole PF}_3} \times \dfrac{6.022 \times 10^{23} \text{ atoms P}}{1 \text{ mole P}}$

$= 1.7113709 \times 10^{23}$ (calc) $= 1.71 \times 10^{23} \text{ atoms P}$ (corr)

b) $25.0 \text{ g Be}_3P_2 \times \dfrac{1 \text{ mole Be}_3P_2}{88.98 \text{ g Be}_3P_2} \times \dfrac{2 \text{ moles P}}{1 \text{ mole Be}_3P_2} \times \dfrac{6.022 \times 10^{23} \text{ atoms P}}{1 \text{ mole P}}$

$= 3.3839065 \times 10^{23}$ (calc) $= 3.38 \times 10^{23} \text{ atoms P}$ (corr)

c) $25.0 \text{ g POCl}_3 \times \dfrac{1 \text{ mole POCl}_3}{153.32 \text{ g POCl}_3} \times \dfrac{1 \text{ mole P}}{1 \text{ mole POCl}_3} \times \dfrac{6.022 \times 10^{23} \text{ atoms P}}{1 \text{ mole P}}$

$= 9.8193321 \times 10^{22}$ (calc) $= 9.82 \times 10^{22} \text{ atoms P}$ (corr)

d) $25.0 \text{ g Na}_5P_3O_{10} \times \dfrac{1 \text{ mole Na}_5P_3O_{10}}{367.86 \text{ g Na}_5P_3O_{10}} \times \dfrac{3 \text{ moles P}}{1 \text{ mole Na}_5P_3O_{10}} \times \dfrac{6.022 \times 10^{23} \text{ atoms P}}{1 \text{ mole P}}$

$= 1.2277769 \times 10^{23}$ (calc) $= 1.23 \times 10^{23} \text{ atoms P}$ (corr)

9.77 a) $2.0 \times 10^{25} \text{ molecules } P_4O_{10} \times \dfrac{1 \text{ mole } P_4O_{10}}{6.022 \times 10^{23} \text{ molecules } P_4O_{10}} \times \dfrac{10 \text{ mole O}}{1 \text{ mole } P_4O_{10}} \times \dfrac{16.00 \text{ g O}}{1 \text{ mole O}}$

$= 5.3138492 \times 10^3$ (calc) $= 5.3 \times 10^3 \text{ g O}$ (corr)

b) $50.00 \text{ g SO}_3 \times \dfrac{1 \text{ mole SO}_3}{32.06 + 3(16.00) \text{ g SO}_3} \times \dfrac{3 \text{ moles O}}{1 \text{ mole SO}_3} \times \dfrac{16.00 \text{ g O}}{1 \text{ mole O}}$

$= 29.977517$ (calc) $= 29.98 \text{ g O}$ (corr)

c) $3.50 \text{ moles KNO}_3 \times \dfrac{3 \text{ moles O}}{1 \text{ mole KNO}_3} \times \dfrac{16.00 \text{ g O}}{1 \text{ mole O}} = 168 \text{ g O}$ (calc and corr)

d) $475 \text{ g Ca}_3(PO_4)_2 \times \dfrac{1 \text{ mole Ca}_3(PO_4)_2}{[3(40.08) \times 2(30.97) + 8(16.00)] \text{ g Ca}_3(PO_4)_2} \times \dfrac{8 \text{ moles O}}{1 \text{ mole Ca}_3(PO_4)_2} \times$

$\dfrac{16.00 \text{ g O}}{1 \text{ mole O}} = 196.01522 \text{ (calc)} = 196 \text{ g O (corr)}$

9.79   a) $1.000 \text{ g S} \times \dfrac{1 \text{ mole S}}{32.06 \text{ g S}} \times \dfrac{1 \text{ mole H}_2S}{1 \text{ mole S}} = 0.0311915 \text{ (calc)} = 0.03119 \text{ mole H}_2S \text{ (corr)}$

b) $1.000 \text{ g S} \times \dfrac{1 \text{ mole S}}{32.06 \text{ g S}} \times \dfrac{1 \text{ mole S}_8}{8 \text{ moles S}} \times \dfrac{6.022 \times 10^{23} \text{ molecules S}_8}{1 \text{ mole S}_8}$

$= 2.3479414 \times 10^{21} \text{ (calc)} = 2.348 \times 10^{21} \text{ molecules S}_8 \text{ (corr)}$

c) $1.000 \text{ g S} \times \dfrac{1 \text{ mole S}}{32.06 \text{ g S}} \times \dfrac{1 \text{ mole S}_3N_3O_3Cl_3}{3 \text{ moles S}} \times \dfrac{292.56 \text{ g S}_3N_3O_3Cl_3}{1 \text{ mole S}_3N_3O_3Cl_3}$

$= 3.0417966 \text{ (calc)} = 3.042 \text{ g S}_3N_3O_3Cl_3 \text{ (corr)}$

d) $1.000 \text{ g S} \times \dfrac{1 \text{ mole S}}{32.06 \text{ g S}} \times \dfrac{6.022 \times 10^{23} \text{ atoms S}}{1 \text{ mole S}} = 1.8783531 \times 10^{22} \text{ (calc)}$

$= 1.878 \times 10^{22} \text{ atoms S (corr)}$

9.81   a) $2.70 \times 10^{25} \text{ atoms O} \times \dfrac{1 \text{ mole 0}}{6.022 \times 10^{23} \text{ atoms O}} \times \dfrac{1 \text{ mole CO}_2}{2 \text{ mole O}} \times \dfrac{44.01 \text{ g CO}_2}{1 \text{ mole CO}_2}$

$= 9.866074394 \times 10^2 \text{ (calc)} = 9.87 \times 10^2 \text{ (corr)}$

b) $2.70 \times 10^{25} \text{ atoms C} \times \dfrac{1 \text{ mole C}}{6.022 \times 10^{23} \text{ atoms C}} \times \dfrac{1 \text{ mole CO}_2}{1 \text{ mole C}} \times \dfrac{44.01 \text{ g CO}_2}{1 \text{ mole CO}_2}$

$= 1.973 \times 10^3 \text{ (calc)} = 1.97 \times 10^3 \text{ (corr)}$

c) There are 3 atoms in 1 molecule of CO_2 (1 atom C + 2 atoms O)

$2.70 \times 10^{25} \text{ atoms total} \times \dfrac{1 \text{ molecule CO}_2}{3 \text{ atoms}} \times \dfrac{1 \text{ mole CO}_2}{6.022 \times 10^{23} \text{ molecule CO}_2} \times \dfrac{44.01 \text{ g CO}_2}{1 \text{ mole CO}_2}$

$= 6.577382929 \times 10^2 \text{ (calc)} = 6.58 \times 10^2 \text{ (corr)}$

d) $2.70 \times 10^{25} \text{ molecules CO}_2 \times \dfrac{1 \text{ mole CO}_2}{6.022 \times 10^{23} \text{ molecules CO}_2} \times \dfrac{44.01 \text{ g CO}_2}{1 \text{ mole CO}_2}$

$= 1.973 \times 10^3 \text{ (calc)} = 1.97 \times 10^3 \text{ (corr)}$

9.83   The molar mass of $C_{21}H_{30}O_2$ is $21(12.01) + 30(1.01) + 2(16.00) = 314.51 \text{ (calc)} = 314.5 \text{ g/mole (corr)}$

a) $25.00 \text{ g C}_{21}H_{30}O_2 \times \dfrac{1 \text{ mole C}_{21}H_{30}O_2}{314.51 \text{ g C}_{21}H_{30}O_2} \times \dfrac{(21 + 30 + 2) \text{ moles atoms}}{1 \text{ mole C}_{21}H_{30}O_2}$

$= 4.2129026 \text{ (calc)} = 4.213 \text{ moles atoms (corr)}$

b) $25.00 \text{ g C}_{21}H_{30}O_2 \times \dfrac{1 \text{ mole C}_{21}H_{30}O_2}{314.51 \text{ g C}_{21}H_{30}O_2} \times \dfrac{21 \text{ mole C}}{1 \text{ mole C}_{21}H_{30}O_2} \times \dfrac{6.022 \times 10^{23} \text{ atoms C}}{\text{mole C}}$

$= 1.0052304 \times 10^{24} \text{ (calc)} = 1.005 \times 10^{24} \text{ atoms C (corr)}$

c) $25.00 \text{ g C}_{21}H_{30}O_2 \times \dfrac{1 \text{ mole C}_{21}H_{30}O_2}{314.51 \text{ g C}_{21}H_{30}O_2} \times \dfrac{2 \text{ mole O}}{1 \text{ mole C}_{21}H_{30}O_2} \times \dfrac{16.00 \text{ g O}}{\text{mole O}}$

$= 2.5436393 \text{ (calc)} = 2.544 \text{ g O (corr)}$

d) $25.00 \text{ g } C_{21}H_{30}O_2 \times \dfrac{1 \text{ mole } C_{21}H_{30}O_2}{314.5 \text{ g } C_{21}H_{30}O_2} \times \dfrac{6.022 \times 10^{23} \text{ molecules } C_{21}H_{30}O_2}{\text{mole } C_{21}H_{30}O_2}$

$$= 4.7869634 \times 10^{22} \text{ (calc)} = 4.787 \times 10^{22} \text{ molecules } C_{21}H_{30}O_2 \text{ (corr)}$$

Purity of Samples (Sec 9.12)

9.85 a) $325 \text{ g sample } Fe_2S_3 \times \dfrac{95.4 \text{ g } Fe_2S_3}{100 \text{ g sample } Fe_2S_3} = 3.1005 \times 10^2 \text{ (calc)}$

$$= 3.10 \times 10^2 \text{ g } Fe_2S_3 \text{ in sample}$$

b) $325 \text{ g sample } Fe_2S_3 - 310 \text{ g } Fe_2S_3 = 15 \text{ g impurities in sample}$

9.87 $100 \text{ g sample } - 62.03 \text{ g of FeS} = 37.97 \text{ g impurities in sample}$

$6.00 \text{ g impurities} \times \dfrac{100 \text{ g sample}}{37.97 \text{ g impurities}} = 15.801948 \text{ (calc)} = 15.8 \text{ g sample}$

9.89 $0.55 \text{ g impurities} + 67.21 \text{ g NaCl} = 67.76 \text{ g sample}$

$\dfrac{67.21 \text{ g NaCl}}{67.76 \text{ g sample}} \times 100 = 99.1883116 \text{ (calc)} = 99.19\% \text{ of sample is pure NaCl}$

9.91 $35.00 \text{ g sample} \times \dfrac{92.35 \text{ g Cu}}{100 \text{ g sample}} \times \dfrac{1 \text{ mole Cu}}{63.55 \text{ g Cu}} \times \dfrac{6.022 \times 10^{23} \text{ atoms Cu}}{1 \text{ mole Cu}}$

$$= 3.062881117 \times 10^{23} \text{(calc)} = 3.063 \times 10^{23} \text{ atoms Cu (calc)}$$

9.93 $25.00 \text{ g sample} \times \dfrac{64.0 \text{ g } Cr_2O_3}{100 \text{ g sample}} \times \dfrac{104.00 \text{ g Cr}}{152.00 \text{ g } Cr_2O_3} = 1.09473684 \times 10^1 \text{(calc)}$

$$= 1.09 \times 10^1 \text{ g Cr (corr)}$$

Empirical and Molecular Formulas (Secs. 9.13 through 9.15)

9.95 a) HO   b) C_4H_7 c) C_3H_8 d) SN

9.97 a) $58.91 \text{ g Na} \times \dfrac{1 \text{ mole Na}}{22.99 \text{ g Na}} = 2.5624184 \text{ (calc)} = 2.562 \text{ moles Na (corr)}$

$41.09 \text{ g S} \times \dfrac{1 \text{ mole S}}{32.06 \text{ g S}} = 1.2816594 \text{ (calc)} = 1.282 \text{ moles S (corr)}$

Na: $\dfrac{2.562}{1.282} = 1.998$ S: $\dfrac{1.282}{1.282} = 1.000$

The empirical formula is Na_2S

b) $24.74 \text{ g K} \times \dfrac{1 \text{ mole K}}{39.10 \text{ g K}} = 0.63273657 \text{ (calc)} = 0.6327 \text{ mole K (corr)}$

$34.76 \text{ g Mn} \times \dfrac{1 \text{ mole Mn}}{54.94 \text{ g Mn}} = 0.6326902 \text{ (calc)} = 0.6327 \text{ mole Mn (corr)}$

$40.50 \text{ g O} \times \dfrac{1 \text{ mole O}}{16.00 \text{ g O}} = 2.53125 \text{ (calc)} = 2.531 \text{ moles O (corr)}$

K: $\dfrac{0.6327}{0.6327} = 1.000$ Mn: $\dfrac{0.6327}{0.6327} = 1.000$ O: $\dfrac{2.531}{0.6327} = 4.000$

The empirical formula is $KMnO_4$.

c) 2.06 g H x $\dfrac{1 \text{ mole H}}{1.01 \text{ g H}}$ = 2.0396039 (calc) = 2.04 moles H (corr)

32.69 g S x $\dfrac{1 \text{ mole S}}{32.06 \text{ g S}}$ = 1.0196507 (calc) = 1.020 moles S (corr)

65.25 g O x $\dfrac{1 \text{ mole O}}{16.00 \text{ g O}}$ = 4.078125 (calc) = 4.078 moles O (corr)

H: $\dfrac{2.04}{1.020} = 2.000$ S: $\dfrac{1.020}{1.020} = 1.000$ O: $\dfrac{4.078}{1.020} = 3.998$

The empirical formula is H_2SO_4.

d) 19.84 g C x $\dfrac{1 \text{ mole C}}{12.01 \text{ g C}}$ = 1.6519567 (calc) = 1.652 moles C (corr)

2.50 g H x $\dfrac{1 \text{ mole H}}{1.01 \text{ g H}}$ = 2.4952475 (calc) = 2.48 moles H (corr)

66.08 g O x $\dfrac{1 \text{ mole O}}{16.00 \text{ g O}}$ = 4.13 (calc) = 4.130 moles O (corr)

11.57 g N x $\dfrac{1 \text{ mole N}}{14.01 \text{ g N}}$ = 0.82583868 (calc) = 0.8258 mole N (corr)

C: $\dfrac{1.652}{0.8258} = 2.000$ H: $\dfrac{2.48}{0.8258} = 3.00$ O: $\dfrac{4.130}{0.8258} = 5.001$ N: $\dfrac{0.8258}{0.8258} = 1.000$

The empirical formula is $C_2H_3O_5N$.

9.99   a) multiply by 3; 3 to 4   b) multiply by 2; 3 to 4
       c) multiply by 4; 7 to 8 to 9   d) multiply by 3; 4 to 7 to 6

9.101 a) 43.64 g P x $\dfrac{1 \text{ mole P}}{30.97 \text{ g P}}$ = 1.4091055 (calc) = 1.409 moles P (corr)

56.36 g O x $\dfrac{1 \text{ mole O}}{16.00 \text{ g O}}$ = 3.5225 (calc) = 3.522 moles O (corr)

P: $\dfrac{1.409}{1.409} = 1.000$ O: $\dfrac{3.502}{1.409} = 2.500$

P: 1.000 x 2 = 2.000   O: 2.500 x 2 = 5.000

The empirical formula is P_2O_5.

b) 72.24 g Mg x $\dfrac{1 \text{ mole Mg}}{24.30 \text{ g Mg}}$ = 2.9728395 (calc) = 2.973 moles Mg (corr)

27.76 g N x $\dfrac{1 \text{ mole N}}{14.01 \text{ g N}}$ = 1.9814418 (calc) = 1.981 moles N (corr)

Mg: $\dfrac{2.973}{1.981} = 1.501$ N: $\dfrac{1.981}{1.981} = 1.000$

Mg: 1.501 x 1 = 3.002   N: 1.000 x 2 = 2.000

The empirical formula is Mg_3N_2.

c) 29.08 g Na x $\dfrac{1 \text{ mole Na}}{22.99 \text{ g Na}}$ = 1.2648977 (calc) = 1.265 moles Na (corr)

40.56 g S x $\dfrac{1 \text{ mole S}}{32.06 \text{ g S}}$ = 1.2651279 (calc) = 1.265 moles S (corr)

$$30.36 \text{ g O} \times \frac{1 \text{ mole O}}{16.00 \text{ g O}} = 1.8975 \text{ (calc)} = 1.898 \text{ moles O (corr)}$$

Na: $\dfrac{1.265}{1.265} = 1.000$ S: $\dfrac{1.265}{1.265} = 1.000$ O: $\dfrac{1.898}{1.265} = 1.500$

Na: $1.000 \times 2 = 2.000$ S: $1.000 \times 2 = 2.000$ O: $1.500 \times 2 = 3.000$

The empirical formula is $Na_2S_2O_3$.

d) $21.85 \text{ g Mg} \times \dfrac{1 \text{ mole Mg}}{24.30 \text{ g Mg}} = 0.89917695 \text{ (calc)} = 0.8992 \text{ mole Mg (corr)}$

$27.83 \text{ g P} \times \dfrac{1 \text{ mole P}}{30.97 \text{ g P}} = 0.89861155 \text{ (calc)} = 0.8986 \text{ mole P (corr)}$

$50.32 \text{ g O} \times \dfrac{1 \text{ mole O}}{16.00 \text{ g O}} = 3.145 \text{ moles O (calc and corr)}$

Mg: $\dfrac{0.8992}{0.8986} = 1.001$ P: $\dfrac{0.8986}{0.8986} = 1.000$ O: $\dfrac{3.145}{0.8986} = 3.500$

Mg: $1.001 \times 2 = 2.002$ P: $1.000 \times 2 = 2.000$ O: $3.500 \times 2 = 7.000$

The empirical formula is $Mg_2P_2O_7$.

9.103   Compound I: Take 100 g compound. %Cl = 100 - 45.3 = 54.7% Cl

$45.3 \text{ g Ni} \times \dfrac{1 \text{ mole Ni}}{58.69 \text{ g Ni}} = 0.7718521 \text{ (calc)} = 0.772 \text{ mole Ni (corr)}$

$54.7 \text{ g Cl} \times \dfrac{1 \text{ mole Cl}}{35.45 \text{ g Cl}} = 1.5430183 \text{ (calc)} = 1.54 \text{ moles Cl}$

Cl: $\dfrac{1.54}{0.772} = 1.9948187 \text{ (calc)} = 1.99 \text{ (corr)}$ Ni: $\dfrac{0.772}{0.772} = 1.00$

Empirical formula is $NiCl_2$.

Compound II: %Cl = 100.0 - 35.5 = 64.5% Cl

$35.5 \text{ g Ni} \times \dfrac{1 \text{ mole Ni}}{58.69 \text{ g Ni}} = 0.604873 \text{ (calc)} = 0.605 \text{ moles Ni}$

$64.5 \text{ g Cl} \times \dfrac{1 \text{ mole Cl}}{35.45 \text{ g Cl}} = 1.819464 \text{ (calc)} = 1.82 \text{ moles Cl}$

Cl: $\dfrac{1.82}{0.605} = 3.0082645 \text{ (calc)} = 3.01 \text{ (corr)}$ Ni: $\dfrac{0.605}{0.605} = 1.00$

Empirical formula is $NiCl_3$.

9.105 $5.798 \text{ g C} \times \dfrac{1 \text{ mole C}}{12.01 \text{ g C}} = 0.48276436 \text{ (calc)} = 0.4828 \text{ mole C (corr)}$

$1.46 \text{ g H} \times \dfrac{1 \text{ mole H}}{1.01 \text{ g H}} = 1.4455445 \text{ (calc)} = 1.45 \text{ moles H (corr)}$

$7.740 \text{ g S} \times \dfrac{1 \text{ mole S}}{32.06 \text{ g S}} = 0.2414223 \text{ (calc)} = 0.2414 \text{ mole S (corr)}$

C: $\dfrac{0.4828}{0.2414} = 2.000$ H: $\dfrac{1.45}{0.2414} = 6.00$ S: $\dfrac{0.2414}{0.2414} = 1.000$

The empirical formula is C_2H_6S.

9.107   Wt oxygen in compound = 5.55 g - 2.00 g = 3.55 g oxygen

$$2.00 \text{ g Be} \times \frac{1 \text{ mole Be}}{9.01 \text{ g Be}} = 0.22197558 \text{ (calc)} = 0.222 \text{ moles Be (corr)}$$

$$3.55 \text{ g O} \times \frac{1 \text{ mole O}}{16.00 \text{ g O}} = 0.221875 \text{ (calc)} = 0.222 \text{ moles O (corr)}$$

Be: $\dfrac{0.222}{0.222} = 1.00$ O: $\dfrac{0.222}{0.222} = 1.00$

The empirical formula is BeO.

9.109   Since this compound has only C and H, find moles C and moles H from data:

a) $0.338 \text{ g CO}_2 \times \dfrac{1 \text{ mole CO}_2}{44.01 \text{ g CO}_2} \times \dfrac{1 \text{ mole C}}{1 \text{ mole CO}_2} = 0.007680072 \text{ (calc)} = 0.00768 \text{ moles C (corr)}$

$0.277 \text{ g H}_2\text{O} \times \dfrac{1 \text{ mole H}_2\text{O}}{18.02 \text{ g H}_2\text{O}} \times \dfrac{2 \text{ moles H}}{1 \text{ mole H}_2\text{O}} = 0.0307436 \text{ (calc)} = .0307 \text{ moles H (corr)}$

H: $= \dfrac{0.0307}{0.00768} = 3.9973958 \text{ (calc)} = 4.00 \text{ (corr)}$ C: $\dfrac{0.00768}{0.00768} = 1.00$

The empirical formula is CH_4.

b) $0.303 \text{ g CO}_2 \times \dfrac{1 \text{ mole CO}_2}{44.01 \text{ g CO}_2} \times \dfrac{1 \text{ mole C}}{1 \text{ mole CO}_2} = 0.006884799 \text{ (calc)} = 0.00688 \text{ moles C (corr)}$

$0.0621 \text{ g H}_2\text{O} \times \dfrac{1 \text{ mole H}_2\text{O}}{18.02 \text{ g H}_2\text{O}} \times \dfrac{2 \text{ mole H}}{1 \text{ mole H}_2\text{O}} = 0.0068923418 \text{ (calc)} = 0.00689 \text{ moles H (corr)}$

H: $\dfrac{0.00689}{0.00688} = 1.0014535 \text{ (calc)} = 1.00 \text{ (corr)}$ C: $\dfrac{0.00688}{0.00688}$

$= 0.9985486 \text{ (calc)} = 1.00 \text{ (corr)}$

The empirical formula is CH.

c) $0.225 \text{ g CO}_2 \times \dfrac{1 \text{ mole CO}_2}{44.01 \text{ g CO}_2} \times \dfrac{1 \text{ mole C}}{1 \text{ mole CO}_2} = 0.00511247 \text{ (calc)}$

$= 0.00511 \text{ moles C (corr)}$

$0.115 \text{ g H}_2\text{O} \times \dfrac{1 \text{ mole H}_2\text{O}}{18.02 \text{ g H}_2\text{O}} \times \dfrac{2 \text{ mole H}}{1 \text{ mole H}_2\text{O}} = 0.0127635 \text{ (calc)} = 0.0128 \text{ moles H (corr)}$

H: $\dfrac{0.0128}{0.00511} = 2.50489237 \text{ (calc)} = 2.50 \text{ (corr)}$ C: $\dfrac{0.00511}{0.00511} = 1$

Multiplying by 2 gives the empirical formula C_2H_5.

d) $0.314 \text{ g CO}_2 \times \dfrac{1 \text{ mole CO}_2}{44.01 \text{ g CO}_2} \times \dfrac{1 \text{ mole C}}{1 \text{ mole CO}_2} = 0.00713474 \text{ (calc)} = 0.00713 \text{ mole C}$

$0.192 \text{ g H}_2\text{O} \times \dfrac{1 \text{ mole H}_2\text{O}}{18.02 \text{ g H}_2\text{O}} \times \dfrac{2 \text{ moles H}}{1 \text{ mole H}_2\text{O}} = 0.0213096 \text{(calc)} = 0.0213 \text{ moles H}$

H: $\dfrac{0.0213}{0.00713} = 2.9873773 \text{ (calc)} = 2.99 \text{ (corr)}$ C: $\dfrac{0.00713}{0.00713} = 1.00$

The empirical formula is CH_3.

9.111 $2.328 \text{ mg } CO_2 \times \dfrac{12.01 \text{ mg C}}{44.01 \text{ mg } CO_2} = 0.6352937 \text{ (calc)} = 0.6353 \text{ mg C (corr)}$

$0.7429 \text{ mg sample} - 0.6353 \text{ mg C} = 0.1076 \text{ mg H}$

$0.6353 \text{ mg C} \times \dfrac{1 \text{ g C}}{10^3 \text{ mg C}} \times \dfrac{1 \text{ mole C}}{12.01 \text{ g C}} = 5.2897587 \times 10^{-5} \text{ (calc)} = 5.290 \times 10^{-5} \text{ moles C (corr)}$

$0.1076 \text{ mg H} \times \dfrac{1 \text{ g C}}{10^3 \text{ mg C}} \times \dfrac{1 \text{ mole H}}{1.01 \text{ g H}} = 1.0653465 \times 10^{-4} \text{ (calc)} = 1.065 \times 10^{-4} \text{ moles H (corr)}$

C: $\dfrac{5.290 \times 10^{-5}}{5.290 \times 10^{-5}} = 1.00 \text{ (corr)}$ H: $\dfrac{1.065 \times 10^{-4}}{5.290 \times 10^{-5}} = 2.013 \text{ (corr)}$

The empirical formula is CH_2.

9.113 The grams of O and the moles of C, H and O are needed.
Carbon:

$10.05 \text{ g } CO_2 \times \dfrac{1 \text{ mole } CO_2}{44.01 \text{ g } CO_2} \times \dfrac{1 \text{ mole C}}{1 \text{ mole } CO_2} = 0.22835719 \text{ (calc)} = 0.2284 \text{ mole C (corr)}$

$0.2284 \text{ mole C} \times \dfrac{12.01 \text{ g C}}{1 \text{ mole C}} = 2.743084 \text{ (calc)} = 2.743 \text{ g C (corr)}$

Hydrogen:

$2.47 \text{ g } H_2O \times \dfrac{1 \text{ mole } H_2O}{18.02 \text{ g } H_2O} \times \dfrac{2 \text{ moles H}}{1 \text{ mole } H_2O} = 0.27413984 \text{ (calc)} = 0.274 \text{ mole H (corr)}$

$0.274 \text{ mole H} \times \dfrac{1.01 \text{ g H}}{1 \text{ mole H}} = 0.27674 \text{ (calc)} = 0.277 \text{ g H (corr)}$

Oxygen:
$3.750 \text{ g compound} - 2.743 \text{ g C} - 0.277 \text{ g H} = 0.73 \text{ (calc)} = 0.730 \text{ g O (corr)}$

$0.730 \text{ g O} \times \dfrac{1 \text{ mole O}}{16.00 \text{ g O}} = 0.045625 \text{ (calc)} = 0.0456 \text{ mole O (corr)}$

C: $\dfrac{0.2284}{0.0456} = 5.00$ H: $\dfrac{0.274}{0.0456} = 6.00$ O: $\dfrac{0.0456}{0.0456} = 1.00$

The empirical formula is C_5H_6O.

9.115 a) Empirical formula mass = $2(30.97) + 5(16.00) = 141.94$ amu
$\dfrac{\text{molecular formula mass}}{\text{empirical formula mass}} = \dfrac{284 \text{ amu}}{141.94 \text{ amu}} = 2.0008454 \text{ (calc)} = 2.00 \text{ (corr)};\quad (P_2O_5)_2 = P_4O_{10}$

b) Empirical formula mass = $32.06 + 14.01 = 46.07$ amu
$\dfrac{\text{molecular formula mass}}{\text{empirical formula mass}} = \dfrac{184 \text{ amu}}{46.07 \text{ amu}} = 3.9939223 \text{ (calc)} = 3.99 \text{ (corr)};\quad (SN)_4 = S_4N_4$

c) Empirical formula mass = $3(12.01) + 6(1.01) + 2(16.00) = 74.09$ amu, which is the molecular formula mass; $(C_3H_6O_2)_1 = C_3H_6O_2$

d) Empirical formula mass = $10.81 + 14.01 + 2(1.01) = 26.84$ amu
$\dfrac{\text{molecular formula mass}}{\text{empirical formula mass}} = \dfrac{80.4 \text{ amu}}{26.84 \text{ amu}} = 2.980625 \text{ (calc)} = 2.98 \text{ (corr)}; (BNH_2)_3 = B_3N_3H_6$

9.117 a) $100.0 \text{ g compound} \times \dfrac{70.57 \text{ g C}}{100 \text{ g compound}} \times \dfrac{1 \text{ mole C}}{12.01 \text{ g C}} = 5.8759367 \text{ (calc)}$

$= 5.876 \text{ mole C (corr)}$

$100.0 \text{ g compound} \times \dfrac{5.93 \text{ g H}}{100 \text{ g compound}} \times \dfrac{1 \text{ mole H}}{1.01 \text{ g H}} = 5.87128713 \text{ (calc)}$

$= 5.87 \text{ mole H (corr)}$

$100.0 \text{ g compound} \times \dfrac{23.49 \text{ g O}}{100 \text{ g compound}} \times \dfrac{1 \text{ mole O}}{16.00 \text{ g O}} = 1.468125 \text{ (calc)}$

$= 1.468 \text{ mole O (corr)}$

C: $\dfrac{5.876}{1.468} = 4.0027246 \text{ (calc)} = 4.00 \text{ (corr)}$ H: $\dfrac{5.87}{1.486} = 4.0260631 \text{ (calc)} = 4.03$

O: $\dfrac{1.486}{1.486} = 1.00$

Empirical formula = C_4H_4O
Empirical formula mass = $4(12.01) + 4(1.01) + 1(16.00) = 68.08 \text{ amu}$

$\dfrac{\text{molecular formula mass}}{\text{empirical formula mass}} = \dfrac{136 \text{ amu}}{68.08 \text{ amu}}\, 1.9976498 = 2.00; \quad (C_4H_4O)_2 = C_8H_8O_2$

b) $1.00 \text{ mole compound} \times \dfrac{136 \text{ g compound}}{1 \text{ mole compound}} \times \dfrac{70.57 \text{ g C}}{100 \text{ g compound}} \times \dfrac{1 \text{ mole C}}{12.01 \text{ g C}}$

$= 7.9912739 \text{ (calc)} = 8.00 \text{ moles C (corr)}$

$1.00 \text{ mole compound} \times \dfrac{136 \text{ g compound}}{1 \text{ mole compound}} \times \dfrac{5.93 \text{ g H}}{100 \text{ g compound}} \times \dfrac{1 \text{ mole H}}{1.01 \text{ g H}}$

$= 7.9849505 \text{ (calc)} = 7.98 \text{ moles H (corr)}$

$1.00 \text{ mole compound} \times \dfrac{136 \text{ g compound}}{1 \text{ mole compound}} \times \dfrac{23.49 \text{ g O}}{100 \text{ g compound}} \times \dfrac{1 \text{ mole O}}{16.00 \text{ g O}}$

$= 1.99665 \text{ (calc)} = 2.00 \text{ moles O (corr)}$

Molecular formula is $C_8H_8O_2$

9.119 a) $100.0 \text{ g compound} \times \dfrac{40.0 \text{ g C}}{100 \text{ g compound}} \times \dfrac{1 \text{ mole C}}{12.01 \text{ g C}} = 3.3305579 \text{ (calc)} = 3.33 \text{ moles C (corr)}$

$100.0 \text{ g compound} \times \dfrac{6.71 \text{ g H}}{100 \text{ g compound}} \times \dfrac{1 \text{ mole H}}{1.01 \text{ g H}} = 6.64356436 \text{ (calc)} = 6.64 \text{ moles H (corr)}$

$100.0 \text{ g compound} \times \dfrac{53.3 \text{ g O}}{100 \text{ g compound}} \times \dfrac{1 \text{ mole O}}{16.00 \text{ g O}} = 3.33125 \text{ (calc)} = 3.33 \text{ moles O (corr)}$

H: $\dfrac{6.64}{3.33} = 1.99399399 \text{ (calc)} = 1.99 \text{ (corr)};$ C: $\dfrac{3.33}{3.33} = 1.00$ H: $\dfrac{3.33}{3.33} = 1.00$

Empirical formula is CH_2O
Empirical formula mass = $12.01 + 2(1.01) + 16.00 = 30.03 \text{ amu}$

$\dfrac{\text{molecular formula mass}}{\text{empirical formula mass}} = \dfrac{90.0 \text{ amu}}{30.03 \text{ amu}} = 2.997003 \text{ (calc)} = 3.00 \text{ (corr)};$

molecular formula = $(CH_2O)_3 = C_3H_6O_3$

b) $1.00 \text{ mole compound} \times \dfrac{90.0 \text{ g compound}}{1 \text{ mole compound}} \times \dfrac{40.0 \text{ g C}}{100 \text{ g compound}} \times \dfrac{1 \text{ mole C}}{12.01 \text{ g C}} = 2.9975021 \text{ (calc)}$

$= 3.00 \text{ moles (corr)}$

$1.00 \text{ mole compound} \times \dfrac{90.0 \text{ g compound}}{1 \text{ mole compound}} \times \dfrac{6.71 \text{ g H}}{100 \text{ g compound}} \times \dfrac{1 \text{ mole H}}{1.01 \text{ g H}} = 5.979200792 \text{ (calc)}$

$= 5.98 \text{ moles H (corr)}$

$$1.00 \text{ mole compound} \times \frac{90.0 \text{ g compound}}{1 \text{ mole compound}} \times \frac{53.3 \text{ g O}}{100 \text{ g compound}} \times \frac{1 \text{ mole O}}{16.00 \text{ g O}}$$
$$= 2.998125 \text{ (calc)} = 3.00 \text{ moles O (corr)}$$

Molecular formula = $C_3H_6O_3$

ADDITIONAL PROBLEMS

9.121 a) gold   b) sulfur   c) Cl_2 molecules   d) Ne

9.123 a) P_4 b) 1.00 mol Na   c) Cu   d) Be

9.125 a) false   b) true   c) true   d) false

9.127 Molecular mass of K_2S = 2(39.10) + 32.06 = 110.26 amu
Method 1:

$$4.000 \text{ g } K_2S \times \frac{1 \text{ mole } K_2S}{110.26 \text{ g } K_2S} \times \frac{2 \text{ mole K}}{1 \text{ mole } K_2S} \times \frac{39.10 \text{ g K}}{1 \text{ mole K}} = 2.8369309 \text{ (calc)}$$
$$= 2.837 \text{ g K (corr)}$$

$$4.000 \text{ g } K_2S \times \frac{1 \text{ mole } K_2S}{110.26 \text{ g } K_2S} \times \frac{1 \text{ mole S}}{1 \text{ mole } K_2S} \times \frac{32.06 \text{ g S}}{1 \text{ mole S}} = 1.1630691 \text{ (calc)}$$
$$= 1.163 \text{ g S (corr)}$$

Method 2:

$$\%K \text{ in } K_2S = \frac{2(39.10) \text{ amu}}{110.26 \text{ amu}} \times 100 = 70.92327 \text{ (calc)} = 70.92\% \text{ K (corr)}$$

$$\%S = \frac{32.06 \text{ amu}}{110.26 \text{ amu}} \times 100 = 29.07672 \text{ (calc)} = 29.08\% \text{ S (corr)}$$

$$4.000 \text{ g } K_2S \times \frac{70.92 \text{ g K}}{100 \text{ g } K_2S} = 2.8368 \text{ (calc)} = 2.837 \text{ g K (corr)}$$

$$4.000 \text{ g } K_2S \times \frac{29.08 \text{ g S}}{100 \text{ g } K_2S} = 1.1632 \text{ (calc)} = 1.163 \text{ g S (corr)}$$

9.129 3.50 moles B contain the same number of atoms as 3.50 moles Xe

$$3.50 \text{ moles B} \times \frac{10.81 \text{ g B}}{\text{mole B}} = 37.835 \text{ (calc)} = 37.8 \text{ g B (corr)}$$

9.131 The same mass of carbon contains the same moles of C atoms.

$$3.44 \text{ g } C_2H_6O \times \frac{1 \text{ mole } C_2H_6O}{46.08 \text{ g } C_2H_6O} \times \frac{2 \text{ moles C}}{1 \text{ mole } C_2H_6O} \times \frac{1 \text{ mole } C_6H_{12}O_6}{6 \text{ moles C}} \times \frac{180.18 \text{ g } C_6H_{12}O_6}{1 \text{ mole } C_6H_{12}O_6}$$
$$= 4.4836458 \text{ (calc)} = 4.48 \text{ g } C_6H_{12}O_6 \text{ (corr)}$$

9.133 a) Basis: Assume each sample contains 10.0 g of Cr

$$Cr_2O_3: \; 10.0 \text{ g Cr} \times \frac{1 \text{ mole Cr}}{52.00 \text{ g Cr}} \times \frac{1 \text{ mole } Cr_2O_3}{2 \text{ moles Cr}} \times \frac{152.00 \text{ g } Cr_2O_3}{1 \text{ mole } Cr_2O_3}$$
$$= 14.615384 \text{ (calc)} = 14.6 \text{ g } Cr_2O_3 \text{ (corr)}$$

$$CrO_2: \; 10.0 \text{ g Cr} \times \frac{1 \text{ mole Cr}}{52.00 \text{ g Cr}} \times \frac{1 \text{ mole } CrO_2}{1 \text{ mole Cr}} \times \frac{84.00 \text{ g } CrO_2}{1 \text{ mole } CrO_2}$$

$$= 16.153846 \text{ (calc)} = 16.2 \text{ g } CrO_2 \text{ (corr)}$$

CrO_3: $10.0 \text{ g } Cr \times \dfrac{1 \text{ mole } Cr}{52.0 \text{ g } Cr} \times \dfrac{1 \text{ mole } CrO_3}{1 \text{ mole } Cr} \times \dfrac{100 \text{ g } CrO_3}{1 \text{ mole } CrO_3}$

$$= 19.230769 \text{ (calc)} = 19.2 \text{ g } CrO_3 \text{ (corr)}$$

CrO_3 sample has the largest mass.

b) Basis: Assume each sample contains 10.0 g of Cr

Cr_2O_3: $10.0 \text{ g } Cr \times \dfrac{1 \text{ mole } Cr}{52.00 \text{ g } Cr} \times \dfrac{3 \text{ moles } O}{2 \text{ moles } Cr} \times \dfrac{6.022 \times 10^{23} \text{ atoms } O}{1 \text{ mole } O}$

$$= 1.7371154 \times 10^{23} \text{ (calc)} = 1.74 \times 10^{23} \text{ atoms O (corr)}$$

CrO_2: $10.0 \text{ g } Cr \times \dfrac{1 \text{ mole } Cr}{52.00 \text{ g } Cr} \times \dfrac{2 \text{ moles } O}{1 \text{ mole } Cr} \times \dfrac{6.022 \times 10^{23} \text{ atoms } O}{1 \text{ mole } O}$

$$= 2.3161538 \times 10^{23} \text{ (calc)} = 2.32 \times 10^{23} \text{ atoms O (corr)}$$

CrO_3: $10.0 \text{ g } Cr \times \dfrac{1 \text{ mole } Cr}{52.00 \text{ g } Cr} \times \dfrac{3 \text{ moles } O}{1 \text{ mole } Cr} \times \dfrac{6.022 \times 10^{23} \text{ atoms } O}{1 \text{ mole } O}$

$$= 3.4742308 \times 10^{23} \text{ (calc)} = 3.47 \times 10^{23} \text{ atoms O (corr)}$$

CrO_3 sample contains the most oxygen atoms.

9.135 $1.00 \times 10^{24} \text{ atoms alloy} \times \dfrac{3 \text{ atoms Au}}{6 \text{ atoms alloy}} \times \dfrac{1 \text{ mole Au}}{6.022 \times 10^{23} \text{ atoms Au}} \times \dfrac{196.97 \text{ g Au}}{1 \text{ mole Au}}$

$$= 163.54201 \text{ (calc)} = 164 \text{ g Au (corr)}$$

$1.00 \times 10^{24} \text{ atoms alloy} \times \dfrac{2 \text{ atoms Cu}}{6 \text{ atoms alloy}} \times \dfrac{1 \text{ mole Cu}}{6.022 \times 10^{23} \text{ atoms Cu}} \times \dfrac{63.55 \text{ g Cu}}{1 \text{ mole Cu}}$

$$= 35.176575 \text{ (calc)} = 35.2 \text{ g Cu (corr)}$$

$1.00 \times 10^{24} \text{ atoms alloy} \times \dfrac{1 \text{ atom Ni}}{6 \text{ atoms alloy}} \times \dfrac{1 \text{ mole Ni}}{6.022 \times 10^{23} \text{ atoms Ni}} \times \dfrac{58.69 \text{ g Ni}}{1 \text{ mole Ni}}$

$$= 16.243219 \text{ (calc)} = 16.2 \text{ g Ni (corr)}$$

Total mass = 164 g + 35.2 g + 16.2 g = 215.4 (calc) = 215 g (corr)

9.137 a) $1.792 \times 10^{-22} \text{ g} \times \dfrac{6.022 \times 10^{23} \text{ amu}}{1 \text{ g}} = 107.91424 \text{ (calc)} = 107.9 \text{ amu (corr)} = Ag$

b) Dividing mass by the number of moles gives:

$\dfrac{0.05232 \text{ g}}{4.840 \times 10^{-3} \text{ mole}} = 10.81 \dfrac{\text{g}}{\text{mole}} \text{ (corr)} = 10.81 \text{ amu} = B$

9.139 a) 3(12.01 amu) + 9(1.01 amu) + 28.09 amu + 35.45 amu = 108.66 amu (calc and corr)

mass % H = $\dfrac{9(1.01 \text{ amu})}{108.66 \text{ amu}} \times 100 = 8.3655439 \text{ (calc)} = 8.37\% \text{ H (corr)}$

b) 1 molecule $(CH_3)_3SiCl \times \dfrac{14 \text{ atoms total}}{1 \text{ molecule } (CH_3)_3SiCl} = 14 \text{ atoms total (calc and corr)}$

1 molecule $(CH_3)_3SiCl \times \dfrac{9 \text{ H atoms}}{1 \text{ molecule } (CH_3)_3SiCl} = 9 \text{ H atoms (calc and corr)}$

atom % H = $\dfrac{9 \text{ H atoms}}{14 \text{ total atoms}} \times 100 = 64.285714 \text{ (calc)} = 60 \% \text{ H (corr)}$

c) $1 \text{ mole } (CH_3)_3SiCl \times \dfrac{14 \text{ moles atoms}}{1 \text{ mole } (CH_3)_3SiCl} = 14 \text{ moles atoms (calc and corr)}$

$1 \text{ mole } (CH_3)_3SiCl \times \dfrac{9 \text{ moles H atoms}}{1 \text{ mole } (CH_3)_3SiCl} = 9 \text{ moles H atoms (calc and corr)}$

$\text{mole } \% \text{ H} = \dfrac{9 \text{ moles H atoms}}{14 \text{ total moles atoms}} \times 100 = 64.285714 \text{ (calc)} = 60 \% \text{ H (corr)}$

9.141 a) Since the ratio of atoms equals the ratio of moles of atoms, the atom ratio can be used instead of the   mole ratio to determine the empirical formula.

Na: $\dfrac{9.0 \times 10^{23}}{3.0 \times 10^{23}} = 3.0$ Al: $\dfrac{3.0 \times 10^{23}}{3.0 \times 10^{23}} = 1.0$ F: $\dfrac{1.8 \times 10^{24}}{3.0 \times 10^{23}} = 6.0$

The empirical formula is Na_3AlF_6.

b) $3.2 \text{ g S} \times \dfrac{1 \text{ mole S}}{32.06 \text{ g S}} = 0.0998128 \text{ (calc)} = 0.10 \text{ mole S (corr)}$

$1.20 \times 10^{23} \text{ atoms O} \times \dfrac{1 \text{ mole O}}{6.022 \times 10^{23} \text{ atoms O}} = 0.1992693 \text{ mole O (calc)}$

$= 0.199 \text{ mole O (corr)}$

S: $\dfrac{0.10}{0.10} = 1.0$ O: $\dfrac{0.199}{0.10} = 2.0$

The empirical formula is SO_2.

c) 0.36 mole Ba, 0.36 mole C

$17.2 \text{ g O} \times \dfrac{1 \text{ mole O}}{16.00 \text{ g O}} = 1.075 \text{ (calc)} = 1.08 \text{ moles O (corr)}$

Ba: $\dfrac{0.36}{0.36} = 1.0$ C: $\dfrac{0.36}{0.36} = 1.0$ O: $\dfrac{1.08}{0.36} = 3.0$

The empirical formula is $BaCO_3$.

d) $1.81 \times 10^{23} \text{ atoms H} \times \dfrac{1 \text{ mole H}}{6.022 \times 10^{23} \text{ atoms H}} = 0.3005646 \text{ mole H (calc)}$

$= 0.301 \text{ mole H (corr)}$

$10.65 \text{ g Cl} \times \dfrac{1 \text{ mole}}{35.45 \text{ g Cl}} = 0.30042313 \text{ (calc)} = 0.3004 \text{ mole Cl (corr)}$

0.30 mole O

H: $\dfrac{0.301}{0.30} = 1.0$ O: $\dfrac{0.30}{0.30} = 1.0$ Cl: $\dfrac{0.3004}{0.30} = 1.0$

The empirical formula is HClO.

9.143 $5.25 \text{ g compound} \times \dfrac{92.26 \text{ g C}}{100 \text{ g compound}} \times \dfrac{1 \text{ mole C}}{12.01 \text{ g C}} \times \dfrac{6.022 \times 10^{23} \text{ atoms C}}{1 \text{ mole C}}$

$= 2.4286811 \times 10^{23} \text{ (calc)} = 2.43 \times 10^{23} \text{ atoms C (corr)}$

9.145 a) The molecular formula has twice as many atoms as the empirical formula, $(C_2H_3O)_2$ or $C_4H_6O_2$.
b) The empirical formula has 6 atoms, so the molecular formula is $(C_2H_3O)_3$ or $C_6H_9O_3$.
c) In the empirical formula, the sum of C and O = 3; the molecular formula is $(C_2H_3O)_6$ or $C_{12}H_{18}O_6$.
d) Divide the mass by the moles to get the molar formula mass.

$\text{molar mass} = \dfrac{0.86 \text{ g}}{0.010 \text{ mole}} = 86 \dfrac{\text{g}}{\text{mole}} \text{ or } 86 \text{ amu}$

empirical formula mass = 2(12.01) + 3(1.01) + 16.00 = 43.05

$$\frac{\text{molecular formula mass}}{\text{empirical formula mass}} = \frac{86}{43.05} = 1.9976771(\text{calc}) = 2.0 \text{ (corr)}, \text{ so } (C_2H_3O)_2 = C_4H_6O_2$$

9.147 Since the compound contains only C and H, the mass of C in 13.75 g CO_2 plus the mass of H in 11.25 g H_2O equals the mass of the compound.

$$\text{mass of C} = 13.75 \text{ g CO}_2 \times \frac{1 \text{ mole CO}_2}{44.01 \text{ g CO}_2} \times \frac{1 \text{ mole C}}{1 \text{ mole CO}_2} \times \frac{12.01 \text{ g C}}{1 \text{ mole C}}$$

$$= 3.75227221 \text{ (calc)} = 3.752 \text{ g C (corr)}$$

$$\text{mass of H} = 11.25 \text{ g H}_2O \times \frac{1 \text{ mole H}_2O}{18.02 \text{ g H}_2O} \times \frac{2 \text{ moles H}}{1 \text{ mole H}_2O} \times \frac{1.01 \text{ g H}}{1 \text{ mole H}}$$

$$= 1.26109878 \text{ (calc)} = 1.261 \text{ g H (corr)}$$

$$\text{mass compound} = 3.752 \text{ g C} + 1.261 \text{ g H} = 5.013 \text{ g compound}$$

9.149 Both the moles and grams of C, H and S are needed.
Carbon:

$$6.60 \text{ g CO}_2 \times \frac{1 \text{ mole CO}_2}{44.01 \text{ g CO}_2} \times \frac{1 \text{ mole C}}{1 \text{ mole CO}_2} = 0.1499659 \text{ (calc)} = 0.150 \text{ mole C (corr)}$$

$$0.150 \text{ mole C} \times \frac{12.01 \text{ g C}}{1 \text{ mole C}} = 1.8015 \text{ (calc)} = 1.80 \text{ g C (corr)}$$

Hydrogen:

$$5.41 \text{ g H}_2O \times \frac{1 \text{ mole H}_2O}{18.02 \text{ g H}_2O} \times \frac{2 \text{ moles H}}{1 \text{ mole H}_2O} = 0.6004439 \text{ (calc)} = 0.600 \text{ mole H (corr)}$$

$$0.600 \text{ mole H} \times \frac{1.01 \text{ g H}}{1 \text{ mole H}} = 0.606 \text{ g H (calc and corr)}$$

Sulfur:

$$9.61 \text{ g SO}_2 \times \frac{1 \text{ mole SO}_2}{64.06 \text{ g SO}_2} \times \frac{1 \text{ mole S}}{1 \text{ mole SO}_2} = 0.1500156 \text{ (calc)} = 0.150 \text{ mole S (corr)}$$

$$0.150 \text{ mole S} \times \frac{32.06 \text{ g S}}{1 \text{ mole S}} = 4.809 \text{ (calc)} = 4.81 \text{ g S (corr)}$$

a) C: $\dfrac{0.150}{0.150} = 1.00$ H: $\dfrac{0.600}{0.150} = 4.00$ S: $\dfrac{0.150}{0.150} = 1.00$

The empirical formula is CH_4S.

b) Sample mass $= 1.80 \text{ g C} + 0.606 \text{ g H} + 4.81 \text{ g S} = 7.216 \text{ (calc)} = 7.22 \text{ g (corr)}$

9.151 Basis: 100.0 g sample:
Since all the F is in NaF,

$$\text{mass NaF} = 100.0 \text{ g sample} \times \frac{18.1 \text{ g F}}{100 \text{ g sample}} \times \frac{1 \text{ mole F}}{19.00 \text{ g F}} \times \frac{1 \text{ mole NaF}}{1 \text{ mole F}} \times \frac{41.99 \text{ g NaF}}{1 \text{ mole NaF}}$$

$$= 40.001 \text{ (calc)} = 40.0 \text{ g NaF (corr)}$$

$$\%\text{NaF} = \frac{40.0 \text{ g NaF}}{100.0 \text{ g sample}} \times 100 = 40.0\% \text{ NaF}$$

Since all the N atoms are in $NaNO_3$,

$$\text{mass NaNO}_3 = 100.0 \text{ g sample} \times \frac{6.60 \text{ g N}}{100 \text{ g sample}} \times \frac{1 \text{ mole N}}{14.01 \text{ g N}} \times \frac{1 \text{ mole NaNO}_3}{1 \text{ mole N}} \times \frac{85.00 \text{ g NaNO}_3}{1 \text{ mole NaNO}_3} =$$

$$40.042827 \text{ (calc)} = 40.0 \text{ g NaNO}_3 \text{ (corr)}$$

$$\%NaNO_3 = \frac{40.0 \text{ g } NaNO_3}{100.0 \text{ g sample}} \times 100 = 40.0 \% NaNO_3$$

Mass Na_2SO_4 = mass sample – mass NaF – mass $NaNO_3$ = 100.0 – 40.0 – 40.0 = 20.0 g Na_2SO_4

$$\%Na_2SO_4 = \frac{20.0 \text{ g } Na_2SO_4}{100.0 \text{ g sample}} \times 100 = 20.0 \% Na_2SO_4$$

9.153 28.9% of the formula mass must be from the chlorine atom.
0.289 x (formula mass) = 35.45 amu
formula mass = 122.66435 amu (calc) = 123 amu (corr)
formula mass = at. mass K + at. mass Cl + X(at. mass O)
123 amu = 39.10 amu + 35.45 amu + X(16.00 amu)
3.028125 = X
The value of X is the integer 3.

9.155 mass O = total mass – mass M
= 10.498 g – 7.503 g = 2.995 g O (calc and corr)

$$2.995 \text{ g O} \times \frac{1 \text{ mole O}}{16.00 \text{ g O}} \times \frac{1 \text{ mole M}}{1 \text{ mole O}} = 0.1871875 \text{ (calc)} = 0.1872 \text{ mole M (corr)}$$

molar mass equals the g of M divided by the moles of M.

$$\frac{7.503 \text{ g}}{0.1872 \text{ mole}} = 40.080128 \text{ (calc)} = 40.08 \frac{\text{g}}{\text{mole}} \text{ (corr)}$$

9.157 Basis: 100.0 g of compound.
Carbon:

$$100.0 \text{ g compound} \times \frac{47.4 \text{ g C}}{100 \text{ g compound}} = 47.4 \text{ g C (calc and corr)}$$

$$47.4 \text{ g C} \times \frac{1 \text{ mole C}}{12.01 \text{ g C}} = 3.9467111 \text{(calc)} = 3.95 \text{ moles C (corr)}$$

OH_4 units:
mass OH_4 = mass compound – mass C
= 100.0 g – 47.4 g = 52.6 g (calc and corr)

$$52.6 \text{ g } OH_4 \times \frac{1 \text{ mole } OH_4}{20.04 \text{ g } OH_4} = 2.6247505 \text{(calc)} = 2.62 \text{ moles } OH_4 \text{ (corr)}$$

C: $\frac{3.95}{2.62} = 1.5076336$ (calc) = 1.51 (corr) $\qquad$ OH_4: $\frac{2.62}{2.62} = 1.00$ (calc and corr)

C: 1.51 x 2 = 3.02 $\qquad\qquad\qquad\qquad$ OH_4: 1.00 x 2 = 2.00
The empirical formula is $C_3(OH_4)_2$ or $C_3H_8O_2$.

CUMULATIVE PROBLEMS

9.159 Add the exact atomic masses and round appropriately:
3(1.00794) amu + 74.9216 amu + 4(15.9994) amu = 141.94302 (calc) = 141.9430 (corr)
a) 142 b) 141.9 c) 141.94 d) 141.943

9.161 $0.422 \text{ mole Pb} \times \frac{207.2 \text{ g Pb}}{1 \text{ mole Pb}} = 87.4384$ (calc) = 87.4 g Pb (corr)

$$d = \frac{87.4 \text{ g}}{7.74 \text{ cm}^3} = 11.291989 \text{ (calc)} = 11.3 \text{ g/cm}^3 \text{ (corr)}$$

9.163 $225 \text{ mL } C_2H_6O \times \dfrac{0.789 \text{ g } C_2H_6O}{1 \text{ mL } C_2H_6O} \times \dfrac{1 \text{ mole } C_2H_6O}{46.08 \text{ g } C_2H_6O} \times \dfrac{6.022 \times 10^{23} \text{ molecules } C_2H_6O}{1 \text{ mole } C_2H_6O} =$

$2.319999 \times 10^{24}(\text{calc}) = 2.32 \times 10^{24}$ molecules C_2H_6O (corr) $= 2.32 \times 10^{24}$ molecules H_2O

2.32×10^{24} molecules $H_2O \times \dfrac{1 \text{ mole } H_2O}{6.022 \times 10^{23} \text{ molecules } H_2O} \times \dfrac{18.02 \text{ g } H_2O}{1 \text{ mole } H_2O} \times \dfrac{1 \text{ mL } H_2O}{1.00 \text{ g } H_2O}$

$= 69.422783 \text{ (calc)} = 69.4 \text{ mL } H_2O \text{ (corr)}$

9.165 $2.50 \text{ moles Zn} \times \dfrac{65.41 \text{ g Zn}}{1 \text{ mole Zn}} \times \dfrac{1 \text{ cm}^3 \text{ Zn}}{7.14 \text{ g Zn}} = 22.902661 \text{ (calc)} = 22.9 \text{ cm}^3 \text{ Zn (corr)}$

9.167 a) magnesium nitrate $= Mg(NO_3)_2$
      24.30 amu $+ 2(14.01$ amu$) + 6(16.00$ amu$) = 148.32$ amu (calcand corr)
      molar mass $= 148.32$ g
    b) sodium azide $= NaN_3$
      22.99 amu $+ 3(14.01$ amu$) = 65.02$ amu (calc and corr)
      molar mass $= 65.02$ g
    c) nickel(II) fluoride $= NiF_2$
      58.69 amu $+ 2(19.00$ amu$) = 96.69$ amu (calc and corr)
      molar mass $= 96.69$ g
    d) ammonium perchlorate $= NH_4ClO_4$
      14.01 amu $+ 4(1.01$ amu$) + 35.45$ amu $+ 4(16.00$ amu$) = 117.50$ amu (calc and corr)
      molar mass $= 117.5$ g

9.169 Assume that the measurement, one cup, has one significant figure.

$1 \text{ cup} \times \dfrac{371 \text{ mg K}}{1 \text{ cup}} \times \dfrac{10^{-3} \text{ g K}}{1 \text{ mg K}} \times \dfrac{1 \text{ mole K}}{39.10 \text{ g K}} \times \dfrac{6.022 \times 10^{23} \text{ atoms K}}{1 \text{ mole K}} \times \dfrac{0.012 \text{ atoms } ^{40}K}{100 \text{ atoms K}}$

$= 6.8567632 \times 10^{17} \text{ (calc)} = 7 \times 10^{17} \text{ atoms } ^{40}K \text{ (corr)}$

9.171 a) $2.33 \text{ moles Al}_2(SO_4)_3 \times \dfrac{6.022 \times 10^{23} \text{ formula units } Al_2(SO_4)_3}{1 \text{ mole } Al_2(SO_4)_3}$

$= 1.403126 \times 10^{24} \text{ (calc)} = 1.40 \times 10^{24} \text{ formula units } Al_2(SO_4)_3 \text{ (corr)}$

    b) $2.33 \text{ moles Al}_2(SO_4)_3 \times \dfrac{2 \text{ moles } Al^{3+} \text{ ions}}{1 \text{ mole } Al_2(SO_4)_3} \times \dfrac{6.022 \times 10^{23} \text{ } Al^{3+} \text{ ions}}{1 \text{ mole } Al^{3+} \text{ ions}}$

$= 2.806252 \times 10^{24} \text{ (calc)} = 2.81 \times 10^{24} \text{ } Al^{3+} \text{ ions (corr)}$

    c) $2.33 \text{ moles Al}_2(SO_4)_3 \times \dfrac{3 \text{ moles } SO_4^{2-} \text{ ions}}{1 \text{ mole } Al_2(SO_4)_3} \times \dfrac{6.022 \times 10^{23} \text{ } SO_4^{2-} \text{ ions}}{1 \text{ mole } SO_4^{2-} \text{ ions}}$

$= 4.209378 \times 10^{24} \text{ (calc)} = 4.21 \times 10^{24} \text{ } SO_4^{2-} \text{ ions (corr)}$

    d) $2.33 \text{ moles Al}_2(SO_4)_3 \times \dfrac{5 \text{ moles ions}}{1 \text{ mole } Al_2(SO_4)_3} \times \dfrac{6.022 \times 10^{23} \text{ ions}}{1 \text{ mole ions}}$

$= 7.01563 \times 10^{24} \text{ (calc)} = 7.02 \times 10^{24} \text{ ions (corr)}$

9.173 $32.5 \text{ g CaCl}_2 \times \dfrac{1 \text{ mole } CaCl_2}{110.98 \text{ g } CaCl_2} \times \dfrac{3 \text{ moles ions}}{1 \text{ mole } CaCl_2} = 0.878536 \text{ (calc)} = 0.879 \text{ moles ions (corr)}$

$0.879 \text{ moles ions} \times \dfrac{1 \text{ mole KCl}}{2 \text{ mole ions}} \times \dfrac{74.55 \text{ g KCl}}{1 \text{ mole KCl}} = 32.764725 \text{ (calc)} = 32.8 \text{ g KCl}$

9.175   a) $SO_2 = \dfrac{32.06 \text{ g S}}{64.06 \text{ g } SO_2} \times 100 = 50.0468311 \text{ (calc)} = 50.05 \text{ % S}$

b) $H_2S = \dfrac{32.06 \text{ g S}}{34.08 \text{ g } H_2S} \times 100 = 94.07276 \text{ (calc)} = 94.07 \text{ % S}$

c) $H_2SO_4 = \dfrac{32.06 \text{ g S}}{98.08 \text{ g } H_2SO_4} \times 100 = 32.68760 \text{ (calc)} = 32.69 \text{ % S}$

d) $H_2SO_3 = \dfrac{32.06 \text{ g S}}{82.08 \text{ g } H_2SO_3} \times 100 = 39.05945 \text{ (calc)} = 39.06 \text{ % S}$

9.177   425 g mixture x $\dfrac{42.0 \text{ g NaCl}}{100 \text{ g mixture}}$ x $\dfrac{1 \text{ mole NaCl}}{58.44 \text{ g NaCl}}$ x $\dfrac{1 \text{ mole } Cl^- \text{ ions}}{1 \text{ mole NaCl}}$ x

$\dfrac{6.022 \times 10^{23} \, Cl^- \text{ ions}}{1 \text{ mole } Cl^- \text{ ions}}$

$= 1.8393686 \times 10^{24} \text{ (calc)} = 1.84 \times 10^{24} \, Cl^- \text{ ions (corr)}$

425 g mixture x $\dfrac{58.0 \text{ g } CaCl_2}{100 \text{ g mixture}}$ x $\dfrac{1 \text{ mole } CaCl_2}{110.98 \text{ g } CaCl_2}$ x $\dfrac{2 \text{ moles } Cl^- \text{ ions}}{1 \text{ mole } CaCl_2}$ x

$\dfrac{6.022 \times 10^{23} \, Cl^- \text{ ions}}{1 \text{ mole } Cl^- \text{ ions}} = 2.675118 \times 10^{24} \text{ (calc)} = 2.68 \times 10^{24} \, Cl^- \text{ ions (corr)}$

Total Cl^- ions $= 1.84 \times 10^{24} + 2.68 \times 10^{24} \, Cl^- \text{ ions}$
$= 4.52 \times 10^{24} \, Cl^- \text{ ions (calc and corr)}$

9.179 $V = 10.0 \text{ cm} \times 30.0 \text{ cm} \times 62.0 \text{ cm} = 18{,}600 \text{ cm}^3 \text{ (calc and corr)}$

18,600 cm^3 x $\dfrac{8.31 \text{ g alloy}}{1 \text{ cm}^3}$ x $\dfrac{43.0 \text{ g Ni}}{100 \text{ g alloy}}$ x $\dfrac{1 \text{ mole Ni}}{58.69 \text{ g Ni}}$ x $\dfrac{6.022 \times 10^{23} \text{ atoms Ni}}{1 \text{ mole Ni}}$

$= 6.8196026 \times 10^{26} \text{ (calc)} = 6.82 \times 10^{26} \text{ atoms Ni (corr)}$

9.181   0.275 mole NaOH x $\dfrac{40.00 \text{ g NaOH}}{1 \text{ mole NaOH}}$ x $\dfrac{100 \text{ g solution}}{12.0 \text{ g NaOH}}$ x $\dfrac{1 \text{ mL solution}}{1.131 \text{ g solution}}$

$= 81.049218 \text{ (calc)} = 81.0 \text{ mL solution (corr)}$

9.183   Ethyl alcohol:

15.0 mL solution x $\dfrac{0.807 \text{ g solution}}{1 \text{ mL solution}}$ x $\dfrac{85.0 \text{ g } C_2H_6O}{100 \text{ g solution}}$ x $\dfrac{1 \text{ mole } C_2H_6O}{46.08 \text{ g } C_2H_6O}$ x $\dfrac{9 \text{ moles atoms}}{1 \text{ mole } C_2H_6O}$

x $\dfrac{6.022 \times 10^{23} \text{ atoms}}{1 \text{ mole atoms}} = 1.2101926 \times 10^{24} \text{ (calc)} = 1.21 \times 10^{24} \text{ atoms (corr)}$

Water:

15.0 mL solution x $\dfrac{0.807 \text{ g solution}}{1 \text{ mL solution}}$ x $\dfrac{15.0 \text{ g } H_2O}{100 \text{ g solution}}$ x $\dfrac{1 \text{ mole } H_2O}{18.02 \text{ g } H_2O}$ x $\dfrac{3 \text{ moles atoms}}{1 \text{ mole } H_2O}$

x $\dfrac{6.022 \times 10^{23} \text{ atoms}}{1 \text{ mole atoms}} = 1.8203851 \times 10^{23} \text{ (calc)} = 1.82 \times 10^{23} \text{ atoms (corr)}$

Total atoms $= (1.21 \times 10^{24}) + (1.82 \times 10^{23}) = 1.392 \times 10^{24} \text{ (calc)} = 1.39 \times 10^{24} \text{ atoms (corr)}$

9.185 $1 \text{ cent} \times \dfrac{1 \text{ dollar}}{100 \text{ cents}} \times \dfrac{1 \text{ lb Cu}}{0.645 \text{ dollar}} \times \dfrac{453.6 \text{ g Cu}}{1 \text{ lb Cu}} \times \dfrac{1 \text{ mole Cu}}{63.55 \text{ g Cu}} \times \dfrac{6.022 \times 10^{23} \text{ atoms Cu}}{1 \text{ mole Cu}}$

$= 6.6640543 \times 10^{22} \text{ (calc)} = 6.66 \times 10^{22} \text{ atoms Cu (corr)}$

(The 1 cent is a counted number)

CHAPTER TEN
Chemical Calculations Involving Chemical Equations

PRACTICE PROBLEMS

The Law of Conservation of Mass (Sec. 10.1)

10.1 The total mass of products = total mass of reactants
x g + 8.50 g = 5.85 g + 16.98 g; x = 16.98 + 5.85 − 8.50; x = 14.33 g

10.3 The law of conservation of mass requires the mass of the reactants to equal the mass of the products 4.2 g + 10.0 g = 12.0 g + X; X = (14.2 − 12.0) g = 2.2 g

Chemical Equation Notation (Secs. 10.2 and 10.4)

10.5 a) yes b) no, Cl should be Cl_2 c) no, He_2 should be He d) yes

10.7 a) *(s)* means solid, and *(g)* means gas
b) *(g)* means gas, *(l)* means liquid, and *(aq)* means water (aqueous) solution

Balancing Chemical Equations (Sec. 10.3)

10.9 a) balanced b) balanced c) unbalanced d) balanced

10.11 a) Reactants: 4 N, 6 O; Products: 4 N, 6 O
b) Reactants: 10 N, 6 O, 12 H; Products: 10 N, 6 O, 12 H
c) Reactants: 1 P, 3 Cl, 6 H; Products: 1 P, 3 Cl, 6 H
d) Reactants: 2 Al, 3 O, 6 H, 6 Cl; Products: 2 Al, 3 O, 6 H, 6 Cl

10.13 a) $2Cu + O_2 \rightarrow 2CuO$ b) $2H_2O \rightarrow 2H_2 + O_2$
c) $BaCl_2 + Na_2S \rightarrow BaS + 2NaCl$ d) $Mg + 2HBr \rightarrow MgBr_2 + H_2$

10.15 a) $3PbO + 2NH_3 \rightarrow 3Pb + N_2 + 3H_2O$
b) $2NaHCO_3 + H_2SO_4 \rightarrow Na_2SO_4 + 2CO_2 + 2H_2O$
c) $TiO_2 + C + 2Cl_2 \rightarrow TiCl_4 + CO_2$
d) $2NBr_3 + 3NaOH \rightarrow N_2 + 3NaBr + 3HBrO$

10.17 a) $CH_4 + 2O_2 \rightarrow CO_2 + 2H_2O$ b) $2C_6H_6 + 15O_2 \rightarrow 12CO_2 + 6H_2O$
c) $C_4H_8O_2 + 5O_2 \rightarrow 4CO_2 + 4H_2O$ d) $C_5H_{10}O + 7O_2 \rightarrow 5CO_2 + 5H_2O$

10.19 a) $Ca(OH)_2 + 2HNO_3 \rightarrow Ca(NO_3)_2 + 2H_2O$ b) $BaCl_2 + (NH_4)_2SO_4 \rightarrow BaSO_4 + 2NH_4Cl$
c) $2Fe(OH)_3 + 3H_2SO_4 \rightarrow Fe_2(SO_4)_3 + 6H_2O$ d) $Na_3PO_4 + 3AgNO_3 \rightarrow 3NaNO_3 + Ag_3PO_4$

10.21 a) divide each coefficient by 3: $AgNO_3 + KCl \rightarrow AgCl + KNO_3$
b) divide each coefficient by 2: $CS_2 + 3O_2 \rightarrow CO_2 + 2SO_2$
c) multiply each coefficient by 2: $2H_2 + O_2 \rightarrow 2H_2O$
d) multiply each coefficient by 2: $2Ag_2CO_3 \rightarrow 4Ag + 2CO_2 + O_2$

Classes of Chemical Reactions (Sec. 10.5)

10.23 a) synthesis b) synthesis c) double replacement d) single replacement

10.25 a) the correct formula for zinc nitrate is $Zn(NO_3)_2$ and the symbol for copper is Cu;
$Zn + Cu(NO_3)_2 \rightarrow Zn(NO_3)_2 + Cu$
b) the correct formula for calcium oxide is CaO; $2Ca + O_2 \rightarrow 2CaO$
c) the correct formula for barium sulfate is $BaSO_4$, and for potassium nitrate it is KNO_3;
$K_2SO_4 + Ba(NO_3)_2 \rightarrow BaSO_4 + 2KNO_3$
d) the correct formula for oxygen is O_2, the symbol for silver is Ag; $2Ag_2O \rightarrow 4Ag + O_2$

10.27 a) $K_2CO_3 \rightarrow K_2O + CO_2$ b) $CaCO_3 \rightarrow CaO + CO_2$
c) $NiCO_3 \rightarrow NiO + CO_2$ d) $Fe_2(CO_3)_3 \rightarrow Fe_2O_3 + 3CO_2$

10.29 a) $CH_4 + 2O_2 \rightarrow CO_2 + 2H_2O$ b) $2C_6H_6 + 15O_2 \rightarrow 12CO_2 + 6H_2O$
c) $C_6H_{12} + 9O_2 \rightarrow 6CO_2 + 6H_2O$ d) $C_3H_4 + 4O_2 \rightarrow 3CO_2 + 2H_2O$

10.31 a) $CH_2O + O_2 \rightarrow CO_2 + H_2O$ b) $C_3H_6O + 4O_2 \rightarrow 3CO_2 + 3H_2O$
c) $2CH_2O_2 + O_2 \rightarrow 2CO_2 + 2H_2O$ d) $C_4H_8O_2 + 5O_2 \rightarrow 4CO_2 + 4H_2O$

10.33 a) $4C_2H_7N + 19 O_2 \rightarrow 8CO_2 + 14H_2O + 4NO_2$
b) $CH_4S + 3O_2 \rightarrow CO_2 + 2H_2O + SO_2$

10.35 a) combination, single-replacement, combustion, and combination
b) single-replacement, and decomposition
c) combination, decomposition, single-replacement, double-replacement, and combustion
d) combination, decomposition, single-replacement, double replacement, and combustion

Chemical Equations and the Mole Concept (Sec. 10.6)

10.37 a) 2 molecules B   b) 9 molecules A   c) 6 molecules D   d) 3 moles A x $\dfrac{2 \text{ moles B}}{3 \text{ moles A}}$ = 2 moles B

10.39

$\dfrac{4 \text{ moles } NH_3}{3 \text{ moles } O_2}$	$\dfrac{3 \text{ moles } O_2}{4 \text{ moles } NH_3}$	$\dfrac{4 \text{ moles } NH_3}{2 \text{ moles } N_2}$	$\dfrac{2 \text{ moles } N_2}{4 \text{ moles } NH_3}$
$\dfrac{4 \text{ moles } NH_3}{6 \text{ moles } H_2O}$	$\dfrac{6 \text{ moles } H_2O}{4 \text{ moles } NH_3}$	$\dfrac{3 \text{ moles } O_2}{2 \text{ moles } N_2}$	$\dfrac{2 \text{ moles } N_2}{3 \text{ moles } O_2}$
$\dfrac{3 \text{ moles } O_2}{6 \text{ moles } H_2O}$	$\dfrac{6 \text{ moles } H_2O}{3 \text{ moles } O_2}$	$\dfrac{2 \text{ moles } N_2}{6 \text{ moles } H_2O}$	$\dfrac{6 \text{ moles } H_2O}{2 \text{ moles } N_2}$

10.41 a) 3.00 moles N_2 x $\dfrac{2 \text{ moles } NaN_3}{3 \text{ moles } N_2}$ = 2 (calc) = 2.00 moles NaN_3 (corr)

b) 3.00 moles N_2 x $\dfrac{3 \text{ moles CO}}{1 \text{ mole } N_2}$ = 9 (calc) = 9.00 moles CO (corr)

c) 3.00 moles N_2 x $\dfrac{2 \text{ moles } NH_2Cl}{1 \text{ mole } N_2}$ = 6 (calc) = 6.00 moles NH_2Cl (corr)

d) 3.00 moles N_2 x $\dfrac{4 \text{ moles } C_3H_5O_9N_3}{6 \text{ moles } N_2}$ = 2 (calc) = 2.00 moles $C_3H_5O_9N_3$ (corr)

10.43 a) $1.42 \text{ moles } O_2 \times \dfrac{1 \text{ mole } C_7H_{16}}{11 \text{ moles } O_2} = 0.1290909 \text{ (calc)} = 0.129 \text{ mole } C_7H_{16} \text{ (corr)}$

b) $1.42 \text{ moles } CaCO_3 \times \dfrac{2 \text{ moles } HCl}{1 \text{ mole } CaCO_3} = 2.84 \text{ moles } HCl \text{ (calc and corr)}$

c) $1.42 \text{ moles } C \times \dfrac{1 \text{ mole } Na_2SO_4}{2 \text{ moles } C} = 0.71 \text{ (calc)} = 0.710 \text{ mole } Na_2SO_4 \text{ (corr)}$

d) $1.42 \text{ moles } Fe_3Br_8 \times \dfrac{4 \text{ moles } Na_2CO_3}{1 \text{ mole } Fe_3Br_8} = 5.68 \text{ moles } Na_2CO_3 \text{ (calc and corr)}$

10.45 a) $1.75 \text{ moles } NH_4NO_3 \times \dfrac{7 \text{ moles products}}{2 \text{ moles } NH_4NO_3} = 6.125 \text{ (calc)} = 6.12 \text{ moles products (corr)}$

b) $1.75 \text{ moles } NaClO_3 \times \dfrac{5 \text{ moles products}}{2 \text{ moles } NaClO_3} = 4.375 \text{ (calc)} = 4.38 \text{ moles products (corr)}$

c) $1.75 \text{ moles } KNO_3 \times \dfrac{3 \text{ moles products}}{2 \text{ moles } KNO_3} = 2.625 \text{ (calc)} = 2.62 \text{ moles products (corr)}$

d) $1.75 \text{ moles } I_4O_9 \times \dfrac{11 \text{ moles products}}{4 \text{ moles } I_4O_9} = 4.8125 \text{ (calc)} = 4.81 \text{ moles products (corr)}$

10.47 a) $4.75 \text{ moles } CCl_4 \times \dfrac{4 \text{ moles } Cl_2}{1 \text{ mole } CCl_4} = 19 \text{ (calc)} = 19.0 \text{ moles } Cl_2 \text{ (corr)}$

b) $0.083 \text{ mole } CH_4 \times \dfrac{4 \text{ moles } HCl}{1 \text{ mole } CH_4} = 0.332 \text{ (calc)} = 0.33 \text{ mole } HCl \text{ (corr)}$

c) $2.30 \text{ moles } Cl_2 \times \dfrac{1 \text{ mole } CH_4}{4 \text{ moles } Cl_2} = 0.575 \text{ mole } CH_4 \text{ (calc and corr)}$

d) $1.23 \text{ moles } HCl \times \dfrac{1 \text{ mole } CCl_4}{4 \text{ moles } HCl} = 0.3075 \text{ (calc)} = 0.308 \text{ mole } CCl_4 \text{ (corr)}$

Balanced Chemical Equations and the Law of Conservation of Mass (Sec. 10.7)

10.49 Law of Conservation of Mass states mass reactants = mass products
a) $5.00 \text{ g A} + 3.20 \text{ g B} = 8.20 \text{ g C}$
b) $2.70 \text{ g A} + X \text{ g B} = 7.50 \text{ g C} \quad \therefore \quad 7.50 \text{ g C} - 2.70 \text{ g A} = 4.80 \text{ g B}$

10.51 a) $SiO_2 + 3C \rightarrow 2CO + SiC$
$60.09 \text{ g } SiO_2 + 3(12.01) \text{ g C} = 2(28.01) \text{ g CO} + 40.10 \text{ g SiC}$
$96.12 \text{ g} = 96.12 \text{ g}$
b) $CH_4 + 4Cl_2 \rightarrow 4HCl + CCl_4$
$16.05 \text{ g } CH_4 + 4(70.90) \text{ g } Cl_2 = 4(36.46) \text{ g HCl} + 153.81 \text{g } CCl_4$
$299.65 \text{ g} = 299.65 \text{ g}$
c) $H_2O_2 + H_2S \rightarrow 2H_2O + S$
$34.02 \text{ g } H_2O_2 + 34.08 \text{ g } H_2S = 2(18.02) \text{ g } H_2O + 32.06 \text{ g S}$
$68.10 \text{ g} = 68.10 \text{ g}$
d) $Mg + 2HCl \rightarrow MgCl_2 + H_2$
$24.30 \text{ g Mg} + 2(36.46) \text{ g HCl} = 95.20 \text{ g } MgCl_2 + 2.02 \text{ g } H_2$
$97.22 \text{ g} = 97.22 \text{ g}$

Stoichiometry (Sec. 10.8)

10.53   a)   7.00 moles $KClO_3$ x $\dfrac{3 \text{ mole } O_2}{2 \text{ moles } KClO_3}$ x $\dfrac{32.00 \text{ g } O_2}{1 \text{ mole } O_2}$ = 336 g O_2 (calc and corr)

     b)   7.00 moles CuO x $\dfrac{1 \text{ mole } O_2}{2 \text{ moles } CuO}$ x $\dfrac{32.00 \text{ g } O_2}{1 \text{ mole } O_2}$ = 112 g O_2 (calc and corr)

     c)   7.00 moles $NaNO_3$ x $\dfrac{1 \text{ mole } O_2}{2 \text{ moles } NaNO_3}$ x $\dfrac{32.00 \text{ g } O_2}{1 \text{ mole } O_2}$ = 112 g O_2 (calc and corr)

     d)   7.00 moles HNO_3 x $\dfrac{1 \text{ mole } O_2}{4 \text{ moles } HNO_3}$ x $\dfrac{32.00 \text{ g } O_2}{1 \text{ mole } O_2}$ = 56.0 g O_2 (calc and corr)

10.55   a)   1.00 mole H_2Ox $\dfrac{4 \text{ mole } HNO_3}{2 \text{ moles } H_2O}$ x $\dfrac{63.02 \text{ g } HNO_3}{1 \text{ mole } HNO_3}$ = 126.04 (calc) = 126 g HNO_3 (corr)

     b)   1.00 mole H_2Ox $\dfrac{6 \text{ mole } HNO_3}{3 \text{ moles } H_2O}$ x $\dfrac{63.02 \text{ g } HNO_3}{1 \text{ mole } HNO_3}$ = 126.04 (calc) = 126 g HNO_3 (corr)

     c)   1.00 mole H_2Ox $\dfrac{1 \text{ mole } HNO_3}{2 \text{ moles } H_2O}$ x $\dfrac{63.02 \text{ g } HNO_3}{1 \text{ mole } HNO_3}$ = 31.51 (calc) = 31.5 g HNO_3 (corr)

     d)   1.00 mole H_2Ox $\dfrac{10 \text{ mole } HNO_3}{3 \text{ moles } H_2O}$ x $\dfrac{63.02 \text{ g } HNO_3}{1 \text{ mole } HNO_3}$ = 210.06666 (calc) = 211 g HNO_3 (corr)

10.57   a) 1.772 g SiO_2 x $\dfrac{1 \text{ mole } SiO_2}{60.09 \text{ g } SiO_2}$ x $\dfrac{3 \text{ moles } C}{1 \text{ mole } SiO_2}$ x $\dfrac{12.01 \text{ g } C}{1 \text{ mole } C}$ = 1.06249226 (calc) = 1.062 g C (corr)

     b) 1.772 g O_2 x $\dfrac{1 \text{ mole } O_2}{32.00 \text{ g } O_2}$ x $\dfrac{1 \text{ mole } C_3H_8}{5 \text{ moles } O_2}$ x $\dfrac{44.11 \text{ g } C_3H_8}{1 \text{ mole } C_3H_8}$ = 0.4885182 (calc)

                                                     = 0.4885 g C_3H_8 (corr)

     c) 1.772 g CH_4 x $\dfrac{1 \text{ mole } CH_4}{16.05 \text{ g } CH_4}$ x $\dfrac{4 \text{ moles } Cl_2}{1 \text{ mole } CH_4}$ x $\dfrac{70.90 \text{ g } Cl_2}{1 \text{ mole } Cl_2}$ = 31.31085358 (calc)

                                                     = 31.31 g Cl_2 (corr)

     d) 1.772 g NO_2 x $\dfrac{1 \text{ mole } NO_2}{46.01 \text{ g } NO_2}$ x $\dfrac{1 \text{ mole } H_2O}{3 \text{ moles } NO_2}$ x $\dfrac{18.02 \text{ g } H_2O}{1 \text{ mole } H_2O}$ = 0.2313369 (calc)

                                                     = 0.2313 g H_2O (corr)

10.59   a) 1.50 moles C x $\dfrac{1 \text{ mole } SiO_2}{3 \text{ moles } C}$ x $\dfrac{60.09 \text{ g } SiO_2}{1 \text{ mole } SiO_2}$ = 30.045 (calc) = 30.0 g SiO_2 (corr)

     b) 1.37 moles SiO_2 x $\dfrac{2 \text{ moles } CO}{1 \text{ mole } SiO_2}$ x $\dfrac{28.01 \text{ g } CO}{1 \text{ mole } CO}$ = 76.7474 (calc) = 76.7 g CO (corr)

     c) 3.33 moles CO x $\dfrac{1 \text{ mole } SiC}{2 \text{ moles } CO}$ x $\dfrac{40.10 \text{ g } SiC}{1 \text{ mole } SiC}$ = 66.7665 (calc) = 66.8 g SiC (corr)

     d) 0.575 mole SiC x $\dfrac{3 \text{ moles } C}{1 \text{ mole } SiC}$ x $\dfrac{12.01 \text{ g } C}{1 \text{ mole } C}$ = 20.71725 (calc) = 20.7 g C (corr)

10.61 a) $4.50 \text{ moles } CO_2 \times \dfrac{2 \text{ moles LiOH}}{1 \text{ mole } CO_2} \times \dfrac{23.95 \text{ g LiOH}}{1 \text{ mole LiOH}} = 215.55 \text{ (calc)} = 216 \text{ g LiOH (corr)}$

b) $3.00 \times 10^{24} \text{ molecules } CO_2 \times \dfrac{1 \text{ mole } CO_2}{6.022 \times 10^{23} \text{ molecules } CO_2} \times \dfrac{2 \text{ moles LiOH}}{1 \text{ mole } CO_2}$

$\times \dfrac{23.95 \text{ g LiOH}}{1 \text{ mole LiOH}} = 238.62504 \text{ (calc)} = 239 \text{ g LiOH (corr)}$

c) $10.0 \text{ g } H_2O \times \dfrac{1 \text{ mole } H_2O}{18.02 \text{ g } H_2O} \times \dfrac{2 \text{ moles LiOH}}{1 \text{ mole } H_2O} \times \dfrac{23.95 \text{ g LiOH}}{1 \text{ mole LiOH}}$

$= 26.581576 \text{ (calc)} = 26.6 \text{ g LiOH (corr)}$

d) $10.0 \text{ g } Li_2CO_3 \times \dfrac{1 \text{ mole } Li_2CO_3}{73.89 \text{ g } Li_2CO_3} \times \dfrac{2 \text{ moles LiOH}}{1 \text{ mole } Li_2CO_3} \times \dfrac{23.95 \text{ g LiOH}}{1 \text{ mole LiOH}}$

$= 6.482603 \text{ (calc)} = 6.48 \text{ g LiOH (corr)}$

10.63 a) $25.00 \text{ g NaF} \times \dfrac{1 \text{ mole NaF}}{41.99 \text{ g NaF}} \times \dfrac{1 \text{ mole } Na_2SiO_3}{2 \text{ moles NaF}}$

$= 0.29768992 \text{ (calc)} = 0.2977 \text{ mole } Na_2SiO_3 \text{ (corr)}$

b) $27.00 \text{ g } H_2O \times \dfrac{1 \text{ mole } H_2O}{18.02 \text{ g } H_2O} \times \dfrac{8 \text{ moles HF}}{3 \text{ moles } H_2O} \times \dfrac{20.01 \text{ g HF}}{1 \text{ mole HF}}$

$= 79.951165 \text{ (calc)} = 79.95 \text{ g HF (corr)}$

c) $2.000 \text{ g } Na_2SiO_3 \times \dfrac{1 \text{ mole } Na_2SiO_3}{122.07 \text{ g } Na_2SiO_3} \times \dfrac{1 \text{ mole } H_2SiF_6}{1 \text{ mole } Na_2SiO_3} \times \dfrac{6.022 \times 10^{23} \text{ molecules } H_2SiF_6}{1 \text{ mole } H_2SiF_6}$

$= 9.8667401 \times 10^{21} \text{ (calc)} = 9.867 \times 10^{21} \text{ molecules } H_2SiF_6 \text{ (corr)}$

d) $50.00 \text{ g } Na_2SiO_3 \times \dfrac{1 \text{ mole } Na_2SiO_3}{122.07 \text{ g } Na_2SiO_3} \times \dfrac{8 \text{ moles HF}}{1 \text{ mole } Na_2SiO_3} \times \dfrac{20.01 \text{ g HF}}{1 \text{ mole HF}}$

$= 65.568936 \text{ (calc)} = 65.57 \text{ g HF (corr)}$

10.65 Balanced equation: $2Na + S \rightarrow Na_2S$

$16.5 \text{ g S} \times \dfrac{1 \text{ mole S}}{32.06 \text{ g S}} \times \dfrac{2 \text{ moles Na}}{1 \text{ mole S}} \times \dfrac{22.99 \text{ g Na}}{1 \text{ mole Na}} = 23.664067 \text{ (calc)} = 23.7 \text{ g Na (corr)}$

10.67 mass of chromium: $200.0 \text{ g } CrCl_3 \times \dfrac{1 \text{ mole } CrCl_3}{158.35 \text{ g } CrCl_3} \times \dfrac{2 \text{ moles Cr}}{2 \text{ moles } CrCl_3} \times \dfrac{52.00 \text{ g Cr}}{1 \text{ mole Cr}}$

$= 65.677297 \text{ (calc)} = 65.68 \text{ g Cr (corr)}$

mass of chlorine: $200.0 \text{ g } CrCl_3 \times \dfrac{1 \text{ mole } CrCl_3}{158.35 \text{ g } CrCl_3} \times \dfrac{3 \text{ moles } Cl_2}{2 \text{ moles } CrCl_3} \times \dfrac{70.90 \text{ g } Cl_2}{1 \text{ mole } Cl_2}$

$= 134.3227 \text{ (calc)} = 134.3 \text{ g } Cl_2 \text{ (corr)}$

Note: the mass of Cl_2 could also be obtained by subtracting 65.68 g Cr from $200.0 \text{ g } CrCl_3$.

Limiting Reactant Calculations (Sec. 10.9)

10.69 $216 \text{ nuts} \times \dfrac{1 \text{ combination}}{3 \text{ nuts}} = 72 \text{ combinations}$

        $284 \text{ bolts} \times \dfrac{1 \text{ combination}}{4 \text{ bolts}} = 71 \text{ combinations}$

The limiting reactant is the 284 bolts.

10.71 $426 \text{ wings} \times \dfrac{1 \text{ kit}}{2 \text{ wings}} = 213 \text{ kits (calc and corr)}$

        $224 \text{ fuselages} \times \dfrac{1 \text{ kit}}{1 \text{ fuselage}} = 224 \text{ kits (calc and corr)}$

        $860 \text{ engines} \times \dfrac{1 \text{ kit}}{4 \text{ engines}} = 215 \text{ kits (calc and corr)}$

        $1578 \text{ wheels} \times \dfrac{1 \text{ kit}}{6 \text{ wheels}} = 263 \text{ kits (calc and corr)}$

$\therefore$ 213 kits can be produced.

10.73   a) $1.25 \text{ moles } N_2 \times \dfrac{2 \text{ moles } NH_3}{1 \text{ mole } N_2} = 2.50 \text{ moles } NH_3 \text{ (calc and corr)}$

          $3.65 \text{ moles } H_2 \times \dfrac{2 \text{ moles } NH_3}{3 \text{ moles } H_2} = 2.4333333 \text{ (calc)} = 2.43 \text{ moles } NH_3 \text{ (corr)}$

          The 3.65 moles H_2 is the limiting reactant.

      b) $2.60 \text{ moles } N_2 \times \dfrac{2 \text{ moles } NH_3}{1 \text{ mole } N_2} = 5.20 \text{ moles } NH_3 \text{ (calc and corr)}$

          $8.00 \text{ moles } H_2 \times \dfrac{2 \text{ moles } NH_3}{3 \text{ moles } H_2} = 5.3333333 \text{ (calc)} = 5.33 \text{ moles } NH_3 \text{ (corr)}$

          The 2.60 moles of N_2 is the limiting reactant.

      c) $327 \text{ molecules } N_2 \times \dfrac{2 \text{ molecules } NH_3}{1 \text{ molecule } N_2} = 654 \text{ molecules } NH_3 \text{ (calc and corr)}$

          $975 \text{ molecules } H_2 \times \dfrac{2 \text{ molecules } NH_3}{1 \text{ molecule } H_2} = 650 \text{ molecules } NH_3 \text{ (calc and corr)}$

          The 975 molecules of H_2 is the limiting reactant.

      d) $44.0 \text{ g } N_2 \times \dfrac{1 \text{ mole } N_2}{28.02 \text{ g } N_2} \times \dfrac{2 \text{ moles } NH_3}{1 \text{ mole } N_2} = 3.1406138 \text{ (calc)} = 3.14 \text{ moles } NH_3 \text{ (corr)}$

          $3.00 \text{ moles } H_2 \times \dfrac{2 \text{ moles } NH_3}{3 \text{ moles } H_2} = 2 \text{ (calc)} = 2.00 \text{ moles } NH_3 \text{ (corr)}$

          The 3.00 moles of H_2 is the limiting reactant.

10.75 Determine the limiting reactant in each part, then convert moles of product to mass of product.

a) Using all of the 10.0 g Mg:

$$10.0 \text{ g Mg} \times \frac{1 \text{ mole Mg}}{24.30 \text{ g Mg}} \times \frac{1 \text{ mole Mg}_3\text{N}_2}{3 \text{ moles Mg}}$$

$$= 0.13717421 \text{ (calc)} = 0.137 \text{ mole Mg}_3\text{N}_2 \text{ (corr)}$$

Using all of the 10.0 g N_2:

$$10.0 \text{ g N}_2 \times \frac{1 \text{ mole N}_2}{28.02 \text{ g N}_2} \times \frac{1 \text{ mole Mg}_3\text{N}_2}{1 \text{ mole N}_2} = 0.3568879 \text{ (calc)} = 0.357 \text{ mole Mg}_3\text{N}_2 \text{ (corr)}$$

The Mg is the limiting reactant.

$$0.137 \text{ mole Mg}_3\text{N}_2 \times \frac{100.92 \text{ g Mg}_3\text{N}_2}{1 \text{ mole Mg}_3\text{N}_2} = 13.82604 \text{ (calc)} = 13.8 \text{ g Mg}_3\text{N}_2 \text{ (corr)}$$

b) Using all of the 20.0 g Mg:

$$20.0 \text{ g Mg} \times \frac{1 \text{ mole Mg}}{24.30 \text{ g Mg}} \times \frac{1 \text{ mole Mg}_3\text{N}_2}{3 \text{ moles Mg}}$$

$$= 0.27434842 \text{ (calc)} = 0.274 \text{ mole Mg}_3\text{N}_2 \text{ (corr)}$$

Using all of the 10.0 g N_2 (from part a) = 0.357 mole Mg_3N_2 (corr)
The Mg is the limiting reactant.

$$0.274 \text{ mole Mg}_3\text{N}_2 \times \frac{100.92 \text{ g Mg}_3\text{N}_2}{1 \text{ mole Mg}_3\text{N}_2} = 27.65208 \text{ (calc)} = 27.7 \text{ g Mg}_3\text{N}_2 \text{ (corr)}$$

c) Using all of the 30.0 g Mg:

$$30.0 \text{ g Mg} \times \frac{1 \text{ mole Mg}}{24.30 \text{ g Mg}} \times \frac{1 \text{ mole Mg}_3\text{N}_2}{3 \text{ moles Mg}} = 0.41152263 \text{ (calc)} = 0.412 \text{ mole Mg}_3\text{N}_2 \text{ (corr)}$$

Using all of the 10.0 g N_2 (from part a) = 0.357 mole Mg_3N_2
The N_2 is the limiting reactant.

$$0.357 \text{ mole Mg}_3\text{N}_2 \times \frac{100.92 \text{ g Mg}_3\text{N}_2}{1 \text{ mole Mg}_3\text{N}_2} = 36.02844 \text{ (calc)} = 36.0 \text{ g Mg}_3\text{N}_2 \text{ (corr)}$$

d) Using all of the 40.0 g Mg:

$$40.0 \text{ g Mg} \times \frac{1 \text{ mole Mg}}{24.30 \text{ g Mg}} \times \frac{1 \text{ mole Mg}_3\text{N}_2}{3 \text{ moles Mg}} = 0.54869685 \text{ (calc)} = 0.549 \text{ mole Mg}_3\text{N}_2 \text{ (corr)}$$

Using all of the 10.0 g N_2 (from part a) = 0.357 mole Mg_3N_2
The N_2 is the limiting reactant.

$$0.357 \text{ mole Mg}_3\text{N}_2 \times \frac{100.92 \text{ g Mg}_3\text{N}_2}{1 \text{ mole Mg}_3\text{N}_2} = 36.02844 \text{ (calc)} = 36.0 \text{ g Mg}_3\text{N}_2 \text{ (corr)}$$

10.77

$$525 \text{ Co atoms} \times \frac{2 \text{ formula units CoCl}_3}{2 \text{ atoms Co}} = 525 \text{ formula units CoCl}_3$$

$$525 \text{ HCl molecules} \times \frac{2 \text{ formula units CoCl}_3}{6 \text{ molecules HCl}} = 175 \text{ formula units}$$

The HCl is the limiting reactant. 175 $CoCl_3$ formula units can be made.

10.79 The limiting reactant will all react. Use the limiting reactant to determine the mass of the other reactant that reacts, and then find the unreacted by difference.

$$70.0 \text{ g Fe}_3O_4 \times \frac{1 \text{ mole Fe}_3O_4}{231.52 \text{ g Fe}_3O_4} \times \frac{6 \text{ moles Fe}_2O_3}{4 \text{ moles Fe}_3O_4}$$

$$= 0.4535245 \text{ (calc)} = 0.454 \text{ mole Fe}_2O_3 \text{ (corr)}$$

$$12.0 \text{ g O}_2 \times \frac{1 \text{ mole O}_2}{32.00 \text{ g O}_2} \times \frac{6 \text{ moles Fe}_2O_3}{1 \text{ mole O}_2} = 2.25 \text{ mole Fe}_2O_3 \text{ (calc and corr)}$$

The Fe_3O_4 is the limiting reactant. There will be none left upon completion.
Calculate the mass of O_2 reacted:

$$0.454 \text{ mole Fe}_2O_3 \times \frac{1 \text{ mole O}_2}{6 \text{ moles Fe}_2O_3} \times \frac{32.00 \text{ g O}_2}{1 \text{ mole O}_2}$$

$$= 2.4213333 \text{ (calc)} = 2.42 \text{ g O}_2 \text{ reacted (corr)}$$

Unreacted: $Fe_3O_4 = 0$
$O_2 = 12.0 \text{ g} - 2.42 \text{ g} = 9.58 \text{ (calc)} = 9.6 \text{ g O}_2 \text{ unreacted (corr)}$

10.81 $8.00 \text{ g SCl}_2 \times \dfrac{1 \text{ mole SCl}_2}{102.96 \text{ g SCl}_2} \times \dfrac{1 \text{ mole SF}_4}{3 \text{ moles SCl}_2} = 0.0259 \text{ mole SF}_4 \text{ (calc and corr)}$

$4.00 \text{ g NaF} \times \dfrac{1 \text{ mole NaF}}{41.99 \text{ g NaF}} \times \dfrac{1 \text{ mole SF}_4}{4 \text{ moles NaF}} = 0.0238151 \text{ (calc)} = 0.0238 \text{ mole SF}_4 \text{ (corr)}$
NaF is the limiting reactant.

$0.0238 \text{ mole SF}_4 \times \dfrac{108.06 \text{ g SF}_4}{1 \text{ mole SF}_4} = 2.571828 \text{ (calc)} = 2.57 \text{ g SF}_4 \text{ (corr)}$

$0.0238 \text{ mole SF}_4 \times \dfrac{1 \text{ mole S}_2Cl_2}{1 \text{ mole SF}_4} \times \dfrac{135.02 \text{ g S}_2Cl_2}{1 \text{ mole S}_2Cl_2} = 3.213476 \text{ (calc)} = 3.21 \text{ g S}_2Cl_2 \text{ (corr)}$

$0.0238 \text{ mole SF}_4 \times \dfrac{4 \text{ moles NaCl}}{1 \text{ mole SF}_4} \times \dfrac{58.44 \text{ g NaCl}}{1 \text{ mole NaCl}} = 5.563488 \text{ (calc)} = 5.56 \text{ g NaCl (corr)}$

Theoretical and Percent Yield (Sec. 10.10)

10.83 $\% \text{ yield} = \dfrac{16.0 \text{ g (actual)}}{52.0 \text{ g (theoretical)}} \times 100 = 30.76923 \text{ (calc)} = 30.8 \% \text{ (corr)}$

10.85 $75.0 \text{ g Al} \times \dfrac{1 \text{ mole Al}}{26.98 \text{ g Al}} \times \dfrac{1 \text{ mole Al}_2S_3}{2 \text{ moles Al}} = 1.3899185 \text{ (calc)} = 1.39 \text{ moles Al}_2S_3 \text{ (corr)}$

$300.0 \text{ g S} \times \dfrac{1 \text{ mole S}}{32.06 \text{ g S}} \times \dfrac{1 \text{ mole Al}_2S_3}{3 \text{ moles S}} = 3.1191516 \text{ (calc)} = 3.119 \text{ moles Al}_2S_3 \text{ (corr)}$
Al is the limiting reactant.

a) $1.39 \text{ moles Al}_2S_3 \times \dfrac{150.14 \text{ g Al}_2S_3}{1 \text{ mole Al}_2S_3} = 208.6946 \text{ (calc)} = 209 \text{ g Al}_2S_3 \text{ (corr)}$

b) $\% \text{ yield} = \dfrac{125 \text{ g Al}_2S_3}{209 \text{ g Al}_2S_3} \times 100 = 59.80861 \text{ (calc)} = 59.8 \% \text{ (calc)}$

10.87 Theoretical yield of HCl:

$$2.13 \text{ g H}_2 \times \frac{1 \text{ mole H}_2}{2.02 \text{ g H}_2} \times \frac{2 \text{ moles HCl}}{1 \text{ mole H}_2} \times \frac{36.46 \text{ g HCl}}{1 \text{ mole HCl}}$$

$$= 76.890891 \text{(calc)} = 76.9 \text{ g HCl (corr)}$$

$$\% \text{ yield} = \frac{74.30 \text{ g HCl}}{76.9 \text{ g HCl}} \times 100 = 96.6189857 \text{ (calc)} = 96.6\% \text{ (corr)}$$

10.89 Theoretical yield of Al_2S_3:

$$55.0 \text{ g Al} \times \frac{1 \text{ mole Al}}{26.98 \text{ g Al}} \times \frac{1 \text{ mole Al}_2S_3}{2 \text{ moles Al}} \times \frac{150.14 \text{ g Al}_2S_3}{1 \text{ mole Al}_2S_3}$$

$$= 153.03373 \text{ (calc)} = 153 \text{ g Al}_2S_3 \text{ (corr)}$$

Actual yield = theoretical yield x % yield

$$= 153 \text{ g Al}_2S_3 \text{ (theor)} \times \frac{85.6 \text{ g Al}_2S_3 \text{ (actual)}}{100 \text{ g Al}_2S_3 \text{ (theor)}} = 130.968 \text{ (calc)} = 131 \text{ g Al}_2S_3 \text{ (corr)}$$

10.91 Find the limiting reactant.

$$35.0 \text{ g CO} \times \frac{1 \text{ mole CO}}{28.01 \text{ g CO}} \times \frac{2 \text{ moles CO}_2}{2 \text{ moles CO}} = 1.2495537 \text{ (calc)} = 1.25 \text{ moles CO}_2 \text{ (calc and corr)}$$

$$35.0 \text{ g O}_2 \times \frac{1 \text{ mole O}_2}{32.00 \text{ g O}_2} \times \frac{2 \text{ moles CO}_2}{1 \text{ mole O}_2} = 2.1875 \text{ (calc)} = 2.19 \text{ moles CO}_2 \text{ (corr)}$$

The CO is the limiting reactant.

$$\text{Theoretical yield} = 1.25 \text{ moles CO}_2 \times \frac{44.01 \text{ g CO}_2}{1 \text{ mole CO}_2} = 55.0125 \text{ (calc)} = 55.0 \text{ g CO}_2 \text{ (corr)}$$

$$\text{Actual yield} = 55.0 \text{ g CO}_2 \text{ (theor)} \times \frac{57.8 \text{ g CO}_2 \text{ (actual)}}{100 \text{ g CO}_2 \text{ (theor)}} = 31.79 \text{ (calc)} = 31.8 \text{ g CO}_2 \text{ (corr)}$$

Simultaneous Chemical Reactions (Sec. 10.11)

10.93 $$82.5 \text{ g mixture} \times \frac{60.0 \text{ g ZnS}}{100 \text{ g mixture}} \times \frac{1 \text{ mole ZnS}}{97.45 \text{ g ZnS}} \times \frac{2 \text{ moles SO}_2}{2 \text{ moles ZnS}} \times \frac{64.06 \text{ g SO}_2}{1 \text{ mole SO}_2}$$

$$= 32.539456 \text{ (calc)} = 32.5 \text{ g SO}_2 \text{ (corr)}$$

$$82.5 \text{ g mixture} \times \frac{40.0 \text{ g CuS}}{100 \text{ g mixture}} \times \frac{1 \text{ mole CuS}}{95.61 \text{ g CuS}} \times \frac{2 \text{ moles SO}_2}{2 \text{ moles CuS}} \times \frac{64.06 \text{ g SO}_2}{1 \text{ mole SO}_2}$$

$$= 22.110449 \text{ (calc)} = 22.1 \text{ g SO}_2 \text{ (corr)}$$

Total SO_2 = 32.5 g + 22.1 g = 54.6 g (calc and corr)

10.95 $$75.0 \text{ g mixture} \times \frac{70.0 \text{ g CH}_4}{100 \text{ g mixture}} \times \frac{1 \text{ mole CH}_4}{16.05 \text{ g CH}_4} \times \frac{2 \text{ moles O}_2}{1 \text{ mole CH}_4} \times \frac{32.00 \text{ g O}_2}{1 \text{ mole O}_2}$$

$$= 209.34579 \text{ (calc)} = 209 \text{ g O}_2 \text{ (corr)}$$

$$75.0 \text{ g mixture} \times \frac{30.0 \text{ g C}_2H_6}{100 \text{ g mixture}} \times \frac{1 \text{ mole C}_2H_6}{30.08 \text{ g C}_2H_6} \times \frac{7 \text{ moles O}_2}{2 \text{ moles C}_2H_6} \times \frac{32.00 \text{ g O}_2}{1 \text{ mole O}_2}$$

$$= 83.776596 \text{ (calc)} = 83.8 \text{ g O}_2 \text{ (corr)}$$

total = 209 g O_2 + 83.8 g O_2 = 292.8 (calc) = 293 g O_2 (corr)

Sequential Chemical Reactions (Sec. 10.11)

10.97 a) $6.00 \text{ moles SO}_2 \times \dfrac{1 \text{ mole O}_2}{1 \text{ mole SO}_2} \times \dfrac{2 \text{ moles NaClO}_3}{3 \text{ moles O}_2} = 4.00 \text{ moles NaClO}_3$ (calc and corr)

b) $20.0 \text{ g SO}_2 \times \dfrac{1 \text{ mole SO}_2}{64.06 \text{ g SO}_2} \times \dfrac{1 \text{ mole O}_2}{1 \text{ mole SO}_2} \times \dfrac{2 \text{ moles NaClO}_3}{3 \text{ moles O}_2} \times \dfrac{106.44 \text{ g NaClO}_3}{1 \text{ mole NaClO}_3}$
$= 22.15423 \text{ (calc)} = 22.2 \text{ g NaClO}_3 \text{ (corr)}$

10.99 a) $2.00 \text{ moles N}_2 \times \dfrac{2 \text{ moles NO}}{1 \text{ mole N}_2} \times \dfrac{2 \text{ moles NO}_2}{2 \text{ moles NO}} \times \dfrac{4 \text{ moles HNO}_3}{4 \text{ moles NO}_2}$
$= 4.00 \text{ moles HNO}_3 \text{ (calc and corr)}$

b) $2.00 \text{ g N}_2 \times \dfrac{1 \text{ mole N}_2}{28.02 \text{ g N}_2} \times \dfrac{2 \text{ moles NO}}{1 \text{ mole N}_2} \times \dfrac{2 \text{ moles NO}_2}{2 \text{ moles NO}} \times \dfrac{4 \text{ moles HNO}_3}{4 \text{ moles NO}_2} \times \dfrac{63.02 \text{ g HNO}_3}{1 \text{ mole HNO}_3}$
$= 8.9964311 \text{ (calc)} = 9.00 \text{ g HNO}_3 \text{ (corr)}$

10.101 $5.00 \text{ g I}_2 \times \dfrac{1 \text{ mole I}_2}{253.80 \text{ g I}_2} \times \dfrac{2 \text{ moles FeI}_2}{2 \text{ moles I}_2} \times \dfrac{2 \text{ moles AgI}}{1 \text{ mole FeI}_2} \times \dfrac{1 \text{ mole AgNO}_3}{1 \text{ mole AgI}} \times \dfrac{169.88 \text{ g AgNO}_3}{1 \text{ mole AgNO}_3}$
$= 6.6934594 \text{ (calc)} = 6.69 \text{ g AgNO}_3 \text{ (corr)}$

ADDITIONAL PROBLEMS

10.103 a) $3.00 \text{ moles CH}_4 \times \dfrac{2 \text{ mole O}_2}{1 \text{ mole CH}_4} = 6.00 \text{ moles O}_2$ (calc and corr)

b) $3.00 \text{ moles PCl}_3 \times \dfrac{3 \text{ mole H}_2\text{O}}{1 \text{ mole PCl}_3} = 9.00 \text{ moles H}_2\text{O}$ (calc and corr)

c) $3.00 \text{ moles NaOH} \times \dfrac{1 \text{ mole H}_3\text{PO}_4}{3 \text{ mole NaOH}} = 1.00 \text{ moles H}_3\text{PO}_4$ (calc and corr)

d) $3.00 \text{ moles NaClO}_2 \times \dfrac{1 \text{ mole Cl}_2}{2 \text{ mole NaClO}_2} = 1.50 \text{ moles Cl}_2$ (calc and corr)

10.105 $75.0 \text{ g (NH}_4)_2\text{Cr}_2\text{O}_7 \times \dfrac{1 \text{ mole (NH}_4)_2\text{Cr}_2\text{O}_7}{252.10 \text{ g (NH}_4)_2\text{Cr}_2\text{O}_7} \times \dfrac{1 \text{ mole N}_2}{1 \text{ mole (NH}_4)_2\text{Cr}_2\text{O}_7} \times \dfrac{28.02 \text{ g N}_2}{1 \text{ mole N}_2}$
$= 8.3359778 \text{ (calc)} = 8.34 \text{ g N}_2 \text{ (corr)}$

$75.0 \text{ g (NH}_4)_2\text{Cr}_2\text{O}_7 \times \dfrac{1 \text{ mole (NH}_4)_2\text{Cr}_2\text{O}_7}{252.10 \text{ g (NH}_4)_2\text{Cr}_2\text{O}_7} \times \dfrac{4 \text{ moles H}_2\text{O}}{1 \text{ mole (NH}_4)_2\text{Cr}_2\text{O}_7} \times \dfrac{18.02 \text{ g H}_2\text{O}}{1 \text{ mole H}_2\text{O}}$
$= 21.443871 \text{ (calc)} = 21.4 \text{ g H}_2\text{O} \text{ (corr)}$

$$75.0 \text{ g (NH}_4)_2\text{Cr}_2\text{O}_7 \times \frac{1 \text{ mole (NH}_4)_2\text{Cr}_2\text{O}_7}{252.10 \text{ g (NH}_4)_2\text{Cr}_2\text{O}_7} \times \frac{1 \text{ mole Cr}_2\text{O}_3}{1 \text{ mole (NH}_4)_2\text{Cr}_2\text{O}_7} \times \frac{152.00 \text{ g Cr}_2\text{O}_3}{1 \text{ mole Cr}_2\text{O}_3}$$
$$= 45.220151 \text{ (calc)} = 45.2 \text{ g Cr}_2\text{O}_3 \text{ (corr)}$$

10.107 Obtain a "conversion factor" with g of product and g of H_2S by finding the mass of products that could be made from 1.000 g H_2S:

$$1.000 \text{ g H}_2\text{S} \times \frac{1 \text{ mole H}_2\text{S}}{34.08 \text{ g H}_2\text{S}} \times \frac{2 \text{ moles SO}_2}{2 \text{ moles H}_2\text{S}} \times \frac{64.06 \text{ g SO}_2}{1 \text{ mole SO}_2}$$
$$= 1.8796948 \text{ (calc)} = 1.880 \text{ g SO}_2 \text{ (corr)}$$

and

$$1.000 \text{ g H}_2\text{S} \times \frac{1 \text{ mole H}_2\text{S}}{34.08 \text{ g H}_2\text{S}} \times \frac{2 \text{ moles H}_2\text{O}}{2 \text{ moles H}_2\text{S}} \times \frac{18.02 \text{ g H}_2\text{O}}{1 \text{ mole H}_2\text{O}}$$
$$= 0.5287558 \text{ (calc)} = 0.5288 \text{ g H}_2\text{O} \text{ (corr)}$$

Total: 1.880 g + 0.5288 = 2.409 g product.

The conversion factor is $\dfrac{2.409 \text{ g product}}{1.000 \text{ g H}_2\text{S}}$

$$100.0 \text{ g product} \times \frac{1.000 \text{ g H}_2\text{S}}{2.409 \text{ g product}} = 41.511 \text{ (calc)} = 41.51 \text{ g H}_2\text{S (corr)}$$

10.109
a) actual ratio A:B (4:1) is greater than the required ratio (3:1) ∴ B is limiting
b) actual ratio A:B (1.33:1) is less than the required ratio (1.5:1) ∴ A is limiting
c) actual ratio A:B (0.51:1) is greater than the required ratio (0.50:1) ∴ B is limiting
d) actual ratio A:B (1.19:1) is less than the required ratio (1.33:1) ∴ A is limiting

10.111 $3A + 2B \rightarrow C + 2D$
6.0 g   8.0 g   9.0 g   5.0 g

a) Let x = molar mass of A and y = molar mass of B

$$\therefore 3 \times \frac{6.0 \text{ g A}}{x} = 2 \times \frac{8.0 \text{ g B}}{y} \qquad \frac{18.0 \text{ g A}}{x} = \frac{16.0 \text{ g B}}{y}$$

$$\therefore x = y \frac{18.0 \text{ g A}}{16.0 \text{ g B}} \text{ and } x > y \text{ and A has a greater molar mass than B}$$

b) Let x = molar mass of A and z = molar mass of C

$$\therefore 3 \times \frac{6.0 \text{ g A}}{x} = 1 \times \frac{9.0 \text{ g C}}{z} \qquad \frac{18.0 \text{ g A}}{x} = \frac{9.0 \text{ g B}}{z}$$

$$\therefore x = z \frac{18.0 \text{ g A}}{9.0 \text{ g C}} \text{ and } x > z \text{ and A has a greater molar mass than C}$$

c) Let x = molar mass of A and w = molar mass of D

$$\therefore 3 \times \frac{6.0 \text{ g A}}{x} = 2 \times \frac{5.0 \text{ g D}}{w} \qquad \frac{18.0 \text{ g A}}{x} = \frac{10.0 \text{ g D}}{w}$$

$$\therefore x = w \frac{18.0 \text{ g A}}{10.0 \text{ g D}} \text{ and } x > w \text{ and A has a greater molar mass than D}$$

d) Let x = molar mass of A and w = molar mass of D

$$x = y \frac{18.0 \text{ g A}}{16.0 \text{ g B}} = z \frac{18.0 \text{ g A}}{9.0 \text{ g C}} = w \frac{18.0 \text{ g A}}{10.0 \text{ g D}}$$

∴ x = 30.0 g/mole and thus y = 26.7 g/mole
z = 15.0 g/mole
w = 16.7 g/mole

10.113 $2.00 \text{ moles KNO}_2 \times \dfrac{4 \text{ moles NO}}{3 \text{ moles KNO}_2} = 2.6666666 \text{ (calc)} = 2.67 \text{ moles NO (corr)}$

$2.00 \text{ moles KNO}_3 \times \dfrac{4 \text{ moles NO}}{1 \text{ mole KNO}_3} = 8 \text{ (calc)} = 8.00 \text{ moles NO (corr)}$

$2.00 \text{ moles Cr}_2\text{O}_3 \times \dfrac{4 \text{ moles NO}}{1 \text{ mole Cr}_2\text{O}_3} = 8 \text{ (calc)} = 8.00 \text{ moles NO (corr)}$

KNO_2 is the limiting reactant.

$2.67 \text{ moles NO} \times \dfrac{30.01 \text{ g NO}}{1 \text{ mole NO}} = 80.1267 \text{ (calc)} = 80.1 \text{ g NO (corr)}$

10.115 $1.33 \text{ g Cu} \times \dfrac{1 \text{ mole Cu}}{63.55 \text{ g Cu}} \times \dfrac{1 \text{ mole CuSO}_4}{1 \text{ mole Cu}} \times \dfrac{159.61 \text{ g CuSO}_4}{1 \text{ mole CuSO}_4}$

$= 3.3403824 \text{ (calc)} = 3.34 \text{ g CuSO}_4 \text{ (corr)}$

$\% \text{ CuSO}_4 = \dfrac{3.34 \text{ g}}{7.53 \text{ g}} \times 100 = 44.35591 \text{ (calc)} = 44.4 \% \text{ (corr)}$

10.117 Balanced equation: $2\text{Ag}_2\text{O} \rightarrow 4\text{Ag} + \text{O}_2$

$0.115 \text{ g O}_2 \times \dfrac{1 \text{ mole O}_2}{32.00 \text{ g O}_2} \times \dfrac{2 \text{ moles Ag}_2\text{O}}{1 \text{ mole O}_2} \times \dfrac{231.74 \text{ g Ag}_2\text{O}}{1 \text{ mole Ag}_2\text{O}}$

$= 1.6656313 \text{ (calc)} = 1.67 \text{ g Ag}_2\text{O (corr)}$

$\% \text{ Ag}_2\text{O} = \dfrac{1.67 \text{ g}}{1.80 \text{ g}} \times 100 = 92.777777 \text{ (calc)} = 92.8\% \text{ (corr)}$

10.119 $113.4 \text{ g I}_2\text{O}_5 \times \dfrac{1 \text{ mole I}_2\text{O}_5}{333.80 \text{ g I}_2\text{O}_5} \times \dfrac{12 \text{ moles IF}_5}{6 \text{ moles I}_2\text{O}_5} = 0.67944877 \text{ (calc)} = 0.6794 \text{ mole IF}_5 \text{ (corr)}$

$132.2 \text{ g BrF}_3 \times \dfrac{1 \text{ mole BrF}_3}{136.90 \text{ g BrF}_3} \times \dfrac{12 \text{ moles IF}_5}{20 \text{ moles BrF}_3} = 0.57940102 \text{ (calc)} = 0.5794 \text{ mole IF}_5 \text{ (corr)}$

BrF_3 is the limiting reactant.
Theoretical yield of IF_5:

$0.5794 \text{ mole IF}_5 \times \dfrac{221.9 \text{ g IF}_5}{1 \text{ mole IF}_5} = 128.56886 \text{ (calc)} = 128.6 \text{ g IF}_5 \text{ (corr)}$

$\% \text{ yield IF}_5 = \dfrac{97.0 \text{ g}}{128.6 \text{ g}} \times 100 = 75.427682 \text{ (calc)} = 75.4 \% \text{ (corr)}$

10.121 $500.0 \text{ lb Cu} \times \dfrac{453.6 \text{ g Cu}}{1 \text{ lb Cu}} \times \dfrac{1 \text{ mole Cu}}{63.55 \text{ g Cu}} \times \dfrac{2 \text{ moles CuCO}_3}{2 \text{ moles Cu}} \times \dfrac{123.56 \text{ g CuCO}_3}{1 \text{ mole CuCO}_3}$

$\times \dfrac{100.0 \text{ g ore}}{13.22 \text{ g CuCO}_3} \times \dfrac{1 \text{ lb ore}}{453.6 \text{ g ore}} \times \dfrac{1 \text{ ton ore}}{2000 \text{ lb ore}}$

$= 3.6768075 \text{ (calc)} = 3.677 \text{ ton ore (corr)}$

10.123 Mass of $NaHCO_3$ present:

$$0.873 \text{ g } H_2O \times \frac{1 \text{ mole } H_2O}{18.02 \text{ g } H_2O} \times \frac{2 \text{ moles } NaHCO_3}{1 \text{ mole } H_2O} \times \frac{84.01 \text{ g } NaHCO_3}{1 \text{ mole } NaHCO_3}$$

$$= 8.1399256 \text{ (calc)} = 8.14 \text{ g } NaHCO_3 \text{ (corr)}$$

Mass of $CaCO_3$ present: $(13.20 - 8.14)$ g $CaCO_3 = 5.06$ g $CaCO_3$ (calc and corr)

% $CaCO_3$: $\frac{5.06 \text{ g}}{13.20 \text{ g}} \times 100 = 38.3333$ (calc) $= 38.3$ % (corr)

CUMULATIVE PROBLEMS

10.125 a) $Zn + 2AgNO_3 \rightarrow Zn(NO_3)_2 + 2Ag$ b) $HCl + NaOH \rightarrow NaCl + H_2O$
c) $PCl_3 + Cl_2 \rightarrow PCl_5$ d) $2Cu + O_2 \rightarrow 2CuO$

10.127 Since the oxygen is balanced with 18 atoms on each side of the equation, the compound cyclopropane contains only C and H: $2C_xH_y + 9O_2 \rightarrow 6CO_2 + 6H_2O$
C balance: $2x = 6$; $x = 3$ H balance: $2y = 6(2)$; $y = 6$
$\therefore$ Cyclopropane $= C_3H_6$

10.129 Take 100.00 g of the copper compound

$$100.00 \text{ g compound} \times \frac{88.82 \text{ g } Cu}{100.0 \text{ g compound}} \times \frac{1 \text{ mole } Cu}{63.55 \text{ g } Cu}$$

$$= 1.3976396 \text{ (calc)} = 1.398 \text{ moles } Cu \text{ (corr)}$$

100.00 g compound $-$ 88.82 g Cu $= 11.18$ g O (calc and corr)

$$11.18 \text{ g O} \times \frac{1 \text{ mole O}}{16.00 \text{ g O}} = 0.69875 \text{ (calc)} = 0.6988 \text{ mole O (corr)}$$

Cu: $\frac{1.398}{0.6988} = 2.000$ O: $\frac{0.6988}{0.6988} = 1.000$

The formula of the copper oxide is Cu_2O.
$2Cu_2S + 3O_2 \rightarrow 2Cu_2O + 2SO_2$

10.131 Empirical formula mass of CH = 13.02 amu

$\frac{78.12 \text{ amu}}{13.02 \text{ amu}} = 6.000$ $\therefore$ the molecular formula $= (CH)_6 = C_6H_6$

$2C_6H_6 + 15O_2 \rightarrow 12CO_2 + 6H_2O$

10.133 Since five significant figures are wanted in part b), work part a) using 5 significant figures and then round as needed for parts b, c and d.

a) $50.000 \text{ g Be} \times \frac{1 \text{ mole Be}}{9.0122 \text{ g Be}} \times \frac{1 \text{ mole } BeF_2}{1 \text{ mole Be}} \times \frac{47.022 \text{ g } BeF_2}{1 \text{ mole } BeF_2} = 260.879696$ (calc)

$$= 261 \text{ g } BeF_2 \text{ (corr)}$$

b) using calculator answer in part a), rounded to 5 significant figures:

$$260.88 \text{ g } BeF_2 \times \frac{1 \text{ kg}}{1 \times 10^3 \text{ g}} = 0.26088 \text{ kg } BeF_2 \text{ (calc and corr)}$$

c) using calculator answer in part a), rounded to 4 significant figures:

$$260.9 \text{ g } BeF_2 \times \frac{1 \text{ } \mu g}{1 \times 10^{-6} \text{ g}} = 2.609 \times 10^8 \text{ } \mu g \text{ } BeF_2 \text{ (calc and corr)}$$

d) using calculator answer in part a), rounded to 4 significant figures:

$$260.9 \text{ g BeF}_2 \times \frac{1 \text{ lb}}{453.6 \text{ g}} = 0.57515432 \text{ (calc)} = 0.5752 \text{ lb BeF}_2 \text{ (corr)}$$

10.135 There are five chlorine-containing product molecules or formula units:
$2(KCl) + 2(ClO_2) + 1 \; Cl_2$
Determine the limiting reactant

$$100.0 \text{ g KClO}_3 \times \frac{1 \text{ mole KClO}_3}{122.55 \text{ g KClO}_3} \times \frac{2 \text{ moles H}_2\text{O}}{2 \text{ moles KClO}_3}$$

$$= 0.8159934 \text{(calc)} = 0.8160 \text{ mole H}_2\text{O (corr)}$$

$$200.0 \text{ g HCl} \times \frac{1 \text{ mole HCl}}{36.46 \text{ g HCl}} \times \frac{2 \text{ moles H}_2\text{O}}{4 \text{ moles HCl}} = 2.7427317 \text{ (calc)} = 2.743 \text{ moles H}_2\text{O (corr)}$$

$KClO_3$ is the limiting reactant.

$$0.8160 \text{ mole H}_2\text{O} \times \frac{5 \text{ moles chlorine-containing products}}{2 \text{ moles H}_2\text{O}}$$

$$= 2.04 \text{ (calc)} = 2.040 \text{ moles chlorine-containing products (corr)}$$

10.137 $$10.0 \text{ g Al} \times \frac{1 \text{ mole Al}}{26.98 \text{ g Al}} \times \frac{1 \text{ mole AlCl}_3}{3 \text{ moles Al}} \times \frac{[13 + 3(17)] \text{ moles electrons}}{1 \text{ mole AlCl}_3}$$

$$= 7.9070917 \text{ (calc)} = 7.91 \text{ moles electrons (corr)}$$

10.139 For the NaCl produced:

$$500.0 \text{ g CaCl}_2 \times \frac{1 \text{ mole CaCl}_2}{110.98 \text{ g CaCl}_2} \times \frac{2 \text{ moles NaCl}}{1 \text{ mole CaCl}_2} \times \frac{1 \text{ mole pos. ions}}{1 \text{ mole NaCl}}$$

$$\times \frac{6.022 \times 10^{23} \text{ pos. ions}}{1 \text{ mole pos. ions}} = 5.4262029 \times 10^{24} \text{ (calc)} = 5.426 \times 10^{24} \text{ pos. ions (corr)}$$

For the $CaCO_3$ produced:

$$500.0 \text{ g CaCl}_2 \times \frac{1 \text{ mole CaCl}_2}{110.98 \text{ g CaCl}_2} \times \frac{1 \text{ mole CaCO}_3}{1 \text{ mole CaCl}_2} \times \frac{1 \text{ mole pos. ions}}{1 \text{ mole CaCO}_3}$$

$$\times \frac{6.022 \times 10^{23} \text{ pos. ions}}{1 \text{ mole pos. ions}} = 2.7131015 \times 10^{24} \text{ (calc)} = 2.713 \times 10^{24} \text{ pos. ions (corr)}$$

Total = $[5.426 \times 10^{24} + 2.713 \times 10^{24}] = 8.139 \times 10^{24}$ positive ions (calc and corr)

10.141 $$10.0 \text{ g AgBr} \times \frac{1 \text{ mole AgBr}}{187.77 \text{ g AgBr}} \times \frac{1 \text{ mole NaBr}}{1 \text{ mole AgBr}} \times \frac{102.89 \text{ g NaBr}}{1 \text{ mole NaBr}} \times \frac{100 \text{ g solution}}{6.00 \text{ g NaBr}}$$

$$\times \frac{1 \text{ mL solution}}{1.046 \text{ g solution}} = 87.310008 \text{ (calc)} = 87.3 \text{ mL solution (corr)}$$

10.143 % yield can be expressed as either $\dfrac{\text{g (actual)}}{\text{g (theoretical)}} \times 100$ or $\dfrac{\text{moles (actual)}}{\text{moles (theoretical)}} \times 100$

$$75.0 \text{ mL NH}_3 \times \frac{10^{-3} \text{ L NH}_3}{1 \text{ mL NH}_3} \times \frac{0.695 \text{ g NH}_3}{1 \text{ L NH}_3} \times \frac{1 \text{ mole NH}_3}{17.04 \text{ g NH}_3} \times \frac{4 \text{ moles NO (theoretical)}}{4 \text{ moles NH}_3}$$

$$x \frac{0.852 \text{ mole NO (actual)}}{1 \text{ mole NO (theoretical)}} \times \frac{2 \text{ moles } NO_2 \text{ (theoretical)}}{2 \text{ moles NO (actual)}} \times \frac{0.827 \text{ mole } NO_2 \text{ (actual)}}{1 \text{ mole } NO_2 \text{ (theoretical)}}$$

$$x \frac{2 \text{ moles } HNO_3 \text{ (theoretical)}}{3 \text{ moles } NO_2 \text{ (actual)}} \times \frac{0.870 \text{ mole } HNO_3 \text{ (actual)}}{1 \text{ mole } HNO_3 \text{ (theoretical)}} \times \frac{63.02 \text{ g } HNO_3 \text{ (actual)}}{1 \text{ mole } HNO_3 \text{ (actual)}}$$

$$= 0.0787821 \text{ (calc)} = 0.0788 \text{ g } HNO_3 \text{ (corr)}$$

10.145 The balanced equations are: $S + O_2 \rightarrow SO_2$ and $CaO + SO_2 \rightarrow CaSO_3$.

$$1.0 \text{ ton coal} \times \frac{2000 \text{ lb coal}}{1.0 \text{ ton coal}} \times \frac{453.6 \text{ g coal}}{1 \text{ lb coal}} \times \frac{4.3 \text{ g S}}{100 \text{ g coal}} \times \frac{1 \text{ mole S}}{32.06 \text{ g S}} \times \frac{1 \text{ mole } SO_2}{1 \text{ mole S}}$$

$$x \frac{1 \text{ mole } CaSO_3}{1 \text{ mole } SO_2} \times \frac{120.14 \text{ g } CaSO_3}{1 \text{ mole } CaSO_3} \times \frac{1 \text{ lb } CaSO_3}{453.6 \text{ g } CaSO_3} \times \frac{1 \text{ ton } CaSO_3}{2000 \text{ lb } CaSO_3}$$

$$= 0.161136 \text{ (calc)} = 0.16 \text{ ton } CaSO_3 \text{ (corr)}$$

CHAPTER ELEVEN
States of Matter

PRACTICE PROBLEMS

States of Matter (Secs. 11.1 and 11.2)

11.1 a) gaseous b) liquid c) gaseous d) gaseous

11.3 a) both gases b) liquid and solid c) both gases d) both solids

Kinetic Molecular Theory (Secs. 11.3 through 11.6)

11.5 a) potential b) kinetic c) potential d) potential

11.7 a) direct; the average velocity increases as the temperature increases and vice versa
b) potential (attractive)
c) direct; the higher the temperature, the higher the disruptive forces
d) all three; the disruptive forces are predominant in gases and the cohesive forces are more dominant in solids

11.9 a) solid b) liquid c) solid d) solid or liquid

11.11 a) The predominant cohesive forces in the solid hold the particles in essentially fixed position.
b) The gas particles are widely separated (disruptive forces). The solid and liquid particles have very little space between them (cohesive forces). The space between the particles can be decreased greatly in gases, but not in solids or liquids.
c) The cohesive forces are dominant enough that changing the temperature has only a small effect on the space between particles.
d) The disruptive forces in a gas are so dominant that each particle can act independently of the others.

Physical Changes of State (Sec. 11.8)

11.13 a) exothermic, endothermic   b) both endothermic
c) both exothermic   d) exothermic, endothermic

11.15 a) solid, liquid b) both gases c) liquid, solid d) solid, gas

11.17 a) opposite changes b) not opposite c) not opposite d) opposite changes

Heat Energy and Specific Heat (Sec. 11.9)

11.19 a) $2290 \text{ kJ} \times \dfrac{10^3 \text{ J}}{1 \text{ kJ}} = 2.29 \times 10^6 \text{ J}$ (calc and corr)

b) $2290 \text{ kJ} \times \dfrac{1 \text{ kcal}}{4.184 \text{ kJ}} = 547.32313$ (calc) $= 547 \text{ kcal}$ (corr)

c) $2290 \text{ kJ} \times \dfrac{1 \text{ kcal}}{4.184 \text{ kJ}} \times \dfrac{10^3 \text{ cal}}{1 \text{ kcal}} = 5.4732313 \times 10^5$ (calc) $= 5.47 \times 10^5 \text{ cal}$ (corr)

d) $2290 \text{ kJ} \times \dfrac{1 \text{ kcal}}{4.184 \text{ kJ}} \times \dfrac{1 \text{ Cal}}{1 \text{ kcal}} = 547.32313$ (calc) $= 547 \text{ Cal}$ (corr)

11.21   a) $2290 \text{ kJ} \times \dfrac{10^3 \text{J}}{1 \text{ kJ}} = 2,290,000 \text{ J (calc)} = 2.29 \times 10^6 \text{ J (corr)}$

      b) $2290 \text{ kJ} \times \dfrac{1.0 \text{ kcal}}{4.181 \text{ kJ}} = 547.32314 \text{ kcal (calc)} = 547 \text{ kcal (corr)}$

      c) $2290 \text{ kJ} \times \dfrac{10^3 \text{ J}}{1 \text{ kJ}} \times \dfrac{1 \text{ calories}}{4.184 \text{ J}} = 547323.14 \text{ calories} = 5.47 \times 10^5 \text{ calories (corr)}$

      d) $2290 \text{ kJ} \times \dfrac{1 \text{ kcal}}{4.184 \text{ kJ}} \times \dfrac{1 \text{ Calorie}}{1 \text{ kcal}} = 547.3425 \text{ Calories (calc)} = 547 \text{ Calories (corr)}$

11.23   In Table 11.2 the specific heat of copper is 0.382 J/g °C
$\Delta t = (34.7 - 23.0) \, ^\circ\text{C} = 11.7 \, ^\circ\text{C}$

$\dfrac{0.382 \text{ J}}{\text{g } ^\circ\text{C}} \times 25.0 \text{ g} \times 11.7 \, ^\circ\text{C} = 111.735 \text{ (calc)} = 112 \text{ J (corr)}$

11.25   In Table 11.2 the specific heat of water is 4.18 J/g °C. Using this as a conversion factor and inverting gives

$\dfrac{145 \text{ J}}{4.18 \dfrac{\text{J}}{\text{g } ^\circ\text{C}} \times 7.73 \text{ g}} = 4.4875802 \text{ (calc)} = 4.5 \, ^\circ\text{C (corr) above } 43.2 \, ^\circ\text{C} = 47.7 \, ^\circ\text{C}$

11.27 $g = \dfrac{422 \text{ J}}{0.908 \dfrac{\text{J}}{\text{g } ^\circ\text{C}} \times 295 \, ^\circ\text{C}} = 1.5754499 \text{ (calc)} = 1.58 \text{ g (corr)}$

11.29   specific heat $= \dfrac{46.9 \text{ J}}{40.0 \text{ g} \times 3.0 \, ^\circ\text{C}} = 0.3908333 \text{ (calc)} = 0.39 \dfrac{\text{J}}{\text{g } ^\circ\text{C}} \text{ (corr)}$

11.31   Heat capacity of 40.0 g gold = 40.0 g × 0.13 J/g °C = 5.2 J/ °C (calc and corr)
Heat capacity of 80.0 g copper = 80.0 g × 0.382 J/g °C = 30.56 (calc) = 30.6 J/°C (corr)
∴ heat capacity of 80.0 g copper is higher.

11.33   Specific heat $= \dfrac{28.7 \dfrac{\text{J}}{^\circ\text{C}}}{75.1 \text{ g}} = 0.3821571 \text{ (calc)} = 0.382 \dfrac{\text{J}}{\text{g } ^\circ\text{C}} \text{ (corr)}$

11.35   Heat gained = heat lost

$0.382 \dfrac{\text{J}}{\text{g } ^\circ\text{C}} \times X \text{ g} \times 20 \, ^\circ\text{C} = 4.18 \dfrac{\text{J}}{\text{g } ^\circ\text{C}} \times 1.0 \text{ g} \times 85 \, ^\circ\text{C}$

Solving for X:

$$X = \frac{4.18 \; \frac{J}{g\, °C} \times 1.0 \text{ g} \times 85 \, °C}{0.382 \; \frac{J}{g\, °C} \times 20 \, °C} = 46.505236 \text{ (calc)} = 47 \text{ g (corr)}$$

Energy and Changes of State (Sec. 11.11)

11.37   Molar mass of benzene, C_6H_6, is 78.11 g/mol. Therefore,

$$395 \; \frac{J}{g} \times \frac{78.11 g}{1 mol} \times \frac{10^{-3} kJ}{1 J} = 30.85345 kJ/mol \text{ (calc)} = 30.9 \, kJ/mol \text{ (corr)}$$

11.39   a) heat of solidification   b) heat of condensation
c) heat of fusion   d) heat of vaporization

11.41   a) 50.0 g Al x $\dfrac{393 \text{ J}}{\text{g Al}}$ = 19650 (calc) = 1.96×10^4 J released (corr)

b) 50.0 g steam x $\dfrac{2260 \text{ J}}{\text{g steam}}$ = 113,000 (calc) or 1.13×10^5 J released (corr)

c) 50.0 g Cu x $\dfrac{205 \text{ J}}{\text{g Cu}}$ = 10,250 (calc) = 1.02×10^4 J absorbed (corr)

d) 50.0 g H_2O x $\dfrac{2260 \text{ J}}{\text{g } H_2O}$ = 113,000 (calc) or 1.13×10^5 J absorbed (corr)

11.43   The same amount, 6680 J

11.45 $\dfrac{1.00 \text{ mole } Na_2SO_4 \times 80.93 \; \frac{kJ}{mole} \; Na_2SO_4}{1.00 \text{ mole NaOH} \times 15.79 \; \frac{kJ}{mole} \; \text{NaOH}}$ = 5.1253958 (calc) = 5.13 times as much (corr)

11.47   115 kJ x $\dfrac{1 \text{ mole } CCl_4}{30.0 \text{ kJ}}$ = 3.8333333 (calc) = 3.83 moles CCl_4 (corr)

11.49   Heat of fusion for A: $\dfrac{1016 \text{ J}}{3.25 \text{ g}}$ = 312.61538 (calc) = 313 J/g (corr)

Heat of fusion for B: $\dfrac{983 \text{ J}}{3.20 \text{ g}}$ = 307.1875 (calc) = 307 J/g (corr)

A has the higher heat of fusion by 6 J/g

11.51   7.00 g Na x $\dfrac{1 \text{ mole Na}}{22.99 \text{ g Na}}$ x $\dfrac{2.40 \text{ kJ}}{1 \text{ mole Na}}$ x $\dfrac{10^3 \text{ J}}{1 \text{ kJ}}$ = 730.7525 (calc) = 7.31×10^2 J (corr)

Heat Energy Calculations (Sec. 11.12)

11.53

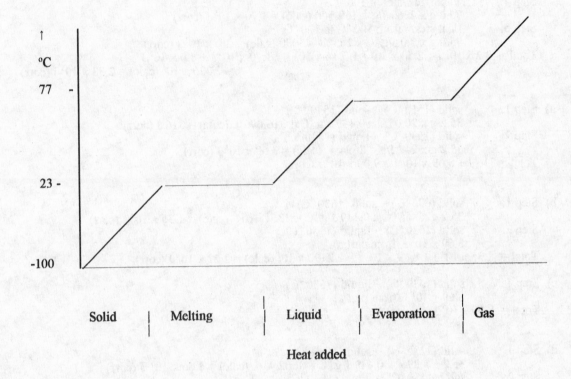

11.55 specific heat ice = 2.1 J/g °C   heat of fusion = 334 J/g
       specific heat water = 4.18 J/g °C   heat of vaporization = 2260 J/g
       specific heat steam = 2.0 J/g °C

a) Step 1:   Heat ice from – 20 °C to ice at – 5 °C.
               Q = 75.0 g ice x 2.1 J/g °C x 15 °C = 2362.5 (calc) = 2.4 x 10^3 J (corr)

b) Step 1:   Heat ice from – 20 °C to ice at 0 °C.
               Q = 75.0 g x 2.1 J/g °C x 20. °C = 3150 (calc) = 3.2 x 10^3 J (corr)
   Step 2:   Melt ice at 0 °C to water at 0 °C.
               Q = 75.0 g x 334 J/g = 25,050 (calc) = 2.50 x 10^4 J (corr)
   Step 3:   Heat water from 0 °C to 25 °C.
               Q = 75.0 g x 4.18 J/g °C x 25 °C = 7837.5 (calc) = 7.8 x 10^3 J (corr)
   Total = 3.2 x 10^3 J + 2.50 x 10^4 J + 7.8 x 10^3 J = 36,000 (calc) = 3.60 x 10^4 J (corr)

c) Step 1:   Heat ice from – 20 °C to ice at 0 °C.
               Q = 75.0 g x 2.1 J/g °C x 20. °C = 3150 (calc) = 3.2 x 10^3 J (corr)
   Step 2:   Melt ice at 0 °C to water at 0 °C.
               Q = 75.0 g x 334 J/g = 25,050 (calc) = 2.50 x 10^4 J (corr)
   Step 3:   Heat water from 0 °C to 100 °C.
               75.0 g H_2O x 4.18 J/g °C x 100 °C = 31,350 (calc) = 3.14 x 10^4 J (corr)
   Step 4:   Vaporize water at 100 °C.
               75.0 g x 2260 J/g = 169,500 (calc) = 1.70 x 10^5 J (corr)
   Total = 0.32 x 10^4 J + 2.50 x 10^4 J + 3.14 x 10^4 J + 17.0 x 10^4 J
                                                    = 2.296 x 10^5 (calc) = 2.30 x 10^5 J (corr)

d) Step 1:   Heat ice from $-20\ ^{\circ}C$ to ice at $0\ ^{\circ}C$.
$Q = 75.0\ g \times 2.1\ J/g\ ^{\circ}C \times 20.\ ^{\circ}C = 3150$ (calc) $= 3.2 \times 10^3$ J (corr)

Step 2:   Melt ice at $0\ ^{\circ}C$ to water at $0\ ^{\circ}C$.
$Q = 75.0\ g \times 334\ J/g = 25,050$ (calc) $= 2.50 \times 10^4$ J (corr)

Step 3:   Heat water from $0\ ^{\circ}C$ to $100\ ^{\circ}C$.
$75.0\ g\ H_2O \times 4.18\ J/g\ ^{\circ}C \times 100\ ^{\circ}C = 31,350$ (calc) $= 3.14 \times 10^4$ J (corr)

Step 4:   Vaporize water at $100\ ^{\circ}C$.
$75.0\ g \times 2260\ J/g = 169,500$ (calc) $= 1.70 \times 10^5$ J (corr)

Step 5:   Heat steam from $100\ ^{\circ}C$ to $120\ ^{\circ}C$.
$75.0\ g \times 2.0\ J/g\ ^{\circ}C \times 20.\ ^{\circ}C = 3000$ (calc) $= 3.0 \times 10^3$ J (corr)

Total $= 3.2 \times 10^3$ J $+ 2.50 \times 10^4$ J $+ 3.14 \times 10^4$ J $+ 1.70 \times 10^5$ J $+ 3.0 \times 10^3$ J
$= 2.326 \times 10^5$ (calc) $= 2.33 \times 10^5$ J (corr)

11.57 a) Step 1:   solid (1510 °C) → solid (1530 °C)
$35.2\ g \times 20.0\ ^{\circ}C \times 0.449\ J/g\ ^{\circ}C = 316.096$ J (calc) $= 316$ J (corr)

Step 2:   solid (1530 °C) → liquid (1530 °C)
$35.2\ g \times 247\ J/g = 8694.4$ (calc) $= 8.69 \times 10^3$ J (corr)

Total $= 316$ J $+ 8.69 \times 10^3$ J $= 9.00 \times 10^3$ J (corr)

b) Step 1:   solid (675 °C) → solid (1530 °C)
$35.2\ g \times 855\ ^{\circ}C \times 0.449\ J/g\ ^{\circ}C = 13513.104$ (calc) $= 1.35 \times 10^4$ J (corr)

Step 2:   solid (1530 °C) → liquid (1530 °C)
8.69×10^3 J (from part a)

Total $= 1.35 \times 10^4$ J $+ 8.69 \times 10^3$ J $= 2.2190 \times 10^4$ (calc) $= 2.22 \times 10^4$ J (corr)

c) Step 1:   solid (1530 °C) → liquid (1530 °C)
8.69×10^3 J (from part a)

Total $= 8.69 \times 10^3$ J

d) Step 1:   solid (1235 °C) → solid (1530 °C)
$35.2\ g \times 295^{\circ} \times 0.449\ J/g\ ^{\circ}C = 4662.416$ (calc) $= 4.66 \times 10^3$ J (corr)

Step 2:   solid (1530 °C) → liquid (1530 °C)
8.69×10^3 J (from part a)

Total $= 4.66 \times 10^3$ J $+ 8.69 \times 10^3$ J $= 1.335 \times 10^4$ (calc) $= 1.34 \times 10^4$ J (corr)

11.59 Step 1: solid (–135 °C) → solid (–117 °C)
$15.0\ g \times 18\ ^{\circ}C \times 0.97\ J/g\ ^{\circ}C = 261.9$ (calc) $= 2.6 \times 10^2$ J (corr)

Step 2: solid (–117 °C) → liquid (–117 °C)
$15.0\ g \times 109\ J/g = 1635$ J (calc) $= 1.64 \times 10^3$ J (corr)

Step 3: liquid (–117 °C) → liquid (78° C)
$15.0\ g \times 195\ ^{\circ}C \times 2.3\ J/g\ ^{\circ}C = 6827$ (calc) $= 6.7 \times 10^3$ J (corr)

Step 4: liquid (78 °C) → gas (78 °C)
$15.0\ g \times 837\ J/g = 12,555$ (calc) $= 1.26 \times 10^4$ J (corr)

Step 5: gas (78 °C) → gas (95 °C)
$15.0\ g \times 17\ ^{\circ}C \times 0.95\ J/g\ ^{\circ}C = 242.25$ J (calc) $= 2.40 \times 10^2$ J (corr)

Total $= 2.6 \times 10^2$ J $+ 1.64 \times 10^3$ J $+ 6.7 \times 10^3$ J $+ 1.26 \times 10^4$ J $+ 2.40 \times 10^2$ J
$= 21,440$ (calc) $= 2.14 \times 10^4$ J (corr)

Properties of Liquids (Sec. 11.13 through 11.15)

11.61 a) boiling point   b) vapor pressure   c) boiling   d) boiling point

11.63 a) Increasing the temperature increases the average kinetic energy of the particles, enabling more molecules to evaporate.
b) The boiling point is lower; reactions occur more slowly at lower temperatures.
c) The boiling point is higher; reactions occur more rapidly at higher temperatures.

d) The particles leaving have higher than average kinetic energy. The particles remaining as liquid have a lower average kinetic energy and a lower temperature.

11.65 a) increase
   b) no change – the rate of evaporation depends on the temperature, the cohesive forces present in the liquid and the surface area where evaporation can occur. The concentration of air molecules above the liquid have a slight effect on the rate at which condensation of the vapor can occur. The *net* evaporation rate, the evaporation rate minus the condensation rate, may increase slightly at higher elevations, but the absolute rate of evaporation would not change.
   c) increase – the liquid surface area has increased
   d) no change

11.67 a) no change   b) decrease   c) no change   d) no change

11.69 a) increase
   b) no change – the rate of evaporation depends on the temperature the cohesive forces present in the liquid, and the surface area where evaporation can occur. The concentration of air molecules above the liquid have a slight effect on the rate at which condensation of the vapor can occur. The *net* evaporation rate, the evaporation rate minus the condensation rate, may increase slightly at higher elevations, but the absolute rate of evaporation would not change. This will make the vapor pressure increase very slightly.
   c) no change
   d) no change

11.71 B must have lower cohesive forces between particles than A to make B evaporate faster.

11.73 In comparing substances, at the same temperature, the substance with the highest vapor pressure is the most volatile. Therefore, CS_2 is more volatile.

Intermolecular Forces in Liquids (Sec. 11.16)

11.75 Since dipole-dipole interactions occur between polar molecules, polar molecules must be present.

11.77 The stronger the intermolecular forces, the higher the boiling point.

11.79 a) London forces   b) hydrogen bonds
   c) dipole-dipole interactions   d) London forces

11.81 a) no   b) yes   c) yes   d) no

11.83 a) Cl_2, larger mass   b) HF, hydrogen bonding
   c) NO, dipole-dipole   d) C_2H_6, larger size

11.85 a) As larger molecules have greater polarizability, $SiH_4 > CH_4$
   b) As larger molecules have greater polarizability, $SiCl_4 > SiH_4$
   c) As larger molecules have greater polarizability, $GeBr_4 > SiCl_4$
   d) As larger molecules have greater polarizability, $C2H_4 > N_2$.

Types of Solids (Sec. 11.17)

11.87 a) true   b) false   c) true   d) false

11.89 a) NaCl, ionic solid vs nonpolar molecular
   b) SiO_2, macromolecular vs nonpolar molecular
   c) Cu, metallic vs polar molecular and Cu is larger
   d) MgO, higher ionic charges on Mg^{2+} and O^{2-} vs Na^+ and F^-

ADDITIONAL PROBLEMS

11.91   a) $SnCl_4$ b) SnI_4 c) SnI_4 d) SnI_4

11.93 $50.0 \text{ g} \times \dfrac{4.18 \text{ J}}{\text{g} \cdot ^\circ\text{C}} \times 80.0 \,^\circ\text{C} = 16{,}720 \text{ (calc)} = 1.6 \times 10^4 \text{ J (corr)}$

$50.0 \text{ g} \times \dfrac{2260 \text{ J}}{\text{g}} = 113{,}000 \text{ (calc)} = 1.13 \times 10^5 \text{ J (corr)}$

The vaporizing takes longer because it requires more heat energy.

11.95   Let X = grams of ice added

Heat gained by ice: $X \text{ g} \times \dfrac{334 \text{ J}}{\text{g}} = 334 \cdot X \text{ J (calc and corr)}$

Heat lost by water: $40.0 \text{ g} \times \dfrac{4.18 \text{ J}}{\text{g} \cdot ^\circ\text{C}} \times 19.0 \,^\circ\text{C} = 3176.8 \text{ (calc)} = 3180 \text{ J (corr)}$

Heat lost = heat gained: $3180 \text{ J} = 334 \cdot X \text{ J}$
$X = 9.520958 \text{ (calc)} = 9.52 \text{ g (corr)}$

11.97   Let X = final temperature of water in °C
Heat lost by water:
Water (80.0 °C) → water (X °C)

$30.0 \text{ g} \times (80.0 - X) \,^\circ\text{C} \times \dfrac{4.18 \text{ J}}{\text{g} \cdot ^\circ\text{C}} = (10{,}032 - 125.4 \cdot X) \text{ (calc)} = (1\overline{0}{,}\overline{0}00 - 125 \cdot X) \text{ J (corr)}$

Heat gained by ice:
Step 1: ice (– 10 °C) → ice (0 °C): $10.0 \text{ g} \times 10.0 \,^\circ\text{C} \times 2.1 \text{ J/g} \,^\circ\text{C} = 210 \text{ J (calc and corr)}$
Step 2: ice (0 °C) → water (0 °C): $10.0 \text{ g} \times 334 \text{ J/g} = 3340 \text{ J (calc and corr)}$
Step 3: water (0 °C) → water (X °C): $10.0 \text{ g} \times X \,^\circ\text{C} \times 4.18 \text{ J/g} \,^\circ\text{C}$
                                                                                                    $= 41.8 \cdot X \text{ J (calc and corr)}$

Total = $(210 \text{ J} + 3340 \text{ J} + 41.8 \cdot X \text{ J}) = (3550 + 41.8 \cdot X) \text{ J (calc and corr)}$
Heat lost = heat gained: $(1\overline{0}{,}\overline{0}00 - 125 \cdot X) \text{ J} = (3550 + 41.8 \cdot X) \text{ J}$
$6450 \text{ J} = (166.8 \cdot X) \text{ J (calc)}$
$6400 \text{ J} = (167 \cdot X) \text{ J (corr)}$
$X = 38.323353 \text{ (calc)} = 38.3 \,^\circ\text{C (corr)}$

11.99   Let X = specific heat of metal
Heat lost = heat gained

$500.0 \text{ g} \times X \dfrac{\text{J}}{\text{g} \cdot ^\circ\text{C}} \times 26.6 \,^\circ\text{C} = 100.0 \text{ g} \times \dfrac{4.18 \text{ J}}{\text{g} \cdot ^\circ\text{C}} \times 13.4 \,^\circ\text{C}$
$13{,}300 \cdot X = 5601.2 \text{ (calc)}$
$13{,}300 \cdot X = 56\overline{0}0 \text{ (corr)}$
$X = 0.42105263 \text{ (calc)} = 0.421 \text{ J/g} \,^\circ\text{C (corr)}$

11.101 $4.3 \text{ min} \times \dfrac{60 \text{ sec}}{1 \text{ min}} \times \dfrac{136 \text{ J}}{\text{sec}} = 35{,}088 \text{ J (calc)} = 35{,}000 \text{ J (corr)}$

$\dfrac{35{,}000 \text{ J}}{25.3 \text{ g}} = 1383.3992 \text{ (calc)} = 1.4 \times 10^3 \text{ J/g (corr)}$

CUMULATIVE PROBLEMS

11.103 $2.50 \text{ moles Ag} \times \dfrac{107.87 \text{ g Ag}}{1 \text{ mole Ag}} \times \dfrac{0.24 \text{ J}}{\text{g }^\circ\text{C}} \times 10.0 \,^\circ\text{C} = 647.22 \text{ (calc)} = 6.5 \times 10^2 \text{ J (corr)}$

11.105 $5.7 \text{ L blood} \times \dfrac{1 \text{ mL}}{10^{-3} \text{ L}} \times \dfrac{1.06 \text{ g}}{1 \text{ mL}} = 6042 \text{ (calc)} = 6\overline{0}00 \text{ g blood (corr)}$

$\text{heat required} = 4.18 \dfrac{\text{J}}{\text{g }^\circ\text{C}} \times 6\overline{0}00 \text{ g} \times 1.0 \text{ C}^\circ \times \dfrac{1 \text{ kJ}}{10^3 \text{ J}} = 25.08 \text{ (calc)} = 25 \text{ kJ (corr)}$

11.107 $\text{specific heat} = \dfrac{59.5 \text{ J}}{35.0 \text{ g} \times 1.0 \,^\circ\text{C}} = 1.7 \dfrac{\text{J}}{\text{g }^\circ\text{C}} \text{ (calc and corr)}$

The unknown is likely a mixture of A and B since the specific heat is intermediate between that for pure A and that for pure B.

11.109 $\dfrac{10.0 \text{ g}}{1485 \text{ J}} \times \dfrac{1151 \text{ J}}{10.0 \text{ mL}} = 0.77508417 \text{ (calc)} = 0.775 \text{ g/mL (corr)}$

11.111 $\dfrac{1.00 \text{ g}}{602 \text{ J}} \times \dfrac{10^3 \text{ J}}{1 \text{ kJ}} \times \dfrac{18.1 \text{ kJ}}{1 \text{ mole}} = 30.066445183 \text{ (calc)} = 30.1 \text{ g/mole (corr)}$

molecular mass = 30.1 amu

11.113 $2Cu_2O \rightarrow 4Cu + O_2$

$52.0 \text{ g Cu}_2\text{O} \times \dfrac{1 \text{ mole Cu}_2\text{O}}{143.10 \text{ g Cu}_2\text{O}} \times \dfrac{4 \text{ moles Cu}}{2 \text{ moles Cu}_2\text{O}} \times \dfrac{13.0 \text{ kJ}}{1 \text{ mole Cu}}$

11.115 $6.32 \times 10^{24} \text{ H atoms} \times \dfrac{1 \text{ mole H}}{6.022 \times 10^{23} \text{ H atoms}} \times \dfrac{1 \text{ mole C}_6\text{H}_6}{6 \text{ moles H}} \times \dfrac{78.12 \text{ g C}_6\text{H}_6}{1 \text{ mole C}_6\text{H}_6}$

$\times \dfrac{1.74 \text{ J}}{\text{g (C}_6\text{H}_6) \,^\circ\text{C}} \times 10 \,^\circ\text{C} = 2377.5878 \text{ (calc)} = 2.38 \times 10^3 \text{ J (corr)}$

11.117 Volume of water per sec:

$\dfrac{3.3 \times 10^6 \text{ kJ}}{\text{sec}} \times \dfrac{10^3 \text{ J}}{1 \text{ kJ}} \times \dfrac{1 \text{ g H}_2\text{O}}{2420 \text{ J}} \times \dfrac{1 \text{ mL H}_2\text{O}}{0.997 \text{ g H}_2\text{O}} \times \dfrac{10^{-3} \text{ L H}_2\text{O}}{1 \text{ mL H}_2\text{O}} \times \dfrac{1 \text{ qt H}_2\text{O}}{0.9463 \text{ L H}_2\text{O}}$

$\times \dfrac{1 \text{ gal H}_2\text{O}}{4 \text{ qt H}_2\text{O}} \times \dfrac{60 \text{ sec}}{1 \text{ min}} \times \dfrac{60 \text{ min}}{1 \text{ hr}} \times \dfrac{24 \text{ hr}}{1 \text{ day}}$

$= 3.1219671 \times 10^7 \text{ (calc)} = 3.1 \times 10^7 \text{ gal/day (corr)}$

CHAPTER TWELVE
Gas Laws

PRACTICE PROBLEMS

Measurement of Pressure (Sec. 12.2)

12.1   a) $6.20 \text{ atm} \times \dfrac{760 \text{ mm Hg}}{1 \text{ atm}} = 4712. \text{ (calc)} = 4.71 \times 10^3 \text{ mm Hg (corr)}$

   b) $6.20 \text{ atm} \times \dfrac{29.92 \text{ in. Hg}}{1 \text{ atm}} = 185.504 \text{ (calc)} = 186 \text{ in. Hg (corr)}$

   c) $6.20 \text{ atm} \times \dfrac{14.68 \text{ psi}}{1 \text{ atm}} = 91.016 \text{ (calc)} = 91.0 \text{ psi (corr)}$

   d) $6.20 \text{ atm} \times \dfrac{760 \text{ mm Hg}}{1 \text{ atm}} \times \dfrac{1 \times 10^{-3} \text{ m}}{1 \text{ mm}} \times \dfrac{1 \text{ cm}}{1 \times 10^{-2} \text{ m}} = 471.2 \text{ (calc)} = 471 \text{ cm Hg (corr)}$

12.3   a) smaller, 1 atm = 760 mm Hg
   b) equal, both 1 atm
   c) larger, 585 mm Hg < 1 atm; 29.92 in. Hg = 1 atm
   d) equal, $4.639 \text{ atm} \times \dfrac{14.68 \text{ psi}}{1 \text{ atm}} = 68.10052 \text{ (calc)} = 68.10 \text{ psi (corr)}$

12.5   (762 + 237) mm Hg = 999 mm Hg (calc and corr)

Boyle's Law (Sec. 12.3)

12.7   a) decrease   b) increase   c) decrease   d) decrease

12.9   For this problem, $V_2 = V_1 \cdot \dfrac{P_1}{P_2}$, where $V_1 = 2.00$ L and $P_1 = 2.00$ atm

   a) $V_2 = 2.00 \text{ L} \times \dfrac{2.00 \text{ atm}}{3.13 \text{ atm}} = 1.2779553 \text{ (calc)} = 1.28 \text{ L (corr)}$

   b) $V_2 = 2.00 \text{ L} \times \dfrac{2.00 \text{ atm}}{0.723 \text{ atm}} = 5.5325035 \text{ (calc)} = 5.53 \text{ L (corr)}$
   c) Convert 762 mm Hg to atm:

   $762 \text{ mm Hg} \times \dfrac{1 \text{ atm}}{760 \text{ mm Hg}} = 1.0026316 \text{ (calc)} = 1.00 \text{ atm (corr)}$

   $V_2 = 2.00 \text{ L} \times \dfrac{2.00 \text{ atm}}{1.00 \text{ atm}} = 4 \text{ (calc)} = 4.00 \text{ L (corr)}$
   d) Convert 37.2 mm Hg to atm:

   $37.2 \text{ mm Hg} \times \dfrac{1 \text{ atm}}{760 \text{ mm Hg}} = 0.0489474 \text{ (calc)} = 0.0489 \text{ atm (corr)}$

   $V_2 = 2.00 \text{ L} \times \dfrac{2.00 \text{ atm}}{0.0489 \text{ atm}} = 81.7995910 \text{ (calc)} = 81.8 \text{ L (corr)}$

12.11   In this problem, V_1 is the unknown original volume in mL. V_2 is the given final volume.

$P_1 = 4.0$ atm, $P_2 = 2.5$ atm. Solve $P_1V_1 = P_2V_2$ for V_1: $V_1 = V_2 \cdot \dfrac{P_2}{P_1}$

a) $V_1 = 425$ mL $\times \dfrac{2.5 \text{ atm}}{4.0 \text{ atm}} = 256.625$ (calc) $= 2.6 \times 10^2$ mL (corr)

b) $V_1 = 25.4$ mL $\times \dfrac{2.5 \text{ atm}}{4.0 \text{ atm}} = 15.875$ (calc) $= 16$ mL (corr)

c) $V_1 = 1.08$ L $\times \dfrac{2.5 \text{ atm}}{4.0 \text{ atm}} = 0.675$ (calc) $= 0.68$ L (corr)

convert L to mL: 0.68 L $\times \dfrac{1 \text{ mL}}{10^{-3} \text{ L}} = 6.8 \times 10^2$ mL

d) $V_1 = 4.68$ L $\times \dfrac{2.5 \text{ atm}}{4.0 \text{ atm}} = 2.925$ (calc) $= 2.9$ L (corr)

convert L to mL: 2.9 L $\times \dfrac{1 \text{ mL}}{10^{-3} \text{ L}} = 2.9 \times 10^3$ mL

12.13 $P_2 = P_1 \cdot \dfrac{V_1}{V_2}$, where $V_2 = \frac{1}{3}V_1$ or $V_1 = 3V_2$

$P_2 = 645$ mm Hg $\times \dfrac{3V_2}{V_2} = 1935$ (calc) $= 1.94 \times 10^3$ mm Hg (corr)

Charles's Law (Sec. 12.4)

12.15   a) increase   b) decrease   c) increase   d) decrease

12.17   Solve $\dfrac{V_1}{T_1} = \dfrac{V_2}{T_2}$ for V_2: $V_2 = V_1 \cdot \dfrac{T_2}{T_1}$ where $V_1 = 5.00$ L and $T_1 = 35\ ^\circ\text{C} + 273 = 308$ K

a) $T_2 = 125\ ^\circ\text{C} + 273 = 398$ K

$V_2 = 5.00$ L $\times \dfrac{398 \text{ K}}{308 \text{ K}} = 6.4610390$ (calc) $= 6.46$ L (corr)

b) $T_2 = 5\ ^\circ\text{C} + 273 = 278$ K

$V_2 = 5.00$ L $\times \dfrac{278 \text{ K}}{308 \text{ K}} = 4.5129870$ (calc) $= 4.51$ L (corr)

c) $T_2 = -5\ ^\circ\text{C} + 273 = 268$ K

$V_2 = 5.00$ L $\times \dfrac{268 \text{ K}}{308 \text{ K}} = 4.3506494$ (calc) $= 4.35$ L (corr)

d) $T_2 = 273 + 985 = 1258$ (calc) $= 1260$ K (corr)

$V_2 = 5.00$ L $\times \dfrac{1260 \text{ K}}{308 \text{ K}} = 20.4545455$ (calc) $= 20.5$ L (corr)

12.19   For this problem, V_1 is the unknown original volume, in mL, V_2 is the given final volume,

$T_1 = 73\ ^\circ\text{C} + 273 = 346$ K, and $T_2 = 273$ K. Solve $\dfrac{V_1}{T_1} = \dfrac{V_2}{T_2}$ for V_1: $V_1 = V_2 \cdot \dfrac{T_1}{T_2}$

a) $V_1 = 15.2$ mL x $\dfrac{346\ K}{273\ K}$ = 19.2644689 (calc) = 19.3 mL (corr)

b) $V_1 = 879$ mL x $\dfrac{346\ K}{273\ K}$ = 1114.043956 (calc) = 1.11 x 10^3 mL (corr)

c) $V_1 = 1.20$ L x $\dfrac{346\ K}{273\ K}$ = 1.5208791 (calc) = 1.52 L (corr)

  Convert L to mL: 1.52 L x $\dfrac{1\ mL}{10^{-3}\ L}$ = 1.52 x 10^3 mL

d) $V_1 = 10.7$ L x $\dfrac{346\ K}{273\ K}$ = 13.5611722 (calc) = 13.6 L (corr)

  Convert L to mL: 13.6 L x $\dfrac{1\ mL}{10^{-3}\ L}$ = 1.36 x 10^4 mL

12.21 Solve $\dfrac{V_1}{T_1} = \dfrac{V_2}{T_2}$ for T_2; $T_2 = T_1 \cdot \dfrac{V_2}{V_1}$ where T_1 = 24 °C + 273 = 297 K, $V_2 = \frac{1}{2}V_1$

T_2 = 297 K x $\dfrac{\frac{1}{2}V_1}{V_1}$ = 148.5 (calc) = 148 K (corr)

Converting to Celsius: 148 K − 273 = − 125 °C (calc and corr)

Gay-Lussac's Law (Sec. 12.5)

12.23 a) increase   b) decrease   c) increase   d) decrease

12.25 Solving $\dfrac{P_1}{T_1} = \dfrac{P_2}{T_2}$ for P_2 gives $P_2 = P_1 \cdot \dfrac{T_2}{T_1}$ where P_1 = 1.00; T_1 = 22 °C + 273 = 295 K

a) T_2 = 122 °C + 273 = 395 K;

  $P_2 = 1.00$ atm x $\dfrac{395\ K}{295\ K}$ = 1.3389831 (calc) = 1.34 atm (corr)

b) T_2 = 222 °C + 273 = 495 K;

  $P_2 = 1.00$ atm x $\dfrac{495\ K}{295\ K}$ = 1.6779661 (calc) = 1.68 atm (corr)

c) T_2 = 422 °C + 273 = 695 K;

  $P_2 = 1.00$ atm x $\dfrac{695\ K}{295\ K}$ = 2.3559322 (calc) = 2.36 atm (corr)

d) T_2 = 722 °C + 273 = 995 K;

  $P_2 = 1.00$ atm x $\dfrac{995\ K}{295\ K}$ = 3.3728814 (calc) = 3.37 atm (corr)

12.27 For this problem, P_1 is the unknown, original pressure, P_2 is the given final pressure, T_1 = 97 °C + 273 = 370 K, and T_2 = 27 °C + 273 = 300 K.

Solve $\dfrac{P_1}{T_1} = \dfrac{P_2}{T_2}$ for P_1; $P_1 = P_2 \cdot \dfrac{T_1}{T_2}$

a) $P_1 = 3.00$ atm x $\dfrac{370\ K}{300\ K}$ = 3.7 (calc) = 3.70 atm (corr)

b) $P_1 = 1.00$ atm x $\dfrac{370 \text{ K}}{300 \text{ K}} = 1.2333333$ (calc) = 1.23 atm (corr)

c) $P_1 = 1394$ mm Hg x $\dfrac{370 \text{ K}}{300 \text{ K}} = 1719.266667$ (calc) = 1719 mm Hg (corr)

Convert mm Hg to atm

1719 mm Hg x $\dfrac{1 \text{ atm}}{760 \text{ mm Hg}} = 2.2621929$ (calc) = 2.262 atm (corr)

d) $P_1 = 375$ mm Hg x $\dfrac{370 \text{ K}}{300 \text{ K}} = 462.5$ (calc) = 462 mm Hg (corr)

Convert mm Hg to atm

462 mm Hg x $\dfrac{1 \text{ atm}}{760 \text{ mm Hg}} = 0.60789474$ (calc) = 0.608 atm (corr)

12.29 $P_2 = P \cdot \dfrac{T_2}{T_1}$ where $T_1 = 24\ °C + 273 = 297$ K and $T_2 = 485\ °C + 273 = 758$ K

$P_2 = 1.2$ atm x $\dfrac{758 \text{ K}}{297 \text{ K}} = 3.0626262$ (calc) = 3.1 atm (corr)

The Combined Gas Law (Sec. 12.6)

12.31 a) $\dfrac{P_1V_1}{T_1} = \dfrac{P_2V_2}{T_2}$ Multiply both sides by T_1 and T_2, divide by P_1 and V_1

$\dfrac{T_2T_1}{P_1V_1} \cdot \dfrac{P_1V_1}{T_1} = \dfrac{P_2V_2}{T_2} \cdot \dfrac{T_2T_1}{P_1V_1}$ gives $T_2 = T_1 \cdot \dfrac{P_2}{P_1} \cdot \dfrac{V_2}{V_1}$

b) $\dfrac{P_1V_1}{T_1} \cdot \dfrac{P_2V_2}{T_2}$ Reverse the equation: $\dfrac{P_2V_2}{T_2} = \dfrac{P_1V_1}{T_1}$

Multiply both sides by T_2 and divide by P_1 and P_2

$\dfrac{P_2V_2}{T_2} \cdot \dfrac{T_2}{P_1P_2} = \dfrac{P_1V_1}{T_1} \cdot \dfrac{T_2}{P_1P_2}$ gives $\dfrac{V_2}{P_1} = \dfrac{V_1}{P_2} \cdot \dfrac{T_2}{T_1}$

12.33 $V_2 = V_1 \cdot \dfrac{P_1}{P_2} \cdot \dfrac{T_2}{T_1}$ where $V_1 = 3.00$ mL; $P_1 = 0.980$ atm; $T_1 = 230\ °C + 273 = 503$ K

a) $P_2 = 1.50$ atm; $T_2 = 185\ °C + 273 = 458$ K

$V_2 = 3.00$ mL x $\dfrac{0.980 \text{ atm}}{1.50 \text{ atm}}$ x $\dfrac{458 \text{ K}}{503 \text{ K}} = 1.7846521$ (calc) = 1.78 mL (corr)

b) $P_2 = 2.00$ atm; $T_2 = 35\ °C + 273 = 308$ K

$V_2 = 3.00$ mL x $\dfrac{0.980 \text{ atm}}{2.00 \text{ atm}}$ x $\dfrac{308 \text{ K}}{503 \text{ K}} = 0.9001193$ (calc) = 0.900 mL (corr)

c) $P_2 = 4.00$ atm; $T_2 = -35\ °C + 273 = 238$ K

$V_2 = 3.00$ mL x $\dfrac{0.980 \text{ atm}}{4.00 \text{ atm}}$ x $\dfrac{238 \text{ K}}{503 \text{ K}} = 0.3477734$ (calc) = 0.348 mL (corr)

d) $P_2 = 5.67$ atm; $T_2 = -125\ °C + 273 = 148$ K

$V_2 = 3.00$ mL x $\dfrac{0.980 \text{ atm}}{5.67 \text{ atm}}$ x $\dfrac{148 \text{ K}}{503 \text{ K}} = 0.1525661$ (calc) = 0.153 mL (corr)

12.35 a) $V_2 = V_1 \cdot \dfrac{P_1}{P_2} \cdot \dfrac{T_2}{T_1} = 15.2 \text{ L} \times \dfrac{1.35 \text{ atm}}{3.50 \text{ atm}} \times \dfrac{308 \text{ K}}{306 \text{ K}} = 5.9011764 \text{ (calc)} = 5.90 \text{ L (corr)}$

b) $15.2 \text{ L} = 15,200 \text{ mL}$

$V_2 = V_1 \cdot \dfrac{P_1}{P_2} \cdot \dfrac{T_2}{T_1} = 15,200 \text{ mL} \times \dfrac{1.35 \text{ atm}}{6.70 \text{ atm}} \times \dfrac{370 \text{ K}}{306 \text{ K}} = 3703.2485 \text{ (calc)}$

$= 3.70 \times 10^3 \text{ mL (corr)}$

c) $P_2 = P_1 \cdot \dfrac{V_1}{V_2} \cdot \dfrac{T_2}{T_1} = 1.35 \text{ atm} \times \dfrac{15.2 \text{ L}}{10.0 \text{ L}} \times \dfrac{315 \text{ K}}{306 \text{ K}} = 2.1123529 \text{ (calc)} = 2.11 \text{ atm (corr)}$

d) $T_2 = T_1 \cdot \dfrac{P_2}{P_1} \cdot \dfrac{V_2}{V_1} = 306 \text{ K} \times \dfrac{7.00 \text{ atm}}{1.35 \text{ atm}} \times \dfrac{0.973 \text{ L}}{15.2 \text{ L}} = 101.56754 \text{ (calc)} = 102 \text{ K (corr)}$

$= -171 \text{ }°C$

12.37 a) $375 \text{ mL} \times \dfrac{10^{-3} \text{ L}}{1 \text{ mL}} = 0.375 \text{ L}$

$P_2 = P_1 \cdot \dfrac{V_1}{V_2} = 1.03 \text{ atm} \times \dfrac{0.375 \text{ L}}{1.25 \text{ L}} = 0.309 \text{ atm (calc and corr)}$

$0.309 \text{ atm} \times \dfrac{760 \text{ mm Hg}}{1 \text{ atm}} = 234.84 \text{ (calc)} = 235 \text{ mm Hg (corr)}$

b) $T_1 = 27 \text{ }°C + 273 = 300 \text{ K}$

$T_2 = T_1 \cdot \dfrac{V_2}{V_1} = 300 \text{ K} \times \dfrac{1.25 \text{ L}}{0.375 \text{ L}} = 1000 \text{ K}$

Converting to Celsius, $1000 \text{ K} - 273 = 727 \text{ }°C$

12.39 $T_2 = T_1 \cdot \dfrac{P_2}{P_1} \cdot \dfrac{V_2}{V_1}$ where $T_1 = 33 \text{ }°C + 273 = 306 \text{ K}$.

a) $P_2 = 3P_1; V_2 = 3V_1$

$T_2 = 306 \text{ K} \times \dfrac{3P_1}{P_1} \times \dfrac{3V_1}{V_1} = 2754 \text{ (calc)} = 2750 \text{ K (corr)}$

Converting to Celsius: $2750 \text{ K} - 273 = 2477 \text{ (calc)} = 2.48 \times 10^3 \text{ }°C$

b) $P_2 = \frac{1}{2}P_1$ or $2P_2 = P_1$; $V_2 = \frac{1}{2}V_1$ or $2V_2 = V_1$

$T_2 = 306 \text{ K} \times \dfrac{\frac{1}{2}P_1}{P_1} \times \dfrac{\frac{1}{2}V_1}{V_1} = 76.5 \text{ K (calc and corr)}$

Converting to Celsius: $76.5 \text{ K} - 273.2 = -196.7 \text{ }°C \text{ (calc and corr)}$

c) $P_2 = 3P_1, V_2 = \frac{1}{2}V_1$

$T_2 = 306 \text{ K} \times \dfrac{3P_1}{P_1} \times \dfrac{\frac{1}{2}V_1}{V_1} = 459 \text{ K (calc and corr)}$

Converting to Celsius: $459 \text{ K} - 273 = 186 \text{ }°C$

d) $P_2 = \frac{1}{2}P_1, V_2 = 2V_1$

$T_2 = 306 \text{ K} \times \dfrac{\frac{1}{2}P_1}{P_1} \times \dfrac{2V_1}{V_1} = 306 \text{ K (no change)}.$

Converting to Celsius: $306 \text{ K} - 273 = 33 \text{ }°C \text{ (no change)}$

GAS LAWS

99

STP Conditions (Sec. 12.7)

12.41 $V_2 = V_1 \cdot \dfrac{P_1}{P_2} \cdot \dfrac{T_2}{T_1}$, where $V_1 = 3.50$ L, $P_2 = 1.00$ atm (or 760 mm Hg), $T_2 = 273$ K

a) $T_1 = 30\ °C + 273 = 303$ K, $P_1 = 1.00$ atm

$V_2 = 3.50$ L $\times \dfrac{1.00\ \text{atm}}{1.00\ \text{atm}} \times \dfrac{273\ \text{K}}{303\ \text{K}} = 3.1534653$ (calc) $= 3.15$ L (corr)

b) $T_1 = 0\ °C + 273 = 273$ K; $P_1 = 3.00$ atm

$V_2 = 3.50$ L $\times \dfrac{3.00\ \text{atm}}{1.00\ \text{atm}} \times \dfrac{273\ \text{K}}{273\ \text{K}} = 10.5$ L (calc and corr)

c) $T_1 = 55\ °C + 273 = 328$ K, $P_1 = 1.25$ atm

$V_2 = 3.50$ L $\times \dfrac{1.25\ \text{atm}}{1.00\ \text{atm}} \times \dfrac{273\ \text{K}}{328\ \text{K}} = 3.6413872$ (calc) $= 3.64$ L (corr)

d) $T_1 = 135\ °C + 273 = 408$ K, $P_1 = 852$ mm Hg

$V_2 = 3.50$ L $\times \dfrac{852\ \text{mm Hg}}{760\ \text{mm Hg}} \times \dfrac{273\ \text{K}}{408\ \text{K}} = 2.6254063$ (calc) $= 2.63$ L (corr)

12.43 $V_2 = V_1 \cdot \dfrac{P_1}{P_2} \cdot \dfrac{T_2}{T_1}$ where $V_1 = 1.00$ L, $P_1 = 1.00$ atm (or 760 mm Hg), $T_1 = 273$ K

a) $P_2 = 1.08$ atm, $T_2 = 8\ °C + 273 = 281$ K

$V_2 = 1.00$ L $\times \dfrac{1.00\ \text{atm}}{1.08\ \text{atm}} \times \dfrac{281\ \text{K}}{273\ \text{K}} = 0.9530593$ (calc) $= 0.953$ L (corr)

b) $P_2 = 6.20$ atm, $T_2 = 875\ °C + 273 = 1148$ K

$V_2 = 1.00$ L $\times \dfrac{1.00\ \text{atm}}{6.20\ \text{atm}} \times \dfrac{1148\ \text{K}}{273\ \text{K}} = 0.6782465$ (calc) $= 0.678$ L (corr)

c) $P_2 = 0.500$ atm, $T_2 = -15\ °C + 273 = 258$ K

$V_2 = 1.00$ L $\times \dfrac{1.00\ \text{atm}}{0.500\ \text{atm}} \times \dfrac{258\ \text{K}}{273\ \text{K}} = 1.8901099$ (calc) $= 1.89$ L (corr)

d) $P_2 = 680$ mm Hg, $T_2 = -30\ °C + 273 = 243$ K

$V_2 = 1.00$ L $\times \dfrac{760\ \text{mm Hg}}{680\ \text{mm Hg}} \times \dfrac{243\ \text{K}}{273\ \text{K}} = 0.9948287$ (calc) $= 0.995$ L (corr)

Gay-Lussac's Law of Combining Volumes (Sec. 12.8)

12.45 The whole-number combining ratio is $\dfrac{2.00\ \text{L O}_2}{1.60\ \text{L NH}_3} = \dfrac{5\ \text{L O}_2}{4\ \text{L NH}_3}$ which matches the coefficients in the second reaction.

12.47 a) 1.30 L $CO_2 \times \dfrac{1\ \text{L C}_3\text{H}_4}{3\ \text{L CO}_2} = 0.43333333$ (calc) $= 0.433$ L C_3H_8 (corr)

b) 1.30 L $H_2O \times \dfrac{1\ \text{L C}_3\text{H}_8}{4\ \text{L H}_2\text{O}} = 0.325$ L C_3H_8 (calc and corr)

12.49   0.75 total volume of products
At constant temperature, pressure 1 L of C_3H_8 produces 3 L CO_2 and 4 L of H_2O, 7 L total products

$$0.75 \text{ L total products} \times \frac{1 \text{ L } C_3H_8}{7 \text{ L Products}} = 0.10714285 \text{ (calc)} = 0.11 \text{ L } C_3H_8 \text{ (corr)}$$

Gas Volumes and Limiting Reactants (Sec. 12.9)

12.51 $N_2 + 3H_2 \rightarrow 2NH_3$

a) $1.00 \text{ L } N_2 \times \dfrac{2 \text{ L } NH_3}{1 \text{ L } N_2} = 2.00 \text{ L } NH_3 \text{ (calc and corr)}$

$1.50 \text{ L } H_2 \times \dfrac{2 \text{ L } NH_3}{3 \text{ L } H_2} = 1.00 \text{ L } NH_3 \text{ (calc and corr)}$ $\therefore 1.50 \text{ L } H_2$ is the limiting reactant

b) $2.00 \text{ L } N_2 \times \dfrac{2 \text{ L } NH_3}{1 \text{ L } N_2} = 4.00 \text{ L } NH_3 \text{ (calc and corr)}$

$5.50 \text{ L } H_2 \times \dfrac{2 \text{ L } NH_3}{3 \text{ L } H_2} = 3.66666 \text{ (calc)} = 3.67 \text{ L } NH_3 \text{ (corr)}$

$\therefore 5.50 \text{ L } H_2$ is the limiting reactant

c) $1.00 \text{ L } N_2 \times \dfrac{2 \text{ L } NH_3}{1 \text{ L } N_2} = 2.00 \text{ L } NH_3 \text{ (calc and corr)}$

$4.00 \text{ L } H_2 \times \dfrac{2 \text{ L } NH_3}{3 \text{ L } H_2} = 2.66666 \text{ (calc)} = 2.67 \text{ L } NH_3 \text{ (corr)}$

$\therefore 1.00 \text{ L } N_2$ is the limiting reactant

d) $3.00 \text{ L } N_2 \times \dfrac{2 \text{ L } NH_3}{1 \text{ L } N_2} = 6.00 \text{ L } NH_3 \text{ (calc and corr)}$

$1.00 \text{ L } H_2 \times \dfrac{2 \text{ L } NH_3}{3 \text{ L } H_2} = 0.66666 \text{ (calc)} = 0.667 \text{ L } NH_3 \text{ (corr)}$

$\therefore 1.00 \text{ L } H_2$ is the limiting reactant

12.53 $CH_4 + 2H_2O \rightarrow CO_2 + 4H_2$

a) $45.0 \text{ L } CH_4 \times \dfrac{1 \text{ L } CO_2}{1 \text{ L } CH_4} = 45.0 \text{ L } CO_2 \text{ (calc and corr)}$

$45.0 \text{ L } H_2O \times \dfrac{1 \text{ L } CO_2}{2 \text{ L } H_2O} = 22.5 \text{ L } CO_2 \text{ (calc and corr)}$

$\therefore 45.0 \text{ L } H_2O$ is the limiting reactant $45.0 \text{ L } H_2O \times \dfrac{4 \text{ L } H_2}{2 \text{ L } H_2O} = 90.0 \text{ L } H_2 \text{ (calc and corr)}$

$\therefore 22.5 \text{ L } CO_2$ and $90.0 \text{ L } H_2$ are produced.

b) $45.0 \text{ L CH}_4 \times \dfrac{1 \text{ L CO}_2}{1 \text{ L CH}_4} = 45.0 \text{ L CO}_2$ (calc and corr)

$66.0 \text{ L H}_2\text{O} \times \dfrac{1 \text{ L CO}_2}{2 \text{ L H}_2\text{O}} = 33.0 \text{ L CO}_2$ (calc and corr)

$\therefore$ 66.0 L H_2O is the limiting reactant $66.0 \text{ L H}_2\text{O} \times \dfrac{4 \text{ L H}_2}{2 \text{ L H}_2\text{O}} = 132 \text{ L H}_2$ (calc and corr)

$\therefore$ 33.0 L CO_2 and 132 L H_2 are produced.

c) $64.0 \text{ L CH}_4 \times \dfrac{1 \text{ L CO}_2}{1 \text{ L CH}_4} = 64.0 \text{ L CO}_2$ (calc and corr)

$134 \text{ L H}_2\text{O} \times \dfrac{1 \text{ L CO}_2}{2 \text{ L H}_2\text{O}} = 67.0 \text{ L CO}_2$ (calc and corr)

$\therefore$ 64.0 L CH_4 is the limiting reactant $64.0 \text{ L CH}_4 \times \dfrac{4 \text{ L H}_2}{1 \text{ L CH}_4} = 256 \text{ L H}_2$ (calc and corr)

$\therefore$ 64.0 L CO_2 and 256 L H_2 are produced.

d) $16.0 \text{ L CH}_4 \times \dfrac{1 \text{ L CO}_2}{1 \text{ L CH}_4} = 16.0 \text{ L CO}_2$ (calc and corr)

$32.0 \text{ L H}_2\text{O} \times \dfrac{1 \text{ L CO}_2}{2 \text{ L H}_2\text{O}} = 16.0 \text{ L CO}_2$ (calc and corr)

$\therefore$ Both 16.0 L CH_4 and 32.0 L H_2O are limiting reactants

$16.0 \text{ L CH}_4 \times \dfrac{4 \text{ L H}_2}{1 \text{ L CH}_4} = 64.0 \text{ L H}_2$ (calc and corr)

Or $32.0 \text{ L H}_2\text{O} \times \dfrac{4 \text{ L H}_2}{2 \text{ L H}_2\text{O}} = 64.0 \text{ L H}_2$ (calc and corr)

$\therefore$ 16.0 L CO_2 and 64 L H_2 are produced.

Avogadro's Law (Sec. 12.10)

12.55 $n_2 = n_1 \cdot \dfrac{V_2}{V_1} = 0.573 \text{ mole} \times \dfrac{50.7 \text{ mL}}{37.2 \text{ mL}} = 0.7809435$ (calc) $= 0.781$ mole (corr)

12.57 $3.75 \text{ g CO} \times \dfrac{1 \text{ mole CO}}{28.01 \text{ g CO}} = 0.133880756$ (calc) $= 0.134$ mole CO gas (corr)

$\dfrac{125 \text{ L CO}}{0.134 \text{ mole CO}} = \dfrac{X \text{ L CO}}{0.300 \text{ mole CO}}$ $X = 279.850746$ (calc) $= 280.$ L CO gas (corr)

12.59 $n_2 = n_1 \cdot \dfrac{V_2}{V_1}$ $n_2 = 1.83 \text{ moles} \times \dfrac{0.811 \text{ L}}{0.673 \text{ L}} = 2.2052451$ (calc) $= 2.21$ moles (corr)

increase in moles $= (2.21 - 1.83)$ moles $= 0.38$ mole (calc and corr)

$0.38 \text{ mole He} \times \dfrac{4.00 \text{ g He}}{1 \text{ mole He}} = 1.52$ (calc) $= 1.5$ g He (corr)

12.61 1.33 L. Equal moles of gas will have equal volume at the same temperature and pressure.

12.63 The one with the larger number of moles will have the larger volume.
a) 0.450 mole O_2 will have the larger volume
b) 2.32 moles CH_4 will have the larger volume

c) $100.0 \text{ g NO}_2 \times \dfrac{1 \text{ mole NO}_2}{46.01 \text{ g NO}_2} = 2.1734406 \text{ (calc)} = 2.173 \text{ moles NO}_2 \text{ (corr)}$

$100.0 \text{ g N}_2\text{O} \times \dfrac{1 \text{ mole N}_2\text{O}}{44.02 \text{ g N}_2\text{O}} = 2.2716947 \text{ (calc)} = 2.272 \text{ moles N}_2\text{O (corr)}$

∴ 100.0 g N_2O will have the larger volume

d) $100.0 \text{ g CO} \times \dfrac{1 \text{ mole CO}}{28.01 \text{ g CO}} = 3.5701535 \text{ (calc)} = 3.570 \text{ moles CO (corr)}$

$100.0 \text{ g CO}_2 \times \dfrac{1 \text{ mole CO}_2}{44.01 \text{ g CO}_2} = 2.2722109 \text{ (calc)} = 2.272 \text{ moles CO}_2$

∴ 100 g CO will have the larger volume.

12.65 Since the volumes are in the whole number ratio of 1 L N_2 : 3 L F_2 : 2 L compound, the mole ratio of each gas must be the same: 1 mole N_2 : 3 moles F_2 : 2 moles compound, and the molecular ratio must also be the same. Thus, 2 molecules of compound gives one molecule N_2 and 3 molecules F_2 and the 2 molecules of compound must contain a total of 2 N atoms and 6 F atoms, so the molecule is NF_3.

12.67 $\dfrac{P_1 V_1}{n_1 T_1} = \dfrac{P_2 V_2}{n_2 T_2}$ $P_1 = 1.5$ atm, $V_1 = 2.0$ L, $n_1 = 0.500$ mole, $T_1 = 27°\text{ C} + 273 \text{ K} = 300.\text{ K}$

$P_2 = 1.5$ atm - 0.50 atm = 1.00 atm
$V_2 = ?$
$n_2 = 0.500$ mole - 0.100 mole = 0.400 mole
$T_2 = 20°\text{ C} + 27°\text{ C} = 47°\text{ C (calc)} = 50°\text{ C (corr)}$
$47°\text{ C} + 273 \text{ K} = 320 \text{ K}$ (2 significant figures)

$\dfrac{1.5 \text{ atm } 2.0 \text{ L}}{0.500 \text{ mole } 300 \text{ K}} = \dfrac{1.00 \text{ atm ? L}}{0.400 \text{ mole } 320 \text{ K}} = 2.56 \text{ (calc)} = 2.6 \text{ L (corr)}$

Molar Volume (Sec. 12.11)

12.69 1.25 mole of *any gas* will have a volume at STP given by:

$1.25 \text{ moles} \times \dfrac{22.41 \text{ L}}{1 \text{ mole}} = 28.0125 \text{ (calc)} = 28.0 \text{ L (corr)}$

a) 28.0 L N_2 b) 28.0 L NH_3 c) 28.0 L CO_2 d) 28.0 L Cl_2

12.71 a) $24.5 \text{ g N}_2 \times \dfrac{1 \text{ mole N}_2}{28.02 \text{ g N}_2} \times \dfrac{22.41 \text{ L N}_2}{1 \text{ mole N}_2} = 19.594754 \text{ (calc)} = 19.6 \text{ L N}_2 \text{ (corr)}$

$24.5 \text{ g NH}_3 \times \dfrac{1 \text{ mole NH}_3}{17.04 \text{ g NH}_3} \times \dfrac{22.41 \text{ L NH}_3}{1 \text{ mole NH}_3} = 32.220951 \text{ (calc)} = 32.2 \text{ L NH}_3 \text{ (corr)}$

∴ the NH_3 has the larger volume

b) $30.0 \text{ g O}_2 \times \dfrac{1 \text{ mole O}_2}{32.00 \text{ g O}_2} \times \dfrac{22.41 \text{ L O}_2}{1 \text{ mole O}_2} = 21.009375 \text{ (calc)} = 21.0 \text{ L O}_2 \text{ (corr)}$

$30.0 \text{ g O}_3 \times \dfrac{1 \text{ mole O}_3}{48.00 \text{ g O}_3} \times \dfrac{22.41 \text{ L O}_3}{1 \text{ mole O}_3} = 14.00625 \text{ (calc)} = 14.0 \text{ L O}_3 \text{ (corr)}$

$\therefore$ the O_2 has the larger volume

c) $10.0 \text{ g SO}_2 \times \dfrac{1 \text{ mole SO}_2}{64.06 \text{ g SO}_2} \times \dfrac{22.41 \text{ L SO}_2}{1 \text{ mole SO}_2} = 3.4982829 \text{ (calc)} = 3.50 \text{ L SO}_2 \text{ (corr)}$

$20.0 \text{ g NO}_2 \times \dfrac{1 \text{ mole NO}_2}{46.01 \text{ g NO}_2} \times \dfrac{22.41 \text{ L NO}_2}{1 \text{ mole NO}_2} = 9.7413606 \text{ (calc)} = 9.74 \text{ L NO}_2 \text{ (corr)}$

$\therefore$ the NO_2 has the larger volume

d) $15.0 \text{ g N}_2\text{O} \times \dfrac{1 \text{ mole N}_2\text{O}}{44.02 \text{ g N}_2\text{O}} \times \dfrac{22.41 \text{ L N}_2\text{O}}{1 \text{ mole N}_2\text{O}} = 7.6363017 \text{ (calc)} = 7.64 \text{ L N}_2\text{O} \text{ (corr)}$

$20.0 \text{ g NO} \times \dfrac{1 \text{ mole NO}}{30.01 \text{ g NO}} \times \dfrac{22.41 \text{ L NO}}{1 \text{ mole NO}} = 14.935022 \text{ (calc)} = 14.9 \text{ L NO} \text{ (corr)}$

$\therefore$ the NO has the larger volume

ALTERNATE METHOD: The one with the smaller molar mass will have the lower density. If the masses are equal, the one with the lower density will have the larger volume.
a) Mass equal, the molar mass of NH_3 is less than N_2, $\therefore$ NH_3 has the larger volume.
b) Mass equal, the molar mass of O_2 is less than O_3, $\therefore$ O_2 has the larger volume.
c) Since NO_2 has smaller molar mass than SO_2, 10.0 g NO_2 would have a larger volume than 10.0 g SO_2, $\therefore$ 20.0 g NO_2 would be even larger.
d) Since NO has smaller molar mass than N_2O, 15.0 g NO would have a larger volume than 15.0 g of N_2O, $\therefore$ 20.0 g NO would be even larger.

12.73 a) $23.7 \text{ L Ar} \times \dfrac{1 \text{ mole Ar}}{22.41 \text{ L Ar}} \times \dfrac{39.95 \text{ g Ar}}{1 \text{ mole Ar}} = 42.249665 \text{ (calc)} = 42.2 \text{ g Ar} \text{ (corr)}$

b) $23.7 \text{ L N}_2\text{O} \times \dfrac{1 \text{ mole N}_2\text{O}}{22.41 \text{ L N}_2\text{O}} \times \dfrac{44.02 \text{ g N}_2\text{O}}{1 \text{ mole N}_2\text{O}} = 46.553949 \text{ (calc)} = 46.6 \text{ g N}_2\text{O} \text{ (corr)}$

c) $23.7 \text{ L SO}_3 \times \dfrac{1 \text{ mole SO}_3}{22.41 \text{ L SO}_3} \times \dfrac{80.06 \text{ g SO}_3}{1 \text{ mole SO}_3} = 84.668541 \text{ (calc)} = 84.7 \text{ g SO}_3 \text{ (corr)}$

d) $23.7 \text{ L PH}_3 \times \dfrac{1 \text{ mole PH}_3}{22.41 \text{ L PH}_3} \times \dfrac{34.00 \text{ g PH}_3}{1 \text{ mole PH}_3} = 35.957162 \text{ (calc)} = 36.0 \text{ g PH}_3 \text{ (corr)}$

12.75 a) $\dfrac{44.02 \text{ g N}_2\text{O}}{1 \text{ mole N}_2\text{O}} \times \dfrac{1 \text{ mole N}_2\text{O}}{22.41 \text{ L N}_2\text{O}} = 1.9643017 \text{ (calc)} = 1.96 \text{ g/L} \text{ (corr)}$

b) $\dfrac{92.02 \text{ g N}_2\text{O}_4}{1 \text{ mole N}_2\text{O}_4} \times \dfrac{1 \text{ mole N}_2\text{O}_4}{22.41 \text{ L N}_2\text{O}_4} = 4.1062026 \text{ (calc)} = 4.11 \text{ g/L} \text{ (corr)}$

c) $\dfrac{46.01 \text{ g NO}_2}{1 \text{ mole NO}_2} \times \dfrac{1 \text{ mole NO}_2}{22.41 \text{ L NO}_2} = 2.0531013 \text{ (calc)} = 2.05 \text{ g/L} \text{ (corr)}$

d) $\dfrac{30.01 \text{ g NO}}{1 \text{ mole NO}} \times \dfrac{1 \text{ mole NO}}{22.41 \text{ L NO}} = 1.3391343 \text{ (calc)} = 1.34 \text{ g/L} \text{ (corr)}$

12.77   The one with the larger molar mass will have the greater density.
a) O_3 b) PH_3 c) CO_2 d) F_2

12.79   a) $1.97 \text{ g/L} \times \dfrac{22.41 \text{ L}}{1 \text{ mole}} = 44.1477 \text{ (calc)} = 44.1 \text{ g/mole (corr)}$

b) $1.25 \text{ g/L} \times \dfrac{22.41 \text{ L}}{1 \text{ mole}} = 28.0125 \text{ (calc)} = 28.0 \text{ g/mole (corr)}$

c) $0.714 \text{ g/L} \times \dfrac{22.41 \text{ L}}{1 \text{ mole}} = 16.00074 \text{ (calc)} = 16.0 \text{ g/mole (corr)}$

d) $3.17 \text{ g/L} \times \dfrac{22.41 \text{ L}}{1 \text{ mole}} = 71.0397 \text{ (calc)} = 71.0 \text{ g/mole (corr)}$

12.81 $22.5 \text{ g XeO}_2\text{F}_2 \times \dfrac{1 \text{ mole XeO}_2\text{F}_2}{201.29 \text{ g XeO}_2\text{F}_2} \times \dfrac{1 \text{ mole Xe}}{1 \text{ mole XeO}_2\text{F}_2} \times \dfrac{22.41 \text{ L Xe}}{1 \text{ mole Xe}}$

$$= 2.504968 \text{ (calc)} = 2.50 \text{ L Xe (corr)}$$

The Ideal Gas Law (Sec. 12.12)

12.83   Solving $PV = nRT$ for V gives: $V = \dfrac{nRT}{P}$ where $n = 1.20$ moles

a) $P = 1$ atm, $T = 273$ K

$V = \dfrac{1.20 \text{ mole}}{1.00 \text{ atm}} \times 0.08206 \dfrac{\text{atm L}}{\text{mole K}} \times 273 \text{ K} = 26.882856 \text{ (calc)} = 26.9 \text{ L (corr)}$

b) $P = 1.54$ atm, $T = 73 \,°\text{C} + 273 = 346$ K

$V = \dfrac{1.20 \text{ moles}}{1.54 \text{ atm}} \times 0.08206 \dfrac{\text{atm L}}{\text{mole K}} \times 346 \text{ K} = 22.124229 \text{ (calc)} = 22.1 \text{ L (corr)}$

c) $P = 15.0$ atm, $T = 525 \,°\text{C} + 273 = 798$ K

$V = \dfrac{1.20 \text{ moles}}{15.0 \text{ atm}} \times 0.08206 \dfrac{\text{atm L}}{\text{mole K}} \times 798 \text{ K} = 5.2387104 \text{(calc)} = 5.24 \text{ L (corr)}$

d) $P = 765$ mm Hg, $T = -23 \,°\text{C} + 273 = 250$ K

$V = \dfrac{1.20 \text{ moles}}{765 \text{ mm Hg}} \times \dfrac{62.36 \text{ mm Hg·L}}{\text{mole K}} \times 250 \text{ K} = 24.454902 \text{ (calc)} = 24.5 \text{ L (corr)}$

12.85 $n = \dfrac{PV}{RT}$, $T = 25 \,°\text{C} + 273 = 298$ K

$n = \dfrac{3.67 \text{ atm} \times 6.00 \text{ L}}{0.08206 \dfrac{\text{atm L}}{\text{mole K}} \cdot 298 \text{ K}} = 0.9004706 \text{ (calc)} = 0.900 \text{ mole (corr)}$

12.87 $T = \dfrac{PV}{nR}$,   Convert volume to liters: $V = 1275 \text{ mL} \times \dfrac{10^{-3} \text{ L}}{1 \text{ mL}} = 1.275 \text{ L}$

$T = \dfrac{5.78 \text{ atm} \times 1.275 \text{ L}}{0.332 \text{ mole} \times 0.08206 \dfrac{\text{atm L}}{\text{mole K}}} = 270.50072 \text{ (calc)} = 271 \text{ K} \therefore \text{Celsius: } 271 - 273 = -2 \,°\text{C}$

12.89 $P = \dfrac{nRT}{V}$ where $V = 6.00$ L, $T = 25\ ^\circ C + 273 = 298$ K

a) $P = \dfrac{0.30\ \text{mole}}{6.00\ \text{L}} \times 0.08206\ \dfrac{\text{atm L}}{\text{mole K}} \times 298\ \text{K} = 1.222694\ (\text{calc}) = 1.2\ \text{atm (corr)}$

b) $P = \dfrac{1.20\ \text{mole}}{6.00\ \text{L}} \times 0.08206\ \dfrac{\text{atm L}}{\text{mole K}} \times 298\ \text{K} = 4.890776\ (\text{calc}) = 4.89\ \text{atm (corr)}$

c) $P = \dfrac{0.30\ \text{g N}_2}{6.00\ \text{L}} \times \dfrac{1\ \text{mole N}_2}{28.02\ \text{g N}_2} \times 0.08206\ \dfrac{\text{atm L}}{\text{mole K}} \times 298\ \text{K}$

$= 0.043636\ (\text{calc}) = 0.044\ \text{atm (corr)}$

d) $P = \dfrac{1.20\ \text{g N}_2}{6.00\ \text{L}} \times \dfrac{1\ \text{mole N}_2}{28.02\ \text{g N}_2} \times 0.08206\ \dfrac{\text{atm L}}{\text{mole K}} \times 298\ \text{K}$

$= 0.1745459\ (\text{calc}) = 0.175\ \text{atm (corr)}$

12.91 $R = \dfrac{PV}{nT} = \dfrac{13.3\ \text{atm} \times 3.00\ \text{L}}{1.14\ \text{moles} \times 425\ \text{K}} = 0.082352941\ (\text{calc}) = 0.0824\ \dfrac{\text{atm L}}{\text{mole K}}\ (\text{corr})$

12.93 $V = \dfrac{nRT}{P} = \dfrac{1.00\ \text{mole} \times 0.08206\ \dfrac{\text{atm L}}{\text{mole K}} \times 400\ \text{K}}{0.908\ \text{atm}} = 36.14978\ (\text{calc}) = 36.1\ \text{L (corr)}$

12.95 $m = (MM)\ \dfrac{PV}{RT}$

a) for C_2H_6 the molar mass (MM) = 30.08 g/mole. $T = 29\ ^\circ C + 273 = 302$ K.

$m = \dfrac{30.08\ \text{g}}{1\ \text{mole}} \times \dfrac{0.972\ \text{atm} \times 25.0\ \text{L}}{0.08206\ \dfrac{\text{atm L}}{\text{mole K}} \times 302\ \text{K}} = 29.494813\ (\text{calc}) = 29.5\ \text{g (corr)}$

b) for HCl, (MM) = 36.46 g/mole, $T = 75\ ^\circ C + 273 = 348$ K.

$m = \dfrac{36.46\ \text{g}}{1\ \text{mole}} \times \dfrac{854\ \text{mm Hg} \times 2.22\ \text{L}}{62.36\ \dfrac{\text{mm Hg·L}}{\text{mole K}} \times 348\ \text{K}} = 3.18524\ (\text{calc}) = 3.19\ \text{g (corr)}$

c) for SO_2, (MM) = 64.07 g/mole, $T = 273$ K.

$m = \dfrac{64.06\ \text{g}}{1\ \text{mole}} \times \dfrac{1\ \text{atm} \times 5.50\ \text{L}}{0.08206\ \dfrac{\text{atm L}}{\text{mole K}} \times 273\ \text{K}} = 15.727347\ (\text{calc}) = 15.7\ \text{g (corr)}$

d) for N_2O, (MM) = 44.02 g/mole, $T = 273\ ^\circ C + 273 = 546$ K,

$V = 783\ \text{mL} \times \dfrac{10^{-3}\ \text{L}}{\text{mL}} = 0.783\ \text{L}$

$m = \dfrac{44.02\ \text{g}}{1\ \text{mole}} \times \dfrac{359\ \text{mm Hg} \times 0.783\ \text{L}}{62.36\ \dfrac{\text{mm Hg·L}}{\text{mole K}} \times 546\ \text{K}} = 0.3634188(\text{calc}) = 0.363\ \text{g (corr)}$

12.97 $m = (MM) \dfrac{PV}{RT}$, T = 23 °C + 273 = 296 K. For Cl_2, (MM) = 70.90 g/mole

$$m = \frac{70.90 \text{ g}}{1 \text{ mole}} \times \frac{1.65 \text{ atm} \times 30.0 \text{ L}}{0.08206 \dfrac{\text{atm L}}{\text{mole K}} \times 296 \text{ K}} = 144.48681 \text{ (calc)} = 144 \text{ g } Cl_2 \text{ after adding (corr)}$$

If there were 100.0 g Cl_2 initially, then 144 − 100.0 = 44 g Cl_2 added.

Molar Mass, Density, and the Ideal Gas Law (Sec. 12.13)

12.99 $(MM) = \dfrac{mRT}{PV}$, $P = 741 \text{ mmHg} \times \dfrac{1 \text{ atm}}{760 \text{ mmHg}} = 0.975 \text{ atm}$, T = 33 °C + 273 = 306 K

$$\frac{1.305 \text{ g} \times 0.08206 \dfrac{\text{atm L}}{\text{mole K}} \times 306 \text{ K}}{1.20 \text{ L} \times 0.975 \text{ atm}} = 28.007709 \text{ (calc)} = 28.01 \text{ g/mole (corr)}$$

12.101 $(MM) = \dfrac{mRT}{PV}$, $V = 125 \text{ mL} \times \dfrac{10^{-3} \text{ L}}{1 \text{ mL}} = 0.125 \text{ L}$, T = 75 °C + 273 = 348 K

$$\frac{0.450 \text{ g} \times 0.08206 \dfrac{\text{atm L}}{\text{mole K}} \times 348 \text{ K}}{0.125 \text{ L} \times 1.00 \text{ atm}} = 102.804768 \text{ (calc)} = 103 \text{ g/mol (corr)}$$

12.103 $(MM) = \dfrac{mRT}{PV}$, $V = 125 \text{ mL} \times \dfrac{10^{-3} \text{ L}}{1 \text{ mL}} = 0.125 \text{ L}$, T = 90 °C + 273 = 363 K

$$\frac{0.4537 \text{ g} \times 0.08206 \dfrac{\text{atm L}}{\text{mole K}} \times 363 \text{ K}}{0.125 \text{ L} \times 1.20 \text{ atm}} = 90.098105 \text{ (calc)} = 90.1 \text{ g/mol (corr)}$$

12.105 $(MM) = \dfrac{mRT}{PV}$, T = 20 °C + 273 = 293 K

$$(MM) = \frac{1.61 \text{ g} \times 0.08206 \dfrac{\text{atm L}}{\text{mole K}} \times 293 \text{ K}}{0.902 \text{ L} \times 1.65 \text{ atm}} = 26.009651 \text{ (calc)} = 26.0 \text{ g/mole (corr)}$$

CO has a molar mass of 26.01 g/mole; CO_2 has 44.01 g/mole. The gas is CO.

12.107 $d = \dfrac{m}{V} = \dfrac{(MM) P}{RT}$, (MM H_2S) = 34.08 g/mole

a)   T = 24 °C + 273 = 297 K.

$$d = \frac{34.08 \text{ g}}{1 \text{ mole}} \times \frac{675 \text{ mm Hg}}{62.36 \dfrac{\text{mm Hg L}}{\text{mole K}} \times 297 \text{ K}} = 1.2420549 \text{ (calc)} = 1.24 \text{ g/L (corr)}$$

b) T = 24 °C + 273 = 297 K.

$$d = \frac{34.08 \text{ g}}{1 \text{ mole}} \times \frac{1.20 \text{ atm}}{0.08206 \frac{\text{atm L}}{\text{mole K}} \times 297 \text{ K}} = 1.6780035 \text{ (calc)} = 1.68 \text{ g/L (corr)}$$

c) T = 370 °C + 273 = 643 K.

$$d = \frac{34.08 \text{ g}}{1 \text{ mole}} \times \frac{1.30 \text{ atm}}{0.08206 \frac{\text{atm L}}{\text{mole K}} \times 643 \text{K}} = 0.8396541 \text{ (calc)} = 0.840 \text{ g/L (corr)}$$

d) T = −25 °C + 273 = 248 K.

$$d = \frac{34.08 \text{ g}}{1 \text{ mole}} \times \frac{452 \text{ mm Hg}}{62.36 \frac{\text{mm Hg·L}}{\text{mole K}} \times 248 \text{ K}} = 0.9960479 \text{ (calc)} = 0.996 \text{ g/L (corr)}$$

12.109 $P = \dfrac{dRT}{(MM)}$; T = 47 °C + 273 = 320 K; d = 1.00 g/L

a) $(MM) = \dfrac{28.02 \text{ g}}{1 \text{ mole}}$; $P = \dfrac{1.00 \text{ g}}{L} \times \dfrac{1 \text{ mole}}{28.02 \text{ g}} \times 0.08206 \dfrac{\text{atm L}}{\text{mole K}} \times 320 \text{ K}$

$$= 0.9371591 \text{ (calc)} = 0.937 \text{ atm (corr)}$$

b) $(MM) = \dfrac{131.29 \text{ g}}{1 \text{ mole}}$; $P = \dfrac{1.00 \text{ g}}{L} \times \dfrac{1 \text{ mole}}{131.29 \text{ g}} \times 0.08206 \dfrac{\text{atm L}}{\text{mole K}} \times 320 \text{ K}$

$$= 0.2000091 \text{ (calc)} = 0.200 \text{ atm (corr)}$$

c) $(MM) = \dfrac{54.45 \text{ g}}{1 \text{ mole}}$; $P = \dfrac{1.00 \text{ g}}{L} \times \dfrac{1 \text{ mole}}{54.45 \text{ g}} \times 0.08206 \dfrac{\text{atm L}}{\text{mole K}} \times 320 \text{ K}$

$$= 0.4822626 \text{ (calc)} = 0.482 \text{ atm (corr)}$$

d) $(MM) = \dfrac{44.02 \text{ g}}{1 \text{ mole}}$; $P = \dfrac{1.00 \text{ g}}{L} \times \dfrac{1 \text{ mole}}{44.02 \text{ g}} \times 0.08206 \dfrac{\text{atm L}}{\text{mole K}} \times 320 \text{ K}$

$$= 0.5965288 \text{ (calc)} = 0.597 \text{ atm (corr)}$$

12.111 T = 27 °C + 273 = 300 K; $(MM) = \dfrac{dRT}{P}$

$$(MM) = \frac{2.27 \text{ g}}{L} \times 0.08206 \frac{\text{atm L}}{\text{mole K}} \times \frac{300 \text{ K}}{2.00 \text{ atm}} = 27.94143 \text{ (calc)} = 27.9 \frac{\text{g}}{\text{mole}} \text{ (corr)}$$

Since CO has a molar mass of 28.01 g/mole and NO has 30.01 g/mole, the gas is CO.

Gas Laws and Chemical Equations (Sec. 12.14)

12.113 $25.0 \text{ g NO} \times \dfrac{1 \text{ mole NO}}{30.01 \text{ g NO}} \times \dfrac{2 \text{ moles NO}_2}{2 \text{ moles NO}} \times \dfrac{22.41 \text{ L NO}_2}{1 \text{ mole NO}_2}$

$$= 18.668777 \text{ (calc)} = 18.7 \text{ L NO}_2 \text{ (corr)}$$

12.115 Method 1. Find moles O_2

$n = \dfrac{PV}{RT}$; T = 27 °C + 273 = 300 K

$$n = \frac{1.00 \text{ atm} \times 25.0 \text{ L}}{0.08206 \frac{\text{atm L}}{\text{mole K}} \times 300 \text{ K}} = 1.0155171 \text{ (calc)} = 1.02 \text{ moles O}_2 \text{ (corr)}$$

$$1.02 \text{ moles } O_2 \times \frac{2 \text{ moles NO}}{1 \text{ mole } O_2} \times \frac{30.01 \text{ g NO}}{1 \text{ mole NO}} = 61.2204 \text{ (calc)} = 61.2 \text{ g NO (corr)}$$

Method 2. Find volume of O_2 at STP (P constant)

$$V_2 = \frac{V_1 T_2}{T_1}. \quad V_2 = 25.0 \text{ L} \times \frac{273 \text{ K}}{300 \text{ K}} = 22.75 \text{ (calc)} = 22.8 \text{ L } O_2 \text{ at STP (corr)}$$

$$22.8 \text{ L } O_2 \times \frac{1 \text{ mole } O_2}{22.41 \text{ L } O_2} \times \frac{2 \text{ moles NO}}{1 \text{ mole } O_2} \times \frac{30.01 \text{ g NO}}{1 \text{ mole NO}} = 61.064525 \text{ (calc)} = 61.1 \text{ g NO (corr)}$$

Rounding in intermediate steps causes the difference.

12.117 $12.0 \text{ g Mg} \times \dfrac{1 \text{ mole Mg}}{24.30 \text{ g Mg}} \times \dfrac{1 \text{ mole } H_2}{1 \text{ mole Mg}} = 0.49382716 \text{ (calc)} = 0.494 \text{ mole } H_2 \text{ (corr)}$

$$V = \frac{0.494 \text{ mole} \times 0.08206 \dfrac{\text{atm L}}{\text{mole K}} \times 296 \text{ K}}{0.980 \text{ atm}} = 12.244022 \text{ (calc)} = 12.2 \text{ L (corr)}$$

12.119 $T = 450 \text{ °C} + 273 = 723 \text{ K}$. Conversion factor: $\dfrac{7 \text{ moles product gases}}{2 \text{ moles NH}_4\text{NO}_3}$

$$100.0 \text{ g NH}_4\text{NO}_3 \times \frac{1 \text{ mole NH}_4\text{NO}_3}{80.06 \text{ g NH}_4\text{NO}_3} \times \frac{7 \text{ moles product}}{2 \text{ moles NH}_4\text{NO}_3}$$
$$= 4.3717212 \text{ (calc)} = 4.37 \text{ moles product (corr)}$$

Method 1: $V = \dfrac{nRT}{P} = \dfrac{4.37 \text{ moles}}{1 \text{ atm}} \times 0.08206 \dfrac{\text{atm L}}{\text{mole K}} \times 723 \text{ K}$

$$= 259.26939 \text{ (calc)} = 259 \text{ L (corr)}$$

Method 2: $4.37 \text{ moles} \times \dfrac{22.41 \text{ L}}{1 \text{ mole}} \times \dfrac{723 \text{ K}}{273 \text{ K}} = 259.35758 \text{ (calc)} = 259 \text{ L (corr)}$

12.121 $n = \dfrac{645 \text{ mm Hg} \times 75.0 \text{ L}}{62.36 \dfrac{\text{mm Hg L}}{\text{mole K}} \times 311 \text{ K}} = 2.4943333 \text{ (calc)} = 2.49 \text{ moles NO (corr)}$

$$2.49 \text{ moles NO} \times \frac{3 \text{ moles NO}_2}{1 \text{ mole NO}} = 7.47 \text{ moles NO}_2 \text{ (calc and corr)}$$

$$V = \frac{7.47 \text{ moles} \times 0.08206 \dfrac{\text{atm L}}{\text{mole K}} \times 294 \text{ K}}{2.31 \text{ atm}} = 78.01668 \text{ L (calc)} = 78.0 \text{ L (corr)}$$

Mixtures of Gases (Sec. 12.15)

12.123   Moles of gas = $3.00 \text{ moles } N_2 + 3.00 \text{ moles } O_2 = 6.00 \text{ moles gas mixture}$
$T = 27 \text{° C} + 273 = 300. \text{ K}$

$$V = \frac{nRT}{P} = \frac{6.00 \text{ mole} \times 0.08206 \dfrac{\text{atm L}}{\text{mole K}} \times 300. \text{ K}}{20.00 \text{ atm}} = 7.3854 \text{ (calc)} = 7.39 \text{ L (corr)}$$

12.125 $T = 27° C + 273 = 300. K$

a) $3.00 \text{ g Ne} \times \dfrac{1 \text{ mole Ne}}{20.18 \text{ g Ne}} = 0.148662 \text{ (calc)} = 0.149 \text{ mole Ne (corr)}$

$3.00 \text{ g Ar} \times \dfrac{1 \text{ mole Ar}}{39.95 \text{ g Ar}} = 0.0750939 \text{ (calc)} = 0.0751 \text{ mole Ar (corr)}$

Total moles of gas $= 0.149 + 0.0751 = 0.2240938 \text{ (calc)} = 0.224 \text{ mole (corr)}$

$V = \dfrac{nRT}{P} = \dfrac{0.224 \text{ mole} \times 0.08206 \dfrac{\text{atm L}}{\text{mole K}} \times 300. \text{ K}}{1.00 \text{ atm}} = 5.514432 \text{ (calc)} = 5.51 \text{ L (corr)}$

b) $4.00 \text{ g Ne} \times \dfrac{1 \text{ mole Ne}}{20.18 \text{ g Ne}} = 0.198216 \text{ (calc)} = 0.198 \text{ mole Ne (corr)}$

$2.00 \text{ g Ar} \times \dfrac{1 \text{ mole Ar}}{39.95 \text{ g Ar}} = 0.0500625 \text{ (calc)} = 0.0501 \text{ mole Ar (corr)}$

Total moles of gas $= 0.198 + 0.0501 = 0.2481 \text{ (calc)} = 0.248 \text{ mole (corr)}$

$V = \dfrac{nRT}{P} = \dfrac{0.248 \text{ mole} \times 0.08206 \dfrac{\text{atm L}}{\text{mole K}} \times 300. \text{ K}}{1.00 \text{ atm}} = 6.105264 \text{ (calc)} = 6.11 \text{ L (corr)}$

c) $5.00 \text{ g Ar} \times \dfrac{1 \text{ mole Ar}}{39.95 \text{ g Ar}} = 0.125156 \text{ (calc)} = 0.125 \text{ mole Ar (corr)}$

Total moles of gas $= 3.00 + 0.0501 = 3.0501 \text{ (calc)} = 3.05 \text{ mole (corr)}$

$V = \dfrac{nRT}{P} = \dfrac{3.05 \text{ mole} \times 0.08206 \dfrac{\text{atm L}}{\text{mole K}} \times 300. \text{ K}}{1.00 \text{ atm}} = 75.0849 \text{ (calc)} = 75.1 \text{ L (corr)}$

d) Total moles of gas $= 4.00 + 4.00 = 8.00 \text{ moles (calc and corr)}$

$V = \dfrac{nRT}{P} = \dfrac{8.00 \text{ mole} \times 0.08206 \dfrac{\text{atm L}}{\text{mole K}} \times 300. \text{ K}}{1.00 \text{ atm}} = 196.944 \text{ (calc)} = 197 \text{ L (corr)}$

12.127 $3.00 \text{ moles Ar} + 3.00 \text{ moles Ne} + 3.00 \text{ more He} = 9.00 \text{ moles (calc and corr)}$
$T = 27° C + 273 = 300. K$

$P = \dfrac{9.00 \text{ mole} \times 0.08206 \dfrac{\text{atm L}}{\text{mole K}} \times 300. \text{ K}}{27.0 \text{ L}} = 8.206 \text{ (calc)} = 8.21 \text{ atm (corr)}$

Dalton's Law of Partial Pressures (Sec. 12.16)

12.129 $P_{He} = 9.0 \text{ atm}$

$P_{Ne} = 14.0 \text{ atm} - 9.0 \text{ atm} = 5.00 \text{ atm}$

$P_{Ar} = 29.0 \text{ atm} - 14.0 \text{ atm} = 15.0 \text{ atm}$

12.131 a) P_{CO_2} = 842 – 675 = 167 mm Hg

b) P_{N_2} = same as before = 354 mm Hg

c) P_{Ar} = same as before = 235 mm Hg

d) P_{H_2} = same as before = 675 – P_{N_2} – P_{Ar} = 675 – 354 – 235 = 86 mm Hg

12.133 a) moles CO = 25.0 g CO x $\dfrac{1 \text{ mole CO}}{28.01 \text{ g CO}}$ = 0.8925383 (calc) = 0.893 mole CO (corr)

moles CO_2 = 25.0 g CO_2 x $\dfrac{1 \text{ mole } CO_2}{44.01 \text{ g } CO_2}$ = 0.5680527 (calc) = 0.568 mole CO_2 (corr)

moles H_2S = 25.0 g H_2S x $\dfrac{1 \text{ mole } H_2S}{34.08 \text{ g } H_2S}$ = 0.733568 (calc) = 0.734 mole H_2S (corr)

Total moles = 0.893 + 0.568 + 0.734 = 2.195 moles total (calc and corr)

Mole fraction CO = $\dfrac{0.893}{2.195}$ = 0.4068337 (calc) = 0.407 mole fraction CO (corr)

Mole fraction CO_2 = $\dfrac{0.568}{2.195}$ = 0.2587699 (calc) = 0.259 mole fraction CO_2 (corr)

Mole fraction H_2S = $\dfrac{0.733}{2.195}$ = 0.3343963 (calc) = 0.334 mole fraction H_2S (corr)

b) Partial pressure = mole fraction x total pressure

P_{CO} = 0.407 x 1.72 atm = 0.70004 (calc) = 0.700 atm (corr)

P_{CO_2} = 0.259 x 1.72 atm = 0.44548 (calc) = 0.445 atm (corr)

P_{H_2S} = 0.334 x 1.72 atm = 0.57448 (calc) = 0.574 atm (corr)

12.135 a) $P_{O_2} = \dfrac{0.50 \text{ mole} \times 0.08206 \frac{\text{atm L}}{\text{mole K}} \times 293 \text{ K}}{2.50 \text{ L}}$ = 4.808716 (calc) = 4.8 atm (corr)

b) 4.8 atm. A change in the amount of N_2 does not affect the partial pressure of O_2.

c) 4.8 atm. A change in the amount of N_2 does not affect the partial pressure of O_2.

d) 0.50 g O_2 x $\dfrac{1 \text{ mole } O_2}{32.00 \text{ g } O_2}$ = 0.01538789 (calc) = 0.016 mole O_2 (corr)

$P_{O_2} = \dfrac{0.016 \text{ mole} \times 0.08206 \frac{\text{atm L}}{\text{mole K}} \times 293 \text{ K}}{2.50 \text{ L}}$ = 0.15395392 (calc) = 0.15 atm (corr)

12.137 Partial pressure = mole fraction x total pressure

a) $P_{O_2} = \dfrac{0.40 \text{ mole}}{0.40 + 0.40 \text{ mole}}$ x 1.20 atm = 0.6 (calc) = 0.60 atm (corr)

b) $P_{O_2} = \dfrac{0.40 \text{ mole}}{0.40 + 0.80 \text{ mole}}$ x 1.20 atm = 0.4 (calc) = 0.40 atm (corr)

c) The mole fraction of O_2 is 1/3.

P_{O_2} = ⅓ x 1.20 atm = 0.4 (calc) = 0.400 atm (corr)

d) 0.400 atm. An equal number of molecules means that there is also an equal number of moles present.

12.139 $P_A = P_T \cdot \dfrac{n_A}{n_T}$ or $P_T = P_A \cdot \dfrac{n_T}{n_A}$

$P_T = 0.40$ atm x $\dfrac{4.0 + 2.0 + 0.50 \text{ moles total}}{0.5 \text{ mole Ne}} = 5.2$ atm (calc and corr)

12.141 a) 1.00 - 0.150 = 0.850 mole fraction of O_2
0.850 x 6.00 atm = 5.10 atm (calc and corr)
b) 2.26 atm = 0.180 (X atm) = 12.5555 (calc) = 12.6 atm total pressure
1.00 - 0.180 = 0.82 mole fraction O_2
0.82 (12.6 atm) = 10.33 (calc) = 10.3 atm (corr)

12.143 0.500atm He + 0.250 atm Ar + 0.350 atm Xe = 1.100 atm total pressure

$X_{He} = \dfrac{0.500 \text{ atm}}{1.100 \text{ atm}} = 0.454545(\text{calc}) = 0.455$ (corr)

$X_{Ar} = \dfrac{0.250 \text{ atm}}{1.100 \text{ atm}} = 0.227272(\text{calc}) = 0.227$ (corr)

$X_{Xe} = \dfrac{0.350 \text{ atm}}{1.100 \text{ atm}} = 0.3181818$ (calc) $= 0.318$ (corr)

12.145 Moles $N_2 = 20.0$ g N_2 x $\dfrac{1 \text{ mole } N_2}{28.02 \text{ g } N_2} = 0.71377588$ (calc) $= 0.714$ moles N_2 (corr)

Moles Ar = 8.00 g Ar x $\dfrac{1 \text{ mole Ar}}{39.95 \text{ g Ar}} = 0.200250$ (calc) $= 0.200$ moles Ar (corr)

Total moles = 0.714 + 0.200 = 0.914 moles

$\dfrac{P_1}{n_1} = \dfrac{P_2}{n_2}$ $\dfrac{1.00 \text{ atm}}{0.714 \text{ mole}} = \dfrac{P_2}{0.914 \text{ mole}}$ $P_2 = 1.280112$ (calc) $= 1.28$ atm (corr)

12.147 From the coefficients in the balanced equation, the mole fraction of $N_2 = \dfrac{1}{1 + 3} = 0.250$ and the

mole fraction of $H_2 = \dfrac{3}{1 + 3} = 0.750$

$P_{N_2} = 0.250$ x 852 mm Hg = 213 mm Hg (calc and corr)

$P_{H_2} = 0.750$ x 852 mm Hg = 639 mm Hg (calc and corr)

12.149 Water vapor pressure values are obtained from Table 12.6 in the text.
a) 743 - 16.5 mm Hg = 726.5 (calc) = 726 mm Hg (corr)
b) 645 - 28.3 mm Hg = 616.7 (calc) = 617 mm Hg (corr)
c) 762 - 39.9 mm Hg = 722.1 (calc) = 722 mm Hg (corr)
d) 0.933 atm x $\dfrac{760 \text{ mm Hg}}{1 \text{ atm}} = 709.08$ (calc) = 709 mm Hg (corr)

709 - 18.7 mm Hg = 690.3 (calc) = $69\overline{0}$ mm Hg (corr)

12.151 a) mole fraction He, $X_{He} = \dfrac{0.100 \text{ mole He}}{0.100 + 0.200 + 0.800 \text{ moles total}}$

$$= 0.09090909 \text{ (calc)} = 0.0909 \text{ (corr)}$$

b) mole % Ar $= \dfrac{0.800 \text{ mole Ar}}{1.100 \text{ moles total}} \times 100 = 72.7272727 \text{ (calc)} = 72.7 \text{ % Ar (corr)}$

c) $P_{Ne} = X_{Ne} \times P_{total} = \dfrac{0.200 \text{ mole}}{1.100 \text{ moles total}} \times 1.00 \text{ atm} = 0.1818182 \text{ (calc)} = 0.182 \text{ atm (corr)}$

pressure % Ne $= \dfrac{P_{Ne}}{P_{total}} \times 100 = \dfrac{0.182 \text{ atm}}{1.00 \text{ atm}} \times 100 = 18.2 \text{ % Ne}$

d) volume He at STP (alone) $= 0.100 \text{ mole He} \times \dfrac{22.41 \text{ L He}}{1 \text{ mole He}} = 2.241 \text{(calc)} = 2.24 \text{ L He (corr)}$

volume % He $= \dfrac{\text{vol He}}{\text{total volume}} \times 100 = \dfrac{2.24 \text{ L He}}{24.64 \text{ L total}} \times 100$

$$= 9.0909091 \text{ (calc)} = 9.09 \text{ % He (corr)}$$

12.153 a) at constant temperature and pressure,

vol % $O_2 = \dfrac{V_{O_2}}{V_{total}} \times 100 = \dfrac{2.0 \text{ L } O_2}{8.0 \text{ L total}} \times 100 = 25 \text{ % } O_2 \text{ (calc and corr)}$

b) mole Ar $= 3.0 \text{ L Ar} \times \dfrac{1 \text{ mole Ar}}{22.41 \text{ L Ar}} = 0.1338688 \text{ (calc)} = 0.13 \text{ mole Ar (corr)}$

mole $O_2 = 2.0 \text{ L } O_2 \times \dfrac{1 \text{ mole } O_2}{22.41 \text{ L } O_2} = 0.0892458 \text{ (calc)} = 0.089 \text{ mole } O_2 \text{ (corr)}$

mole Ne $= 3.0 \text{ L Ne} \times \dfrac{1 \text{ mole Ne}}{22.41 \text{ L Ne}} = 0.1338688 \text{ (calc)} = 0.13 \text{ mole Ne (corr)}$

total moles $= 0.13 + 0.089 + 0.13 = 0.349 \text{ (calc)} = 0.35 \text{ mole (corr)}$

mole % Ar $= \dfrac{\text{moles Ar}}{\text{total moles}} \times 100 = \dfrac{0.13}{0.35} \times 100 = 37.142857 \text{ (calc)} = 37 \text{ % Ar (corr)}$

c) In the final container, $P_{Ne} = X_{Ne} \times P_{total} = \dfrac{0.13 \text{ mole Ne}}{0.35 \text{ moles total}} \times 1.00 \text{ atm}$

$$= 0.37142857 \text{ (calc)} = 0.37 \text{ atm (corr)}$$

Pressure % Ne $= \dfrac{0.37 \text{ atm Ne}}{1.0 \text{ atm total}} \times 100 = 37 \text{ % Ne (calc and corr)}$

d) $P_{O_2} = X_{O_2} \times P_{total}$ in final container

$$= \dfrac{0.089 \text{ mole } O_2}{0.35 \text{ mole total}} \times 1.0 \text{ atm} = 0.25428571 \text{ (calc)} = 0.25 \text{ atm (corr)}$$

ADDITIONAL PROBLEMS

12.155 $1.00 \text{ L } CO_2 \times \dfrac{1 \text{ mole } CO_2}{22.41 \text{ L } CO_2} \times \dfrac{6.022 \times 10^{23} \text{ molecules } CO_2}{1 \text{ mole } CO_2}$

$$= 2.6871932 \times 10^{22} \text{ (calc)} = 2.69 \times 10^{22} \text{ molecules } CO_2 \text{ (corr)}$$

12.157 $n = \dfrac{0.0010 \text{ mm Hg} \times 0.00100 \text{ L}}{62.36 \dfrac{\text{mm Hg L}}{\text{mole K}} \times 296 \text{ K}} = 5.4175407 \times 10^{-11} \text{ (calc)} = 5.4 \times 10^{-11} \text{ mole } O_2 \text{ (corr)}$

$5.4 \times 10^{-11} \text{ mole } O_2 \times \dfrac{6.022 \times 10^{23} \text{ molecules } O_2}{1 \text{ mole } O_2}$

$= 3.25188 \times 10^{13} \text{ (calc)} = 3.3 \times 10^{13} \text{ molecules } O_2 \text{ (corr)}$

12.159 $8.00 \text{ g } N_2 \times \dfrac{1 \text{ mole } N_2}{28.02 \text{ g } N_2} = 0.2855103 \text{ (calc)} = 0.286 \text{ mole } N_2 \text{ (corr)}$

$1.00 \times 10^{23} \text{ molecules } NH_3 \times \dfrac{1 \text{ mole } NH_3}{6.022 \times 10^{23} \text{ molecules } NH_3}$

$= 0.1660577 \text{ (calc)} = 0.166 \text{ mole } NH_3 \text{ (corr)}$

$V_{NH_3} = V_{N_2} \times \dfrac{n_{NH_3}}{n_{H_2}} = 6.00 \text{ L} \times \dfrac{0.166 \text{ mole}}{0.286 \text{ mole}} = 3.4825174 \text{ (calc)} = 3.48 \text{ L } NH_3 \text{ (corr)}$

12.161 $n_1 = \dfrac{1.00 \text{ atm} \times 1.00 \text{ L}}{0.08206 \dfrac{\text{atm L}}{\text{mole K}} \times 298 \text{ K}} = 0.0408933 \text{ (calc)} = 0.0409 \text{ mole } O_2 \text{ (corr)}$

$n_2 = \dfrac{0.880 \text{ atm} \times 1.00 \text{ L}}{0.08206 \dfrac{\text{atm L}}{\text{mole K}} \times 295 \text{ K}} = 0.036352 \text{ (calc)} = 0.0364 \text{ mole } O_2 \text{ (corr)}$

$\Delta n = (0.0409 - 0.0364) \text{ mole } O_2 = 0.0045 \text{ mole } O_2 \text{ (calc and corr)}$

$0.0045 \text{ mole } O_2 \times \dfrac{32.00 \text{ g } O_2}{1 \text{ mole } O_2} = 0.144 \text{ (calc)} = 0.14 \text{ g } O_2 \text{ (corr)}$

12.163 Let V_1 = original volume in mL, $V_2 = V_1 - 25.0$ mL

Applying Boyles Law: $V_2 = V_1 \cdot \dfrac{P_1}{P_2}$

$V_1 - 25.0 = V_1 \times \dfrac{1.50 \text{ atm}}{3.50 \text{ atm}}$

Rearranging gives: $V_1 - V_1 \times \dfrac{1.50}{3.50} = 25.0$ or $V_1 \left(1 - \dfrac{1.50}{3.50} \right) = 25.0$

or $V_1 \dfrac{3.50 - 1.50}{3.50} = 25.0$ or $V_1 \times \dfrac{2.00}{3.50} = 25.0$

$V_1 = 25.0 \dfrac{3.50}{2.00} = 43.75 \text{ (calc)} = 43.8 \text{ mL (corr)}$

12.165 $P_1 V_1 = P_2 V_2$, $P_1 = 3.6$ atm, $V_1 = ?$, $P_2 = 2.6$ atm, $V_2 = (5.21 + V_1)$
$3.6 \ V_1 = 2.6(5.21 + V_1)$
$3.6 \ V_1 = 13.5 + 2.6 \ V_1$
$1.0 \ V_1 = 13.5 \text{ mL}$
$V_1 = 14 \text{ mL}$

12.167 $P_1V_1 = P_2V_2 \quad V_2 = 0.800\ V_1$

$$P_2 = P_1 \cdot \frac{V_1}{V_2} = P_1 \frac{V_1}{0.800\ V_1} = 1.25\ P_1 \text{ (calc and corr)}$$

$$\Delta P = (1.25\ P_1 - P_1) = 0.25\ P_1$$

$$\% \text{ change} = \frac{\Delta P}{P_1} \times 100 = \frac{0.25\ P_1}{P_1} \times 100 = 25\ \% \text{ (calc and corr)}$$

12.169 $V_2 = 1.500\ V_1$

$$T_2 = T_1 \cdot \frac{V_2}{V_1} = T_1 \frac{1.500\ V_1}{V_1} = 1.500\ T_1$$

$$\Delta T = 1.500\ T_1 - T_1 = 0.500\ T_1$$

$$\% \text{ change} = \frac{\Delta T}{T_1} \times 100 = \frac{0.500\ T_1}{T_1} \times 100 = 50\ \% \text{ (calc)} = 50.0\ \% \text{ (corr)}$$

12.171 a) $\dfrac{d_{O_2}}{d_{N_2}} = \dfrac{\dfrac{\text{molar mass}_{O_2}}{\text{molar volume (STP)}}}{\dfrac{\text{molar mass}_{N_2}}{\text{molar volume (STP)}}} = \dfrac{\text{molar mass}_{O_2}}{\text{molar mass}_{N_2}} = \dfrac{32.00\ \text{g/mole}}{28.02\ \text{g/mole}}$

$$= 1.1420414 \text{ (calc)} = 1.14{:}1 \text{ (corr)}$$

b) $\dfrac{d_{O_2}}{d_{N_2}} = \dfrac{\dfrac{(MM)_{O_2}P_{O_2}}{RT}}{\dfrac{(MM)_{N_2}P_{N_2}}{RT}} = \dfrac{(MM)_{O_2} \times 1.25\ \text{atm}}{(MM)_{N_2} \times 1.25\ \text{atm}} = \dfrac{32.00\ \text{g/mole}}{28.02\ \text{g/mole}}$

$$= 1.1420414 \text{ (calc)} = 1.14{:}1 \text{ (corr)}$$

12.173 Add the partial pressures of each gas in the new container.

$$P_{N_2} = 350.0\ \text{mm Hg} \times \frac{1.000\ \text{L}}{2.000\ \text{L}} = 175 \text{ (calc)} = 175.0\ \text{mm Hg (corr)}$$

$$P_{O_2} = 300.0\ \text{mm Hg} \times \frac{6.000\ \text{L}}{2.000\ \text{L}} = 900. \text{ (calc)} = 900.0\ \text{mm Hg (corr)}$$

$$P_{H_2} = 250.0\ \text{mm Hg} \times \frac{1.000\ \text{L}}{2.000\ \text{L}} = 125 \text{ (calc)} = 125.0\ \text{mm Hg (corr)}$$

Total pressure = 175.0 + 900.0 + 125.0 = 1200.0 mm Hg

12.175 Find the pressure of SF_6 in the new container. This is its partial pressure.

$$P_{SF_6} = 0.97\ \text{atm} \times \frac{376\ \text{mL}}{275\ \text{mL}} = 1.3262545 \text{ (calc)} = 1.3\ \text{atm (corr)}$$

12.177 $P = \dfrac{g\ RT}{V(MM)} = \dfrac{15.0\ \text{g} \times 0.08206\ \dfrac{\text{atm L}}{\text{mole K}} \times 327\ \text{K}}{4.0\ \text{L} \times 39.95\ \text{g/mole}} = 2.5188004 \text{ (calc)} = 2.5\ \text{atm (corr)}$

12.179 N_2 pressure in He container at 37 °C (310 K):

$$P_2 = 645 \text{ mm Hg} \times \frac{30.0 \text{ mL}}{40.0 \text{ mL}} \times \frac{310 \text{ K}}{300 \text{ K}} = 499.875 \text{ (calc)} = 5\overline{00} \text{ mm Hg (corr)}$$

Total pressure in 40.0 mL container at 37 °C:

$$P_{total} = 765 + 5\overline{00} \text{ mm Hg} = 1265 \text{ mm Hg (calc and corr)}$$

Total pressure at 32 °C:

$$P_2 = 1265 \text{ mm Hg} \times \frac{305 \text{ K}}{310 \text{ K}} = 1244.5968 \text{ (calc)} = 1240 \text{ mm Hg (corr)}$$

CUMULATIVE PROBLEMS

12.181 steam: use $n = \dfrac{PV}{RT}$; T = 135 °C + 273 = 408 K

$$n = \frac{1.02 \text{ atm} \times 20.0 \text{ L}}{0.08206 \dfrac{\text{atm L}}{\text{mole K}} \times 408 \text{ K}} = 0.6093102 \text{ (calc)} = 0.609 \text{ moles}$$

$$0.609 \text{ moles} \times \frac{6.022 \times 10^{23} \text{ molecules}}{1 \text{ mole}} = 3.667398 \times 10^{23} \text{ (calc)} = 3.67 \times 10^{23} \text{ molecules (corr)}$$

ice: $10.5 \text{ mL} \times \dfrac{0.917 \text{ g}}{\text{mL}} \times \dfrac{1 \text{ mole } H_2O}{18.02 \text{ g } H_2O} \times \dfrac{6.022 \times 10^{23} \text{ molecules}}{1 \text{ mole } H_2O}$

$$= 3.217693 \times 10^{23} \text{ (calc)} = 3.22 \times 10^{23} \text{ molecules (corr)}$$

The steam has more molecules.

12.183 $2.24 \text{ L} \times \dfrac{1 \text{ mole gas}}{22.41 \text{ L}} = 0.0999553 \text{ (calc)} = 0.100 \text{ mole (corr)}$

Molar mass $= \dfrac{7.5 \text{ g}}{0.100 \text{ mole}} = 75 \text{ g/mole (calc and corr)}$

Molecular mass = 75 amu

12.185 molar mass = density (STP) x molar volume (STP)

$$= \frac{1.517 \text{ g}}{1 \text{ L}} \times \frac{22.41 \text{ L}}{1 \text{ mole}} = 33.99597 \text{ (calc)} = 34.00 \text{ g/mole (corr)}$$

molar mass P + X(molar mass H)   = 34.00 g/mole
30.97 + X(1.01)   = 34.00
1.01X   = 3.03
X   = 3

12.187 Take 100 g mixture, giving 75.0 g HCl, 5.00 g H_2 and 20.0 g He.

a) moles HCl = $75.0 \text{ g HCl} \times \dfrac{1 \text{ mole}}{36.46 \text{ g}} = 2.0570488 \text{ (calc)} = 2.06 \text{ moles HCl (corr)}$

moles H_2 = $5.00 \text{ g } H_2 \times \dfrac{1 \text{ mole } H_2}{2.02 \text{ g } H_2} = 2.4752475 \text{ (calc)} = 2.48 \text{ moles } H_2 \text{ (corr)}$

moles He = $20.0 \text{ g He} \times \dfrac{1 \text{ mole He}}{4.00 \text{ g He}} = 5 \text{ (calc)} = 5.00 \text{ mole He (corr)}$

total moles = 2.06 + 2.48 + 5.00 = 9.54 moles (calc and corr)

$$X_{HCl} = \frac{2.05}{9.54} = 0.2159329 \text{ (calc)} = 0.216 \text{ (corr)}$$

$$X_{H_2} = \frac{2.48}{9.54} = 0.259958 \text{ (calc)} = 0.260 \text{ (corr)}$$

$$X_{He} = \frac{5.00}{9.54} = 0.524109 \text{ (calc)} = 0.524 \text{ (corr)}$$

b) $P_{HCl} = X_{HCl} \cdot P_{total} = 0.216 \times 1.20 \text{ atm} = 0.2592 \text{ (calc)} = 0.259 \text{ atm (corr)}$
   $P_{H_2} = 0.260 \times 1.20 \text{ atm} = 0.312 \text{ atm (calc and corr)}$
   $P_{He} = 0.524 \times 1.20 \text{ atm} = 0.6288 \text{ (calc)} = 0.629 \text{ atm (corr)}$

c) weighted average molar mass $(\overline{MM})$ = sum of the product of each mole fraction times the molar mass
   $(\overline{MM}) = 0.216 \times 36.46 \text{ g/mole} + 0.260 \times 2.02 \text{ g/mole} + 0.525 \times 4.00 \text{ g/mole}$
   $$= 10.50056 \text{ (calc)} = 10.50 \text{ g/mole (corr)}$$

d) density $= \dfrac{10.50 \text{ g/mole}}{22.41 \text{ L/mole}} = 0.4685408 \text{ (calc)} = 0.4685 \text{ g/L (corr)}$

12.189 $0.480 \text{ g C} \times \dfrac{1 \text{ mole C}}{12.01 \text{ g C}} = 0.0399666 \text{ (calc)} = 0.0400 \text{ mole C (corr)}$

$0.101 \text{ g H} \times \dfrac{1 \text{ mole H}}{1.01 \text{ g H}} = 0.1 \text{ (calc)} = 0.100 \text{ mole H (corr)}$

C: $\dfrac{0.0400}{0.0400} = 1.00$ H $= \dfrac{0.100}{0.0400} = 2.50$ C: $1.00 \times 2 = 2.00$ H: $2.50 \times 2 = 5.00$

Empirical formula $= C_2H_5$ Empirical formula mass = 29.05 amu

$\dfrac{0.0869 \text{ g}}{33.6 \text{ mL}} \times \dfrac{1 \text{ mL}}{10^{-3} \text{ L}} \times \dfrac{22.41 \text{ L}}{1 \text{ mole}} = 57.959196 \text{ (calc)} = 58.0 \text{ g/mole (corr)}$

$\dfrac{\text{formula mass}}{\text{empirical formula mass}} = \dfrac{58.0 \text{ amu}}{29.05 \text{ amu}} = 1.9965517 \text{ (calc)} = 2.00 \text{ (corr)}$

Molecular formula $= (C_2H_5)_2 = C_4H_{10}$

12.191 Basis: 100.0 g compound

$24.3 \text{ g C} \times \dfrac{1 \text{ mole C}}{12.01 \text{ g C}} = 2.0233139 \text{ (calc)} = 2.02 \text{ moles C (corr)}$

$4.1 \text{ g H} \times \dfrac{1 \text{ mole H}}{1.01 \text{ g H}} = 4.0594059 \text{ (calc)} = 4.1 \text{ moles H (calc and corr)}$

$71.6 \text{ g Cl} \times \dfrac{1 \text{ mole Cl}}{35.46 \text{ g Cl}} = 2.0197461 \text{ (calc)} = 2.02 \text{ moles Cl (corr)}$

C: $\dfrac{2.02}{2.02} = 1.00$ H: $\dfrac{4.1}{2.02} = 2.0$ Cl: $\dfrac{2.02}{2.02} = 1.00$

Empirical formula is CH_2Cl Empirical formula mass = 49.48 amu

$(MM) = \dfrac{mRT}{PV}$, $T = 96\ ^\circ C + 273 = 369 \text{ K}$

$$(MM) = \frac{0.132 \text{ g} \times 62.36 \dfrac{\text{mm Hg L}}{\text{mole L}} \times 369 \text{ K}}{741 \text{ mm Hg} \times 0.0414 \text{ L}} = 99.012004 \text{ (calc)} = 99.0 \text{ g/mole (corr)}$$

$$\frac{\text{formula mass}}{\text{empirical formula mass}} = \frac{99.0 \text{ amu}}{49.48 \text{ amu}} = 2.00008084 \text{ (calc)} = 2.00 \text{ (corr)}$$

Molecular formula = $(CH_2Cl)_2 = C_2H_4Cl_2$

12.193 Calculate the limiting reactant.

$$60.0 \text{ L NH}_3 \times \frac{4 \text{ L NO}}{4 \text{ L NH}_3} = 60.0 \text{ L NO} \qquad 60.0 \text{ L O}_2 \times \frac{4 \text{ L NO}}{5 \text{ L O}_2} = 48.0 \text{ L NO}$$

∴ Therefore O_2 is limiting and $60.0 \text{ L O}_2 \times \dfrac{6 \text{ L H}_2\text{O}}{5 \text{ L O}_2} = 72.0 \text{ L H}_2\text{O}$

$72.0 \text{ L H}_2\text{O} + 48.0 \text{ L NO} = 120.0 \text{ L total gas products.}$

12.195 Calculate the limiting reactant:

H_2S: $n = \dfrac{625 \text{ mm Hg} \times 1.75 \text{ L}}{62.36 \dfrac{\text{mm Hg L}}{\text{mole K}} \times 298 \text{ K}} = 0.0588566 \text{ (calc)} = 0.0589 \text{ mole H}_2S \text{ (corr)}$

$$0.0589 \text{ mole H}_2S \times \frac{2 \text{ moles H}_2\text{O}}{2 \text{ moles H}_2S} = 0.0589 \text{ mole H}_2\text{O (calc and corr)}$$

O_2: $n = \dfrac{715 \text{ mm Hg} \times 5.75 \text{ L}}{62.36 \dfrac{\text{mm Hg L}}{\text{mole K}} \times 283 \text{ K}} = 0.2329599 \text{ (calc)} = 0.233 \text{ mole O}_2 \text{ (corr)}$

$$0.233 \text{ mole O}_2 \times \frac{2 \text{ moles H}_2\text{O}}{3 \text{ moles O}_2} = 0.15533333 \text{ (calc)} = 0.155 \text{ mole H}_2\text{O (corr)}$$

H_2S is the limiting reactant.

$$0.0589 \text{ mole H}_2\text{O} \times \frac{18.02 \text{ g H}_2\text{O}}{1 \text{ mole H}_2\text{O}} = 1.061378 \text{ (calc)} = 1.06 \text{ g H}_2\text{O (corr)}$$

12.197 $22.0 \text{ g NH}_3 \times \dfrac{1 \text{ mole NH}_3}{17.04 \text{ g NH}_3} \times \dfrac{6 \text{ moles HCl}}{2 \text{ moles NH}_3} \times \dfrac{22.41 \text{ L HCl}}{1 \text{ mole HCl}} \times \dfrac{1 \text{ mL HCl}}{10^{-3} \text{ L HCl}} \times \dfrac{1 \text{ cm}^3 \text{ HCl}}{1 \text{ mL HCl}}$

$$\times \left(\frac{10^{-2} \text{ m HCl}}{1 \text{ cm HCl}}\right)^3 = 0.0867992 \text{ (calc)} = 0.0868 \text{ m}^3 \text{ HCl (corr)}$$

12.199 Calculate the limiting reactant:

NH_3: $n = 7.00 \text{ g NH}_3 \times \dfrac{1 \text{ mole NH}_3}{17.04 \text{ g NH}_3} \times \dfrac{1 \text{ mole NH}_4\text{Cl}}{1 \text{ mole NH}_3}$

$$= 0.4107981 \text{ (calc)} = 0.411 \text{ mole NH}_4\text{Cl (corr)}$$

HCl: $n = 12.0 \text{ g HCl} \times \dfrac{1 \text{ mole HCl}}{36.46 \text{ g HCl}} \times \dfrac{1 \text{ mole NH}_4\text{Cl}}{1 \text{ mole HCl}}$

$$= 0.3291278 \text{ (calc)} = 0.329 \text{ mole NH}_4\text{Cl (corr)}$$

HCl is the limiting reactant.
0.329 mole NH_3 react (one-to-one ratio).

NH_3 originally present: $7.00 \text{ g NH}_3 \times \dfrac{1 \text{ mole NH}_3}{17.04 \text{ g NH}_3} = 0.4107981 \text{ (calc)}$

$$= 0.411 \text{ mole NH}_3 \text{ (corr)}$$

NH_3 is the only gas that remains after the reaction.
$\Delta n = (0.411 - 0.329)$ mole $NH_3 = 0.082$ mole NH_3 (calc and corr)

$$P = \frac{0.082 \text{ mole} \times 0.08206 \dfrac{\text{atm L}}{\text{mole K}} \times 298 \text{ K}}{1.00 \text{ L}} = 2.0052182 \text{ (calc)} = 2.0 \text{ atm (corr)}$$

12.201 $4.22 \text{ L O}_2 \times \dfrac{1 \text{ mole O}_2}{22.41 \text{ L O}_2} \times \dfrac{2 \text{ moles KNO}_3}{1 \text{ mole O}_2} \times \dfrac{101.11 \text{ g KNO}_3}{1 \text{ mole KNO}_3} = 38.07980 \text{ (calc)}$

$$= 38.1 \text{ g KNO}_3 \text{ (corr)}$$

Percent KNO_3 in sample: $\dfrac{38.1 \text{ g KNO}_3}{60.2 \text{ g sample}} \times 100 = 63.25549 \text{ (calc)} = 63.3 \% \text{ KNO}_3$

12.203 The N_2 gas is at STP.

$$\frac{5.20 \text{ \$}}{1000 \text{ ft}^3} \times \left(\frac{1 \text{ ft}}{12 \text{ in.}}\right)^3 \times \left(\frac{1 \text{ in.}}{2.540 \text{ cm}}\right)^3 \times \frac{1 \text{ cm}^3}{1 \text{ mL}} \times \frac{1 \text{ mL}}{10^{-3} \text{ L}} \times \frac{22.41 \text{ L N}_2}{1 \text{ mole N}_2}$$

$$\times \frac{1 \text{ mole N}_2}{28.02 \text{ g N}_2} \times \frac{100 \text{ ¢}}{1 \text{ \$}} = 0.0146869 \text{ (calc)} = 0.0147 \text{ ¢/g (corr)}$$

CHAPTER THIRTEEN
Solutions

PRACTICE PROBLEMS

Characteristics of Solutions (Sec. 13.1)

13.1 a) true, solutions may have multiple solutes
b) true, if it a solution it is heterogeneous by definition.
c) true, all parts of a homogeneous solution have the same properties
d) false, solutes will not settle out of solution

13.3 a) solute = sodium chloride, solvent = water
b) solute = sucrose, solvent = water
c) solute = water, solvent = ethyl alcohol
d) solute = ethyl alcohol, solvent = methyl alcohol

Solubility (Sec. 13.2)

13.5 a) $\dfrac{455 \text{ g AgNO}_3}{100 \text{ g water}}$ at 100 °C = unsaturated

b) $\dfrac{465 \text{ g AgNO}_3}{100 \text{ g water}}$ at 50 °C = supersaturated

c) $\dfrac{910 \text{ g AgNO}_3}{200 \text{ g water}} = \dfrac{455 \text{ g AgNO}_3}{100 \text{ g water}}$ at 50 °C = saturated

d) $\dfrac{55 \text{ g AgNO}_3}{50 \text{ g water}} = \dfrac{110 \text{ g AgNO}_3}{100 \text{ g water}}$ at 0 °C = unsaturated

13.7 a) $\dfrac{1.94 \text{ g PbBr}_2}{100 \text{ g water}} = 0.0194$, insoluble at 50 °C

b) $\dfrac{161.4 \text{ g CsCl}}{100 \text{ g water}} = 1.614$, soluble at 0 °C

c) $\dfrac{952 \text{ g AgNO}_3}{100 \text{ g water}} = 9.52$, soluble at 100 °C

d) $\dfrac{0.573 \text{ g Ag}_2\text{SO}_4}{100 \text{ g water}} = 0.00573$, insoluble at 0 °C

13.9 a) concentrated b) concentrated c) concentrated d) dilute

13.11 a) ammonia gas in water with P = 1atm and T = 50 °C is more soluble
b) carbon dioxide gas in water with P = 2 atm and T = 50 °C is more soluble
c) table salt in water with P = 1 atm and T = 60 °C is more soluble
d) table sugar in water with P = 1 atm and T = 70 °C is more soluble

13.13 $200 \text{ mL H}_2\text{O} \times \dfrac{1 \text{ g H}_2\text{O}}{1 \text{ mL H}_2\text{O}} = 200 \text{ g H}_2\text{O}$

a) at 70 °C, solubility $\dfrac{110 \text{ g Pb(NO}_3)_2}{100 \text{ g water}}$ if $\dfrac{200 \text{ g Pb(NO}_3)_2}{200 \text{ g water}}$ present, none will settle out of water

b) at 40 °C, solubility $\dfrac{78 \text{ g Pb(NO}_3)_2}{100 \text{ g water}}$ $\dfrac{200 \text{ g Pb(NO}_3)_2}{200 \text{ g water}}$ present, then

200g - 2(78 g) = 44 g $Pb(NO_3)_2$ will settle out of water

Solution Formation (Sec. 13.3)

13.15   a) hydrated ion   b) hydrated ion   c) oxygen atom   d) hydrogen atom

13.17   a) decrease   b) increase   c) increase   d) increase

Solubility Rules (Sec. 13.4)

13.19   a) very soluble   b) slightly soluble   c) slightly soluble   d) very soluble

13.21   a) soluble b) soluble   c) insoluble   d) soluble

13.23   a) carbonates are insoluble with the exception of group IA and NH_4^+
b) sulfides are insoluble with the exception of group IA and IIA and NH_4^+
c) ammonium is always soluble
d) sulfates are soluble with the exception of Ca^{+2}, Sr^{+2}, Ba^{+2}, Pb^{+2}

13.25   a) chlorides and sulfates are soluble with exceptions
b) Nitrates and ammonium-ions are soluble
c) carbonates and phosphates are insoluble with exceptions
d) sodium and potassium ions are soluble

13.27   a) both soluble   b) soluble and insoluble, c) both soluble   d) both insoluble

13.29   a) no, $MgSO_4$ soluble   b) yes   c) no, both soluble   d) no, both soluble

Mass Percent (Sec. 13.6)

13.31   a) $\dfrac{6.43 \text{ g NaI}}{85.0 + 6.43 \text{ g solution}} \times 100 = 7.0327026 \text{ (calc)} = 7.03 \text{ % NaI (corr)}$

b) $\dfrac{3.23 \text{ g NaI}}{175.00 + 3.23 \text{ g solution}} \times 100 = 1.8122651 \text{ (calc)} = 1.81\% \text{ NaI (corr)}$

c) $\dfrac{10.3 \text{ g NaI}}{53.0 \text{ g solution}} \times 100 = 19.4339623 \text{ (calc)} = 19.4 \text{ % NaI (corr)}$

d) 0.030 mole NaI x $\dfrac{149.89 \text{ g NaI}}{1 \text{ mole NaI}} = 4.4967 \text{ (calc)} = 4.5 \text{ g NaI (corr)}$

$\dfrac{4.5 \text{ g NaI}}{100.0 + 4.5 \text{ g solution}} \times 100 = 4.30622 \text{ (calc)} = 4.3 \text{ % NaI}$

13.33   a) 35.0 g solution x $\dfrac{2.00 \text{ g NaCl}}{100 \text{ g solution}} = 0.7 \text{ (calc)} = 0.700 \text{ g NaCl (corr)}$

b) $125 \text{ g solution} \times \dfrac{3.50 \text{ g AgNO}_3}{100 \text{ g solution}} = 4.375 \text{ (calc)} = 4.38 \text{ g AgNO}_3 \text{ (corr)}$

c) $1355 \text{ g solution} \times \dfrac{10.00 \text{ g K}_2\text{SO}_4}{100.0 \text{ g solution}} = 135.5 \text{ g K}_2\text{SO}_4 \text{ (calc and corr)}$

d) $43.3 \text{ g solution} \times \dfrac{8.25 \text{ g HCl}}{100 \text{ g solution}} = 3.57225 \text{ (calc)} = 3.57 \text{ g HCl (corr)}$

13.35 a) $5.75 \text{ g solution} \times \dfrac{10.00 \text{ g CaCl}_2}{100.0 \text{ g solution}} = 0.575 \text{ g CaCl}_2 \text{ (calc and corr)}$

$5.75 \text{ g solution} - 0.575 \text{ g CaCl}_2 = 5.175 \text{ (calc)} = 5.18 \text{ g H}_2\text{O (corr)}$

Alternate method: If the solution is 10.00 % $CaCl_2$, it is 90.00 % H_2O

$5.75 \text{ g solution} \times \dfrac{90.00 \text{ g H}_2\text{O}}{100.0 \text{ g solution}} = 5.175 \text{ (calc)} = 5.18 \text{ g H}_2\text{O (corr)}$

b) $57.5 \text{ g solution} \times \dfrac{10.00 \text{ g CaCl}_2}{100.0 \text{ g solution}} = 5.75 \text{ g CaCl}_2 \text{ (calc and corr)}$

$57.5 \text{ g solution} - 5.75 \text{ g CaCl}_2 = 51.75 \text{ g (calc)} = 51.8 \text{ g H}_2\text{O (corr)}$

c) $57.5 \text{ g solution} \times \dfrac{1.00 \text{ g CaCl}_2}{100 \text{ g solution}} = 0.575 \text{ g CaCl}_2 \text{ (calc and corr)}$

$57.5 \text{ g solution} - 0.575 \text{ g CaCl}_2 = 56.925 \text{ (calc)} = 56.9 \text{ g H}_2\text{O (corr)}$

d) $2.3 \text{ g solution} \times \dfrac{0.80 \text{ g CuCl}_2}{100 \text{ g solution}} = 0.0184 \text{ (calc)} = 0.018 \text{ g CaCl}_2 \text{ (corr)}$

$2.3 \text{ g solution} - 0.018 \text{ g CaCl}_2 = 2.282 \text{ (calc)} = 2.3 \text{ g H}_2\text{O (corr)}$

13.37 a) $50.0 \text{ g NaCl} \times \dfrac{95.00 \text{ g H}_2\text{O}}{5.00 \text{ g NaCl}} = 950 \text{ (calc)} = 9.50 \times 10^2 \text{ g H}_2\text{O (corr)}$

b) $50.0 \text{ g KCl} \times \dfrac{95.00 \text{ g H}_2\text{O}}{5.00 \text{ g KCl}} = 950 \text{ (calc)} = 9.50 \times 10^2 \text{ g H}_2\text{O (corr)}$

c) $50.0 \text{ g Na}_2\text{SO}_4 \times \dfrac{95.00 \text{ g H}_2\text{O}}{5.00 \text{ g Na}_2\text{SO}_4} = 950 \text{ (calc)} = 9.50 \times 10^2 \text{ g H}_2\text{O (corr)}$

d) $50.0 \text{ g LiNO}_3 \times \dfrac{95.00 \text{ g H}_2\text{O}}{5.00 \text{ g LiNO}_3} = 950 \text{ (calc)} = 9.50 \times 10^2 \text{ g H}_2\text{O (corr)}$

Volume Percent (Sec. 13.6)

13.39 a) $\dfrac{257 \text{ mL ethyl alcohol}}{325 \text{ mL solution}} \times 100 = 79.0769231 \text{ (calc)} = 79.1 \text{ % ethyl alcohol (corr)}$

b) $\dfrac{257 \text{ mL ethyl alcohol}}{675 \text{ mL solution}} \times 100 = 38.0740741 \text{ (calc)} = 38.1 \text{ % ethyl alcohol (corr)}$

c) $\dfrac{257 \text{ mL ethyl alcohol}}{1.23 \text{ L} \times \dfrac{1 \text{ mL}}{10^{-3} \text{ L}} \text{ solution}} \times 100 = 20.8943089 \text{ (calc)} = 20.9 \text{ % ethyl alcohol (corr)}$

d) $\dfrac{257 \text{ mL ethyl alcohol}}{5.000 \text{ L} \times \dfrac{1 \text{ mL}}{1 \times 10^{-3} \text{ L}} \text{ solution}} \times 100 = 5.14\%$ ethyl alcohol (calc and corr)

13.41 a) $\dfrac{360.6 \text{ mL methyl alcohol}}{1000.0 \text{ mL solution}} \times 100 = 36.06 \%$ methyl alcohol (calc and corr)

b) $\dfrac{667.2 \text{ mL } H_2O}{1000.0 \text{ mL solution}} \times 100 = 66.72 \% H_2O$ (calc and corr)

13.43 $375 \text{ mL solution} \times \dfrac{3.00 \text{ mL } H_2O_2}{100 \text{ mL solution}} = 11.25 \text{ (calc)} = 11.2 \text{ mL } H_2O_2$ (corr)

13.45 $4.00 \text{ gal solution} \times \dfrac{35.0 \text{ gal } H_2O}{100.0 \text{ gal solution}} = 1.40 \text{ gal } H_2O$ (calc and corr)

Mass-Volume Percent (Sec. 13.6)

13.47 Mass in grams, volume in mL

a) $\dfrac{2.00 \text{ g KI}}{75.0 \text{ mL solution}} \times 100 = 2.6666667 \text{ (calc)} = 2.67 \%$ (corr)

b) $\dfrac{15.0 \text{ g KI}}{1.25 \text{ L} \times \dfrac{1 \text{ mL}}{1 \times 10^{-3} \text{ L}} \text{ solution}} \times 100 = 1.2 \text{ (calc)} = 1.20 \%$ (corr)

c) $\dfrac{2.00 \text{ mole KI} \times \dfrac{166.00 \text{ g KI}}{1 \text{ mole KI}}}{10.00 \text{ L} \times \dfrac{1 \text{ mL}}{1 \times 10^{-3} \text{ L}} \text{ solution}} \times 100 = 3.32 \%$ (calc and corr)

d) $\dfrac{0.0020 \text{ mole KI} \times \dfrac{166.00 \text{ g KI}}{1 \text{ mole KI}}}{5.00 \text{ mL solution}} \times 100 = 6.64 \text{ (calc)} = 6.6 \%$ (corr)

13.49 a) $45.0 \text{ g } NaNO_3 \times \dfrac{100 \text{ mL solution}}{6.0 \text{ g } NaNO_3} = 75\overline{0} \text{ mL solution}$ (calc and corr)

b) $2.00 \text{ g } NaNO_3 \times \dfrac{100 \text{ mL solution}}{6.0 \text{ g } NaNO_3} = 33.3333333 \text{ (calc)} = 33 \text{ mL solution}$ (corr)

13.51 a) $455 \text{ mL solution} \times \dfrac{2.50 \text{ g } Na_3PO_4}{100 \text{ mL solution}} = 11.375 \text{ (calc)} = 11.4 \text{ g } Na_3PO_4$ (corr)

b) $50.0 \text{ L solution} \times \dfrac{1 \text{ mL}}{1 \times 10^{-3} \text{ L}} \times \dfrac{7.50 \text{ g } Na_3PO_4}{100 \text{ mL solution}}$

$= 3750 \text{ (calc)} = 3.75 \times 10^3 \text{ g } Na_3PO_4$ (corr)

13.53   Volume of solution = 5.0 g CsCl + 20.0 g H_2O = 25.0 g solution x $\dfrac{1 \text{ mL solution}}{1.18 \text{ g solution}}$

$\qquad\qquad\qquad$ = 21.1864407 (calc) = 21.2 mL (corr)

$\%\left(\dfrac{m}{v}\right) = \dfrac{5.0 \text{ g CsCl}}{21.2 \text{ mL solution}} \times 100 = 23.5849057 \text{ (calc)} = 24 \% \text{ (corr)}$

Parts per Million and Parts per Billion (Sec. 13.7)

13.55   a) 37.5 mg NaCl x $\dfrac{1 \text{ mg}}{1 \times 10^{-3} \text{ g}}$ = 0.0375 g NaCl

$\qquad$ 21.0 kg H_2O x $\dfrac{1 \times 10^3 \text{ g}}{1 \text{ kg}}$ = 21,$\overline{0}$00 g H_2O

$\qquad$ solution mass = 0.0375 g + 21,$\overline{0}$00 g = 21,$\overline{0}$00 g

$\qquad \dfrac{0.0375 \text{ g NaCl}}{21,\overline{0}00 \text{ g solution}} \times 10^6 = 1.7857143 \text{ (calc)} = 1.79 \text{ ppm (corr)}$

$\qquad$ b) 2.12 cg NaCl x $\dfrac{1 \times 10^{-2} \text{ g}}{1 \text{ cg}}$ = 0.0212 g NaCl

$\qquad$ solution mass = 0.0212 g NaCl + 125 g H_2O = 125.0212 (calc) = 125 g solution (corr)

$\qquad \dfrac{0.0212 \text{ g NaCl}}{125 \text{ g solution}} \times 10^6 = 169.6 \text{ (calc)} = 17\overline{0} \text{ ppm}$

$\qquad$ c) 1.00 μg NaCl = 1.00 x 10^{-6} g NaCl; 32.0 dg H_2O x $\dfrac{1 \times 10^{-1} \text{ g}}{1 \text{ dg}}$ = 3.20 g H_2O

$\qquad$ solution mass = 3.20 g H_2O + 1 x 10^{-6} g NaCl = 3.200001 (calc) = 3.20 g solution

$\qquad \dfrac{1.00 \times 10^{-6} \text{ g NaCl}}{3.20 \text{ g solution}} \times 10^6 = 0.3125 \text{ (calc)} = 0.312 \text{ ppm (corr)}$

$\qquad$ d) 35.7 mg NaCl x $\dfrac{1 \times 10^{-3} \text{ g}}{1 \text{ mg}}$ = 0.0357 g NaCl

$\qquad$ solution mass = 15.7 g H_2O + 0.0325 g NaCl = 15.7325 (calc) = 15.7 g solution (corr)

$\qquad \dfrac{0.0357 \text{ g NaCl}}{15.7 \text{ g solution}} \times 10^6 = 2273.88535 \text{ (calc)} = 2270 \text{ ppm (corr)}$

13.57   The only difference in set-up for ppb compared with ppm is changing the factor 10^6 to 10^9. The ppb value is 1000 times the ppm value.

$\qquad$ a) 1790 ppb   b) 17$\overline{0}$,000 **ppb**   c) 312 ppb   d) 2,270,000 ppb

13.59   Take the ratio between the mass of O_2 (in g) and the volume of water (in mL) times 10^6.

$\qquad \dfrac{7 \text{ mg } O_2 \times \dfrac{1 \times 10^{-3} \text{ g}}{1 \text{ mg}}}{1 \text{ L} \times \dfrac{1 \text{ mL}}{1 \times 10^{-3} \text{ L}}} \times 10^6 = 7 \text{ ppm.}$ Yes, 7 ppm is above the minimum.

13.61 $5.000 \text{ L air} \times \dfrac{1 \text{ mL}}{1 \times 10^{-3} \text{ L}} \times \dfrac{0.087 \text{ mL SO}_2}{10^6 \text{ mL air}} = 0.000435 \text{ (calc)} = 0.00044 \text{ mL SO}_2 \text{ (corr)}$

13.63   a) $725 \text{ mL air} \times \dfrac{3.6 \text{ g NH}_3}{10^6 \text{ mL air}} = 0.00261 \text{ (calc)} = 2.6 \times 10^{-3} \text{ g NH}_3 \text{ (corr)}$

          b) $725 \text{ mL air} \times \dfrac{7.5 \text{ g NH}_3}{10^9 \text{ mL air}} = 5.4375 \times 10^{-6} \text{ (calc)} = 5.4 \times 10^{-6} \text{ g NH}_3 \text{ (corr)}$

          c) $725 \text{ mL air} \times \dfrac{1.2 \text{ g NH}_3}{100 \text{ g air}} = 8.7 \text{ g NH}_3 \text{ (calc and corr)}$

Molarity (Sec. 13.8)

13.65   a) $\dfrac{2.0 \text{ moles NaOH}}{0.50 \text{ L solution}} = 4 \text{ (calc)} = 4.0 \text{ M (corr)}$

          b) $\dfrac{13.7 \text{ g NaOH} \times \dfrac{1 \text{ mole NaOH}}{40.00 \text{ g NaOH}}}{90.0 \text{ mL solution} \times \dfrac{1 \times 10^{-3} \text{ L}}{1 \text{ mL}}} = 3.8055556 \text{ (calc)} = 3.81 \text{ M (corr)}$

          c) $\dfrac{53.0 \text{ g NaOH} \times \dfrac{1 \text{ mole NaOH}}{40.00 \text{ g NaOH}}}{1.255 \text{ L solution}} = 1.0557769 \text{ (calc)} = 1.06 \text{ M (corr)}$

          d) $\dfrac{0.0020 \text{ mole NaOH}}{5.00 \text{ mL solution} \times \dfrac{1 \times 10^{-3} \text{ L}}{1 \text{ mL}}} = 0.4 \text{ (calc)} = 0.40 \text{ M (corr)}$

13.67   a) $35.0 \text{ mL solution} \times \dfrac{1 \times 10^{-3} \text{ L}}{1 \text{ mL}} \times \dfrac{6.00 \text{ moles HNO}_3}{1 \text{ L solution}} \times \dfrac{63.02 \text{ g HNO}_3}{1 \text{ mole HNO}_3}$

                               $= 13.2342 \text{ (calc)} = 13.2 \text{ g HNO}_3 \text{ (corr)}$

          b) $10.0 \text{ mL solution} \times \dfrac{1 \times 10^{-3} \text{ L}}{1 \text{ mL}} \times \dfrac{0.600 \text{ moles HNO}_3}{1 \text{ L solution}} \times \dfrac{63.02 \text{ g HNO}_3}{1 \text{ mole HNO}_3}$

                               $= 0.37812 \text{ (calc)} = 0.378 \text{ g HNO}_3 \text{ (calc and corr)}$

          c) $375 \text{ L solution} \times \dfrac{1.00 \text{ mole HNO}_3}{1 \text{ L solution}} \times \dfrac{63.02 \text{ g HNO}_3}{1 \text{ mole HNO}_3}$

                               $= 23632.5 \text{ (calc)} = 2.36 \times 10^4 \text{ g HNO}_3 \text{ (corr)}$

          d) $375 \text{ g solution} \times \dfrac{1 \text{ mL solution}}{1.25 \text{ g solution}} \times \dfrac{1 \times 10^{-3} \text{ L}}{1 \text{ mL}} \times \dfrac{7.91 \text{ moles HNO}_3}{1 \text{ L solution}} \times \dfrac{63.02 \text{ g HNO}_3}{1 \text{ mole HNO}_3}$

                               $= 149.54646 \text{ (calc)} = 150. \text{ g HNO}_3 \text{ (corr)}$

13.69 a) $2.50 \text{ g of Na}_2\text{S}_2\text{O}_3 \times \dfrac{1 \text{ mole Na}_2\text{S}_2\text{O}_3}{158.10 \text{ g Na}_2\text{S}_2\text{O}_3} \times \dfrac{1 \text{ L solution}}{0.468 \text{ moles Na}_2\text{S}_2\text{O}_3} \times \dfrac{1 \text{ mL}}{1 \times 10^{-3} \text{ L}}$

$= 33.787984 \text{ (calc)} = 33.8 \text{ mL (corr)}$

b) $125 \text{ g Na}_2\text{S}_2\text{O}_3 \times \dfrac{1 \text{ mole Na}_2\text{S}_2\text{O}_3}{158.10 \text{ g Na}_2\text{S}_2\text{O}_3} \times \dfrac{1 \text{ L solution}}{3.50 \text{ moles Na}_2\text{S}_2\text{O}_3} \times \dfrac{1 \text{ mL}}{1 \times 10^{-3} \text{ L}}$

$= 225.89681 \text{ (calc)} = 226 \text{ mL (corr)}$

c) $4.50 \text{ moles Na}_2\text{S}_2\text{O}_3 \times \dfrac{1 \text{ L solution}}{2.50 \text{ moles Na}_2\text{S}_2\text{O}_3} \times \dfrac{1 \text{ mL}}{1 \times 10^{-3} \text{ L}}$

$= 1800 \text{ (calc)} = 1.80 \times 10^3 \text{ mL (corr)}$

d) $0.0015 \text{ mole Na}_2\text{S}_2\text{O}_3 \times \dfrac{1 \text{ L solution}}{0.990 \text{ moles Na}_2\text{S}_2\text{O}_3} \times \dfrac{1 \text{ mL}}{1 \times 10^3 \text{ L}}$

$= 1.5151515 \text{ (calc)} = 1.52 \text{ mL (corr)}$

13.71 a) $55.0 \text{ g HBr} \times \dfrac{1 \text{ mole HBr}}{80.91 \text{ g HBr}} \times \dfrac{1 \text{ L solution}}{0.775 \text{ mole HBr}} = 0.8771195 \text{ (calc)} = 0.877 \text{ L (corr)}$

b) $55.0 \text{ g NH}_4\text{Br} \times \dfrac{1 \text{ mole NH}_4\text{Br}}{97.95 \text{ g NH}_4\text{Br}} \times \dfrac{1 \text{ L solution}}{0.775 \text{ mole NH}_4\text{Br}}$

$= 0.7245302 \text{ (calc)} = 0.725 \text{ L (corr)}$

c) $55.0 \text{ g MgBr}_2 \times \dfrac{1 \text{ mole MgBr}_2}{184.10 \text{ g MgBr}_2} \times \dfrac{1 \text{ L solution}}{0.775 \text{ mole MgBr}_2} = 0.3854847 \text{ (calc)} = 0.385 \text{ L (corr)}$

d) $55.0 \text{ g CsBr} \times \dfrac{1 \text{ mole CsBr}}{212.81 \text{ g CsBr}} \times \dfrac{1 \text{ L solution}}{0.775 \text{ mole CsBr}} = 0.3334793 \text{ (calc)} = 0.333 \text{ L (corr)}$

13.73 $\dfrac{88.00 \text{ g CH}_4\text{O}}{100.0 \text{ g solution}} \times \dfrac{0.8274 \text{ g solution}}{1 \text{ mL solution}} \times \dfrac{1 \text{ mL}}{1 \times 10^{-3} \text{ L}} \times \dfrac{1 \text{ mole CH}_4\text{O}}{32.05 \text{ g CH}_4\text{O}}$

$= 22.7180031 \text{ (calc)} = 22.72 \text{ M (corr)}$

13.75 $\dfrac{2.019 \text{ moles NaBr}}{1 \text{ L solution}} \times \dfrac{102.89 \text{ g NaBr}}{1 \text{ mole NaBr}} \times \dfrac{1 \times 10^{-3} \text{ L solution}}{1 \text{ mL solution}} \times \dfrac{1 \text{ mL solution}}{1.157 \text{ g solution}} \times 100$

$= 17.954616 \text{ (calc)} = 17.96 \text{ \% (corr)}$

13.77 $\dfrac{15.0 \text{ g NaOH}}{100 \text{ mL solution}} \times \dfrac{1 \text{ mL solution}}{1 \times 10^{-3} \text{ L solution}} \times \dfrac{1 \text{ mole NaOH}}{40.00 \text{ g NaOH}} = 3.75 \text{ M (calc and corr)}$

Molality (Sec. 13.9)

13.79 a) $\dfrac{16.5 \text{ g C}_{12}\text{H}_{22}\text{O}_{11} \times \dfrac{1 \text{ mole C}_{12}\text{H}_{22}\text{O}_{11}}{342.34 \text{ g C}_{12}\text{H}_{22}\text{O}_{11}}}{1.35 \text{ kg H}_2\text{O}} = 0.0357019 \text{ (calc)} = 0.0357 \text{ } m \text{ (corr)}$

b) $\dfrac{3.15 \text{ moles } C_{12}H_{22}O_{11}}{455 \text{ g } H_2O \times \dfrac{1 \text{ kg}}{1 \times 10^3 \text{ g}}} = 6.9230769 \text{ (calc)} = 6.92 \; m \text{ (corr)}$

c) $\dfrac{0.0356 \text{ g } C_{12}H_{22}O_{11} \times \dfrac{1 \text{ mole } C_{12}H_{22}O_{11}}{342.34 \text{ g } C_{12}H_{22}O_{11}}}{13.0 \text{ g } H_2O \times \dfrac{1 \text{ kg}}{1 \times 10^3 \text{ g}}} = 0.007999245 \text{ (calc)} = 0.00800 \; m \text{ (corr)}$

d) Moles sucrose = $45.0 \text{ g} \times \dfrac{1 \text{ mole } C_{12}H_{22}O_{11}}{342.34 \text{ g } C_{12}H_{22}O_{11}} = 0.1314482 \text{ (calc)} = 0.131 \text{ mole (corr)}$

Mass solution = $318 \text{ mL solution} \times \dfrac{1.06 \text{ g solution}}{1 \text{ mL solution}} = 337.08 \text{ g (calc)} = 337 \text{ g solution}$

Mass H_2O = 337 g solution − 45.0 g $C_{12}H_{22}O_{11}$

$= 292 \text{ g } H_2O \text{ (calc and corr)} \times \dfrac{1 \text{ kg } H_2O}{1 \times 10^3 \text{ g } H_2O} = 0.292 \text{ kg } H_2O$

$\dfrac{0.131 \text{ mole } C_{12}H_{22}O_{11}}{0.292 \text{ kg } H_2O} = 0.4486301 \text{ (calc)} = 0.449 \; m \text{ (corr)}$

13.81 a) $\dfrac{0.400 \text{ mole } Al(NO_3)_3}{1 \text{ kg } H_2O} \times 125 \text{ g } H_2O \times \dfrac{1 \text{ kg } H_2O}{1 \times 10^3 \text{ g } H_2O} \times \dfrac{213.01 \text{ g } Al(NO_3)_3}{1 \text{ mole } Al(NO_3)_3}$

$= 10.6505 \text{ (calc)} = 10.7 \text{ g } Al(NO_3)_3 \text{ (corr)}$

b) $\dfrac{0.400 \text{ mole } MgCl_2}{1 \text{ kg } H_2O} \times 125 \text{ g } H_2O \times \dfrac{1 \text{ kg } H_2O}{1 \times 10^3 \text{ g } H_2O} \times \dfrac{95.20 \text{ g } MgCl_2}{1 \text{ mole } MgCl_2}$

$= 4.761 \text{ (calc)} = 4.76 \text{ g } MgCl_2 \text{ (corr)}$

c) $\dfrac{0.400 \text{ mole } Na_3PO_4}{1 \text{ kg } H_2O} \times 125 \text{ g } H_2O \times \dfrac{1 \text{ kg } H_2O}{1 \times 10^3 \text{ g } H_2O} \times \dfrac{163.94 \text{ g } Na_3PO_4}{1 \text{ mole } Na_3PO_4}$

$= 8.197 \text{ (calc)} = 8.20 \text{ g } Na_3PO_4 \text{ (corr)}$

d) $\dfrac{0.400 \text{ mole } K_2SO_4}{1 \text{ kg } H_2O} \times 125 \text{ g } H_2O \times \dfrac{1 \text{ kg } H_2O}{1 \times 10^3 \text{ g } H_2O} \times \dfrac{174.26 \text{ g } K_2SO_4}{1 \text{ mole } K_2SO_4}$

$= 8.713 \text{ (calc)} = 8.71 \text{ g } K_2SO_4 \text{ (corr)}$

13.83 Moles NaCl = $80.0 \text{ g NaCl} \times \dfrac{1 \text{ mole NaCl}}{58.44 \text{ g NaCl}} = 1.3689254 \text{ (calc)} = 1.37 \text{ moles NaCl (corr)}$

a) $1.37 \text{ moles NaCl} \times \dfrac{1 \text{ kg } H_2O}{0.050 \text{ mole NaCl}} \times \dfrac{1 \times 10^3 \text{ g}}{1 \text{ kg}} = 27,400 \text{ (calc)} = 2.7 \times 10^4 \text{ g } H_2O \text{ (corr)}$

b) $1.37 \text{ moles NaCl} \times \dfrac{1 \text{ kg } H_2O}{0.23 \text{ mole NaCl}} \times \dfrac{1 \times 10^3 \text{ g}}{1 \text{ kg}}$

$= 5956.521739 \text{ (calc)} = 6.0 \times 10^3 \text{ g } H_2O \text{ (corr)}$

c) $1.37 \text{ moles NaCl} \times \dfrac{1 \text{ kg } H_2O}{1.345 \text{ moles NaCl}} \times \dfrac{1 \times 10^3 \text{ g}}{1 \text{ kg}}$

$= 1018.587361 \text{ (calc)} = 1.02 \times 10^3 \text{ g } H_2O \text{ (corr)}$

d) 1.37 moles NaCl $\times \dfrac{1 \text{ kg } H_2O}{2.8 \text{ moles NaCl}} \times \dfrac{1 \times 10^3 \text{ g}}{1 \text{ kg}}$

$$= 489.2857143 \text{ (calc)} = 4.9 \times 10^2 \text{ g } H_2O \text{ (corr)}$$

13.85 Basis: 1 L solution
Mass of solute:

$1 \text{ L solution} \times \dfrac{0.568 \text{ mole } H_2C_2O_4}{1 \text{ L solution}} \times \dfrac{90.04 \text{ g } H_2C_2O_4}{1 \text{ mole } H_2C_2O_4} = 51.14272 \text{ (calc)} = 51.1 \text{ g } H_2C_2O_4 \text{ (corr)}$

Mass of solution:

$1 \text{ L solution} \times \dfrac{1 \text{ mL solution}}{10^{-3} \text{ L solution}} \times \dfrac{1.022 \text{ g solution}}{1 \text{ mL solution}} = 1022 \text{ g solution (calc and corr)}$

Mass of solvent:
$(1022 - 51.1) \text{ g} = 970.9 \text{ (calc)} = 971 \text{ g (corr)}$
Molality:

$\dfrac{51.1 \text{ g } H_2C_2O_4}{971 \text{ g } H_2O} \times \dfrac{1 \text{ mole } H_2C_2O_4}{90.04 \text{ g } H_2C_2O_4} \times \dfrac{10^3 \text{ g } H_2O}{1 \text{ kg } H_2O} = 0.5844753 \text{ (calc)} = 0.584 \text{ } m \text{ (corr)}$

13.87 Basis: 1 kg solvent = 1000 g solvent
Mass of solute:

$1 \text{ kg solvent} \times \dfrac{0.796 \text{ mole } HC_2H_3O_2}{1 \text{ kg solvent}} \times \dfrac{60.06 \text{ g } HC_2H_3O_2}{1 \text{ mole } HC_2H_3O_2}$

$$= 47.80776 \text{ (calc)} = 47.8 \text{ g } HC_2H_3O_2 \text{ (corr)}$$

Mass of solution: $(1000 + 47.8) \text{ g} = 1047.8 \text{ g (calc and corr)}$
Volume of solution:

$1047.8 \text{ g solution} \times \dfrac{1 \text{ mL solution}}{1.004 \text{ g solution}} \times \dfrac{10^{-3} \text{ L solution}}{1 \text{ mL solution}}$

$$= 1.0436254 \text{ (calc)} = 1.044 \text{ L solution (corr)}$$

Molarity:

$\dfrac{47.8 \text{ g } HC_2H_3O_2}{1.044 \text{ L solution}} \times \dfrac{1 \text{ mole } HC_2H_3O_2}{60.06 \text{ g } HC_2H_3O_2} = 0.7623283 \text{ (calc)} = 0.762 \text{ M (corr)}$

13.89 Take 100.0 g solution, containing 14.0 g HNO_3 and $(100.0 - 14.0) = 86.0$ g H_2O

$$\dfrac{14.0 \text{ g } HNO_3 \times \dfrac{1 \text{ mole } HNO_3}{63.02 \text{ g } HNO_3}}{86.0 \text{ g } H_2O \times \dfrac{1 \text{ kg}}{1 \times 10^3 \text{ g}}} = 2.5831593 \text{ (calc)} = 2.58 \text{ } m \text{ (corr)}$$

Dilution (Sec. 13.10)

13.91 $M_1V_1 = M_2V_2$ where $M_1 = 0.400$ M, $V_1 = 25.0$ L and

a) $V_2 = 50.0$ mL; $M_2 = 0.400 \text{ M} \times \dfrac{25.0 \text{ mL}}{50.0 \text{ mL}} = 0.2 \text{ (calc)} = 0.200 \text{ M (corr)}$

b) $V_2 = 83.0$ mL; $M_2 = 0.400 \text{ M} \times \dfrac{25.0 \text{ mL}}{83.0 \text{ mL}} = 0.1204819 \text{ (calc)} = 0.120 \text{ M (corr)}$

c) $V_2 = 375$ mL; $M_2 = 0.400$ M x $\dfrac{25.0 \text{ mL}}{375 \text{ mL}} = 0.0266667$ (calc) $= 0.0267$ M (corr)

d) $V_2 = 2.67$ L x $\dfrac{1 \text{ mL}}{1 \times 10^{-3} \text{ L}} = 2670$ mL;

$M_2 = 0.400$ M x $\dfrac{25.0 \text{ mL}}{2670 \text{ mL}} = 0.0037453$ (calc) $= 0.00375$ M (corr)

13.93 $M_2 = M_1 \cdot \dfrac{V_1}{V_2}$ where $M_1 = 0.500$ M, $V_1 = 1353$ mL and

a) $V_2 = 1125$ mL; $M_2 = 0.500$ M x $\dfrac{1353 \text{ mL}}{1125 \text{ mL}} = 0.6013333$ (calc) $= 0.601$ M (corr)

b) $V_2 = 1.06$ L x $\dfrac{1 \text{ mL}}{1 \times 10^{-3} \text{ L}} = 1060$ mL;

$M_2 = 0.500$ M x $\dfrac{1353 \text{ mL}}{1060 \text{ mL}} = 0.6382075$ (calc) $= 0.638$ M (corr)

c) $V_2 = 975$ mL; $M_2 = 0.500$ M x $\dfrac{1353 \text{ mL}}{975 \text{ mL}} = 0.6938462$ (calc) $= 0.694$ M (corr)

d) $V_2 = 297.5$ mL; $M_2 = 0.500$ M x $\dfrac{1353 \text{ mL}}{297.5 \text{ mL}} = 2.2739496$ (calc) $= 2.27$ M (corr)

13.95 $V_1 = V_2 \cdot \dfrac{M_2}{M_1}$ where $M_1 = 6.0$ M and

a) $V_2 = 30.0$ mL; $M_2 = 5.0$ M; $V_1 = 30.0$ mL x $\dfrac{5.0 \text{ M}}{6.0 \text{ M}} = 25$ mL (calc and corr)

b) $V_2 = 6.5$ L x $\dfrac{1 \text{ mL}}{1 \times 10^{-3} \text{ L}} = 6500$ mL; $M_2 = 1.0$ M;

$V_1 = 6500$ mL x $\dfrac{1.0 \text{ M}}{6.0 \text{ M}} = 1083.33333$ (calc) $= 1.1 \times 10^3$ mL (corr)

c) $V_2 = 275$ mL; $M_2 = 5.9$ M;

$V_1 = 275$ mL x $\dfrac{5.9 \text{ M}}{6.0 \text{ M}} = 270.4166667$ (calc) $= 2.7 \times 10^2$ mL (corr)

d) $V_2 = 3.0$ mL; $M_2 = 0.10$ M;

$V_1 = 3.0$ mL x $\dfrac{0.10 \text{ M}}{6.0 \text{ M}} = 0.05$ (calc) $= 0.050$ mL (corr)

13.97   a) $V_1 = 20.0$ mL; $M_1 = 2.00$ M;

$V_2 = 20.0$ mL x $\dfrac{2.00 \text{ M}}{0.100 \text{ M}} = 4\overline{0}0$ mL (calc and corr)

$V_{H_2O} = 4\overline{0}0$ mL $- 20.0$ mL $= 38\overline{0}$ mL H_2O

b) $V_1 = 20.0$ mL; $M_1 = 0.250$ M;

$V_2 = 20.0$ mL x $\dfrac{0.250 \text{ M}}{0.100 \text{ M}} = 50$ mL (calc) $= 50.0$ mL (corr)

$V_{H_2O} = 50.0 - 20.0 = 30.0$ mL H_2O

c) $V_1 = 358$ mL; $M_1 = 0.950$ M;

$V_2 = 358$ mL x $\dfrac{0.950\ M}{0.100\ M}$ = 3401 mL (calc) = $34\overline{0}0$ mL (corr)

$V_{H_2O} = 34\overline{0}0 - 358 = 3042$ (calc) = 3040 mL H_2O (corr)

d) $V_1 = 2.3$ L; $M_1 = 6.00$ M;

$V_2 = 2.3$ L x $\dfrac{6.00\ M}{0.100\ M}$ = 138 L (calc) = 140 L (corr)

$V_{H_2O} = 140$ L $- 2.3$ L $= 137.7$ (calc) = 140 (corr) x $\dfrac{1\ mL}{1 \times 10^{-3}\ L}$ = 1.4×10^5 mL H_2O

13.99 a) 6.0 M x $\dfrac{25.0\ mL}{45.0\ mL}$ = 3.3333333 (calc) = 3.3 M (corr)

b) 3.0 M x $\dfrac{100.0\ mL}{120.0\ mL}$ = 2.5 M (calc and corr)

c) 10.0 M x $\dfrac{155\ mL}{175\ mL}$ = 8.8571429 (calc) = 8.86 M (corr)

d) 0.100 M x $\dfrac{2.00\ mL}{22.0\ mL}$ = 0.009090909 (calc) = 0.00909 M (corr)

13.101 a) $V_2 = 275$ mL $+ 3.254$ L x $\dfrac{1\ mL}{1 \times 10^{-3}\ L}$ = 3529 mL

$M_2 = 6.00$ M x $\dfrac{275\ mL}{3529\ mL}$ = 0.4675545 (calc) = 0.468 M (corr)

b) simple method: 6.00 M. Both solutions are 6.00 M, hence the mixture is 6.00 M. See part c) for a model to work the problem rigorously.

c) moles NaOH (solution #1) = 6.00 $\dfrac{\text{moles NaOH}}{\text{1 L solution}}$ x 275 mL x $\dfrac{1 \times 10^{-3}\ L}{1\ mL}$

= 1.65 moles (calc and corr)

moles NaOH (solution #2) = 2.00 $\dfrac{\text{moles NaOH}}{\text{1 L solution}}$ x 125 mL x $\dfrac{1 \times 10^{-3}\ L}{1\ mL}$

= 0.250 moles (calc and corr)

total moles = 1.65 + 0.250 = 1.90 moles NaOH

total volume = 275 + 125 = 400 mL x $\dfrac{1\ L}{1 \times 10^{-3}\ mL}$ = 0.400 L solution

$M_{final} = \dfrac{1.90\ \text{moles NaOH}}{0.400\ \text{L solution}}$ = 4.75 M (calc and corr)

d) moles NaOH (solution #1) = $\dfrac{6.00\ \text{moles NaOH}}{\text{1 L solution}}$ x 275 mL x $\dfrac{1 \times 10^{-3}\ L}{1\ mL}$

= 1.65 moles (calc and corr)

moles NaOH (solution #2) = $\dfrac{5.80\ \text{moles NaOH}}{\text{1 L solution}}$ x 27 mL x $\dfrac{1 \times 10^{-3}\ L}{1\ mL}$

= 0.1566 (calc) = 0.157 moles (corr)

total moles = 1.65 + 0.157 = 1.807 (calc) = 1.81 moles (corr)

total volume (L) = 275 mL + 27 mL = 302 mL x $\dfrac{1 \times 10^{-3}\ L}{1\ mL}$ = 0.302 L

$$M_{final} = \frac{1.81 \text{ moles NaOH}}{0.302 \text{ L solution}} = 5.9933775 \text{ (calc)} = 5.99 \text{ M (corr)}$$

Molarity and Chemical Equations (Sec. 13.11)

13.103 $0.500 \text{ L NaCl} \times \dfrac{4.00 \text{ moles NaCl}}{1 \text{ L NaCl}} \times \dfrac{1 \text{ mole Pb(NO}_3)_2}{2 \text{ moles NaCl}} \times \dfrac{1 \text{ L Pb(NO}_3)_2 \text{ solution}}{1.00 \text{ mole Pb(NO}_3)_2}$

$$= 1 \text{ (calc)} = 1.00 \text{ L (corr)}$$

13.105 $30.0 \text{ mL} \times \dfrac{1 \times 10^{-3} \text{ L}}{1 \text{ mL}} \times \dfrac{12.0 \text{ moles HNO}_3}{1 \text{ L}} \times \dfrac{3 \text{ moles S}}{2 \text{ moles HNO}_3} \times \dfrac{32.06 \text{ g S}}{1 \text{ mole S}}$

$$= 17.3124 \text{ (calc)} = 17.3 \text{ g S (corr)}$$

13.107 $18.0 \text{ g Ni} \times \dfrac{1 \text{ mole Ni}}{58.69 \text{ g Ni}} \times \dfrac{1 \text{ mole H}_2\text{SO}_4}{1 \text{ mole Ni}} \times \dfrac{1 \text{ L H}_2\text{SO}_4 \text{ solution}}{0.50 \text{ mole H}_2\text{SO}_4} \times \dfrac{1 \text{ mL}}{1 \times 10^{-3} \text{ L}}$

$$= 613.3924 \text{ (calc)} = 610 \text{ mL (corr)}$$

13.109 $\text{moles HNO}_3 = 23.7 \text{ mL NaOH solution} \times \dfrac{1 \times 10^{-3} \text{ L}}{1 \text{ mL}} \times \dfrac{0.100 \text{ mole NaOH}}{1 \text{ L solution}} \times \dfrac{1 \text{ mole HNO}_3}{1 \text{ mole NaOH}}$

$$= 0.00237 \text{ moles HNO}_3 \text{ (calc and corr)}$$

$\text{volume HNO}_3 = 37.5 \text{ mL} \times \dfrac{1 \times 10^{-3} \text{ L}}{1 \text{ mL}} = 0.0375 \text{ L solution}$

$$M = \frac{0.00237 \text{ mole HNO}_3}{0.0375 \text{ L solution}} = 0.0632 \text{ M (calc and corr)}$$

13.111 $50.0 \text{ mL solution} \times \dfrac{1 \times 10^{-3} \text{ L}}{1 \text{ mL}} \times \dfrac{6.0 \text{ moles HNO}_3}{1 \text{ L solution}} \times \dfrac{2 \text{ moles NO}}{8 \text{ moles HNO}_3} \times \dfrac{22.41 \text{ L NO}}{1 \text{ mole NO}}$

$$= 1.68075 \text{ (calc)} = 1.7 \text{ L NO (corr)}$$

13.113 $2.00 \text{ L CO}_2 \times \dfrac{1 \text{ mole CO}_2}{22.41 \text{ L CO}_2} \times \dfrac{1 \text{ mole Ca(OH)}_2}{1 \text{ mole CO}_2}$

$$= 0.0892458 \text{ (calc)} = 0.0892 \text{ mole Ca(OH)}_2 \text{ (corr)}$$

$$M = \frac{0.0892 \text{ mole Ca(OH)}_2}{1.75 \text{ L solution}} = 0.0509714 \text{ (calc)} = 0.0510 \text{ M (corr)}$$

ADDITIONAL PROBLEMS

13.115 a) $(NH_4)_3PO_4$ b) $Ca(OH)_2$ c) $AgNO_3$ d) CaS, $Ca(NO_3)_2$, $Ca(C_2H_3O_2)_2$

13.117 Since the solution is 75% saturated, it contains
$0.75 \times 33.3 \text{ g CuSO}_4 = 24.975 \text{ (calc)} = 25 \text{ g CuSO}_4$ in $100 \text{ g H}_2\text{O}$.

$$\text{The mass \%} = \frac{25.\ g}{(100 + 25)\ g} \times 100 = 2\bar{0}\ \% \text{ (calc and corr)}$$

$$400.0\ g\ \text{solution} \times \frac{2\bar{0}.\ g\ CuSO_4}{100\ g\ \text{solution}} = 8\bar{0}\ g \text{ (calc and corr)}$$

13.119 a) $\% \dfrac{m}{v} = \dfrac{45.2\ g\ AgNO_3}{254\ mL\ \text{solution}} \times 100 = 17.7952756 \text{ (calc)} = 17.8\ \% \text{ (m/v) (corr)}$

b) $\dfrac{45.2\ g\ AgNO_3 \times \dfrac{1\ \text{mole}\ AgNO_3}{169.88\ g\ AgNO_3}}{254\ mL\ \text{solution} \times \dfrac{1 \times 10^{-3}\ L}{1\ mL}} = 1.0475203 \text{ (calc)} = 1.05\ M \text{ (corr)}$

13.121 $425\ mL\ \text{solution} \times \dfrac{1.02\ g\ \text{solution}}{1\ mL\ \text{solution}} \times \dfrac{1.55\ g\ Na_2SO_4}{100\ g\ \text{solution}} = 6.71925 \text{ (calc)} = 6.72\ g\ Na_2SO_4 \text{ (corr)}$

13.123 Grams of solvent = grams of solution – grams of solute

Grams of solution:

$1375\ mL\ \text{solution} \times \dfrac{1.161\ g\ \text{solution}}{1\ mL\ \text{solution}} = 1596.375 \text{ (calc)} = 1596\ g\ \text{solution (corr)}$

Grams of solute:

$1.375\ L\ \text{solution} \times \dfrac{3.000\ \text{moles}\ NaNO_3}{1\ L\ \text{solution}} \times \dfrac{85.00\ g\ NaNO_3}{1\ \text{mole}\ NaNO_3}$

$$= 350.625 \text{ (calc)} = 350.6\ g\ NaNO_3 \text{ (corr)}$$

Grams of solvent:
$(1596 - 350.6)\ g = 1245.4 \text{ (calc)} = 1245\ g\ H_2O \text{ (corr)}$

13.125 a) $10.0\ g\ Na_2SO_4 \times \dfrac{1\ \text{mole}\ Na_2SO_4}{142.04\ g\ Na_2SO_4} \times \dfrac{1\ L\ \text{solution}}{0.125\ \text{mole}\ Na_2SO_4} \times \dfrac{1\ mL\ \text{solution}}{10^{-3}\ L\ \text{solution}}$

$$= 563.22163 \text{ (calc)} = 563\ mL\ \text{solution (corr)}$$

b) $2.5\ g\ Na^+ \times \dfrac{1\ \text{mole}\ Na^+}{22.99\ g\ Na^+} \times \dfrac{1\ \text{mole}\ Na_2SO_4}{2\ \text{moles}\ Na^+} \times \dfrac{1\ L\ \text{solution}}{0.125\ \text{mole}\ Na_2SO_4} \times \dfrac{1\ mL\ \text{solution}}{10^{-3}\ L\ \text{solution}}$

$$= 434.97173 \text{ (calc)} = 435\ mL\ \text{solution (corr)}$$

c) $0.567\ \text{mole}\ Na_2SO_4 \times \dfrac{1\ L\ \text{solution}}{0.125\ \text{mole}\ Na_2SO_4} \times \dfrac{1\ mL\ \text{solution}}{10^{-3}\ L\ \text{solution}}$

$$= 4536 \text{ (calc)} = 4540\ mL\ \text{solution (corr)}$$

d) $0.112\ \text{mole}\ SO_4^{2-} \times \dfrac{1\ \text{mole}\ Na_2SO_4}{1\ \text{mole}\ SO_4^{2-}} \times \dfrac{1\ L\ \text{solution}}{0.125\ \text{mole}\ Na_2SO_4} \times \dfrac{1\ mL\ \text{solution}}{10^{-3}\ L\ \text{solution}}$

$$= 896\ mL\ \text{solution (calc and corr)}$$

13.127 a) $\dfrac{0.245 \text{ mole Al(NO}_3)_3}{1 \text{ L solution}} \times \dfrac{1 \text{ mole Al}^{3+}}{1 \text{ mole Al(NO}_3)_3} = 0.245 \text{ M Al}^{3+}$ (calc and corr)

$\dfrac{0.245 \text{ mole Al(NO}_3)_3}{1 \text{ L solution}} \times \dfrac{3 \text{ moles NO}_3^-}{1 \text{ mole Al(NO}_3)_3} = 0.735 \text{ M NO}_3^-$ (calc and corr)

b) $M_2 = 0.245 \text{ M} \times \dfrac{225 \text{ mL}}{750 \text{ mL}} = 0.0735 \text{ M Al(NO}_3)_3$ (calc and corr)

$\dfrac{0.0735 \text{ mole Al(NO}_3)_3}{1 \text{ L solution}} \times \dfrac{1 \text{ mole Al}^{3+}}{1 \text{ mole Al(NO}_3)_3} = 0.0735 \text{ M Al}^{3+}$ (calc and corr)

$\dfrac{0.0735 \text{ mole Al(NO}_3)_3}{1 \text{ L solution}} \times \dfrac{3 \text{ moles NO}_3^-}{1 \text{ mole Al(NO}_3)_3} = 0.2205 \text{ (calc)} = 0.221 \text{ M NO}_3^-$ (corr)

13.129 The total volume is 202 mL.
a) $0.100 \text{ M K}_3\text{PO}_4 = 0.300 \text{ M K}^+$; $0.200 \text{ M KCl} = 0.200 \text{ M K}^+$

$M = 0.300 \text{ M K}^+ \times \dfrac{175 \text{ mL}}{202 \text{ mL}} + 0.200 \text{ M K}^+ \times \dfrac{27 \text{ mL}}{202 \text{ mL}}$

$= 0.28663366 \text{ (calc)} = 0.29 \text{ M K}^+$ (corr)

b) $0.200 \text{ M KCl} = 0.200 \text{ M Cl}^-$

$M_2 = 0.200 \text{ M Cl}^- \times \dfrac{27 \text{ mL}}{202 \text{ mL}} = 0.026732673 \text{ (calc)} = 0.027 \text{ M Cl}^-$ (corr)

c) $0.100 \text{ M K}_3\text{PO}_4 = 0.100 \text{ M PO}_4^{3-}$

$M_2 = 0.100 \text{ M PO}_4^{3-} \times \dfrac{175 \text{ mL}}{202 \text{ mL}} = 0.08663366 \text{ (calc)} = 0.0866 \text{ M PO}_4^{3-}$ (corr)

13.131 $3.74 \text{ ppm (m/m)} = \dfrac{3.74 \text{ mg solute}}{10^6 \text{ mg solution}}$

$\dfrac{3.74 \text{ mg solute}}{10^6 \text{ mg solution}} \times \dfrac{1 \text{ mg solution}}{10^{-3} \text{ g solution}} \times \dfrac{10^3 \text{ g solution}}{1 \text{ kg solution}} = 3.74 \; \dfrac{\text{mg solute}}{\text{kg solution}}$ (calc and corr)

13.133 $1.00 \text{ g NaCl} \times \dfrac{1 \text{ mole NaCl}}{58.44 \text{ g NaCl}} = 0.0171115 \text{ (calc)} = 0.0171 \text{ mole NaCl}$ (corr)

$M = \dfrac{0.0171 \text{ mole NaCl}}{0.01000 \text{ L solution}} = 1.71 \text{ M}$ (calc and corr)

$M_2 = 1.71 \text{ M} \times \dfrac{1.00 \text{ mL}}{10.00 \text{ mL}} = 0.171 \text{ M}$ (calc and corr)

13.135 Molarity of a 38.0% (m/m) HCl solution
Basis: $10\overline{0}0$ g of solution

$10\overline{0}0 \text{ g solution} \times \dfrac{38.0 \text{ g HCl}}{100 \text{ g solution}} \times \dfrac{1 \text{ mole HCl}}{36.46 \text{ g HCl}}$

$= 10.422381 \text{ (calc)} = 10.4 \text{ moles HCl}$ (corr)

$10\overline{0}0 \text{ g solution} \times \dfrac{1 \text{ mL solution}}{1.19 \text{ g solution}} \times \dfrac{10^{-3} \text{ L solution}}{1 \text{ mL solution}}$

$$= 0.84033613 \ \text{(calc)} = 0.840 \ \text{L solution (corr)}$$

$$M_1 = \frac{10.4 \ \text{moles HCl}}{0.840 \ \text{L solution}} = 12.380952 \ \text{(calc)} = 12.4 \ \text{M (corr)}$$

Dilution

$$V_1 = 1000 \ \text{mL} \times \frac{0.100 \ \text{M}}{12.4 \ \text{M}} = 8.0645161 \ \text{(calc)} = 8.06 \ \text{mL (corr)}$$

13.137 Moles of NaCl in original solution:

$$1.50 \ \text{kg H}_2\text{O} \times \frac{1.23 \ \text{moles NaCl}}{1 \ \text{kg H}_2\text{O}} = 1.845 \ \text{(calc)} = 1.84 \ \text{moles NaCl (corr)}$$

Mass of H$_2$O in final solution:

$$1.84 \ \text{moles NaCl} \times \frac{1 \ \text{kg H}_2\text{O}}{1.00 \ \text{mole NaCl}} = 1.84 \ \text{kg H}_2\text{O (calc and corr)}$$

$$(1.84 - 1.50) \ \text{kg H}_2\text{O} = 0.34 \ \text{kg H}_2\text{O} \times \frac{10^3 \ \text{g H}_2\text{O}}{1 \ \text{kg H}_2\text{O}} = 340 \ \text{g H}_2\text{O (calc and corr)}$$

13.139 Mass of solution = mass of solute + mass of solvent;
Mass of solute = 52.0 g
Mass of solvent:

$$52.0 \ \text{g H}_3\text{PO}_4 \times \frac{1 \ \text{mole H}_3\text{PO}_4}{98.00 \ \text{g H}_3\text{PO}_4} \times \frac{1 \ \text{kg solvent}}{2.16 \ \text{moles H}_3\text{PO}_4} \times \frac{10^3 \ \text{g solvent}}{1 \ \text{kg solvent}}$$
$$= 245.65381 \ \text{(calc)} = 246 \ \text{g solvent (corr)}$$

Mass of solution = (52.0 + 246) g = 298 g solution (calc and corr)
Volume of solution:

$$298 \ \text{g solution} \times \frac{1 \ \text{mL solution}}{1.12 \ \text{g solution}} = 266.07142 \ \text{(calc)} = 266 \ \text{mL solution (corr)}$$

13.141 a) $11.3 \ \text{mL CH}_3\text{OH} \times \dfrac{0.793 \ \text{g CH}_3\text{OH}}{1 \ \text{mL CH}_3\text{OH}} = 8.9609 \ \text{(calc)} = 8.96 \ \text{g CH}_3\text{OH (corr)}$

$$\% \ (\text{m/v}) = \frac{8.96 \ \text{g CH}_3\text{OH}}{75.0 \ \text{mL solution}} \times 100 = 11.946666 \ \text{(calc)} = 11.9 \ \% \ (\text{m/v}) \ (\text{corr})$$

b) $75.0 \ \text{mL solution} \times \dfrac{0.980 \ \text{g solution}}{1 \ \text{mL solution}} = 73.5 \ \text{g solution (calc and corr)}$

$$\% \ (\text{m/m}) = \frac{8.96 \ \text{g CH}_3\text{OH}}{73.5 \ \text{g solution}} \times 100 = 12.1904076 \ \text{(calc)} = 12.2 \ \% \ (\text{m/m}) \ (\text{corr})$$

c) $\% \ (\text{v/v}) = \dfrac{11.3 \ \text{mL CH}_3\text{OH}}{75.0 \ \text{mL solution}} \times 100 = 15.066666 \ \text{(calc)} = 15.1 \ \% \ (\text{v/v}) \ (\text{corr})$

13.143 Basis: 1 mole KCl
Volume of solution:

$$1 \ \text{mole KCl} \times \frac{1 \ \text{L solution}}{0.271 \ \text{mole KCl}} \times \frac{1 \ \text{mL solution}}{10^{-3} \ \text{L solution}} = 3690.0369 \ \text{(calc)} = 3690 \ \text{mL solution (corr)}$$

Mass of solution = mass of solute + mass of solvent

Mass of solute: $1 \ \text{mole KCl} \times \dfrac{74.55 \ \text{g KCl}}{1 \ \text{mole KCl}} = 74.55 \ \text{g KCl} \ \text{(calc and corr)}$

Mass of solvent:

$$1 \text{ mole KCl} \times \frac{1 \text{ kg solvent}}{0.273 \text{ mole KCl}} \times \frac{10^3 \text{ g solvent}}{1 \text{ kg solvent}} = 3663.0036 \text{ (calc)} = 3660 \text{ g solvent (corr)}$$

Mass of solution: $(3660 + 74.55) \text{ g} = 3734.55 \text{ (calc)} = 3730 \text{ g (corr)}$

$$\text{density} = \frac{\text{mass solution}}{\text{volume solution}} = \frac{3730 \text{ g solution}}{3690 \text{ mL solution}} = 1.0108401 \text{ (calc)} = 1.01 \text{ g/mL (corr)}$$

CUMULATIVE PROBLEMS

13.145 a) $NaCl + AgNO_3 \rightarrow AgCl + NaNO_3$ AgCl is insoluble
       b) $3Ba(C_2H_3O_2)_2 + 2K_3PO_4 \rightarrow 6KC_2H_3O_2 + Ba_3(PO_4)_2$ $Ba_3(PO_4)_2$ is insoluble
       c) $Pb(NO_3)_2 + Ag_2SO_4 \rightarrow 2AgNO_3 + PbSO_4$ $PbSO_4$ is insoluble
       d) $CuSO_4 + BaS \rightarrow BaSO_4 + CuS$ $BaSO_4$ and CuS are insoluble

13.147 Calculate moles NH_3 needed:

$$2.00 \text{ L } NH_3 \times \frac{3.50 \text{ moles } NH_3}{1 \text{ L } NH_3} = 7 \text{ (calc)} = 7.00 \text{ moles } NH_3 \text{ (corr)}$$

$$V = \frac{nRT}{P} = \frac{7.00 \text{ moles} \times 0.08206 \frac{\text{atm L}}{\text{mole K}} \times 298 \text{ K}}{1.46 \text{ atm}} = 117.24463 \text{ (calc)} = 117 \text{ L (corr)}$$

13.149 Find the limiting reactant:

$$6.41 \text{ g } ZnCl_2 \times \frac{1 \text{ mole } ZnCl_2}{136.31 \text{ g } ZnCl_2} \times \frac{2 \text{ moles AgCl}}{1 \text{ mole } ZnCl_2}$$

$$= 0.0940503 \text{ (calc)} = 0.0941 \text{ mole AgCl (corr)}$$

$$40.0 \text{ mL } AgNO_3 \times \frac{0.404 \text{ moles } AgNO_3}{1000 \text{ mL } AgNO_3} \times \frac{2 \text{ moles AgCl}}{2 \text{ moles } AgNO_3}$$

$$= 0.01616 \text{ (calc)} = 0.0162 \text{ mole AgCl (corr)}$$

$AgNO_3$ is the limiting reactant.

$$0.0162 \text{ mole AgCl} \times \frac{143.32 \text{ g AgCl}}{1 \text{ mole AgCl}} = 2.321784 \text{ (calc)} = 2.32 \text{ g AgCl (corr)}$$

13.151 Find the limiting reactant:

$$3\overline{5}0 \text{ mL } BaCl_2 \times \frac{3.25 \text{ moles } BaCl_2}{1000 \text{ mL } BaCl_2} \times \frac{1 \text{ mole } BaCrO_4}{1 \text{ mole } BaCl_2}$$

$$= 1.1375 \text{ (calc)} = 1.14 \text{ moles } BaCrO_4 \text{ (corr)}$$

$$4\overline{5}0 \text{ mL } K_2CrO_4 \times \frac{4.50 \text{ moles } K_2CrO_4}{1000 \text{ mL } K_2CrO_4} \times \frac{1 \text{ mole } BaCrO_4}{1 \text{ mole } K_2CrO_4}$$

$$= 2.025 \text{ (calc)} = 2.02 \text{ moles } BaCrO_4 \text{ (corr)}$$

$BaCl_2$ is the limiting reactant.

$$1.14 \text{ moles } BaCrO_4 \times \frac{253.33 \text{ g } BaCrO_4}{1 \text{ mole } BaCrO_4} = 288.7962 \text{ (calc)} = 289 \text{ g } BaCrO_4 \text{ (corr)}$$

13.153 $70.0 \text{ mL HCl} \times \dfrac{0.125 \text{ mole HCl}}{1000 \text{ mL HCl}} \times \dfrac{1 \text{ mole Na}_2\text{CO}_3}{2 \text{ moles HCl}} \times \dfrac{105.99 \text{ g Na}_2\text{CO}_3}{1 \text{ mole Na}_2\text{CO}_3}$

$$= 0.4637062 \text{ (calc)} = 0.464 \text{ g Na}_2\text{CO}_3 \text{ (corr)}$$

$\% \text{ Na}_2\text{CO}_3 = \dfrac{0.464 \text{ g Na}_2\text{CO}_3}{1.25 \text{ g sample}} \times 100 = 37.12 \text{ (calc)} = 37.1 \% \text{ (m/m) (corr)}$

13.155 $27.9 \text{ mL HCl} \times \dfrac{2.48 \text{ moles HCl}}{1000 \text{ mL HCl}} \times \dfrac{1 \text{ mole MCl}_2}{2 \text{ moles HCl}}$

$$= 0.034596 \text{ (calc)} = 0.0346 \text{ mole MCl}_2 \text{ (corr)}$$

$\text{Molar mass of MCl}_2 = \dfrac{4.72 \text{ g}}{0.0346 \text{ mole}} = 136.41618 \text{ (calc)} = 136 \text{ g/mole (corr)}$

at. mass M + 2(at. mass Cl)	= 136 amu
M + 2(35.45 amu)	= 136 amu
M	= 65 amu
M	= zinc
M	= nickel

13.157 $70.0 \text{ mL O}_2 \times \dfrac{10^{-3} \text{ L O}_2}{1 \text{ mL O}_2} \times \dfrac{1 \text{ mole O}_2}{22.41 \text{ L O}_2} \times \dfrac{4 \text{ moles NaOH}}{1 \text{ mole O}_2}$

$$= 0.0124944 \text{ (calc)} = 0.0125 \text{ mole NaOH (corr)}$$

$M = \dfrac{0.0125 \text{ mole NaOH}}{0.150 \text{ L solution}} = 0.083333333 \text{ (calc)} = 0.0833 \text{ M (corr)}$

CHAPTER FOURTEEN
Acids, Bases, and Salts

PRACTICE PROBLEMS

Acid-Base Definitions (Sec. 14.1 and 14.2)

14.1 a) The species responsible for the properties of acidic solutions is the hydrogen ion, $H^+(aq)$.
b) The term used to describe formation of ions, in aqueous solution, from an ionic compound is dissociation.

14.3 a) Arrhenius acid   b) Arrhenius acid

14.5 a) $HBr \rightarrow H^+ + Br^-$ b) $HClO_2 \rightarrow H^+ + ClO_2^-$
c) $LiOH \rightarrow Li^+ + OH^-$ d) $Ba(OH)_2 \rightarrow Ba^{2+} + 2OH^-$

14.7 a) acid, NH_4^+ donates a proton   b) base, HS^- accepts a proton
c) acid, $HClO_4$ donates a proton   d) base, H_2O accepts a proton

14.9 a) $HBr + H_2O \rightarrow H_3O^+ + Br^-$ b) $H_2O + N_3^- \rightarrow HN_3 + OH^-$
c) $H_2S + H_2O \rightarrow H_3O^+ + HS^-$ d) $HClO_4 + NO_2^- \rightarrow HNO_2 + ClO_4^-$

Conjugate Acids and Bases (Sec. 14.3)

14.11 a) HSO_3^- b) HCN c) HS^- d) ClO^-

14.13 a) $H_2C_2O_4$ and $HC_2O_4^-$; $HClO$ and ClO^- b) HSO_4^- and SO_4^{2-}; H_3O^+ and H_2O
c) $H_2PO_4^-$ and HPO_4^{2-}; NH_4^+ and NH_3 d) H_2CO_3 and HCO_3^-; H_2O and OH^-

14.15 a) yes   b) no   c) no   d) yes

14.17 a) (1) $HS^- + H_3O^+ \rightarrow H_2S + H_2O$ (2) $HS^- + OH^- \rightarrow H_2O + S^{2-}$
b) (1) $HPO_4^{2-} + H_3O^+ \rightarrow H_2PO_4^- + H_2O$ (2) $HPO_4^{2-} + OH^- \rightarrow H_2O + PO_4^{3-}$
c) (1) $HCO_3^- + H_3O^+ \rightarrow H_2CO_3 + H_2O$ (2) $HCO_3^- + OH^- \rightarrow H_2O + CO_3^{2-}$
d) (1) $H_2PO_3^- + H_3O^+ \rightarrow H_3PO_3 + H_2O$ (2) $H_2PO_3^- + OH^- \rightarrow H_2O + HPO_3^{2-}$

Polyprotic Acids (Sec. 14.4)

14.19 a) monoprotic   b) diprotic   c) monoprotic   d) diprotic

14.21 a) 1   b) 2   c) 1   d) 0

14.23 a) $H_2C_4H_4O_4 + H_2O \rightarrow H_3O^+ + HC_4H_4O_4^-$
$HC_4H_4O_4^- + H_2O \rightarrow H_3O^+ + C_4H_4O_4^{2-}$
b) $H_3SO_3 + H_2O \rightarrow H_3O^+ + HSO_3^-$
$HSO_3^- + H_2O \rightarrow H_3O^+ + SO_3^{2-}$

14.25 To emphasize the acidic hydrogen as being different from the nonacidic ones.

14.27 Monoprotic. Hydrogens attached to carbon atoms are not acidic.

Strength of Acids and Bases (Sec. 14.5)

14.29 a) $HClO_3$ - strong   b) $H_3C_2O_4$ - weak   c) $HC_3H_3O_3$ - weak   d) $H_2C_3H_2O_4$ - weak

14.31   a) strong, weak   b) strong, weak   c) weak, strong   d) both weak

14.33   a) strong, strong   b) strong, strong   c) weak, strong   d) weak, strong

14.35   a) HNO_3 b) $HClO_4$ c) H_3PO_4 d) HF

Salts (Sec. 14.6)

14.37   a) salt   b) base   c) salt   d) acid

14.39   a) Na^+ - sodium; PO_4^{3-} - phosphate   b) Li^+ - lithium; NO_3^- - nitrate
        c) NH_4^+ - ammonium; Cl^- - chloride   d) K^+ - potassium; CN^- - cyanide

14.41   Each salt is soluble in water.

14.43   a) $NaI \rightarrow Na^+(aq) + I^-(aq)$ b) $BaS \rightarrow Ba^{2+}(aq) + S^{2-}(aq)$
        c) $Li_2SO_4 \rightarrow 2Li^+(aq) + SO_4^{2-}(aq)$ d) $Al(NO_3)_3 \rightarrow Al^{3+}(aq) + 3NO_3^-(aq)$

Ionic and Net Ionic Equations (Sec. 14.7)

14.45   a) molecular   b) net ionic   c) ionic   d) net ionic

14.47   a) $2Na^+ + 2Br^- + Pb^{2+} + 2NO_3^- \rightarrow 2Na^+ + 2NO_3^- + PbBr_2$
           $Pb^{2+} + 2Br^- \rightarrow PbBr_2$
      b) $Fe^{3+} + 3Cl^- + 3Na^+ + 3OH^- \rightarrow Fe(OH)_3 + 3Na^+ + 3Cl^-$
           $Fe^{3+} + 3\ OH^- \rightarrow Fe(OH)_3$
      c) $Zn + 2H^+ + 2Cl^- \rightarrow Zn^{2+} + 2Cl^- + H_2$
           $Zn + 2H^+ \rightarrow Zn^{2+} + H_2$
      d) $H_2S + 2K^+ + 2OH^- \rightarrow 2K^+ + S^{2-} + 2H_2O$
           $H_2S + 2OH^- \rightarrow S^{2-} + 2H_2O$

14.49   a) $Pb + 2Ag^+ + 2NO_3 \rightarrow 2Ag + Pb^{2+} + 2NO_3^-$
           $2Ag^+ + Pb \rightarrow 2Ag + Pb^{2+}$
      b) $Cl_2 + 2Na^+ + 2Br^- \rightarrow 2Na^+ + 2Cl^- + Br_2$
           $Cl_2 + 2Br^- \rightarrow 2Cl^- + Br_2$
      c) $2Al^{3+} + 6NO_3^- + 6Na^+ + 3S^{2-} \rightarrow Al_2S_3 + 6Na^+ + 6NO_3^-$
           $2Al^{3+} + 3S^{2-} \rightarrow Al_2S_3$
      d) $Na^+ + C_2H_3O_2^- + NH_4^+ + Cl^- \rightarrow NH_4^+ + C_2H_3O_2^- + Na^+ + Cl^-$
           (no net ionic reaction - dissociation only)

Reactions of Acids and Bases (Secs. 14.8 and 14.9)

14.51   a) yes   b) yes   c) no   d) yes

14.53   a) $Ni + 2HCl \rightarrow NiCl_2 + H_2$ b) $Ca + 2H_2O \rightarrow Ca(OH)_2 + H_2$
      c) $Mg + 2HCl \rightarrow MgCl_2 + H_2$ d) $Zn + 2H_2O \rightarrow Zn(OH)_2 + H_2$

14.55   a) No   b) Yes   c) Yes   d) No

14.57   a) 1:1   b) 1:2   c) 1:1   d) 2:1

14.59   a) $2HBr + Sr(OH)_2 \rightarrow SrBr_2 + 2H_2O$ b) $HC_2H_3O_2 + LiOH \rightarrow LiC_2H_3O_2 + H_2O$
      c) $H_2SO_4 + Mg(OH)_2 \rightarrow MgSO_4 + 2H_2O$ d) $H_3PO_4 + 3KOH \rightarrow K_3PO_4 + 3H_2O$

14.61   a) $H^+ + OH^- \rightarrow H_2O$ b) $HC_2H_3O_2 + OH^- \rightarrow H_2O + C_2H_3O_2^-$
      c) $H^+ + OH^- \rightarrow H_2O$ d) $H_3PO_4 + 3\ OH^- \rightarrow 3H_2O + PO_4^{3-}$

14.63 a) H_3PO_4, NaOH   b) HCN, KOH   c) HCl, $Be(OH)_2$ d) $HC_2H_3O_2$, $Ca(OH)_2$

14.65 a) $Zn + 2HCl \rightarrow ZnCl_2 + H_2$ b) $HCl + NaOH \rightarrow NaCl + H_2O$
        c) $2HCl + Na_2CO_3 \rightarrow 2NaCl + CO_2 + H_2O$ d) $HCl + NaHCO_3 \rightarrow NaCl + CO_2 + H_2O$

Reactions of Salts (Sec. 14.10)

14.67 a) no   b) yes   c) no   d) yes

14.69 a) $Fe + CuSO_4 \rightarrow FeSO_4 + Cu$
        $Fe + Cu^{2+} + SO_4^{2-} \rightarrow Fe^{2+} + SO_4^{2-} + Cu$
        $Fe + Cu^{2+} \rightarrow Fe^{2+} + Cu$
    b) $Sn + 2AgNO_3 \rightarrow Sn(NO_3)_2 + 2Ag$
        $Sn + 2Ag^+ + 2NO_3^- \rightarrow Sn^{2+} + 2NO_3^- + 2Ag$
        $Sn + 2Ag^+ \rightarrow Sn^{2+} + 2Ag$
    c) $Zn + NiCl_2 \rightarrow ZnCl_2 + Ni$
        $Zn + Ni^{2+} + 2Cl^- \rightarrow Zn^{2+} + 2Cl^- + Ni$
        $Zn + Ni^{2+} \rightarrow Zn^{2+} + Ni$
    d) $Cr + Pb(C_2H_3O_2)_2 \rightarrow Cr(C_2H_3O_2)_2 + Pb$
        $Cr + Pb^{2+} + 2C_2H_3O_2^- \rightarrow Cr^{2+} + 2C_2H_3O_2^- + Pb$
        $Cr + Pb^{2+} \rightarrow Cr^{2+} + Pb$

14.71 a) an insoluble salt is formed
    b) an insoluble salt is formed
    c) an insoluble salt is formed, weak acid is formed
    d) a gas is evolved

14.73 a) $2Al(NO_3)_3 + 3(NH_4)_2S \rightarrow Al_2S_3 + 6NH_4NO_3$
        $2Al^{3+} + 6NO_3^- + 6NH_4^+ + 3S^{2-} \rightarrow Al_2S_3 + 6NH_4^+ + 6NO_3^-$
        $2Al^{3+} + 3S^{2-} \rightarrow Al_2S_3$
    b) $2HCl + Ba(OH)_2 \rightarrow 2H_2O + BaCl_2$
        $2H^+ + 2Cl^- + Ba^{2+} + 2OH^- \rightarrow 2H_2O + Ba^{2+} + 2Cl^-$
        $H^+ + OH^- \rightarrow H_2O$
    c) no reaction
    d) no reaction

Hydronium Ion and Hydroxide Ion Concentrations (Sec. 14.11)

14.75 $[H_3O^+] = \dfrac{1.00 \times 10^{-14}}{[OH^-]}$ M

    a) 5.0×10^{-11} M
    b) 1.3698630×10^{-8} (calc) = 1.4×10^{-8} M (corr)
    c) 3.3333333×10^{-5} (calc) = 3.3×10^{-5} M (corr)
    d) 4×10^{-7} (calc) = 4.0×10^{-7} M (corr)

14.77 a) basic   b) basic   c) acidic   d) acidic

14.79 $[OH^-] = \dfrac{1.00 \times 10^{-14}}{[H_3O^+]}$

    a) $3.7037037 \times 10^{-11}$ (calc) = 3.7×10^{-11} M (corr)
    b) 1.3333333×10^{-6} (calc) = 1.3×10^{-6} M (corr)
    c) 1×10^{-7} (calc) = 1.0×10^{-7} M (corr)
    d) 2×10^{-7} (calc) = 2.0×10^{-7} M (corr)

14.81   a) acidic   b) basic   c) neutral   d) basic

The pH Scale (Sec. 14.12)

14.83   a) pH = 4.0   b) pH = 9.0   c) pH = 5.0   d) pH = 9.0

14.85   a) 1.3979400 (calc) = 1.4 (corr)
b) 3.15490196 (calc) = 3.2 (corr)
c) 9.09691001 (calc) = 9.1 (corr)
d) 6.3010300 (calc) = 6.3 (corr)

14.87   The calculator answer will be the same for all of these: 2.52287875. The difference is the number of significant figures in the mantissa.
a) 2.5   b) 2.52   c) 2.523   d) 2.5229

14.89   a) both acidic   b) acidic, basic   c) both basic   d) acidic, neutral

14.91   a) 1×10^{-3} M
b) 1×10^{-5} M
c) 1.9952623×10^{-6} (calc) = 2×10^{-6} M (corr)
d) 5.0118723×10^{-7} (calc) = 5×10^{-7} M (corr)

14.93   a) 3.7153523×10^{-3} (calc) = 3.7×10^{-3} M (corr)
b) 3.7153523×10^{-4} (calc) = 3.7×10^{-4} M (corr)
c) 3.7153523×10^{-8} (calc) = 3.7×10^{-8} M (corr)
d) 3.5481339×10^{-8} (calc) = 3.5×10^{-8} M (corr)

14.95 $[H_3O^+]_A = \dfrac{1.0 \times 10^{-14}}{4.3 \times 10^{-4}} = 2.3255813 \times 10^{-11}$ (calc) = 2.3×10^{-11} M (corr)

a) Solution A is more basic. The smaller the $[H_3O^+]$ the more basic the solution.
b) Solution B has the lower pH. The larger the $[H_3O^+]$ the lower the pH.

14.97   The original solution has a $[H_3O^+] = 3.1622777 \times 10^{-5}$ (calc) = 3.16×10^{-5} M (corr)
a) New $[H_3O^+] = 2 \times 3.16 \times 10^{-5} = 6.32 \times 10^{-5}$ M (calc and corr)
pH = 4.1992829 (calc) = 4.199 (corr)
b) New $[H_3O^+] = 4 \times 3.16 \times 10^{-5} = 1.264 \times 10^{-4}$ (calc) = 1.26×10^{-4} M (corr)
pH = 3.8996295 (calc) = 3.900 (corr)
c) New $[H_3O^+] = 10 \times 3.16 \times 10^{-5} = 3.16 \times 10^{-4}$ M (calc and corr)
pH = 3.5003129 (calc) = 3.500 (corr)
d) New $[H_3O^+] = 1000 \times 3.16 \times 10^{-5} = 3.16 \times 10^{-2}$ M (calc and corr)
pH = 1.5003129 (calc) = 1.500 (corr)

14.99   a) HNO_3 is a strong acid and ionizes to give 1 H_3O^+ per HNO_3.
$[H_3O^+] = 6.3 \times 10^{-3}$ M;   pH = 2.2006595 (calc) = 2.20 (corr)
b) HCl is a strong acid and ionizes to give 1 H_3O^+ per HCl.
$[H_3O^+] = 0.20$ M;   pH = 0.6989700 (calc) = 0.70 (corr)
c) H_2SO_4 is a strong acid and ionizes to give 2 H_3O^+ per H_2SO_4.
$[H_3O^+] = 2 \times 0.000021 = 0.000042$ M;   pH = 4.3767507 (calc) = 4.38 (corr)
d) NaOH is a strong base containing 1 OH^- per NaOH.
$[OH^-] = 2.3 \times 10^{-4}$ M;

$[H_3O^+] = \dfrac{1.00 \times 10^{-14}}{2.3 \times 10^{-4}} = 4.3478261 \times 10^{-11}$ (calc) = 4.3×10^{-11} M (corr)

pH = 10.3665315 (calc) = 10.37 (corr)

Hydrolysis of Salts (Sec. 14.13)

14.101 a) PO_4^{3-} b) CN^- c) NH_4^+ d) none

14.103 a) neutral   b) basic   c) acidic   d) neutral

14.105 a) $NH_4^+ + H_2O \rightarrow H_3O^+ + NH_3$
b) $C_2H_3O_2^- + H_2O \rightarrow OH^- + HC_2H_3O_2$
c) $F^- + H_2O \rightarrow OH^- + HF$
d) $CN^- + H_2O \rightarrow OH^- + HCN$

Buffers (Sec. 14.14)

14.107 a) No, have mixture of strong acid and conjugate base
b) Yes, have mixture of weak acid and conjugate base
c) No, do not have an acid in mixture
d) Yes, have mixture of weak acid and conjugate base

14.109 a) HCN and CN-   b) H_3PO_4 and $H_2PO_4^-$ c) H_2CO_3 and HCO_3^- d) HCO_3^- and CO_3^{2-}

14.111 a) $HF + OH^- \rightarrow F^- + H_2O$
b) $HCO_3^- + H_3O^+ \rightarrow H_2CO_3 + H_2O$
c) $CO_3^{2-} + H_3O^+ \rightarrow HCO_3^- + H_2O$
d) $H_3PO_4 + OH^- \rightarrow H_2PO_4^- + H_2O$

Acid-Base Titrations (Sec. 14.15)

14.113

a) $10.00 \text{ mL} \times \dfrac{10^{-3} \text{ L}}{1 \text{ mL}} \times \dfrac{0.350 \text{ moles } H_2SO_4}{1 \text{ L}} \times \dfrac{2 \text{ moles NaOH}}{1 \text{ mole } H_2SO_4} \times \dfrac{1 \text{ L NaOH}}{0.100 \text{ mole NaOH}}$

$\times \dfrac{10^3 \text{ mL}}{1 \text{ L}} = 70 \text{ (calc)} = 70.0 \text{ mL (corr)}$

b) $50.00 \text{ mL} \times \dfrac{10^{-3} \text{ L}}{1 \text{ mL}} \times \dfrac{1.500 \text{ moles } H_3PO_4}{1 \text{ L}} \times \dfrac{3 \text{ moles NaOH}}{1 \text{ mole } H_3PO_4} \times \dfrac{1 \text{ L NaOH}}{0.100 \text{ mole NaOH}}$

$\times \dfrac{10^3 \text{ mL}}{1 \text{ L}} = 2250 \text{ (calc)} = 2.25 \times 10^3 \text{ mL (corr)}$

c) $5.00 \text{ mL} \times \dfrac{10^{-3} \text{ L}}{1 \text{ mL}} \times \dfrac{0.500 \text{ moles } HNO_3}{1 \text{ L}} \times \dfrac{1 \text{ moles NaOH}}{1 \text{ mole } HNO_3} \times \dfrac{1 \text{ L NaOH}}{0.100 \text{ mole NaOH}}$

$\times \dfrac{10^3 \text{ mL}}{1 \text{ L}} = 25.0 \text{ mL (calc and corr)}$

d) $75.00 \text{ mL} \times \dfrac{10^{-3} \text{ L}}{1 \text{ mL}} \times \dfrac{0.00030 \text{ moles } HCl}{1 \text{ L}} \times \dfrac{1 \text{ moles NaOH}}{1 \text{ mole } HCl} \times \dfrac{1 \text{ L NaOH}}{0.100 \text{ mole NaOH}} =$

$\times \dfrac{10^3 \text{ mL}}{1 \text{ L}} \; 0.225 \text{ (calc)} = 0.22 \text{ mL (corr)}$

14.115 a) $10.00 \text{ mL} \times \dfrac{10^{-3} \text{ L}}{1 \text{ mL}} \times \dfrac{2.00 \text{ moles HNO}_3}{1 \text{ L}} \times \dfrac{1 \text{ mole NH}_3}{1 \text{ mole HNO}_3} \times \dfrac{1 \text{ L NH}_3}{2.50 \text{ mole NH}_3}$

$$\times \dfrac{10^3 \text{ mL}}{1 \text{ L}} = 8.00 \text{ (calc and corr)}$$

b) $20.00 \text{ mL} \times \dfrac{10^{-3} \text{ L}}{1 \text{ mL}} \times \dfrac{6.00 \text{ moles H}_2\text{SO}_4}{1 \text{ L}} \times \dfrac{2 \text{ mole NH}_3}{1 \text{ mole H}_2\text{SO}_4} \times \dfrac{1 \text{ L NH}_3}{2.50 \text{ mole NH}_3}$

$$\times \dfrac{10^3 \text{ mL}}{1 \text{ L}} = 96.0 \text{ mL (calc and corr)}$$

c) $30.00 \text{ mL} \times \dfrac{10^{-3} \text{ L}}{1 \text{ mL}} \times \dfrac{7.50 \text{ moles H}_3\text{PO}_4}{1 \text{ L}} \times \dfrac{3 \text{ mole NH}_3}{1 \text{ mole H}_3\text{PO}_4} \times \dfrac{1 \text{ L NH}_3}{2.50 \text{ mole NH}_3}$

$$\times \dfrac{10^3 \text{ mL}}{1 \text{ L}} = 270. \text{ mL (calc and corr)}$$

d) $100.00 \text{ mL} \times \dfrac{10^{-3} \text{ L}}{1 \text{ mL}} \times \dfrac{0.100 \text{ moles HCl}}{1 \text{ L}} \times \dfrac{1 \text{ mole NH}_3}{1 \text{ mole HCl}} \times \dfrac{1 \text{ L NH}_3}{2.50 \text{ mole NH}_3}$

$$\times \dfrac{10^3 \text{ mL}}{1 \text{ L}} = 4.00 \text{ (calc and corr)}$$

14.117 a)

$34.5 \text{ mL} \times \dfrac{10^{-3} \text{ L}}{1 \text{ mL}} \times \dfrac{0.102 \text{ moles NaOH}}{1 \text{ L}} \times \dfrac{1 \text{ mole H}_2\text{SO}_4}{2 \text{ mole NaOH}} = \dfrac{1.7595 \times 10^{-3} \text{ mole H}_2\text{SO}_4}{0.02500 \text{ L}}$

$$= 7.038 \times 10^{-2} \text{ (calc)} = 7.04 \times 10^{-2} \text{ M H}_2\text{SO}_4 \text{ (corr)}$$

b) $34.5 \text{ mL} \times \dfrac{10^{-3} \text{ L}}{1 \text{ mL}} \times \dfrac{0.102 \text{ moles NaOH}}{1 \text{ L}} \times \dfrac{1 \text{ mole HClO}}{1 \text{ mole NaOH}} = \dfrac{3.519 \times 10^{-3} \text{ mole HClO}}{0.02000 \text{ L}}$

$$= 0.17595 \text{ (calc)} = 0.176 \text{ M HClO (corr)}$$

c)

$34.5 \text{ mL} \times \dfrac{10^{-3} \text{ L}}{1 \text{ mL}} \times \dfrac{0.102 \text{ moles NaOH}}{1 \text{ L}} \times \dfrac{1 \text{ mole H}_3\text{PO}_4}{3 \text{ mole NaOH}} = \dfrac{1.173 \times 10^{-3} \text{ mole H}_3\text{PO}_4}{0.02000 \text{ L}}$

$$= 5.865 \times 10^{-2} \text{ (calc)} = 5.87 \times 10^{-2} \text{ M H}_3\text{PO}_4 \text{ (corr)}$$

d)

$34.5 \text{ mL} \times \dfrac{10^{-3} \text{ L}}{1 \text{ mL}} \times \dfrac{0.102 \text{ moles NaOH}}{1 \text{ L}} \times \dfrac{1 \text{ mole HNO}_3}{1 \text{ mole NaOH}} = \dfrac{3.519 \times 10^{-3} \text{ mole HNO}_3}{0.01000 \text{ L}}$

$$= 3.519 \times 10^{-1} \text{ (calc)} = 3.52 \times 10^{-1} \text{ M HNO}_3 \text{ (corr)}$$

Acid and Base Stock Solutions (Sec. 14.16)

14.119 a) 3 M   b) 6 M   c) 16 M   d) 6 M

Additional Problems

14.121 a) strong   b) weak   c) weak   d) strong

14.123 $[H_3O^+]_1$ = antilog (-2.2) = 6.3095734×10^{-3} (calc) = 6×10^{-3} (corr)

$[H_3O^+]_2$ = antilog (-4.5) = 3.1622776×10^{-5} (calc) = 3×10^{-5} (corr)

$$\frac{[H_3O^+]_1}{[H_3O^+]_2} = \frac{6 \times 10^{-3}}{3 \times 10^{-5}} = 200 \text{ (calc and corr)}$$

14.125 If we let the hydroxide concentration, $[OH^-]$ = x, then $[H_3O^+]$ = 3x
From the ion product constant for water, we know that $[H_3O^+] \times [OH^-] = 1.00 \times 10^{-14}$
so $x \times 3x = 1.00 \times 10^{-14}$
giving x = 5.773503×10^{-8}
Therefore $[H_3O^+]$ = 3x = 1.732051×10^{-7} and pH = -log $[H_3O^+]$ = 6.76144 (calc) = 6.76 (corr).

14.127 a) The lower the pH value, the more acidic the solution. So in decreasing acidity: A, B, D, C.
b) In increasing $[H_3O^+]$: C, D, B, A.
c) The higher the pH value, the more basic the solution. So in decreasing $[OH^-]$: C, D, B, A
d) In increasing basicity: A, B, D, C.

14.129 The more concentrated H_3O^+ has a lower pH.
a) no, higher pH   b) no, higher pH   c) yes   d) yes

14.131 NaCl, a soluble salt, does not hydrolyze (no pH effect). HNO_3, a strong acid, produces 0.1 mole H_3O^+ ion. HCl, a strong acid, produces 0.1 mole H_3O^+ ion. NaOH, a strong base, produces 0.1 mole OH^- ion. The 0.1 mole of OH^- ion will neutralize 0.1 mole H_3O^+ ion, with the other 0.1 mole H_3O^+ ion remaining in solution.

$$[H_3O^+] = \frac{0.1 \text{ mole}}{3.00 \text{ L solution}} = 3.3333333 \times 10^{-2} \text{ (calc)} = 3 \times 10^{-2} \text{ M (corr)}$$
pH = -log (3×10^{-2}) = 1.5228787 (calc) = 1.5 (corr)

14.133 NH_4Br (salt of a weak base) hydrolyzes to produce a slightly acid solution. $Ba(OH)_2$ (strong base) produces a strongly basic solution. $HClO_4$ (strong acid) produces a strongly acidic solution. K_2SO_4 (salt of a strong acid and strong base) does not hydrolyze and produces a neutral solution. LiCN (salt of a weak acid) hydrolyzes to produce a slightly basic solution.

The order of decreasing pH will put the most basic solution first (highest pH) and the most acidic solution last (lowest pH): $Ba(OH)_2$, LiCN, K_2SO_4, NH_4Br, $HClO_4$

14.135 a) HCN and NaCN, HCN and KCN   b) HF and NaF

14.137 Buffer 1: $H_2PO_4^-$, H_3PO_4 Buffer 2: $H_2PO_4^-$, HPO_4^{2-}

14.139 Balanced equation: $3Ca(OH)_2 + 2H_3PO_4 \rightarrow Ca_3(PO_4)_2 + 6H_2O$ Molar mass H_3PO_4 = 98.00 g/mol
$$0.40 \text{ g } H_3PO_4 \times \frac{1 \text{ mol } H_3PO_4}{98.00 \text{ g } H_3PO_4} \times \frac{3 \text{ mole } Ca(OH)_2}{2 \text{ mole } H_3PO_4} = 0.061224 \text{ (calc)}$$
$$= 0.062 \text{ mol } Ca(OH)_2 \text{ (calc and corr)}$$

14.141 Balanced equation: $HNO_3 + NaOH \rightarrow NaNO_3 + H_2O$
Moles HNO_3 = 0.125 L × 5.00 M = 0.625
Moles NaOH = 0.125L × 6.00 M = 0.750
Therefore after reaction we have 0.125 moles of NaOH left in the total volume (0.250 L)

Concentration of NaOH left is $\dfrac{0.125 \text{ moles}}{0.250 \text{ L}}$ = 0.500 M

a) As $[H_3O^+] \times [OH^-] = 1.00 \times 10^{-14}$, $[H_3O^+]$ = $1.00 \times 10^{-14}/0.50$ = 2.00×10^{-14} M
b) [NaOH] = 0.500 M
c) pH = -log $[H_3O^+]$ = 13.69897 (calc) = 13.7 (corr)

Cummulative Problems

14.143 a) the iodide, I^-, ion
b) the hydrogen phosphate, HPO_4^{2-}, ion
c) the hydroxide, OH^-, ion
d) the hydronium, H_3O^+, ion

14.145 $H : C : : : N :$ and $[: C : : : N :]^-$

14.147 a) $M_{HCl} = \dfrac{4.8 \text{ g HCl} \times \dfrac{1 \text{ mole HCl}}{36.46 \text{ g HCl}}}{0.40 \text{ L solution}} = 0.3291278 \text{ (calc)} = 0.33 \text{ M (corr)}$

$[H_3O^+] = 0.33 \text{ M}.$ $pH = -\log 0.33 = 0.4814861 \text{ (calc)} = 0.48 \text{ (corr)}$

b) $M_{LiOH} = \dfrac{12.5 \text{ g LiOH} \times \dfrac{1 \text{ mole LiOH}}{23.95 \text{ g LiOH}}}{255 \text{ mL solution} \times \dfrac{10^{-3} \text{ L}}{1 \text{ mL}}} = 2.0467477 \text{ (calc)} = 2.05 \text{ M (corr)}$

$[OH^-] = 2.05 \text{ M}$

$[H_3O^+] = \dfrac{1.00 \times 10^{-14}}{2.05} = 4.8780488 \times 10^{-15} \text{ (calc)} = 4.88 \times 10^{-15} \text{ M (corr)}$

$pH = -\log(4.88 \times 10^{-15}) = 14.31158 \text{ (calc)} = 14.312 \text{ (corr)}$

c) $M_2 = 0.10 \text{ M} \times \dfrac{75 \text{ mL}}{125 \text{ mL}} = 0.06 \text{ (calc)} = 0.060 \text{ M (corr)} = [H_3O^+]$

$pH = -\log 0.060 = 1.2218487 \text{ (calc)} = 1.22 \text{ (corr)}$

d) When you mix two solutions, each is diluted.
Since $V_{HCl} = V_{HNO_3}$, the total $V_{tot} = 2 V_{HCl} = 2 V_{HNO_3}$

$M_{HCl} = 0.20 \times \dfrac{V_{HCl}}{2V_{HCl}} = 0.10 \text{ M } H_3O^+$ from HCl in new solution.

$M_{HNO_3} = 0.50 \times \dfrac{V_B}{2V_B} = 0.25 \text{ M } H_3O^+$ from HNO_3 in new solution.

Total $[H_3O^+] = 0.10 + 0.25 = 0.35 \text{ M}.$
$pH = -\log 0.35 = 0.4559320 \text{ (calc)} = 0.46 \text{ (corr)}$

14.149 a) The initial $[H_3O^+] = [HNO_3] = 0.10 \text{ M}$

b) After dilution, the $[H_3O^+] = 0.10 \times \dfrac{1.00 \text{ mL}}{100.0 \text{ mL}} = 0.0010 \text{ M}$

c) $pH = -\log [H_3O^+] = -\log (0.10) = 1.00$
d) $pH = -\log [H_3O^+] = -\log (0.0010) = 3.00$

14.151 $[H_3O^+] = \text{antilog} (-3.40) = 3.9810717 \times 10^{-4} \text{ (calc)} = 4.0 \times 10^{-4} \text{ M (corr)}$
a) HCl is a strong monoprotic acid. For this type of acid $[H_3O^+]$ and acid molarity are the same. Therefore, the solution is 4.0×10^{-4} M HCl.
b) Basis: 1 L solution
Mass of solute:

$4.0 \times 10^{-4} \text{ mole HCl} \times \dfrac{36.46 \text{ g HCl}}{1 \text{ mole HCl}} = 0.014584 \text{ (calc)} = 0.015 \text{ g HCl (corr)}$

Mass of solution:

$$1 \text{ L solution} \times \frac{1 \text{ mL solution}}{10^{-3} \text{ L solution}} \times \frac{1.10 \text{ g solution}}{1 \text{ mL solution}} = 1100 \text{ g solution (calc and corr)}$$

$$\% \text{ (m/m)} = \frac{\text{mass solute}}{\text{mass solution}} \times 100 = \frac{0.015 \text{ g}}{1100 \text{ g}} \times 100$$
$$= 0.0013636364 \text{ (calc)} = 0.0014 \% \text{ (m/m) (corr)}$$

14.153 from pH, $[H_3O^+] = 3.8018940 \times 10^{-6}$ (calc) $= 3.8 \times 10^{-6}$ M $[H_3O^+]$

$$10.00 \text{ mL solution} \times \frac{10^{-3} \text{ L}}{1 \text{ mL}} \times \frac{3.8 \times 10^{-6} \text{ mole } H_3O^+}{1 \text{ L solution}} \times \frac{6.022 \times 10^{23} \text{ } H_3O^+ \text{ ions}}{1 \text{ mole } H_3O^+}$$
$$= 2.28836 \times 10^{16} \text{ (calc)} = 2.3 \times 10^{16} \text{ } H_3O^+ \text{ ions (corr)}$$

14.155 $[H_3O^+] = $ antilog $(-2.37) = 4.2657951 \times 10^{-3}$ (calc) $= 4.3 \times 10^{-3}$ M H_3O^+ (corr)

$$236 \text{ mL solution} \times \frac{10^{-3} \text{ L solution}}{1 \text{ mL solution}} \times \frac{4.3 \times 10^{-3} \text{ mole } H_3O^+}{1 \text{ L solution}}$$
$$= 0.0010148 \text{ (calc)} = 0.0010 \text{ mole } H_3O^+ \text{ (corr)}$$

moles NO_3^-:
HNO_3 is a strong acid that dissociates 100%. $HNO_3 + H_2O \rightarrow H_3O^+ + NO_3^-$
so moles $NO_3^- = $ moles $H_3O^+ = 0.0010$ mole NO_3^-
moles Na^+:
Na_2SO_4 is a soluble salt that dissociates 100%. $Na_2SO_4 \rightarrow 2Na^+ + SO_4^{2-}$

$$0.100 \text{ mole } Na_2SO_4 \times \frac{2 \text{ moles } Na^+}{1 \text{ mole } Na_2SO_4} = 0.2 \text{ (calc)} = 0.200 \text{ mole } Na^+ \text{ (corr)}$$

moles SO_4^{2-}: $\quad 0.100 \text{ mole } Na_2SO_4 \times \frac{1 \text{ mole } SO_4^{2-}}{1 \text{ mole } Na_2SO_4} = 0.1 \text{ (calc)} = 0.100 \text{ mole } SO_4^{2-} \text{ (corr)}$

total moles ions:
$(0.0010 + 0.0010 + 0.200 + 0.100)$ mole $= 0.302$ mole (calc and corr)
total ions present:

$$0.302 \text{ mole ions} \times \frac{6.022 \times 10^{23} \text{ ions}}{1 \text{ mole ions}} = 1.818644 \times 10^{23} \text{ (calc)} = 1.82 \times 10^{23} \text{ ions (corr)}$$

14.157 As HCl is a strong acid, in this solution, $[H_3O^+] = $ antilog $(-2.40) = 3.98107 \times 10^{-3}$ M.

Therefore number of moles of $H_3O^+ = 3.98107 \times 10^{-3} \times 7.50$ L $= 0.029858$ (calc) $= 0.0299$ (corr)

Using the ideal gas equation PV = nRT and having STP conditions, we get

$$V = \frac{nRT}{P} = \frac{0.0299 \text{ moles} \times 0.08206 \text{ L atm mol}^{-1} \text{ K}^{-1} \times 273 \text{ K}}{1 \text{ atm}} = 0.66889 \text{ L (calc)}$$
$$= 0.669 \text{ L (corr)}$$
$$= 2.66 \times 10^{-4} \text{ L (corr)}$$

14.159 equivalents acid = equivalents base $= V_b \times N_b = 0.0323$ L $\times 0.1000$ equiv/L
$$= 0.00323 \text{ equiv acid (calc and corr)}$$

$$0.00323 \text{ equiv } KHC_8H_4O_4 \times \frac{1 \text{ mole } KHC_8H_4O_4}{1 \text{ equiv } KHC_8H_4O_4} \times \frac{204.23 \text{ g } KHC_8H_4O_4}{1 \text{ mole } KHC_8H_4O_4}$$
$$= 0.6596629 \text{ (calc)} = 0.660 \text{ g } KHC_8H_4O_4 \text{ (corr)}$$

$$\% KHC_8H_4O_4 = \frac{0.660 \text{ g}}{1.00 \text{ g}} \times 100 = 66.0 \% \text{ (m/m) (calc and corr)}$$

CHAPTER FIFTEEN
Oxidation and Reduction

PRACTICE PROBLEMS

Oxidation-Reduction Terminology (Secs. 15.1 and 15.2)

15.1   a) oxidation occurs when an atom loses electrons
          b) oxidation occurs when the oxidation number of an atom increases

15.3   a) an oxidizing agent gains electrons from another substance
          b) an oxidizing agent contains the atom that shows an oxidation number decrease
          c) an oxidizing agent is itself reduced

15.5   a) oxidized   b) decrease   c) reducing agent   d) loses

Assignment of Oxidation Numbers (Sec. 15.2)

15.7   a) $N = -3, H = +1$ b) $H = +1, S = +4, O = -2$
          c) $H = +1, N = +3, O = -2$ d) $Na = +1, P = +5, O = -2$

15.9   a) $P = -3$ b) $Mg = +2$ c) $N = -3, H = +1$ d) $P = +5, O = -2$

15.11   a) $+4$ b) $+3$ c) -2 d) $-2\frac{2}{3}$

15.13   a) $+2$ b) $+2$ c) $+3$ d) $+2$

15.15   a) $Rh = +3, C = +4, O = -2$ b) $Ni = +3, S = +4, O = -2$
          c) $Co = +2, P = +5, O = -2$ d) $Cu = +1, S = +6, O = -2$

15.17   a) -2 b) $+2$ c) -1 d) -2

Characteristics of Oxidation-Reduction Reactions (Sec. 15.2)

15.21   a) H_2 oxidized (0 to +1), N_2 reduced (0 to −3)
          b) I^- oxidized (−1 to 0), Cl_2 reduced (0 to −1)
          c) Fe oxidized (0 to +2), Sb in Sb_2O_3 reduced (+3 to 0)
          d) S in H_2SO_3 oxidized (+4 to +6), N in HNO_3 reduced (+5 to +2)

15.23   a) H_2 is reducing agent, N_2 is oxidizing agent
          b) I^- is reducing agent, Cl_2 is oxidizing agent
          c) Fe is reducing agent, Sb_2O_3 is oxidizing agent
          d) H_2SO_3 is reducing agent, HNO_3 is oxidizing agent

15.25   a) Sulfur SO_2 is oxidized
          b) HNO_3 is oxidizing agent
          c) HNO_3 contains N that decreases from +5 to +2
          d) SO_2 contains S that loses electrons +4 to +6

15.27   a) metal is oxidized, nonmetal is reduced
          b) metal is oxidized, nonmetal is reduced
          c) metal is oxidized, nonmetal is reduced
          d) metal is oxidized, nonmetal is reduced

Types of Chemical Reactions (Sec. 15.3)

15.29 a) redox, synthesis   b) redox, single replacement
c) nonredox, decomposition   d) nonredox, double replacement

15.31 a) redox   b) redox   c) can't classify   d) redox

Balancing Redox Equations: Oxidation-Number Method (Sec. 15.5)

15.33 a)   0   2(+3)   +3

$$2Cr + 6HCl \rightarrow 2CrCl_3 + 3H_2$$

+1   3[2(-1)]   0

b)   0   3(+4)   +4

$$2Cr_2O_3 + 3C \rightarrow 4Cr + 3CO_2$$

+3   2[2(-3)]   0

c)   +4   (+2)   +6

$$SO_2 + NO_2 \rightarrow SO_3 + NO$$

+4   (-2)   +2

d)   0   4(+2)   +2

$$BaSO_4 + 4C \rightarrow BaS + 4CO$$

+6   (-8)   -2

15.35 a)   +4   (+2)   +6

$$Br_2 + 2H_2O + SO_2 \rightarrow 2HBr + H_2SO_4$$

0   2(-1)   -1

b)   -2   3(+2)   0

$$3H_2S + 2HNO_3 \rightarrow 3S + 2NO + 4H_2O$$

$$\text{c)} \qquad \overset{+2}{\underset{+2}{}} \quad \overset{2(+1)}{\underset{(-2)}{}} \quad \overset{+3}{\underset{0}{}}$$

$$\text{SnSO}_4 + 2\text{FeSO}_4 \rightarrow \text{Sn} + \text{Fe}_2(\text{SO}_4)_3$$

(annotations above: +5, 2(−3), +2)

$$\text{d)} \qquad \overset{-1}{\underset{+4}{}} \qquad \overset{2[2(+1)]}{\underset{(-4)}{}} \qquad \overset{0}{\underset{0}{}}$$

$$\text{Na}_2\text{TeO}_3 + 4\text{NaI} + 6\text{HCl} \rightarrow 6\text{NaCl} + \text{Te} + 3\text{H}_2\text{O} + 2\text{I}_2$$

15.37 a) $\overset{0}{}$ $1[2(+5)]$ $+5$

$$\text{I}_2 + 5\text{Cl}_2 + 6\text{H}_2\text{O} \rightarrow 2\text{HIO}_3 + 10\,\text{Cl}^- + 10\,\text{H}^+$$

$0 \qquad\qquad 5[2(1)] \qquad\qquad -1$

b) -3 $5(+8)$ $+5$

$$8\text{MnO}_4^- + 5\text{AsH}_3 + 24\text{H}^+ \rightarrow 5\text{H}_3\text{AsO}_4 + 8\text{Mn}^{2+} + 12\text{H}_2\text{O}$$

$+7 \qquad\qquad 8(-5) \qquad\qquad +2$

c) -1 $2(+1)$ 0

$$2\text{Br}^- + \text{SO}_4^{2-} + 4\text{H}^+ \rightarrow \text{Br}_2 + \text{SO}_2 + 2\text{H}_2\text{O}$$

$+6 \qquad\qquad (-2) \qquad\qquad +4$

d) 0 $(+3)$ $+3$

$$\text{Au} + 4\text{Cl}^- + 3\text{NO}_3^- + 6\text{H}^+ \rightarrow \text{AuCl}_4^- + 3\text{NO}_2 + 3\text{H}_2\text{O}$$

$+5 \qquad\qquad 3(-1) \qquad\qquad +4$

15.39

a) -2 $(+8)$ $+6$

$$8\,\text{OH}^- + \text{S}^{2-} + 4\text{Cl}_2 \rightarrow \text{SO}_4^{2-} + 8\text{Cl}^- + 4\text{H}_2\text{O}$$

$0 \qquad\qquad 4[2(-1)] \qquad\qquad -1$

b)   +4   3(+2)   +6

$$5H_2O + 3SO_3^{2-} + 2CrO_4^{2-} \rightarrow 2Cr(OH)_4^- + 3SO_4^{2-} + 2\,OH^-$$

+6   2(−3) +3

c)   +5   3(+2)   +7

$$H_2O + 2MnO_4^- + 3IO_3^- \rightarrow 2MnO_2 + 3IO_4^- + 2\,OH^-$$

+7   2(−3)   +4

d)   0   2(+7)   +7

$$18\,OH^- + I_2 + 7Cl_2 \rightarrow 2H_3IO_6^{2-} + 14Cl^- + 6H_2O$$

0   7[2(−1)]   −1

Balancing Redox Equations: Half-Reaction Method (Sec. 15.6)

15.41   a) $MnO_2 + e^-$ $\rightarrow Mn^{3+}$ (ox #: +4→ +3)
             $MnO_2 + 4H^+ + e^-$ $\rightarrow Mn^{3+}$
             $MnO_2 + 4H^+ + e^-$ $\rightarrow Mn^{3+} + 2H_2O$

        b) $H_3MnO_4 + 5e^-$ $\rightarrow Mn$ (ox #: +5 → 0)
             $H_3MnO_4 + 5H^+ + 5e^-$ $\rightarrow Mn$
             $H_3MnO_4 + 5H^+ + 5e^-$ $\rightarrow Mn + 4H_2O$

        c) $MnO_4^- + 5e^-$ $\rightarrow Mn^{2+}$ (ox #: +7 → +2)
             $MnO_4^- + 8H^+ + 5e^-$ $\rightarrow Mn^{2+}$
             $MnO_4^- + 8H^+ + 5e^-$ $\rightarrow Mn^{2+} + 4H_2O$

        d) $MnO_4^- + 3e^-$ $\rightarrow MnO_2$ (ox #: +7 → +4)
             $MnO_4^- + 4H^+ + 3e^-$ $\rightarrow MnO_2$
             $MnO_4^- + 4H^+ + 3e^-$ $\rightarrow MnO_2 + 2H_2O$

15.43   a) $SeO_4^{2-} + 6e^-$ $\rightarrow Se$ (ox #: +6 → 0)
             $SeO_4^{2-} + 6e^-$ $\rightarrow Se + 8\,OH^-$
             $SeO_4^{2-} + 4H_2O + 6e^-$ $\rightarrow Se + 8\,OH^-$

        b) Se^{2-} $\rightarrow SeO_3^{2-} + 6e^-$ (ox #: −2 → +4)
             $Se^{2-} + 6\,OH^-$ $\rightarrow SeO_3^{2-} + 6e^-$
             $Se^{2-} + 6\,OH^-$ $\rightarrow SeO_3^{2-} + 6e^- + 3H_2O$

        c) $SeO_4^{2-} + 2e^-$ $\rightarrow SeO_3^{2-}$ (ox #: +6 → +4)
             $SeO_4^{2-} + 2e^-$ $\rightarrow SeO_3^{2-} + 2\,OH^-$
             $SeO_4^{2-} + H_2O + 2e^-$ $\rightarrow SeO_3^{2-} + 2\,OH^-$

        d) Se $\rightarrow SeO_3^{2-} + 4e^-$ (ox #: 0 → +4)
             $Se + 6\,OH^-$ $\rightarrow SeO_3^{2-} + 4e^-$
             $Se + 6\,OH^-$ $\rightarrow SeO_3^{2-} + 4e^- + 3H_2O$

15.45 a) oxidation:

$$Zn \rightarrow Zn^{2+} + 2e^-$$

reduction:

$$Cu^{2+} + 2e^- \rightarrow Cu$$

combining:

$$Zn \rightarrow Zn^{2+} + 2e^- \quad + \quad Cu^{2+} + 2e^- \rightarrow Cu$$
$$Zn + Cu^{2+} + 2e^- \rightarrow Zn^{2+} + 2e^- + Cu$$
$$Zn + Cu^{2+} \rightarrow Zn^{2+} + Cu$$

b) oxidation:

$$2I^- \rightarrow I_2 + 2e^-$$

reduction:

$$Br_2 + 2e^- \rightarrow 2Br^-$$

combining:

$$2I^- \rightarrow I_2 + 2e^- \quad + \quad Br_2 + 2e^- \rightarrow 2Br^-$$
$$2I^- + Br_2 + 2e^- \rightarrow I_2 + 2e^- + 2Br^-$$
$$2I^- + Br_2 \rightarrow I_2 + 2Br^-$$

c) oxidation:

$$S_2O_3^{2-} \rightarrow 2HSO_4^-$$
$$S_2O_3^{2-} \rightarrow 2\,HSO_4^- + 8e^- \text{ (ox \#: } +2 \rightarrow +6 \text{ per S atom)}$$
$$S_2O_3^{2-} \rightarrow 2HSO_4^- + 8e^- + 8\,H^+$$
$$S_2O_3^{2-} + 5H_2O \rightarrow 2HSO_4^- + 8e^- + 8\,H^+$$

reduction:

$$Cl_2 + 2e^- \rightarrow 2Cl^- \text{ (balanced)}$$

combining:

$$S_2O_3^{2-} + 5H_2O \rightarrow 2HSO_4^- + 8e^- + 8\,H^+ \quad + \quad 4(Cl_2 + 2e^- \rightarrow 2Cl^-)$$
$$S_2O_3^{2-} + 5H_2O + 4Cl_2 + 8e^- \rightarrow 2H_2SO_4^- + 8e^- + 8\,H^+ + 8Cl^-$$
$$S_2O_3^{2-} + 5H_2O + 4Cl_2 \rightarrow 2HSO_4^- + 8\,H^+ + 8Cl^-$$

d) oxidation:

$$Zn \rightarrow Zn^{2+} + 2e^- \text{ (balanced)}$$

reduction:

$$As_2O_3 \rightarrow 2AsH_3 \text{ (balance As)}$$
$$As_2O_3 + 12e^- \rightarrow 2AsH_3 \text{ (ox \#: } +3 \rightarrow -3 \text{ per As atom)}$$
$$As_2O_3 + 12e^- + 12H^+ \rightarrow 2AsH_3$$
$$As_2O_3 + 12e^- + 12H^+ \rightarrow 2AsH_3 + 3H_2O$$

combining:

$$6(Zn \rightarrow Zn^{2+} + 2e) \quad + \quad As_2O_3 + 12e^- + 12H^+ \rightarrow 2AsH_3 + 3H_2O$$
$$6Zn + As_2O_3 + 12e^- + 12H^+ \rightarrow 6Zn^{2+} + 12e^- + 2AsH_3 + 3H_2O$$
$$6Zn + As_2O_3 + 12H^+ \rightarrow 6Zn^{2+} + 2AsH_3 + 3H_2O$$

15.47 a) oxidation:

$$I_2 \rightarrow 2HIO_3 \text{ (balance I)}$$
$$I_2 \rightarrow 2HIO_3 + 10e^- \text{ (ox \#: } 0 \rightarrow +5 \text{ per I atom)}$$
$$I_2 \rightarrow 2HIO_3 + 10e^- + 10\,H^+$$
$$I_2 + 6H_2O \rightarrow 2HIO_3 + 10e^- + 10\,H^+$$

reduction:

$$Cl_2 + 2e^- \rightarrow 2Cl^-$$

combining:

$$I_2 + 6H_2O \rightarrow 2HIO_3 + 10e^- + 10\,H^+ \quad + \quad 5(Cl_2 + 2e^- \rightarrow 2Cl^-)$$
$$I_2 + 6H_2O + 5Cl_2 + 10e^- \rightarrow 2HIO_3 + 10e^- + 10\,H^+ + 10\,Cl^-$$
$$I_2 + 6H_2O + 5Cl_2 \rightarrow 2HIO_3 + 10\,H^+ + 10\,Cl^-$$

b) oxidation:

$AsH_3 \rightarrow H_3AsO_4 + 8e^-$ (ox #: $-3 \rightarrow +5$)

$AsH_3 \rightarrow H_3AsO_4 + 8e^- + 8H^+$

$AsH_3 + 4H_2O \rightarrow H_3AsO_4 + 8e^- + 8H^+$

reduction:

$MnO_4^- + 5e^- \rightarrow Mn^{2+}$ (ox #: $+7 \rightarrow +2$)

$MnO_4^- + 5e^- + 8H^+ \rightarrow Mn^{2+} + 4H_2O$

combining:

$5(AsH_3 + 4H_2O \rightarrow H_3AsO_4 + 8e^- + 8H^+) + 8(MnO_4^- + 5e^- + 8H^+ \rightarrow Mn^{2+} + 4H_2O)$

$5AsH_3 + 20 H_2O + 8MnO_4^- + 40e^- + 64H^+$

$\rightarrow 5H_3AsO_4 + 40e^- + 40 H^+ + 8Mn^{2+} + 32H_2O$

$5AsH_3 + 8MnO_4^- + 24H^+ \rightarrow 5H_3AsO_4 + 8Mn^{2+} + 12H_2O$

c) oxidation:

$2Br^- \rightarrow Br_2 + 2e^-$

reduction:

$SO_4^{2-} + 2e^- \rightarrow SO_2$ (ox #: $+6 \rightarrow +4$)

$SO_4^{2-} + 2e^- + 4H^+ \rightarrow SO_2$

$SO_4^{2-} + 2e^- + 4H^+ \rightarrow SO_2 + 2H_2O$

combining:

$2Br^- \rightarrow Br_2 + 2e^- + SO_4^{2-} + 2e^- + 4H^+ \rightarrow SO_2 + 2H_2O$

$2Br^- + SO_4^{2-} + 2e^- + 4H^+ \rightarrow Br_2 + 2e^- + SO_2 + 2H_2O$

$2Br^- + SO_4^{2-} + 4H^+ \rightarrow Br_2 + SO_2 + 2H_2O$

d) oxidation:

$Au + 4Cl^- \rightarrow AuCl_4^-$

$Au + 4Cl^- \rightarrow AuCl_4^- + 3e^-$ (ox #: $0 \rightarrow +3$)

reduction:

$NO_3^- + e^- \rightarrow NO_2$ (ox #: $+5 \rightarrow +4$)

$NO_3^- + e^- + 2H^+ \rightarrow NO_2$

$NO_3^- + e^- + 2H^+ \rightarrow NO_2 + H_2O$

combining:

$Au + 4Cl^- \rightarrow AuCl_4^- + 3e^- + 3(NO_3^- + e^- + 2H^+ \rightarrow NO_2 + H_2O)$

$Au + 4Cl^- + 3NO_3^- + 3e^- + 6H^+ \rightarrow AuCl_4^- + 3e^- + 3NO_2 + 3H_2O$

$Au + 4Cl^- + 3NO_3^- + 6H^+ \rightarrow AuCl_4^- + 3NO_2 + 3H_2O$

15.49 a) oxidation:

$2NH_3 \rightarrow N_2H_4$ (balance N)

$2NH_3 \rightarrow N_2H_4 + 2e^-$ (ox #: $-3 \rightarrow -2$ per N atom)

$2NH_3 + 2 OH^- \rightarrow N_2H_4 + 2e^-$

$2NH_3 + 2 OH^- \rightarrow N_2H_4 + 2e^- + 2H_2O$

reduction:

$ClO^- + 2e^- \rightarrow Cl^-$ (ox #: $+1 \rightarrow -1$)

$ClO^- + 2e^- \rightarrow Cl^- + 2 OH^-$

$ClO^- + 2e^- + H_2O \rightarrow Cl^- + 2 OH^-$

combining:

$2NH_3 + 2 OH^- \rightarrow N_2H_4 + 2e^- + 2H_2O + ClO^- + 2e^- + H_2O \rightarrow Cl^- + 2 OH^-$

$2NH_3 + 2 OH^- + ClO^- + 2e^- + H_2O \rightarrow N_2H_4 + 2e^- + 2H_2O + Cl^- + 2 OH^-$

$2NH_3 + ClO^- \rightarrow N_2H_4 + Cl^- + H_2O$

b) oxidation:

$Cr(OH)_2 \rightarrow CrO_4^{2-} + 4e^-$ (ox #: $+2 \rightarrow +6$)

$Cr(OH)_2 + 6 OH^- \rightarrow CrO_4^{2-} + 4e^-$

$Cr(OH)_2 + 6 OH^- \rightarrow CrO_4^{2-} + 4H_2O + 4e^-$

reduction:

$BrO^- + 2e^- \rightarrow Br^-$ (ox #: $+1 \rightarrow -1$)

$BrO^- + 2e^- \rightarrow 2 OH^-$

$BrO^- + H_2O + 2e^- \rightarrow Br^- + 2 OH^-$

combining:

$$Cr(OH)_2 + 6\,OH^- \rightarrow CrO_4^- + 4H_2O + 4e^- \quad + \quad 2(BrO^- + H_2O + 2e^- \rightarrow Br^- + 2\,OH^-)$$
$$Cr(OH)_2 + 6\,OH^- + 2BrO^- + 2H_2O + 4e^- \quad \rightarrow CrO_4^{2-} + 2H_2O + 4e^- + 2Br^- + 4\,OH^-$$
$$Cr(OH)_2 + 2\,OH^- + 2BrO^- \quad \rightarrow CrO_4^{2-} + 2H_2O + 2Br^-$$

c) oxidation:

$$CrO_2^- \qquad\qquad \rightarrow CrO_4^{2-} + 3e^- \;(\text{ox \#: } +3 \rightarrow +6)$$
$$CrO_2^- + 4\,OH^- \qquad\qquad \rightarrow CrO_4^{2-} + 3e^-$$
$$CrO_2^- + 4\,OH^- \qquad\qquad \rightarrow CrO_4^{2-} + 3e^- + 2H_2O$$

reduction:

$$H_2O_2 + 2e^- \qquad\qquad \rightarrow 2\,OH^- \;(\text{ox \#: } -1 \rightarrow -2 \text{ per O atom})$$

combining:

$$2(CrO_2^- + 4\,OH^- \rightarrow CrO_4^{2-} + 3e^- + 2H_2O) \quad + \quad 3(H_2O_2 + 2e^- \rightarrow 2\,OH^-)$$
$$2CrO_2^- + 8\,OH^- + 3H_2O_2 + 6e^- \quad \rightarrow 2CrO_4^{2-} + 6e^- + 4H_2O + 6\,OH^-$$
$$2CrO_2^- + 2\,OH^- + 3H_2O_2 \quad \rightarrow 2CrO_4^{2-} + 4H_2O$$

d) oxidation:

$$Sn(OH)_3^- \qquad\qquad \rightarrow Sn(OH)_6^{2-} + 2e^- \;(\text{ox \#: } +2 \rightarrow +4)$$
$$Sn(OH)_3^- + 3\,OH^- \qquad\qquad \rightarrow Sn(OH)_6^{2-} + 2e^-$$

reduction:

$$Bi(OH)_3 + 3e^- \qquad\qquad \rightarrow Bi \;(\text{ox \#: } +3 \rightarrow 0)$$
$$Bi(OH)_3 + 3e^- \qquad\qquad \rightarrow Bi + 3\,OH^-$$

combining:

$$3(Sn(OH)_3^- + 3\,OH^- \rightarrow Sn(OH)_6^{2-} + 2e^-) \quad + \quad 2(Bi(OH)_3 + 3e^- \rightarrow Bi + 3\,OH^-)$$
$$3Sn(OH)_3^- + 9\,OH^- + 2Bi(OH)_3 + 6e^- \quad \rightarrow 3Sn(OH)_6^{2-} + 6e^- + 2Bi + 6\,OH^-$$
$$3Sn(OH)_3^- + 3\,OH^- + 2Bi(OH)_3 \quad \rightarrow 3Sn(OH)_6^{2-} + 2Bi$$

15.51 a) oxidation:

$$S^{2-} \qquad\qquad \rightarrow SO_4^{2-} + 8e^- \;(\text{ox \#: } -2 \rightarrow +6)$$
$$S^{2-} + 8\,OH^- \qquad\qquad \rightarrow SO_4^{2-} + 8e^-$$
$$S^{2-} + 8\,OH^- \qquad\qquad \rightarrow SO_4^{2-} + 8e^- + 4H_2O$$

reduction:

$$Cl_2 + 2e^- \qquad\qquad \rightarrow 2Cl^-$$

combining:

$$S^{2-} + 8\,OH^- \rightarrow SO_4^{2-} + 8e^- + 4H_2O \quad + \quad 4(Cl_2 + 2e^- \rightarrow 2Cl^-)$$
$$S^{2-} + 8\,OH^- + 4Cl_2 + 8e^- \quad \rightarrow SO_4^{2-} + 8e^- + 4H_2O + 8Cl^-$$
$$S^{2-} + 8\,OH^- + 4Cl_2 \quad \rightarrow SO_4^{2-} + 4H_2O + 8Cl^-$$

b) oxidation:

$$SO_3^{2-} \qquad\qquad \rightarrow SO_4^{2-} + 2e^- \;(\text{ox \#: } +4 \rightarrow +6)$$
$$SO_3^{2-} + 2\,OH^- \qquad\qquad \rightarrow SO_4^{2-} + 2e^-$$
$$SO_3^{2-} + 2\,OH^- \qquad\qquad \rightarrow SO_4^{2-} + 2e^- + H_2O$$

reduction:

$$CrO_4^{2-} + 3e^- \qquad\qquad \rightarrow Cr(OH)_4^- \;(\text{ox \#: } +6 \rightarrow +3)$$
$$CrO_4^{2-} + 3e^- \qquad\qquad \rightarrow Cr(OH)_4^- + 4\,OH^-$$
$$CrO_4^{2-} + 3e^- + 4H_2O \qquad\qquad \rightarrow Cr(OH)_4^- + 4\,OH^-$$

combining:

$$3(SO_3^{2-} + 2\,OH^- \rightarrow SO_4^{2-} + 2e^- + H_2O)$$
$$+ \quad 2(CrO_4^{2-} + 3e^- + 4H_2O \rightarrow Cr(OH)_4^- + 4\,OH^-)$$
$$3SO_3^{2-} + 6\,OH^- + 2CrO_4^{2-} + 6e^- + 8H_2O$$
$$\rightarrow 3SO_4^{2-} + 6e^- + 3H_2O + 2Cr(OH)_4^- + 8\,OH^-$$
$$3SO_3^{2-} + 2CrO_4^{2-} + 5H_2O \quad \rightarrow 3SO_4^{2-} + 2Cr(OH)_4^- + 2\,OH^-$$

c) oxidation:

$$IO_3^- \qquad\qquad \rightarrow IO_4^- + 2e^- \;(\text{ox \#: } +5 \rightarrow +7)$$
$$IO_3^- + 2\,OH^- \qquad\qquad \rightarrow IO_4^- + 2e^-$$
$$IO_3^- + 2\,OH^- \qquad\qquad \rightarrow IO_4^- + 2e^- + H_2O$$

reduction:

$$MnO_4^- + 3e^- \qquad\qquad\qquad \rightarrow MnO_2 \ (ox\ \#:\ +7 \rightarrow +4)$$
$$MnO_4^- + 3e^- \qquad\qquad\qquad \rightarrow MnO_2 + 4\ OH^-$$
$$MnO_4^- + 3e^- + 2H_2O \qquad\qquad \rightarrow MnO_2 + 4\ OH^-$$

combining:

$$3(IO_3^- + 2\ OH^- \rightarrow IO_4^- + 2e^- + H_2O) \ + \ 2(MnO_4^- + 3e^- + 2H_2O \rightarrow MnO_2 + 4\ OH^-)$$
$$3IO_3^- + 6\ OH^- + 2MnO_4^- + 6e^- + 4H_2O \qquad \rightarrow 3IO_4^- + 6e^- + 3H_2O + 2MnO_2 + 8\ OH^-$$
$$3IO_3^- + 2MnO_4^- + H_2O \qquad\qquad\qquad \rightarrow 3IO_4^- + 2MnO_2 + 2\ OH^-$$

d) oxidation:

$$I_2 \qquad\qquad\qquad\qquad \rightarrow 2H_3IO_6^{2-}\ (balance\ I)$$
$$I_2 \qquad\qquad\qquad\qquad \rightarrow 2H_3IO_6^{2-} + 14e^-\ (ox\ \#:\ 0 \rightarrow +7\ per\ I\ atom)$$
$$I_2 + 18\ OH^- \qquad\qquad \rightarrow 2H_3IO_6^{2-} + 14e^-$$
$$I_2 + 18\ OH^- \qquad\qquad \rightarrow 2H_3IO_6^{2-} + 14e^- + 6H_2O$$

reduction:

$$Cl_2 + 2e^- \qquad\qquad \rightarrow 2Cl^-$$

combining:

$$I_2 + 18\ OH^- \rightarrow 2H_3IO_6^{2-} + 14e^- + 6H_2O \ + \ 7(Cl_2 + 2e^- \rightarrow 2Cl^-)$$
$$I_2 + 18\ OH^- + 7Cl_2 + 14e^- \qquad\qquad \rightarrow 2H_3IO_6^{2-} + 14e^- + 6H_2O + 14Cl^-$$
$$I_2 + 18\ OH^- + 7Cl_2 \qquad\qquad \rightarrow 2H_3IO_6^{2-} + 6H_2O + 14Cl^-$$

Balancing Redox Reactions: Disproportionation Reactions (Sec. 15.7)

15.53 a)

$$\qquad\qquad\qquad +3 \qquad (+2) \qquad +5$$
$$2HNO_2 + HNO_2 \rightarrow 2NO + NO_3^- + H_2O + H^+$$
$$\qquad +3 \qquad 2(-1) \qquad +2$$

$$3HNO_2 \rightarrow 2NO + NO_3^- + H_2O + H^+$$

b) $\quad -1 \qquad\quad 2(+1) \qquad\qquad 0$

$$2Cl^- + 2ClO^- + 4H^+ \rightarrow Cl_2 + Cl_2 + 2H_2O$$
$$\qquad\qquad +1 \qquad 2(-1) \qquad\qquad 0$$

$$2Cl^- + 2ClO^- + 4H^+ \rightarrow 2Cl_2 + 2H_2O$$
$$Cl^- + ClO^- + 2H^+ \rightarrow Cl_2 + H_2O$$

c) $\qquad\qquad\qquad 0 \qquad (+4) \qquad +4$

$$6\ OH^- + 2S + S \rightarrow 2S^{2-} + SO_3^{2-} + 3H_2O$$
$$\qquad\qquad 0 \quad 2(-2) \quad -2$$

$$6\ OH^- + 3S \rightarrow 2S^{2-} + SO_3^{2-} + 3H_2O$$

d)

$$0 \qquad 2(+5) \qquad +5$$

$$12\ OH^- + Br_2 + 5Br_2 \rightarrow 2BrO_3^- + 10\ Br^- + 6H_2O$$

$$0 \qquad 5[2(-1)] \qquad -1$$

$$12\ OH^- + 6Br_2 \rightarrow 2BrO_3^- + 10\ Br^- + 6H_2O$$
$$6\ OH^- + 3Br_2 \rightarrow BrO_3^- + 5Br^- + 3H_2O$$

15.55

a) oxidation:

HNO_2	$\rightarrow NO_3^- + 2e^-$
HNO_2	$\rightarrow NO_3^- + 2e^- + 3H^+$
$HNO_2 + H_2O$	$\rightarrow NO_3^- + 2e^- + 3H^+$

reduction:

$HNO_2 + e^-$	$\rightarrow NO$
$HNO_2 + e^- + H^+$	$\rightarrow NO$
$HNO_2 + e^- + H^+$	$\rightarrow NO + H_2O$

combining:

$$HNO_2 + H_2O \rightarrow NO_3^- + 3H^+ + 2e^- \quad + \quad 2(HNO_2 + e^- + H^+ \rightarrow NO + H_2O)$$
$$HNO_2 + H_2O + 2HNO_2 + 2H^+ + 6e^- \rightarrow NO_3^- + 6e^- + 3H^+ + 2NO + 2H_2O$$
$$3HNO_2 \rightarrow NO_3^- + 2NO + H^+ + H_2O$$

b) oxidation:

$2Cl^-$	$\rightarrow Cl_2$
$2Cl^-$	$\rightarrow Cl_2 + 2e^-$

reduction:

$2ClO^-$	$\rightarrow Cl_2$
$2ClO^- + 2e^-$	$\rightarrow Cl_2$
$2ClO^- + 2e^- + 4H^+$	$\rightarrow Cl_2$
$2ClO^- + 2e^- + 4H^+$	$\rightarrow Cl_2 + 2H_2O$

combining:

$$2Cl^- \rightarrow Cl_2 + 2e^- \quad + \quad 2ClO^- + 2e^- + 4H^+ \rightarrow Cl_2 + 2H_2O$$
$$2Cl^- + 2ClO^- + 2e^- + 4H^+ \rightarrow Cl_2 + 2e^- + Cl_2 + 2H_2O$$
$$2Cl^- + 2ClO^- + 4H^+ \rightarrow 2Cl_2 + 2H_2O$$
$$Cl^- + ClO^- + 2H^+ \rightarrow Cl_2 + H_2O$$

c) oxidation:

S	$\rightarrow SO_3^{2-} + 4e^-$
$S + 6\ OH^-$	$\rightarrow SO_3^{2-} + 4e^-$
$S + 6\ OH^-$	$\rightarrow SO_3^{2-} + 4e^- + 3H_2O$

reduction:

$S + 2e^-$	$\rightarrow S^{2-}$

combining:

$$S + 6\ OH^- \rightarrow SO_3^{2-} + 4e^- + 3H_2O \quad + \quad 2(S + 2e^- \rightarrow S^{2-})$$
$$S + 6\ OH^- + 2S + 4e^- \rightarrow SO_3^{2-} + 4e^- + 2S^{2-} + 3H_2O$$
$$3S + 6\ OH^- \rightarrow SO_3^{2-} + 2S^{2-} + 3H_2O$$

d) oxidation:

Br_2	$\rightarrow 2BrO_3^-$
Br_2	$\rightarrow 2BrO_3^- + 10e^-$
$Br_2 + 12\ OH^-$	$\rightarrow 2BrO_3^- + 10e^-$
$Br_2 + 12\ OH^-$	$\rightarrow 2BrO_3^- + 10e^- + 6H_2$

reduction:

$Br_2 + 2e^-$	$\rightarrow 2Br^-$

combining:

$$Br_2 + 12\,OH^- \rightarrow 2BrO_3^- + 10e^- + 6H_2O \quad + \quad 5(Br_2 + 2e^- \rightarrow 2Br^-)$$
$$Br_2 + 12\,OH^- + 5Br_2 + 10e^- \rightarrow 2BrO_3^- + 10e^- + 6H_2O + 10\,Br^-$$
$$6Br_2 + 12\,OH^- \rightarrow 2BrO_3^- + 10\,Br^- + 6H_2O$$
$$3Br_2 + 6\,OH^- \rightarrow BrO_3^- + 5Br^- + 3H_2O$$

Important Oxidation-Reduction Processes (Sec. 15.8)

15.57   a) $Pb(s) \rightarrow Pb(aq)^{2+} + 2e^-$
      b) $Cu(aq)^{2+} + 2e^- \rightarrow Cu(s)$
      c) anode = oxidation site = $Pb(s)$; cathode = reduction site = $Cu(s)$
      d) electrons flow from anode to cathode in the external circuit or from the $Pb(s)$ to the $Cu(s)$

15.59   anode: $Zn(s) \rightarrow Zn^{2+}(aq) + 2e^-$
      cathode: $2MnO_2(s) + 2NH_4^+(aq) + 2e^- \rightarrow Mn_2O_3(s) + 2NH_3(aq) + H_2O(\ell)$

15.61   anode: $Pb(s) + SO_4^{2-}(aq) \rightarrow PbSO_4(s) + 2e^-$
      cathode: $PbO_2(s) + 4H^+(aq) + SO_4^{2-}(aq) + 2e^- \rightarrow PbSO_4(s) + 2H_2O(\ell)$

15.63   The H_2SO_4 in solution is consumed, producing $PbSO_4$, which is deposited on the electrodes, and H_2O. This lowers the amount of H_2SO_4 dissolved, and lowers the density of the solution.

15.65 $2Cl^-(aq) \rightarrow Cl_2(g) + 2e^-$

ADDITIONAL PROBLEMS

15.67 N_2O (+1), NO (+2), N_2O_3 (+3), NO_2 (+4), N_2O_5 (+5)

15.69   a) S^{2-} only loses electrons, thereby acting as a reducing agent
      b) SO_4^{2-} ion, S has a +6 charge, can only gain electrons, acting as oxidizing agent
      c) SO_2, S has charge of +4, can either lose or gain electrons acting as reducing agent or oxidizing agent
      d) SO_3, S has a +6 charge, can only gain electrons, acting as an oxidizing agent

15.71   a) +2, +1   b) +3 in both   c) +1 in both   d) +3 in both

15.73   a) two reduction half-reactions
      b) one reduction and one oxidation half-reaction
      c) two oxidation half-reactions
      d) one reduction and one oxidation half-reaction

15.75   1) $5(2H_2O + PH_3 \rightarrow H_3PO_2 + 4H^+ + 4e^-) \quad + \quad 4(MnO_4^- + 8H^+ + 5e^- \rightarrow Mn^{2+} + 4H_2O)$ $10\,H_2O +$
      $5PH_3 + 4MnO_4^- + 32H^+ + 20e^-$
                             $\rightarrow 5H_3PO_2 + 20\,H^+ + 20e^- + 4Mn^{2+} + 16H_2O$
      $5PH_3 + 4MnO_4^- + 12H^+ \qquad \rightarrow 5H_3PO_2 + 4Mn^{2+} + 6H_2O$

      2) $2H_2O + PH_3 \rightarrow H_3PO_2 + 4H^+ + 4e^- \quad + \quad 2(SO_4^{2-} + 4H^+ + 2e^- \rightarrow SO_2 + 2H_2O)$
      $2H_2O + PH_3 + 2SO_4^{2-} + 8H^+ + 4e^- \qquad \rightarrow H_3PO_2 + 4H^+ + 4e^- + 2SO_2 + 4H_2O$
      $PH_3 + 2SO_4^{2-} + 4H^+ \qquad \rightarrow H_3PO_2 + 2SO_2 + 2H_2O$

3) $5(3H_2O + As \rightarrow H_3AsO_3 + 3H^+ + 3e^-)$ $+$ $3(MnO_4^- + 8H^+ + 5e^- \rightarrow Mn^{2+} + 4H_2O)$ $15H_2O +$
$5As + 3MnO_4^- + 24H^+ + 15e^-$

$\qquad\qquad\qquad\qquad\qquad \rightarrow 5H_3AsO_3 + 15H^+ + 15e^- + 3Mn^{2+} + 12H_2O$

$5As + 3MnO_4^- + 3H_2O + 9H^+ \rightarrow 5H_3AsO_3 + 3Mn^{2+}$

4) $2(3H_2O + As \rightarrow H_3AsO_3 + 3H^+ + 3e^-)$ $+$ $3(SO_4^{2-} + 4H^+ + 2e^- \rightarrow SO_2 + 2H_2O)$
$6H_2O + 2As + 3SO_4^{2-} + 12H^+ + 6e^- \rightarrow 2H_3AsO_3 + 6H^+ + 6e^- + 3SO_2 + 6H_2O$
$2As + 3SO_4^{2-} + 6H^+ \rightarrow 2H_3AsO_3 + 3SO_2$

15.77 $4Zn + 10\,H^+ + NO_3^- \qquad \rightarrow 4Zn^{2+} + NH_4^+ + 3H_2O$
oxidation:
$\quad Zn \qquad\qquad\qquad\qquad \rightarrow Zn^{2+} + 2e^-$
reduction:
$\quad NO_3^- + 8e^- \qquad\qquad \rightarrow NH_4^+$
$\quad NO_3^- + 8e^- + 10\,H^+ \qquad \rightarrow NH_4^+$
$\quad NO_3^- + 10\,H^+ + 8e^- \qquad \rightarrow NH_4^+ + 3H_2O$

CUMULATIVE PROBLEMS

15.79 a) redox, HNO_3 is the oxidizing agent
   b) acid-base, H_2S is the acid
   c) redox, H_2O_2 is the oxidizing agent
   d) acid-base, H_2SO_4 is the acid

15.81 a) $Sn^{2+} + SO_4^{2-} + 2Fe^{2+} + 2SO_4^{2-} \rightarrow Sn + 2Fe^{3+} + 3SO_4^{2-}$
     $Sn^{2+} + 2Fe^{2+} \rightarrow Sn + 2Fe^{3+}$
   b) $PH_3 + 2NO_2 \rightarrow H_3PO_4 + N_2$
   c) $S + 3H_2O + 2Pb^{2+} + 4NO_3^- \rightarrow 2Pb + H_2SO_3 + 4H^+ + 4NO_3^-$
     $S + 3H_2O + 2Pb^{2+} \rightarrow 2Pb + H_2SO_3 + 4H^+$
   d) $4Zn + 10\,H^+ + 10\,NO_3^- \rightarrow 4Zn^{2+} + 8NO_3^- + NH_4^+ + NO_3^- + 3H_2O$
     $4Zn + 10\,H^+ + NO_3^- \rightarrow 4Zn^{2+} + NH_4^+ + 3H_2O$

15.83 a)
$$8H^+ + 3H_2S + Cr_2O_7^{2-} \rightarrow 2Cr^{3+} + 3S + 7H_2O$$
with labels: -2, $3(+2)$, 0 above H_2S and S; $+6$, $2(-3)$, $+3$ below $Cr_2O_7^{2-}$ and Cr^{3+}

   b)
$$3\,H_2O + 5ClO_3^- + 3I_2 \rightarrow 5Cl^- + 6IO_3^- + 6H^+$$
with labels: 0, $3[2(+5)]$, $+5$ above I_2 and IO_3^-; $+5$, $5(-6)$, -1 below ClO_3^- and Cl^-

   c)
$$8\,OH^- + S^{2-} + 4Br_2 \rightarrow SO_4^{2-} + 8Br^- + 4H_2O$$
with labels: -2, $(+8)$, $+6$ above S^{2-} and SO_4^{2-}; 0, $4[2(-1)]$, -1 below Br_2 and Br^-

d) +4   (+1)   +5

$$2\ OH^- + NO_2 + NO_2 \rightarrow NO_3^- + NO_2^- + H_2O$$

+4   (−1)   +3

15.85 43.2 mL solution $\times \dfrac{10^{-3}\ \text{L solution}}{1\ \text{mL solution}} \times \dfrac{0.300\ \text{mole S}_2\text{O}_3^{2-}}{1\ \text{L solution}} \times \dfrac{1\ \text{mole I}_3^-}{2\ \text{moles S}_2\text{O}_3^{2-}}$

= 0.00648 mole I_3^- (calc and corr)

$$M = \dfrac{0.00648\ \text{mole I}_3^-}{20.0\ \text{mL solution}} \times \dfrac{1\ \text{mL solution}}{10^{-3}\ \text{L solution}} = 0.324\ M\ I_3^-\ (\text{calc and corr})$$

15.87 18.03 mL $S_2O_3^{2-}$ solution $\times \dfrac{10^{-3}\ \text{L S}_2\text{O}_3^{2-}\ \text{solution}}{1\ \text{mL S}_2\text{O}_3^{2-}\ \text{solution}} \times \dfrac{0.00200\ \text{mole S}_2\text{O}_3^{2-}}{1\ \text{L S}_2\text{O}_3^{2-}} \times \dfrac{1\ \text{mole I}_2}{2\ \text{moles S}_2\text{O}_3^{2-}}$

$\times \dfrac{1\ \text{mole O}_3}{1\ \text{mole I}_2} \times \dfrac{48.00\ \text{g O}_3}{1\ \text{mole O}_3} = 0.00086544\ (\text{calc}) = 0.000865\ \text{g O}_3\ (\text{corr})$

$$\dfrac{0.000865\ \text{g O}_3}{28.09\ \text{g sample}} \times 10^6 = 30.793877\ (\text{calc}) = 30.8\ \text{ppm (corr)}$$

CHAPTER SIXTEEN
Reaction Rates and Chemical Equilibrium

PRACTICE PROBLEMS

Theory of Reaction Rates (Sec. 16.1)

16.1 The solute molecules have more motion in the solution, allowing more frequent collisions with other reactant molecules throughout the solution. Only those molecules on the surface of a solid can collide with other reactant molecules.

16.3 The reaction with the lower activation energy, 45 kJ/mole, will have the faster rate. At any given temperature, there will be a greater fraction of collisions with a combined energy equal to or exceeding the lower activation energy.

16.5 (1) The combined kinetic energies of the colliding particles must equal or exceed a minimum value, the activation energy, and (2) the orientation of the particles must be favorable.

16.7

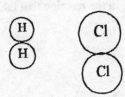

Endothermic and Exothermic Reactions (Sec. 16.2)

16.9   a) exothermic   b) endothermic   c) endothermic   d) endothermic

16.11

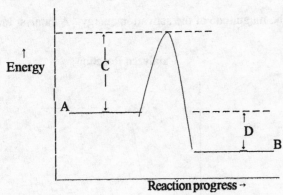

a) average energy of the reactants = (A)
b) average energy of the products = (B)
c) the activation energy = (C)
d) the energy liberated = (D)

16.13

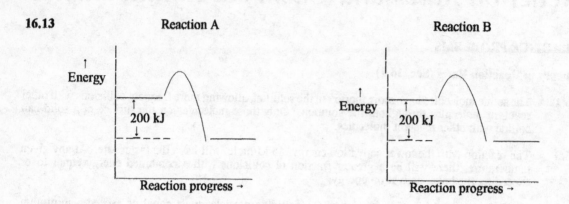

Similarities: Both reactions are exothermic and the energy difference between reactants and products is the same in both reactions. Differences: The activation energy is lower in the reaction that takes place at room temperature, Reaction A.

Factors That Influence Reaction Rates (Sec. 16.3)

16.15   a) A temperature change causes the collision frequency to change and also causes the molecular energy to change.
   b) A catalyst provides an alternate pathway with a lower activation energy.

16.17   The coal dust has much more surface area exposed to the air than does the same mass of charcoal. The reaction with the O_2 in the air will be much faster for the coal dust.

16.19   a) 1 - The lower the activation energy, the faster the reaction.
   b) 3 - The higher the temperature, the faster the reaction.
   c) 4 - The higher the concentration of a reactant, the faster the reaction.
   d) 3 - The higher the temperature and the lower the activation energy, the faster the reaction.

16.21   Diagrams are the same except for the magnitude of the activation energy. A catalyst lowers the activation energy.

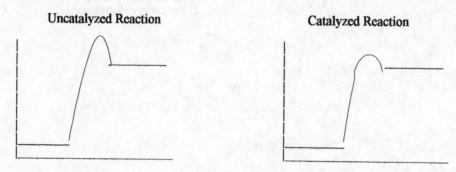

Chemical Equilibrium (Sec. 16.4)

16.23 The rate of the forward reaction must equal the rate of the reverse reaction.

16.25 A physical equilibrium involves a physical change; a chemical equilibrium involves chemical change.

Equilibrium Mixture Stoichiometry (Sec. 16.5)

16.27

	$2SO_3$	$\rightleftharpoons$	$2SO_2$	+	O_2
start	0.0200 mole		0 mole		0 mole
change	?		?		?
equilibrium	?		?		0.0029 mole

The change in O_2 = +0.0029 moles to get from 0 at start to 0.0029 at equilibrium
The change in SO_2 must be twice as great as O_2 or +0.0058 mole (produced)
The change in SO_3 must be twice as great as O_2 or -0.0058 mole (consumed)
At equilibrium the O_2 is 0.0029 moles (given)
At equilibrium the SO_2 is 0 + 0.0058 mole (start + change)
At equilibrium the SO_3 is 0.200 - 0.0058 = 0.1942 (calc) = 0.194 mole (corr)

The full table becomes:

	$2SO_3$	$\rightleftharpoons$	$2SO_2$	+	O_2
start	0.0200 mole		0 mole		0 mole
change	-0.0058 mole		+0.0058 mole		0.0029 mole
equilibrium	0.0142 mole		0.0058 mole		0.0029 mole

16.29

	$2NH_3(g)$	$\rightleftharpoons$	$N_2(g)$	+	$3H_2(g)$
start	0.296 mole		0.1700 mole		0.095 mole
change	-0.028 mole		+0.014 mole		+0.042 mole
equilibrium	0.268 mole		0.184 mole		0.137 mole

Equilibrium Constants (Sec. 16.6)

16.31

a) $$Keq = \frac{[SO_2Cl_2]}{[SO_2][Cl_2]}$$

b) $$Keq = \frac{[N_2][O_2]^2}{[NO_2]^2}$$

c) $K_{eq} = \dfrac{[CS_2][O_2]^4}{[SO_3]^2[CO_2]}$ d) $K_{eq} = \dfrac{[CH_4][H_2S]^2}{[H_2]^4[CS_2]}$

16.33 a) $K_{eq} = [NO_2]^4[O_2]$ b) $K_{eq} = [O_2]^3$ c) $K_{eq} = \dfrac{1}{[Cl_2]}$ d) $K_{eq} = [Cl_2]$

16.35 a) $K_{eq} = \dfrac{[B]^2[C]}{[A]} = \dfrac{(2.00)^2(5.00)}{3.00} = 6.6666667 \text{ (calc)} = 6.67 \text{ (corr)}$

b) $K_{eq} = \dfrac{[C]^2}{[A][B]^3} = \dfrac{(5.00)^2}{(3.00)(2.00)^3} = 1.0416667 \text{ (calc)} = 1.04 \text{ (corr)}$

c) $K_{eq} = \dfrac{[A][C]}{[B]^2} = \dfrac{(3.00)(5.00)}{(2.00)^2} = 3.75 \text{ (calc and corr)}$

d) $K_{eq} = \dfrac{[A]^3}{[C]^4[B]} = \dfrac{(3.00)^3}{(5.00)^4(2.00)} = 0.0216 \text{ (calc and corr)}$

16.37 $K_{eq} = \dfrac{[CH_4][H_2S]^2}{[CS_2][H_2]^4}$; or $0.0280 = \dfrac{(0.00100)(1.43)^2}{[CS_2](0.100)^4}$

Solving for $[CS_2]$ gives: $[CS_2] = \dfrac{(0.00100)(1.43)^2}{(0.0280)(0.100)^4} = 730.3214 \text{ (calc)} = 730. \text{ M (corr)}$

16.39 Find the molar concentration of each gas by dividing the moles by the volume,

$K_{eq} = \dfrac{[PCl_5]}{[PCl_3][Cl_2]} = \dfrac{\left(\dfrac{0.0189}{6.00}\right)}{\left(\dfrac{0.0222}{6.00}\right)\left(\dfrac{0.1044}{6.00}\right)} = 48.928238 \text{ (calc)} = 48.9 \text{ (corr)}$

16.41 a) mostly reactants   b) mostly products
c) mostly products   d) significant amounts of both
                                     reactants and products

Le Chatelier's Principle (Sec. 16.7)

16.43 a) shift to right   b) shift to left   c) shift to left   d) shift to right

16.45 a) shift to right   b) shift to left   c) shift to left   d) shift to right

16.47 a) shift to right   b) shift to left   c) no effect   d) shift to right

16.49 Increased product formation is a shift to the right. Higher temperatures will shift endothermic reactions to the right, so only in c) would high temperature favor product formation.

ADDITIONAL PROBLEMS

16.51   a) $N_2 + 3H_2 \rightleftharpoons 2NH_3$
      b) $4NH_3 + 3\,O_2 \rightleftharpoons 2N_2 + 6H_2O$
      c) $2NO \rightleftharpoons N_2 + O_2$
      d) $N_2 + O_2 \rightleftharpoons 2NO$

16.53   a) $K = \dfrac{[0.350]^2[0.190]}{[0.0300]^2} = 25.861111$ (calc) $= 25.9$ (corr); system is at equilibrium

      b) $K = \dfrac{[0.700]^2[0.380]}{[0.0600]^2} = 51.722222$ (calc) $= 51.7$ (corr)
      K value is too high for equilibrium; a shift to the left will reduce the size of K

      c) $K = \dfrac{[0.356]^2[0.160]}{[0.0280]^2} = 25.864489$ (calc) $= 25.9$ (corr); system is at equilibrium

      d) $K = \dfrac{[0.330]^2[0.180]}{[0.0100]^2} = 196.02$ (calc) $= 196$ (corr)
      K value is too high for equilibrium; a shift to the left will reduce the size of K

16.55   Since the numerator and denominator are reversed, the second K is the reciprocal of the first K.

$$K_{reverse\ reaction} = \frac{1}{K_{forward\ reaction}} = \frac{1}{2 \times 10^3} = 0.0005 \text{ (calc and corr)}$$

16.57   a) no change   b) no change   c) change in equilibrium constant value   d) no change

16.59   a) right   b) no change   c) right   d) right

CUMULATIVE PROBLEMS

16.61   a) $2SO_3(g) \rightleftharpoons 2SO_2(g) + O_2(g)$ $K = \dfrac{[SO_2]^2[O_2]}{[SO_3]^2}$

      b) $7H_2(g) + 2NO_2(g) \rightleftharpoons 2NH_3(g) + 4H_2O(g)$ $K = \dfrac{[NH_3]^2[H_2O]^4}{[H_2]^7[NO_2]^2}$

      c) $FeO(s) + CO(g) \rightleftharpoons Fe(s) + CO_2(g)$ $K = \dfrac{[CO_2]}{[CO]}$

      d) $MgCO_3(s) \rightleftharpoons MgO(s) + CO_2(g)$ $K = [CO_2]$

16.63 $M_{CH_4} = \dfrac{17.6 \text{ g CH}_4 \times \dfrac{1 \text{ mole CH}_4}{16.05 \text{ g CH}_4}}{1.725 \text{ L}} = 0.6356946$ (calc) $= 0.636$ M (corr)

$M_{H_2S} = \dfrac{50.8 \text{ g H}_2\text{S} \times \dfrac{1 \text{ mole H}_2\text{S}}{34.08 \text{ g H}_2\text{S}}}{1.725 \text{ L}} = 0.8641219$ (calc) $= 0.864$ M (corr)

$$M_{CS_2} = \frac{83.8 \text{ g CS}_2 \times \dfrac{1 \text{ mole CS}_2}{76.13 \text{ g CS}_2}}{1.725 \text{ L}} = 0.6381152 \text{ (calc)} = 0.638 \text{ M (corr)}$$

$$M_{H_2} = \frac{8.10 \text{ g H}_2 \times \dfrac{1 \text{ mole H}_2}{2.02 \text{ g H}_2}}{1.725 \text{ L}} = 2.3245803 \text{ (calc)} = 2.32 \text{ M (corr)}$$

$$K = \frac{[CS_2][H_2]^4}{[CH_4][H_2S]^2} = \frac{[0.638][2.32]^4}{[0.636][0.864]^2} = 38.93032 \text{ (calc)} = 38.9 \text{ (corr)}$$

16.65

$$M_{SbCl_5} = \frac{2.48 \times 10^{20} \text{ molecules SbCl}_5 \times \dfrac{1 \text{ mole SbCl}_5}{6.022 \times 10^{23} \text{ molecules SbCl}_5}}{1.00 \text{ L}}$$

$$= 0.00041182331 \text{ (calc)} = 0.000412 \text{ M (corr)}$$

$$M_{SbCl_3} = \frac{0.723 \text{ g SbCl}_3 \times \dfrac{1 \text{ mole SbCl}_3}{228.11 \text{ g SbCl}_3}}{1.00 \text{ L}} = 0.0031695235 \text{ (calc)} = 0.00317 \text{ M (corr)}$$

$$M_{Cl_2} = \frac{0.00317 \text{ mole Cl}_2}{1.00 \text{ L}} = 0.00317 \text{ M (calc and corr)}$$

$$K = \frac{[SbCl_3][Cl_2]}{[SbCl_5]} = \frac{[0.00317][0.00317]}{[0.000412]} = 0.024390534 \text{ (calc)} = 0.0244 \text{ (corr)}$$

16.67 Pressures may be treated in the same way as moles since the number of moles present determines the pressure.

	$N_2O_4(g)$	$\rightleftharpoons$	$2NO_2(g)$
start	1.50 atm		0 atm
change	-0.70 atm		+1.40 atm
equilibrium	0.80 atm		1.40 atm

Total pressure = 0.80 atm + 1.40 atm = 2.2 (calc) = 2.20 atm (corr)

16.69 Basis: 100 g of gaseous mixture (87.43% CO and 12.57% CO_2)

$$100 \text{ g mixture} \times \frac{87.43 \text{ g CO}}{100 \text{ g mixture}} \times \frac{1 \text{ mole CO}}{28.01 \text{ g CO}} = 3.1213852 \text{ (calc)} = 3.121 \text{ moles CO (corr)}$$

$$100 \text{ g mixture} \times \frac{12.57 \text{ g CO}_2}{100 \text{ g mixture}} \times \frac{1 \text{ mole CO}_2}{44.01 \text{ g CO}_2} = 0.2856169 \text{ (calc)} = 0.2856 \text{ mole CO}_2 \text{ (corr)}$$

Total moles = 3.121 moles CO + 0.2856 moles CO_2 = 3.4066 (calc) = 3.407 moles (corr)

$$V_T = \frac{nRT}{P} = \frac{3.407 \text{ moles} \times 0.0821 \dfrac{\text{atm L}}{\text{mole K}} \times 1023 \text{ K}}{1.000 \text{ atm}} = 286.14813 \text{ (calc)} = 286 \text{ L (corr)}$$

$$M_{CO} = \frac{3.121 \text{ moles}}{286 \text{ L}} = 0.010912587 \text{ (calc)} = 0.0109 \text{ M (corr)}$$

$$M_{CO_2} = \frac{0.2856 \text{ mole}}{286 \text{ L}} = 0.00099860139 \text{ (calc)} = 0.000999 \text{ M (corr)}$$

$$K = \frac{[CO]^2}{[CO_2]} = \frac{(0.0109)^2}{0.000999} = 0.11892892 \text{ (calc)} = 0.119 \text{ (corr)}$$

CHAPTER SEVENTEEN
Nuclear Chemistry

PRACTICE PROBLEMS

Atomic Nuclei (Sec. 17.1)

17.1 A radioactive nuclide has an unstable nucleus and a nonradioactive nuclide has a stable nucleus.

17.3 a) $^{9}_{5}B$ or boron-9 b) $^{44}_{19}K$ or potassium-44

c) $^{96}_{45}Rh$ or rhodium-96 d) $^{182}_{73}Ta$ or tantalum-182

17.5 a) $^{14}_{7}N$ b) $^{197}_{79}Au$ c) Rubidium- 92 d) Tin- 121

The Nature of Naturally Occurring Radioactive Emissions (Sec. 17.3)

17.7 a) $^{4}_{2}\alpha$ b) $^{0}_{-1}\beta$ c) $^{0}_{0}\gamma$

17.9 2 protons and 2 neutrons

Alpha-Particle Decay and Beta-Particle Decay (Sec. 17.4)

17.11 a) $^{192}_{78}Pt \rightarrow ^{4}_{2}\alpha + ^{188}_{76}Os$ b) $^{217}_{86}Rn \rightarrow ^{4}_{2}\alpha + ^{213}_{84}Po$

c) $^{212}_{85}At \rightarrow ^{4}_{2}\alpha + ^{208}_{83}Bi$ d) $^{244}_{96}Cm \rightarrow ^{4}_{2}\alpha + ^{240}_{94}Pu$

17.13 a) $^{48}_{21}Sc \rightarrow ^{0}_{-1}\beta + ^{48}_{22}Ti$ b) $^{117}_{47}Ag \rightarrow ^{0}_{-1}\beta + ^{117}_{48}Cd$

c) $^{92}_{36}Kr \rightarrow ^{0}_{-1}\beta + ^{92}_{37}Rb$ d) $^{138}_{55}Cs \rightarrow ^{0}_{-1}\beta + ^{138}_{56}Ba$

17.15 The atomic number decreases by 2 and the mass number decreases by 4.

17.17 a) $^{0}_{-1}\beta$ b) $^{125}_{52}Te$ c) $^{4}_{2}\alpha$ d) $^{229}_{90}Th$

17.19 a) $^{199}_{79}Au \rightarrow ^{0}_{-1}\beta + ^{199}_{80}Hg$ b) $^{120}_{48}Cd \rightarrow ^{0}_{-1}\beta + ^{120}_{49}In$

c) $^{152}_{67}Ho \rightarrow ^{4}_{2}\alpha + ^{148}_{65}Tb$ d) $^{226}_{88}Ra \rightarrow ^{4}_{2}\alpha + ^{222}_{86}Rn$

Half-Life (Sec. 17.5)

17.21 a) $12 \text{ min} \times \dfrac{1 \text{ half-life}}{2.4 \text{ min}} = 5$ half-lives. The fraction left $= \dfrac{1}{(2)^n} = \dfrac{1}{2^5} = \dfrac{1}{32}$

b) The fraction left $= \dfrac{1}{2^4} = \dfrac{1}{16}$

c) $7.2 \text{ min} \times \dfrac{1 \text{ half-life}}{2.4 \text{ min}} = 3 \text{ half-lives.}$ The fraction left $= \dfrac{1}{2^3} = \dfrac{1}{8}$

d) The fraction left $= \dfrac{1}{2^8} = \dfrac{1}{256}$

17.23 a) $\dfrac{1}{4} = \dfrac{1}{2^2}$ $\therefore$ 12 years is 2 half-lives. $\dfrac{12 \text{ yrs}}{2 \text{ half-lives}} = 6 \text{ (calc)} = \dfrac{6.0 \text{ yrs}}{\text{half-life}}$ (corr)

b) $\dfrac{1}{32} = \dfrac{1}{2^5}$ $\therefore$ 12 years is 5 half-lives. $\dfrac{12 \text{ yrs}}{5 \text{ half-lives}} = \dfrac{2.4 \text{ yrs}}{\text{half-life}}$ (calc and corr)

c) $\dfrac{1}{256} = \dfrac{1}{2^8}$ $\therefore$ 12 years is 8 half-lives. $\dfrac{12 \text{ yrs}}{8 \text{ half-lives}} = \dfrac{1.5 \text{ hrs}}{\text{half-life}}$ (calc and corr)

d) $\dfrac{1}{1024} = \dfrac{1}{2^{10}}$ $\therefore$ 12 years is 10 half-lives. $\dfrac{12 \text{ yrs}}{10 \text{ half-lives}} = \dfrac{1.2 \text{ yrs}}{\text{half-life}}$ (calc and corr)

17.25 Amount left = initial amount x fraction left

a) $4.8 \text{ min} \times \dfrac{1 \text{ half-life}}{2.4 \text{ min}} = 2 \text{ half-lives.}$ Amount left $= 8.0 \text{ g} \times \dfrac{1}{2^2} = 2 \text{ (calc)} = 2.0 \text{ g (corr)}$

b) $9.6 \text{ min} \times \dfrac{1 \text{ half-life}}{2.4 \text{ min}} = 4 \text{ half-lives.}$ Amount left $= 8.0 \text{ g} \times \dfrac{1}{2^4} = 0.5 \text{ (calc)} = 0.50 \text{ g (corr)}$

c) $16.8 \text{ min} \times \dfrac{1 \text{ half-life}}{2.4 \text{ min}} = 7 \text{ half-lives.}$

Amount left $= 8.0 \text{ g} \times \dfrac{1}{2^7} = 0.0625 \text{ (calc)} = 0.062 \text{ g (corr)}$

d) $24.0 \text{ min} \times \dfrac{1 \text{ half-life}}{2.4 \text{ min}} = 10 \text{ half-lives.}$

Amount left $= 8.0 \text{ g} \times \dfrac{1}{2^{10}} = 0.0078125 \text{ (calc)} = 0.0078 \text{ g (corr)}$

17.27 Fraction decayed = (1 – fraction left)
Amount decayed = initial amount x fraction decayed

a) $6.4 \text{ hr} \times \dfrac{1 \text{ half-life}}{3.2 \text{ hr}} = 2 \text{ half-lives.}$ Fraction left $= \dfrac{1}{2^2} = \dfrac{1}{4}.$ Fraction decayed $= \dfrac{3}{4}.$

Amount decayed $= 10.0 \text{ g} \times \dfrac{3}{4} = 7.5 \text{ g (calc)} = 7.50 \text{ g (corr)}$

b) $19.2 \text{ hr} \times \dfrac{1 \text{ half-life}}{3.2 \text{ hr}} = 6 \text{ half-lives.}$ Fraction left $= \dfrac{1}{2^6} = \dfrac{1}{64}.$ Fraction decayed $= \dfrac{63}{64}.$ Amount

decayed $= 10.0 \text{ g} \times \dfrac{63}{64} = 9.84375 \text{ (calc)} = 9.84 \text{ g (corr)}$

c) $28.8 \text{ hr} \times \dfrac{1 \text{ half-life}}{3.2 \text{ hr}} = 9 \text{ half-lives.}$ Fraction left $= \dfrac{1}{2^9} = \dfrac{1}{512}.$

Fraction decayed $= \dfrac{511}{512}.$

Amount decayed = 10.0 g x $\frac{511}{512}$ = 9.9804688 (calc) = 9.98 g (corr)

d) 48 hr x $\frac{1 \text{ half-life}}{3.2 \text{ hr}}$ = 15 half-lives. Fraction left = $\frac{1}{2^{15}} = \frac{1}{32,768}$.

Fraction decayed = $\frac{32,767}{32,768}$.

Amount decayed = 10.0 g x $\frac{32,757}{32,768}$ = 9.99966430 (calc) = 10.0 g (corr)

17.29 a) If $\frac{3}{4}$ decayed, $\frac{1}{4}$ left = $\frac{1}{2^2}$.

2 half-lives x $\frac{8.0 \text{ hrs}}{\text{half-life}}$ = 16 hr (calc and corr)

b) If $\frac{15}{16}$ decayed, $\frac{1}{16}$ left = $\frac{1}{2^4}$.

4 half-lives x $\frac{8.0 \text{ hrs}}{\text{half-life}}$ = 32 hr (calc and corr)

c) If $\frac{31}{32}$ decayed, $\frac{1}{32}$ left = $\frac{1}{2^5}$.

5 half-lives x $\frac{8.0 \text{ hrs}}{\text{half-life}}$ = 40. hr (calc and corr)

d) If $\frac{127}{128}$ decayed, $\frac{1}{128}$ left = $\frac{1}{2^7}$.

7 half-lives x $\frac{8.0 \text{ hrs}}{\text{half-life}}$ = 56 hr (calc and corr)

Bombardment Reactions (Sec. 17.6)

17.31 a) $^4_2\alpha$ b) ^2_1H c) $^{81}_{34}Se$ d) ^9_4Be

17.33 a) $^9_4Be + ^4_2\alpha \rightarrow ^1_0n + ^{12}_6C$ b) $^{58}_{28}Ni + ^1_1H \rightarrow ^4_2\alpha + ^{55}_{27}Co$

c) $^{113}_{48}Cd + ^1_0n \rightarrow ^{114}_{48}Cd + ^0_0\gamma$ d) $^{27}_{13}Al + ^4_2\alpha \rightarrow ^{30}_{15}P + ^1_0n$

17.35 a) $^{242}_{96}Cm$ b) $^{238}_{92}U$ c) $^{252}_{98}Cf$ d) $^{209}_{83}Bi$

17.37 nine

17.39 over 2000

Positron Emission and Electron Capture (Sec. 17.7)

17.41 The mass number remains the same; the atomic number decreases by 1

17.43 Beta decay, $^0_{-1}\beta$

17.45 a) $^{29}_{15}P \rightarrow ^{0}_{1}\beta + ^{29}_{14}Si$ b) $^{112}_{51}Sb \rightarrow ^{0}_{1}\beta + ^{112}_{50}Sn$

c) $^{46}_{23}V \rightarrow ^{0}_{1}\beta + ^{46}_{22}Ti$ d) $^{132}_{58}Ce \rightarrow ^{0}_{1}\beta + ^{132}_{57}La$

17.47 a) $^{76}_{36}Kr + ^{0}_{-1}e \rightarrow ^{76}_{35}Br$ b) $^{122}_{54}Xe + ^{0}_{-1}e \rightarrow ^{122}_{53}I$

c) $^{100}_{46}Pd + ^{0}_{-1}e \rightarrow ^{100}_{45}Rh$ d) $^{175}_{73}Ta + ^{0}_{-1}e \rightarrow ^{175}_{72}Hf$

17.49 a) $^{0}_{1}\beta$ b) $^{0}_{-1}e$ c) $^{103}_{47}Ag$ d) $^{133}_{55}Cs$

17.51 $^{63}_{30}Zn \rightarrow ^{0}_{1}\beta + ^{63}_{29}Cu$ $^{63}_{30}Zn + ^{0}_{-1}e \rightarrow ^{63}_{29}Cu$

Nuclear Stability (Sec. 17.8)

17.53 Beta emission

17.55 a) $^{65}_{28}Ni \rightarrow ^{0}_{-1}\beta + ^{65}_{29}Cu$

^{65}Ni: 28p, 37n.   n/p = 37/28 = 1.32142857 (calc and corr)
^{65}Cu: 29p, 36n.   n/p = 36/29 = 1.24137931 (calc and corr)

b) $^{192}_{78}Pt \rightarrow ^{4}_{2}\alpha + ^{188}_{76}Os$

^{192}Pt: 78p, 114n.   n/p = 114/78 = 1.46153846 (calc and corr)
^{188}Os: 76p, 112n.   n/p = 112/76 = 1.47368421 (calc and corr)

c) $^{165}_{69}Tm + ^{0}_{-1}e \rightarrow ^{165}_{68}Er$

^{165}Tm: 69p, 96n.   n/p = 96/69 = 1.39130435 (calc and corr)
^{165}Er: 68p, 97n   n/p = 97/68 = 1.42647059 (calc and corr)

d) $^{107}_{49}In \rightarrow ^{0}_{1}\beta + ^{107}_{48}Cd$

^{107}In: 49p, 58n   n/p = 58/49 = 1.18367347 (calc and corr)
^{107}Cd: 48p, 59n   n/p = 59/48 = 1.22916667 (calc and corr)

17.57 Beta emission occurs in nuclides with too high neutron-proton ratio. Positron emission occurs in nuclides with too low neutron-proton ratio. Radioactive nuclides with a mass number greater than the atomic mass of that element (the mass of the stable nuclides) will decay by beta emission. Those with mass number less than the atomic mass will decay by positron emission.

a) $^{74}_{34}Kr$ = positron; $^{87}_{36}Kr$ = beta   b) $^{68}_{33}As$ = positron; $^{84}_{34}Se$ = beta

c) $^{74}_{31}Ga$ = beta; $^{64}_{31}Ga$ = positron   d) $^{99}_{41}Nb$ = beta; $^{99}_{46}Pd$ = positron

Radioactive Decay Series (Sec. 17.9)

17.59 Stable. The series terminates when a stable nuclide is reached.

17.61 $^{238}_{92}U \rightarrow ^{4}_{2}\alpha + ^{234}_{90}Th \rightarrow ^{0}_{-1}\beta + ^{234}_{91}Pa$

17.63 (1) $^{220}_{86}Rn \rightarrow ^{4}_{2}\alpha + ^{216}_{84}Po$ (2) $^{216}_{84}Po \rightarrow ^{4}_{2}\alpha + ^{212}_{82}Pb$

(3) $^{212}_{82}Pb \rightarrow ^{0}_{-1}\beta + ^{212}_{83}Bi$ (4) $^{212}_{83}Bi \rightarrow ^{0}_{-1}\beta + ^{212}_{84}Po$

Effects of Radiation (Sec. 17.10 and 17.11)

17.65   An ion-pair is the electron and positive ion produced by the ionization interaction between radiation and an atom or molecule.

17.67   a) H_2O^+ is a free radical   b) H_3O^+ is not a free radical
c) OH is a free radical   d) OH^- is not a free radical

17.69   A thick sheet of paper stops only the alpha particles.

17.71   Alpha, 0.1 the speed of light; beta, 0.9 the speed of light; gamma, the speed of light

Nuclear Medicine (Sec. 17.14)

17.73   Alpha and beta particles have too low of a penetrating power and cannot be detected by instrumentation placed outside the body. The high penetrating power of gamma radiation makes it detectable.

17.75   a) cancer therapy: implant
b) diagnostic: intercellular spaces
c) cancer therapy: external beam
d) diagnostic: blood volume, red blood cell lifetime

Nuclear Fission and Nuclear Fusion (Sec. 17.15)

17.77   a) 4 neutrons   b) 4 neutrons   c) 2 neutrons   d) 3 neutrons

17.79 $^{240}_{93}Np \rightarrow 3\,^{1}_{0}n + ^{143}_{56}Ba + ^{94}_{37}Rb$

17.81   a) $2\,^{3}_{2}He^{2+} \rightarrow 2\,^{1}_{1}H^{+} + ^{4}_{2}He$

b) $^{7}_{3}Li + ^{2}_{1}H \rightarrow 2\,^{4}_{2}He + ^{1}_{0}n$

c) $2\,^{1}_{1}H \rightarrow ^{2}_{1}H + ^{0}_{1}\beta$

d) $^{1}_{1}H + ^{2}_{1}H \rightarrow ^{3}_{2}He$

17.83   a) fusion   b) both   c) both   d) fusion

17.85   a) fusion   b) neither   c) neither   d) fission

ADDITIONAL PROBLEMS

17.87   a) emission of beta particle does not change the mass number
b) positron emission does not change the mass number
c) emission of alpha particles change the mass number by 4
d) nucleus captures an extranuclear electron, mass number does not change

17.89

a) $^{232}_{90}Th \xrightarrow{\alpha} ^{228}_{88}Ra \xrightarrow{\beta^-} ^{228}_{89}Ac \xrightarrow{\beta^-} ^{228}_{90}Th$

b) $^{228}_{89}Ac \xrightarrow{\beta^-} ^{228}_{90}Th \xrightarrow{\alpha} ^{224}_{88}Ra \xrightarrow{\alpha} ^{220}_{86}Rn$

17.91 1) Mass number decreases by 24.   6 α particles needed.

2) 6 α particles would decrease atomic number by 12; actual change = 8, so $4_{-1}^{0}\beta$ needed

$$_{90}^{232}\text{Th} \rightarrow \,_{82}^{208}\text{Pb} \,+\, 6_2^4\alpha \,+\, 4_{-1}^0\beta$$

17.93 ^{28}P has too low a neutron-to-proton ratio; the decay mode should be positron emission or electron capture. ^{34}P has too high a neutron-to-proton ratio; the decay mode should be beta emission.

17.95 For the decay A → B, the half-life = 3.2 minutes.
This decay will be complete (to 3 significant figuress) in less than 10 half-lives, 32 minutes. The amount of A left is 0 mole.
For the decay B → C, the half-life = 25 days.
We can assume that the 1.00 mole B was all made at day 0 (to 3 significant figures), so after 50 days (2 half-lives), $\frac{1}{4}$ of B will be left, and $\frac{3}{4}$ of B will have decayed.

For the decay C → D, the half-life is 9 sec.
Compared to the 50 days duration, this half-life is so small that we can assume all the C produced decays instantly. The amount of C = 0 mole and D will be the amount of C made (or B lost) in 50 days.
The amount of D = 0.750 mole.
A = 0; B = 0.250 mole; C = 0; D = 0.750 mole.

17.97 For nuclide A:

$$\frac{1}{64} = \frac{1}{2^6}, \therefore 6 \text{ half-lives of A have passed.}$$

$$\frac{16 \text{ hrs}}{6 \text{ half-lives}} = 2.6666666 \text{ (calc)} = \frac{2.7 \text{ hrs}}{\text{half-life}} \text{ (corr)}$$

For nuclide B:

$$0.45 \times \frac{2.7 \text{ hrs}}{\text{half-life}} = \frac{1.485 \text{ hrs}}{\text{half-life}} \text{ (calc)} = \frac{1.2 \text{ hrs}}{\text{half-life}} \text{ (corr)}$$

$$\frac{1}{16} = \frac{1}{2^4}, \therefore 4 \text{ half-lives have elapsed for B}$$

$$\frac{1.2 \text{ hrs}}{\text{half-life}} \times 4 \text{ half-lives} = 4.8 \text{ hrs (calc and corr)}$$

$$\frac{1.8 \text{ hrs}}{\text{half-life}} \times 5 \text{ half-lives} = 9 \text{ (calc)} = 9.0 \text{ hrs (corr)}$$

17.99 $\dfrac{4.000 \text{ g}}{0.125 \text{ g}} = 32.0, \therefore \dfrac{1}{32}$ of the sample remains after 35 days

a) $\dfrac{1}{32} = \dfrac{1}{2^5}, \therefore 5$ half-lives have elapsed.

$$\frac{35 \text{ days}}{5 \text{ half-lives}} = 7 \text{ (calc)} = \frac{7.0 \text{ days}}{\text{half-life}} \text{ (corr)}$$

b) $4.000 - 0.125 \text{ g} = 3.875 \text{ g X that has decayed}$
Assuming that isotopic masses can be approximated by using mass numbers.

$$3.875 \text{ g X} \times \frac{206 \text{ g Q}}{210 \text{ g X}} = 3.8011904 \text{ (calc)} = 3.80 \text{ g Q (corr)}$$

CUMULATIVE PROBLEMS

17.101

a) $^A_Z Q \rightarrow {}^0_1\beta + {}^A_{Z-1}R$ Q and R are isobars

b) $^A_Z Q \rightarrow {}^4_2\alpha + {}^{A-4}_{Z-2}R$ Q and R are neither isobars nor isotopes

c) $^A_Z Q + {}^1_0 n \rightarrow {}^{A+1}_Z R$ Q and R are isotopes

d)   Q and T are isotopes

$$^A_Z Q \xrightarrow{\alpha} {}^{A-4}_{Z-2}R \xrightarrow{\beta} {}^{A-4}_{Z-1}S \xrightarrow{\beta} {}^{A-4}_Z T$$

17.103 $\dfrac{7.2 \times 10^5 \text{ dps}}{4.5 \times 10^4 \text{ dps}} = 16 \text{ (calc and corr)}$

$\dfrac{1}{16} = \dfrac{1}{2^4}$, therefore, 4 half-lives have elapsed

$$4 \text{ half-lives} \times \frac{4.7 \text{ days}}{1 \text{ half-life}} = 18.8 \text{ (calc)} = 19 \text{ days (corr)}$$

17.105 a) $50.0 \text{ g UF}_6 \times \dfrac{1 \text{ mole UF}_6}{352.03 \text{ g UF}_6} \times \dfrac{1 \text{ mole U}}{1 \text{ mole UF}_6} = 0.1420333 \text{ (calc)} = 0.142 \text{ mole U (corr)}$

$50.0 \text{ g UBr}_4 \times \dfrac{1 \text{ mole UBr}_4}{557.63 \text{ g UBr}_4} \times \dfrac{1 \text{ mole U}}{1 \text{ mole UBr}_4} = 0.0896652 \text{ (calc)} = 0.0897 \text{ mole U(corr)}$

The UF$_6$ sample contains more Uatoms and will produce a greater amount of radioactivity.

b) $0.250 \text{ mole UF}_6 \times \dfrac{1 \text{ mole U}}{1 \text{ mole UF}_6} = 0.25 \text{ (calc)} = 0.250 \text{ mole U (corr)}$

$0.200 \text{ mole UBr}_4 \times \dfrac{1 \text{ mole U}}{1 \text{ mole UBr}_4} = 0.2 \text{ (calc)} = 0.200 \text{ mole U (corr)}$

The UF$_6$ sample contains more Uatoms and will produce a greater amount of radioactivity.

17.107   Time elapsed = 1 half-life
One-half of the Po-210 has decayed = 2.50 g

$$2.50 \text{ g Po-210} \times \frac{1 \text{ mole Po-210}}{210 \text{ g Po-210}} \times \frac{1 \text{ mole } \alpha}{1 \text{ mole Po-210}} \times \frac{1 \text{ mole He}}{1 \text{ mole } \alpha}$$
$$= 0.011904762 \text{ (calc)} = 0.0119 \text{ mole He (corr)}$$

$$V = \frac{nRT}{P} = \frac{0.0119 \text{ mole} \times 0.08206 \dfrac{\text{atm L}}{\text{mole K}} \times 298 \text{ K}}{0.800 \text{ atm}} = 0.3637515 \text{ (calc)} = 0.364 \text{ L (corr)}$$

17.109 1.01×10^{11} kJ x $\dfrac{1 \text{ mole C}}{394 \text{ kJ}}$ x $\dfrac{12.01 \text{ g C}}{1 \text{ mole C}}$ x $\dfrac{1 \text{ kg C}}{10^3 \text{ g C}}$

$= 3.0787056 \times 10^6$ (calc) $= 3.08 \times 10^6$ kg C (corr)